# HEROES OF THE GAME

## A HISTORY OF THE GREY CUP

# HEROES OF THE GAME

# A HISTORY OF THE GREY CUP

*Stephen Thiele*

**Moulin**

Moulin Publishing Limited
P.O. Box #560
Norval, Ontario
Canada L0P 1K0

First Edition

**Canadian Cataloguing in Publication Data**

Thiele, Stephen, 1964–
 Heroes of the game : a history of the Grey Cup

Includes bibliographical references.
ISBN 1-896867-04-9

1. Grey Cup (Football) — History. I. Title.

GV948.T48 1997    796.335'648    C97-900410-1

Front cover illustration: Hugh "Bummer" Stirling of the 1934 and
 1936 Sarnia Imperials

Front cover photo of Hugh Stirling, courtesy of the Canadian
 Football Hall of Fame and Museum.
Back cover photo of the Grey Cup, courtesy of C.F.L. Photos.

Moulin Publishing Limited and Stephen Thiele thank John Tory, Jeff Giles and the Canadian Football League for permission to use the C.F.L. logo on the back cover.

Cover design: Andrew Smith Graphics
Text design: Heidy Lawrance Associates
Printed and bound in Canada

97 98 99 00 01 FC 5 4 3 2 1

# Table of Contents

*This book is dedicated to all the heroes;*
*and*
*to my wife, Prema.*

# FOREWORD

The *Concise Oxford Dictionary* defines a 'hero' as a man noted or admired for nobility, courage or outstanding achievements. Although in sports a team effort is required in order to produce championships, we cannot help but remember the heroic accomplishments of the few gifted athletes whose shoulders have carried fame and who have taken their teammates to glory.

In Canadian football every Grey Cup game has its heroes: Warren Moon and Tommy Scott playing pitch and catch in the 1980 game ... J.C. Watts almost guiding the Ottawa Rough Riders to an incredible upset victory against the heavily favoured Edmonton Eskimos in 1981 ... Roy Dewalt producing big plays for the B.C. Lions in 1985 ... Henry 'Gizmo' Williams sprinting for a 115-yard touchdown return on a missed field goal in 1987 ... The Toronto Argonauts fighting back in 1987, and then losing on a last-minute field goal by Jerry Kauric ... Tony Champion twisting, turning and leaping backward to haul in a touchdown pass in 1989 ... Dave Ridgway finishing that greatest Grey Cup game ever played with a perfect field goal ... Doug Flutie rolling left and right in 1992 and passing for 480 yards ... The Baltimore Stallions becoming the first American team to win the Grey Cup in 1995.

As a former Canadian Football League player with the Saskatchewan Roughriders and the Hamilton Tiger-Cats, and as a football analyst with CTV and currently with The Sports Network, I have experienced the excitement and the intensity of many Grey Cup games and have witnessed the heroes who have made these games memorable.

For me personally, the 1976 Grey Cup holds both the fondest and the saddest memories that I have from the two championships in which I played. As a third-year Saskatchewan Roughrider, I had one of the best games of my career, catching seven passes for 80 yards. It is an achievement that I cherish and one that every player dreams about: to be able to perform at the highest level in the biggest game of the year was exhilarating ... But then in the same game to see it all slip away with one pass from Tom Clements to Tony Gabriel in the dying minutes, brought me from a feeling

Leif Pettersen celebrates a touchdown as a member of the Hamilton Tiger-Cats. (*Toronto Sun*/Barry Gray)

of ecstasy to one of despair knowing that the opportunity to be a champion might never come again. I had been part of one of the greatest Grey Cup games ever played but, I always felt, for the wrong reason: Ottawa 23, Saskatchewan 20.

*Heroes of the Game* captures all of the foregoing memories and many more in an exciting and colourful manner. It celebrates the Canadian gridiron heroes and a Canadian institution by taking you through a fast-paced blend of the play of the games and quotes from those who have participated in the games. The history of the Grey Cup is rich and inspiring; *Heroes of the Game* will ensure that this history is never forgotten.

*Leif A. Pettersen*

# INTRODUCTION

In 1909 Albert George Grey, the fourth Earl and Canada's ninth Governor-General, donated a trophy for the 'Amateur rugby football championship of Canada.' This trophy would later become popularized as the Grey Cup, and be acknowledged as the symbol of Canadian professional football supremacy.

Over the years many men have competed for this glorious prize. They have battled their opponents and the elements of wind, rain, snow, mud and fog. Throughout these battles there have been spectacular passes, outstanding catches, bone-crunching tackles, and awe-inspiring runs. And what for? To hold aloft the $48 Grey Cup, to drink from its lip, and to be Canadian or, historically, Dominion football champions.

The Canadian game is a great one, deep in history and tradition. The Grey Cup, its trophy, is testament to that.

Originally, the Grey Cup was not intended to be the major trophy for Canadian football but a hockey trophy for the amateur senior championship of Canada. However, Sir H. Montague Allan had already donated the Allan Cup to hockey. Accordingly Earl Grey made his trophy available for football.

When the first Grey Cup champion was crowned in 1909, the Cup was not ready for presentation. It was not until March of 1910, three months after the first historic game, that the Cup was officially given to the University of Toronto club. The Grey Cup's adventure had begun.

The Grey Cup remained at the University of Toronto until 1914. But it should not have been so, because in 1912 and 1913 the University did not win the coveted prize. In fact, they did not make it to the final in either year. For some unknown reason the University believed it could keep the Cup until another team defeated Varsity in the championship game. The Toronto Argonauts accomplished this in 1914 and made the Cup available to all subsequent champions.

In 1915 the Hamilton Tigers won its second Grey Cup championship. The players were thrilled with their victory, but they wanted revenge for Varsity's retaining of the trophy in 1912 and 1913. The rumour is that some members of the 1915 championship team commissioned a shield to be made on behalf of the 1908 Senior Football Championship Hamilton Tiger

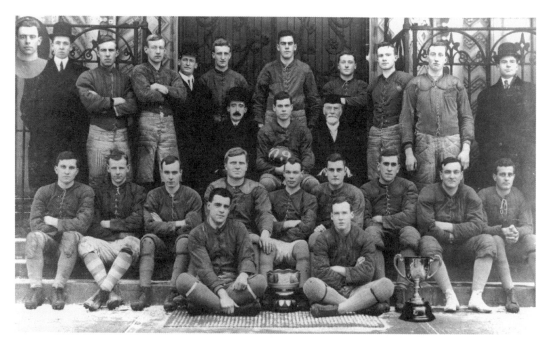

Back row, left to right: J.M. Lajoie (inset), J.J. Pearson (President), W.D. Cruikshank, Dr. J.W. Barton (Physical Director), H. Gall, A.S. Lawson, E.G. Dixon, F.S. Park, C.E. Gage, A.E. Alison (Manager).Second row: H.C. Griffith (Hon. Coach), J. Newton (Captain), Prof. McCurdy (Hon. President). Third row: E.M. Thomson, J.B. MacDonald, G.A. Kingston, H.C. Ritchie (Vice-president), J.S. Bell, G.A. Rankin, A.E. Muir, W.W. Hume, J.R. Dickson. Front row: G.R. Jones, W.C. Foulds.

The Grey Cup was not awarded to the first Cup champion until March 1910. A close examination of the photograph reveals that the Grey Cup was added after the 1909 University of Toronto Varsity Blues players had their picture taken. (University of Toronto Archives)

team. The shield was then secured to the trophy's base to mislead football followers that the first Grey Cup champion was the Tigers. To this day the 1908 shield remains affixed to the original base of the Cup.

Following the 1915 championship the Cup was forgotten as the championship game was cancelled from 1916 to 1919. The Cup was stuck in a vault at a Toronto trust company, to be rediscovered according to Bob Dunn of the *Montreal Gazette* "as one of the family heirlooms of one of the trustees." It is said that upon rediscovering the Cup, the trustee's brother declared dismissively: "Get that thing out of here!"

The Cup then travelled from the vault to a closet. In 1928, the Hamilton Tigers won the trophy. Len Back, the Hamilton manager, took possession of the prize and stuck it in his hall closet. The Cup did not see the light of day again until the 1929 final.

Less than 20 years later, in 1947, tragedy almost struck when a blaze gutted the Toronto Argonaut Rowing Club clubhouse. All the trophies in the building were either melted down or badly scarred by the flames – except the Grey Cup. All of the other trophies fell from the shelves to their destruction, but the Grey Cup caught onto a large nail and never reached the floor. Although blackened, its base badly charred, the Cup survived.

The Cup's adventure continued in 1964 when the British Columbia Lions won its first championship. Apparently, the team held a wild party back at its hotel after the victory. When British Columbia checked out of its hotel the next day, the team left without the Cup. At the airport it was realized that the trophy had been forgotten, and someone was hurriedly dispatched to retrieve it from the Park Plaza Hotel in Toronto.

On December 20, 1969 the Cup was stolen from the trophy case at Lansdowne Park, now Frank Clair Stadium, in Ottawa. A ransom letter demanded a large sum of money but the Canadian Football League (the 'C.F.L.') refused.

On February 16, 1970 Greg Fulton, Secretary-Treasurer of the C.F.L., was advised that the Metropolitan Toronto Police had received a "strange call" instructing the police to proceed to a telephone booth at the corner of Parliament and Dundas Streets, in Toronto. There, the police were to search the coin-return box for a key that would fit a locker at the Royal York Hotel. In that locker the Grey Cup was found.

In 1983 Grey Cup custodians suffered another scare. This time a fraternity at the University of British Columbia threatened to kidnap the prize. The fraternity said that it would hold the Cup for ransom, with the proceeds going to charity. The Cup was never kidnapped. Following the 1983 championship game a Toronto Argonaut, Jan Carinci, had the trophy when, en route to a post-game celebration, his car broke down. Realizing that he had to get to the function in a hurry, Carinci hitch-hiked. A driver going in the opposite direction stopped to help the wayward Argonaut and upon finding that Carinci was carrying the Grey Cup, turned his car around and took him directly to his destination.

Then in 1984 Paul Robson, General Manager of the Winnipeg Blue Bombers, left the Cup behind after a celebration at the Winnipeg Arena. When Robson realized that he had forgotten the trophy, he rushed back to the stadium. In the silent, empty arena stood the Cup, at centre stage.

There are many other colourful stories surrounding the trophy some of which include it being dismembered or beheaded. In 1987, in a post-game celebration, the Cup was sat on and broken. After the 1993 game, Blake Dermott head-butted the Cup for 'tradition' – and cracked the trophy at the neck.

However, this book is not intended to be an historical study of the Grey Cup's misadventures. The purpose is to present the football players who have competed for this prize and have made the Cup the symbol of national pride and unity that it is today. The Grey Cup is a Canadian football institution, and within this book are the plays, and most of all, the heroes of the Grey Cup.

Why would anyone wish to undertake this endeavour, one may ask, especially when the C.F.L. has so many problems? The answer for this author is simple. I love Canadian football. Canadian football is a wide open and fast game, packed with excitement from the opening kick-off to the final gun. Everyone who has watched a Grey Cup game is impressed by the spectacular and electrifying play of Canadian football. Following one final, American

Henry McLemore, a United Press sports journalist, wrote:

> There's no two ways about it – Canadian football is a much more vivid spectacle than our [American] game. I hadn't watched more than a quarter of Saturday's battle for the Grey Cup before realizing that... American spectators, I believe, would like to see more razzle-dazzle running and less highly specialized line play and nobody will ever convince me that watching a guard guard, say, is a heart-stopping sight. I'd rather see a swivel-hipped back sashay along through a swarm of tackles in an open field than to watch all the line play in a month of Sundays.
>
> I talked to several Americans before the game and they all agreed … the Canadian game was twice as much fun to play as the American game.

A similar sentiment was shared by Canadian Football Hall of Fame member Jackie Parker. After the 1954 Grey Cup game Parker stated: "I was a little apprehensive about the brand of football in Canada when I first came to this country from Mississippi State. But I think now the game here is just as good as professional football in the States. There are a lot of boys up here who could lead the league in the States without any trouble. The different rules we have here give you more chance to operate and provide better fan entertainment."

John Steadman, a sports columnist for the *Baltimore Sun*, has also provided his view of Canadian football. He wrote: "It was so good from purely an entertainment viewpoint that the NFL pales by comparison. The Canadian game is faster, more wide open, and higher scoring. The NFL, with one team resembling another courtesy of boring coaches and situation substitutions, has a higher profile and, of course, more acceptability."

Despite such opinions that Canadian football is exciting and fun, the sport is the subject of much criticism. Most commentators favour the American game. However, perhaps it is not fair to compare the two games. While most of the rules are the same, there are many differences which make each style unique.

Recently the excitement and fun of Canadian football have been displayed in some of the greatest Grey Cup games ever played. National media headlines have read:

> 1994: "The Lions are king: Last-second kick by Passaglia beats Baltimore in heart-stopping 82nd Grey Cup"
> "B.C. wins Grey Cup thriller"
>
> 1989: "Roughriders win Cup thriller"
> "Roughriders storm to win in 'most exciting' Grey Cup"

1988:   "Bombers win thriller"

1987:   "Eskimos win Grey Cup classic"
        "Allen offers Esks relief: Kauric's FG beats Argonauts in
        Grey Cup thriller"

Canadian football is going through many changes. Expansion into American cities such as Baltimore, Memphis, and Birmingham, has ended in failure. While the Baltimore franchise had plenty of fan support, football fans in Sacramento, San Antonio, Shreveport, Memphis and Birmingham were never comfortable with the Canadian brand. The American fan did not understand the rules, and was never told about the history of the game. The failed experiment has led to more criticism being directed at the sport. It is time, however, for the criticism to end. It is time to promote the Canadian game and remember the rich tradition that it has created. It is for this reason that I have written this book.

As a Canadian, I am proud of Canadian football, proud of the players, whether Canadian or American, who have made Canadian football great, and proud of the Grey Cup tradition that these players have left other Canadian football players to carry into the future. These players have established a Canadian sports institution and are heroes of one of the best sports played in this world.

*Stephen Thiele*

## Chapter One

# SETTING THE SCENE
## 1861-1908

**F**or many Canadian football fans life begins and ends with the Grey Cup. However, there is more to this great sport than just Grey Cup games. Every year there are pre-season, regular season and playoff games, and prior to the 1909 season, the first year in which a Grey Cup champion was crowned, the game had already developed a rich tradition.

Canadian football can trace its roots to rugby, and the first developments of the modern game pre-date Confederation. Historians suggest that as early as 1861 football was played in Upper Canada, now Ontario, at the University of Toronto. Seven years later football was being played in Quebec when British soldiers stationed in Montreal met a team comprised primarily of McGill University students.

From 1861 through 1908 football grew throughout Ontario and Quebec, and in the West. The Ontario Rugby Football Union (the 'O.R.F.U.') and the Quebec Rugby Football Union (the 'Q.R.F.U.') were two of the earliest organized provincial bodies for football, while the Canadian Rugby Football Union (the 'C.R.F.U.') was the first national body. The unions established rules of play, organized teams into divisions, and developed uniform point-scoring systems. Championship games were also organized, and on November 10, 1883 the Toronto Argonauts defeated the Ottawa Football Club 9 to 7 to become the inaugural O.R.F.U champion. A year later the Montreal Football Club trounced the Argonauts 30 to 0 and won the first national championship.

Football during this period resembled rugby more than it did the game as we know it today. There was no direct snap from centre to the quarterback, and the rules did not permit a forward pass. Further, the game was dominated by kickers and fleet-footed halfbacks. Games often featured kicking duels, risky lateral passes, and thrilling onside kicks. The scoring system promoted the kicking game. For example, as outlined in the 1996

(C.F.L.) *Facts, Figures and Records* guide the 1883 O.R.F.U. scoring system was as follows: six points for a Goal from the Field; four points for a Touchdown and Goals from a Touchdown, Penalties and Free Kicks; two points for a Safety Touch; and one point for a Kick to the Deadline, a Rouge, and a Touch in Goal.

The emphasis on kicking led to what modern sports fans would consider low-scoring games. Exciting games in this period would have produced scores such as 8 to 7 and 11 to 8. A 14-point lead would have been considered insurmountable. In today's game a team trailing by 14 points with less than three minutes to play still has an opportunity of winning.

Another feature of the game was dribbling. Instead of pouncing on loose or fumbled balls, players would kick, or dribble, downfield in wild scrambles. Finally, two-way play, with players participating on both offence and defence, was the norm. Some of the early features continued into the mid-20th century but it is now extremely rare for a player to dribble a ball or play on both offence and defence.

Administratively, the game was controlled by Ontario and Quebec. Although teams were formed in Manitoba, Alberta and Saskatchewan, the clubs from these provinces never participated in national championships. The Western Canada Rugby Football Union was not a recognized member of the national football body, and in 1912 a formal application for membership in the Canadian Rugby Union (the 'C.R.U.') was not entertained because as described in Frank Cosentino's book *Canadian Football: The Grey Cup Years* there were "many difficulties in playing final games (involving western teams) owing to great distances that intervene."

The game began to break away from its rugby influences on Friday, May 15, 1874 when McGill University played Harvard at Boston. McGill had developed new rules for football and the teams battled to a scoreless draw. Harvard was extremely impressed by the 'McGill Rules', and accordingly the rules were adopted into the Ivy League. By 1879 the United States Intercollegiate Football Association endorsed 11-man football. In Canada, the various unions were slow to adopt the 'McGill Rules'. Games were still played with 14 or 15 men per side.

By the turn of the century the Canadian Intercollegiate Rugby Football Union (the 'C.I.R.F.U.') and the C.R.U. had been formed, and the C.R.U. was organizing championship games. On November 10, 1892 Osgoode Hall, representing the O.R.F.U., played the Q.R.F.U.'s Montreal Football Club in the first C.R.U. championship. Osgoode Hall played brilliantly, and it crushed Montreal 45 to 5.

The next significant event in the evolution of Canadian football occurred in 1905. John T.M. Burnside, a former captain of the Toronto Varsity Blues, proposed more new rules for football. Known as the 'Thrift Burnside Rules', they established the foundation for the modern game. Generally, Burnside's rules reduced teams to 12 men per side, introduced a 'snap-back' system, and required a team to gain 10 yards on three downs. Also, the rules abolished throw-ins from the sidelines. However, it was not until after the end of World War I that they were accepted for all football play in Canada.

The stage was set for the first Grey Cup championship with the creation of the Interprovincial Rugby Football Union (the 'Big Four') in 1907. Prohibited from using university players, the strongest teams from the O.R.F.U. and the Q.R.F.U. craved better competition. Accordingly the Hamilton Tigers, Toronto Argonauts, Ottawa Rough Riders, and Montreal Football Club formed the Big Four. But the other amateur unions (the O.R.F.U. and the C.I.R.F.U.) were still able to field strong teams and often defeated the Big Four clubs.

In 1908 the strength of the Big Four was shown in the play-downs for the Dominion championship. While the Toronto Amateur Athletic Club (T.A.A.C.) had won O.R.F.U. honours, the Hamilton Tigers defeated the Ottawa Rough Riders 11 to 9 to win the Big Four senior championship. The game was vigorously contested with Hamilton falling behind 5 to 0 in the first quarter. But strong kicking by Ben Simpson resulted in the Tigers taking an 11 to 6 lead by the fourth quarter. Ottawa's kicking game then produced three points and threatened to score at least three more. But with Ottawa in possession on the Hamilton 15 time expired, and the Tigers won 11 to 9.

A week later the Tigers faced the T.A.A.C. in one semi-final game, while the University of Toronto and Queen's University (Kingston, Ontario) met to decide the intercollegiate championship in the other semi-final. The T.A.A.C. was comprised of good players, but they lacked teamwork. Accordingly, even though the Tigers played carelessly, they easily mauled T.A.A.C. 31 to 8. In the intercollegiate game, the University of Toronto played superbly on special teams. Moon Lee, Andy Duncanson and Jack Ramsey prevented Queen's from gaining ground on punt returns which eventually resulted in

**The Hamilton Tigers won the 1908 Dominion Championship. In the 1910 final (seen here) the Tigers lost to the University of Toronto.** (CFL Photos)

Varsity obtaining scoring position. The game ended Varisty 12, Queen's University 0.

In the national final, played on Saturday, November 28, 1908, the scoring prowess displayed by the Tigers in the semi-final match continued. The Tigers roared to a 19 to 9 first half lead on three touchdowns, two converts, and two singles. One touchdown came when Toronto quarterback Coryell mistakenly lateralled the ball to the referee and Hamilton recovered in the end zone.

But in the second half, Toronto played better. It chipped away at Hamilton's 10-point lead, and by the mid-point of the fourth quarter Toronto had reduced the lead to two points. Yet the Tigers responded to Varsity's comeback and scored two singles in the final moments to win the championship 21 to 17.

The victory by the Tigers marked the end of the initial era of Canadian football. While the rules of the game did not make any significant changes until 1921 and the Big Four and the C.I.R.F.U. remained the largest unions in Canada, the spotlight of the game became fixed on Grey Cup champions. Lord Grey's donation lifted Canadian football to a new height and put Canadian football on the road to becoming a cultural institution.

But for the next 40 years the game underwent tremendous growing pains. Although the Grey Cup was a coveted prize, participation in the game fluctuated greatly. In 1909 the University of Toronto (C.I.R.F.U. champion) was expected to play the Big Four champion Ottawa Football Club for the Cup. But trustees of the trophy determined that neither Varsity nor Ottawa could play for the Cup without first defeating the winner of the O.R.F.U. In 1912 and 1913 the C.I.R.F.U. champions refused to play and in 1915 the C.I.R.F.U. suspended operations for the duration of World War I. In 1921 the West was admitted into the membership of the C.R.U. and East versus West Grey Cup competition began. Yet while the three existing eastern unions (the C.I.R.F.U., Big Four and O.R.F.U.) followed an alternating playoff structure to determine an eastern representative for the Cup, the West did not always compete. On some occasions the C.I.R.F.U. champions also refused to compete and by 1934 the C.I.R.F.U. had completely withdrawn from Cup competition. The withdrawal left the Big Four champion to play the O.R.F.U. champion in the eastern final. The playoff format was then interrupted from 1942 through 1944, and then in 1953 and 1954 the western champion was required to play the O.R.F.U. champion before competing for the Cup. The O.R.F.U. subsequently withdrew from Cup competition leaving the eastern champion to face the western champion for the national title. The formation of the C.F.L. crystallized the playoff format and with the exception of the 1995 final, the Cup has been billed as an East versus West showdown.

## Chapter Two

# THE GREY CUP QUEST BEGINS

## 1909-1915

**T**he quest for the Grey Cup began with the 1909 Canadian football season. For the first seven Grey Cup championship games from 1909 to 1915, teams from Toronto and Hamilton were featured. The University of Toronto, the Toronto Argonauts, and the Hamilton Tigers were the most prominent teams competing for the $48 trophy and national title, and these three won six of the first seven Grey Cups, the other going to the Hamilton Alerts. This initial period was also highlighted by the most controversial Grey Cup game in history.

## 1909 UNIVERSITY OF TORONTO 26 PARKDALE CANOE CLUB 6

The University of Toronto started the quest brilliantly. Led by Hugh Gall, Jack Maynard, Pete Campbell and Smirle Lawson the youthful Varsity Blues captured the first three championships. On December 4, 1909, Varsity deflated the Toronto Parkdale Canoe Club. It was a bleak and chilly Saturday afternoon, but this did not discourage the 3,800 spectators who filled the stands at the Rosedale Field in Toronto to cheer on the young men who would become the first Grey Cup heroes.

The University jumped into an early 6 to 0 lead due to the play of Gall. After an opening exchange of kicks, Gall scored the first point in Grey Cup competition when he drilled the football 65 yards downfield and across Parkdale's goal line. Brady retrieved the ball in his own end zone, but he was smothered by a horde of Varsity tacklers for a rouge: Varsity 1, Parkdale 0. Then Parkdale committed a turnover deep in its own zone. Varsity gained possession and, following an offside penalty against Parkdale, Gall scooted around the end for a touchdown.

Varsity supporters believed that victory was on its way. However, Parkdale showed flashes of brilliance and before the end of the half Gall committed

A University of Toronto ball carrier breaks through the line in the 1909 final against the Parkdale Canoe Club. (Canadian Football Hall of Fame & Museum)

an error which reduced Varsity's lead. Pinned deep in his own zone, Varsity's Billy Foulds tossed a lateral to Gall. Gall mishandled the ball, and Parkdale's Tom Meighan pounced on it for a touchdown.

The score unnerved the Varsity players but in the third quarter a mistake by Parkdale restored Varsity's confidence. Moore lost control of the ball on his own 40-yard line, and Varsity dribbled it downfield. Near the Parkdale goal line, Murray Thomson picked up the ball, shook off Moore, and raced into the Parkdale end zone for the major. Bill Ritchie kicked the convert, and Varsity led 12 to 5.

After the score became 14 to 6, Gall took control of the game. Parkdale could not defend against his long punts, and in the latter part of the third quarter and early in the fourth Gall scored six consecutive singles. 'Big Train' Lawson then added another single before scattering his opponents right and left in the broken field en route to a touchdown on the last play of the game. There was no convert on the play, and the first Grey Cup game ended Varsity 26, Parkdale 6.

**The outstanding player in this game was Varsity's Hugh Gall. His running and kicking single-handedly defeated Parkdale. He out-punted his rival by 10 to 15 yards on every exchange. Consequently, Varsity always gained better and better field position. After the game a member of the Varsity coaching staff said, "Hugh Gall actually won the game for Varsity. He is a wonderful punter, and we are proud of him. He is a member of the Parkdale Canoe Club, you know. He lives in Parkdale, and learned to play football out there, and he is the greatest player on the Varsity team." Gall's tremendous performance in the 1909 game features prominently in the history of the Cup. His eight singles are still a Cup record.**

Gall reproduced his 1909 performance in the 1910 final against the Hamilton Tigers, and thereby led the Varsity speedsters to its second crown.

The first quarter was plagued with lost opportunities. Varsity threatened when Gall and Maynard combined for a spectacular gain, Gall busting through the line for 30 yards. Then as he was tackled, Gall tossed the ball to Maynard, who rambled for an additional few yards. However, a few plays later, a Varsity penalty ended the threat.

Hamilton took advantage of the penalty, and it moved the ball to the Varsity 25. From there, Hamilton's Kid Smith tried a drop on goal but Varsity defenders broke through the line and blocked the kick.

After an exchange of kicks Varsity finally opened the scoring. Scrimmaging from inside the Hamilton 15-yard line, Billy Foulds took the ball and ran along the line toward teammate 'Reddy' Dixon, on a criss-cross. In a strong Hamilton rush the ball was knocked free, but fortunately for Varsity the ball bounced perfectly into the arms of Dixon, who skirted around Varsity's left end for a major.

Varsity increased its lead in the second quarter with the assistance of a favourable ruling by the officials. Gall fired a long lateral to Dixon, but Hamilton's Gatenby intercepted. Gatenby then threw the ball to Awrey, who sprinted toward the Varsity goal line. However, the play was called back. The referees ruled that Gatenby had thrown the ball forward, and thus Varsity retained possession. On the next play, an exchange of kicks ended with Varsity's Bell catching the ball on the Hamilton 30. Surrounded, Bell lateralled to Gall, who broke to the outside for a return of 15 yards before tossing the ball to Maynard. In full flight, Maynard side-stepped Hamilton's Glassford, eluded Moore, and dove into Hamilton's end zone for the score. Maynard converted the touchdown to give Varsity an 11 to 0 lead.

In the second half Hamilton reduced the lead to 11 to 7, and then Gall secured Varsity's second consecutive Cup victory by abandoning Varsity's running attack in favour of a rapid kicking game, which soon produced five unanswered singles to make the final score Varsity 16, Hamilton 7.

**Hugh Gall's intelligent play was the largest contributing factor to**

**Hughie Gall holds the ball for Varsity teammate Jack Maynard in the 1910 Cup.**
(Canadian Football Hall of Fame & Museum)

Varsity's victory. When it became clear to Gall that Hamilton was gaining momentum through the third quarter, he changed Varsity's strategy in order to preserve Varsity's lead. His contribution was also seen in his combined runs with Maynard and Dixon. They took all kinds of chances at top speed, and often produced outstanding lateral passes. On many occasions, while surrounded by yellow and black striped Tigers, they tossed the ball to each other with such lightning speed that Hamilton's defenders were frequently left breathless. Such was their passing that it was not uncommon for all three to handle the ball twice in one run. On one occasion Gall and Dixon exchanged passes three times in astonishing fashion.

## 1911 UNIVERSITY OF TORONTO 14
## TORONTO ARGONAUTS 7

The Varsity Blues continued its dominance in 1911, advancing to its third consecutive Dominion final. Varsity's opponent in this Cup game, played Saturday, November 25, was the Toronto Argonauts. In a titanic struggle Varsity again emerged as champion.

After falling behind 1 to 0 in the first quarter, Varsity took the lead as a result of two Argonaut miscues. First Varsity recovered an Argonaut fumble deep inside enemy territory, and then the Argos' Billy Mallett shanked a kick out of bounds at his own 15-yard line. Varsity moved the ball to the 5, and from there Allan Ramsay charged through a huge opening in the Argonaut defence for a touchdown. Jack Maynard kicked the convert and Varsity led 6 to 1.

The Argonauts battled back to make the score 6 to 3, but in the third quarter Varsity received a break which sealed its victory. With the Argos in possession in its own half, Ross Binkley punted the ball to Varsity's Greene. When Greene ran the ball back to midfield the Argo tacklers were bunched on the northeast side of the gridiron, so he booted the ball to the northwest side of the field. The ball rolled to the Argonaut 10 where Binkley retrieved it, only for Varsity's Bell to jar the ball loose. Frank Knight recovered the fumble for Varsity, and he scrambled across the goal line for a touchdown.

The Argonauts answered this touchdown with a field goal and a rouge. However, it was not enough. Varsity closed the game's scoring with a single, and thereby won the 1911 championship 14 to 7.

While Varsity's Jack Maynard and the Argos' Ross Binkley were two of the game's best players, the star of this game was Varsity's quarterback Pete Campbell. Campbell started every run for Varsity, and he often worked the 'hidden ball' effect to great advantage. Frequently Argonaut defenders were fooled. In the fourth quarter the Argos were so bewildered by Campbell's fakes that Argonaut defenders were tackling every possible Varsity ball carrier. Campbell also exploited every opening in the Argonaut defensive line, squirming through holes to combine with Maynard for long gains. Dr. Thompson, President of the Hamilton Tigers remarked, "In Peter

Campbell, Varsity has the greatest [quarterback] Canadian Rugby ever saw. He is as smart as a steel trap and gets the ball away so fast his opponents can't keep track of it ... The Tigers will have to steal Pete Campbell for next year."

## 1912 HAMILTON ALERTS 11
## TORONTO ARGONAUTS 4

The Argonauts should have stolen Campbell because in 1912 the Boatmen again sailed to the Grey Cup game and lost. However, the game, played Saturday, November 30, was not remembered mainly for Toronto's defeat at the hands of the Hamilton Alerts, but as the game that was almost never played.

While the two combatants and 6,000 fans eagerly awaited the start, word came that a football could not be found! According to officials at the Hamilton Cricket Grounds the person in charge of the ball had locked it in a dressing room and disappeared with the key. Finally, one hour later, someone decided to kick in the dressing room door to retrieve the ball. This act later cost the C.R.U. $1.75 to replace the damaged door, but it allowed the 1912 Grey Cup game to be played.

The delay produced a slow start, and after 15 minutes the Alerts held a slim 2 to 0 lead. Then early in the second quarter Toronto squandered two chances to take the lead. On the first opportunity Hamilton's Norm 'Tout' Leckie mishandled a punt on his own 10-yard line. Toronto's Jimmy Dissette chased the loose ball into the Hamilton end zone, but just as he stooped for the ball Hamilton's Carr kicked it out of play. Instead of five points the Argos had to be satisfied with a 2-point safety.

Toronto's next missed opportunity was the game's turning point. With Hamilton leading 3 to 2, and Toronto in possession on the Hamilton 10, the Argos called an onside kick. Dissette lofted the ball a few yards beyond the scrimmage line to teammate Jack O'Connor. A clear field awaited O'Connor, but as he reached to catch the ball a teammate collided with him. The ball fell free, and a wild scramble ensued. The ball was swatted into the open field to Toronto's Reaume, who tore down the field for an easy touchdown. The Argos celebrated, but only until the officials ruled that O'Connor had illegally batted the ball forward. The touchdown was nullified, and the score remained Hamilton 3, Toronto 2.

The Argonauts never recovered, and early in the third quarter the Alerts scored the game's only touchdown. Toronto had possession on its own 5-yard line, and faced a third down punting situation. Crossen Clarke accepted the ball from centre, but just as he was about to drop the ball to punt, Hamilton's Fisher roared around the end of the line and hammered him for a loss. The ball was turned over to the Alerts on the Toronto 5, and three plays later Hamilton's Ross Craig crashed into the Toronto end zone.

In the fourth quarter, Toronto squandered most of its numerous chances and Hamilton won the 1912 Cup 11 to 4.

Sam Manson of the Hamilton Tigers. In the 1913 Cup against the Parkdale Canoe Club, Manson was one of the best players. (Canadian Football Hall of Fame & Museum)

The outstanding player in this game was Norman Leckie. Leckie's marvellous kicking was responsible for Hamilton's victory as he showed excellent judgment throughout the game in punting high so Hamilton tacklers could get downfield to limit Argonaut returns. Leckie also excelled in kicking back Argonaut punts. Half a dozen times Leckie was surrounded by would-be Argo tacklers inside the Hamilton end zone while awaiting Argo punts but he always caught the ball cleanly, and created enough room for himself to kick the ball downfield. Leckie finished the game with five singles.

## 1913 HAMILTON TIGERS 44
PARKDALE CANOE CLUB 2

A Hamilton team returned to the Grey Cup in 1913. This time the Hamilton representative was the Hamilton Tigers, Inter-Provincial champion. The Tigers fielded many of the best players ever to play Canadian football. Accordingly, Hamilton's opponent, Parkdale Canoe Club (the O.R.F.U. champion) was not given much of a chance. Many fans predicted that Hamilton would win by more than 20 points, and they were right as on November 29 Hamilton trounced Parkdale 44 to 2.

Both of Parkdale's points were scored by ex-Varsity Blue Hugh Gall. After Parkdale fell behind 6 to 0, Gall punted the ball twice into the Hamilton end zone. On each occasion, Hamilton's Sam Manson was tackled for a rouge. Gall's effort in scoring these points was extremely courageous considering his ailments. Before the start of the 1913 season Gall had sustained a hip injury in a motorcycle accident. He had undergone electric treatment, but in the early going of the Grey Cup game the hip was re-injured. In addition, Gall played with a badly crushed right index finger. A week before the game Gall had caught the finger in the engine of an automobile. The finger was encased in a splint, and heavily bandaged.

Following Gall's singles, Hamilton's Art Wilson scored two touchdowns to help increase the Tigers' lead to 20 to 2. Parkdale's last scoring chance came with a few minutes remaining in the second quarter. Bickle busted through the Hamilton line for a run of 30 yards, drew a tackle and lateralled the ball to Zimmerman for an apparent easy score. Only Manson, not noted as a strong tackler, stood between Zimmerman and the Hamilton goal line. However, Manson stretched out a leg, and tripped Zimmerman. Manson was penalized for five minutes, but the touchdown had been prevented.

There was no scoring in the third quarter. Hamilton made up for the drought with an incredible offensive display in the final quarter. Bob Isbister Sr. scored a 5-yard touchdown early on, then Harry Glassford intercepted an errant Parkdale lateral and galloped down the field for another major. Next, Wilson established a Grey Cup record by scoring his third touchdown of the game. In the last minute Manson faked a lateral outside, and took off around the right end to advance the ball to the Parkdale 10. From there, Craig smashed through the line for a touchdown. Final score: 44 to 2.

**The running by Art Wilson and Ross Craig in the 1913 final was phenomenal. From the opening kick-off to the end of the game, their running ripped the Parkdale defensive line to shreds. They helped set up many Hamilton scoring opportunities, and together they directly accounted for 25 of Hamilton's 44 points.**

## 1914 TORONTO ARGONAUTS 14
## UNIVERSITY OF TORONTO 2

In 1914, teams from Toronto were again the best in Canadian football. The national final pitted the University of Toronto Varsity Blues against the Toronto Argonauts. The Argonauts, not expected to win the Cup, entered the game with many battered players. However, the Argonauts defence played a tremendous game, and with the assistance of some luck, led the team to an upset victory over the Blues on December 5.

The Argonauts opened a huge 14-point lead in the first half of the game by capitalizing on two Varsity turnovers. In the first minute Varsity's Red McKenzie misjudged an Argonaut punt, the ball deflecting off his arms. As he stooped for the ball, 'Mac' Murray tackled him and Glad Murphy recovered for the Boatmen. With three Varsity players blocking Murphy's path Frank Knight raced behind Murphy, thrust him forward over the Blues and over the goal line.

In the second quarter, with Varsity in possession in its own half, Stratton took the ball from centre and motioned to lateral it to McKenzie, but Stratton was hammered before he could release the ball. Freddie Mills recovered the loose ball for the Boatmen and romped downfield with the ball tucked securely under his arm for a touchdown.

The strength of the Argonaut defence was displayed in the fourth quarter. With Toronto deep in its own half, O'Connor's punt was blocked by Varsity's 'Laddie' Cassels as he charged through the line. Bryans recovered the ball to give the Blues possession on the Argonaut 5.

On first down, Cassels and Charlie Gage headed a four-man buck into the Argo line for a gain of two yards. Then McKenzie plunged into the line for another yard. Varsity gambled on third down, and Cassels headed another tandem buck which rammed the Argo defence – but did the ball cross the line? As the referee blew his whistle to stop play, a rough and tumble culminated in a pile-up of about 20 players on the Argonaut goal line. The players were unpiled one by one, and Referee Frank Robbins knelt beside the ball. He found just enough room to insert his open hand vertically between the ball and the Argonaut goal line. Varsity's third down gamble had failed, and an Argo team won its first Grey Cup title 14 to 2.

**The best player in this game was the Argos' Jack O'Connor, whose kicking was instrumental in guiding the Boatmen to victory. He showed excellent judgment in placing his kicks, and in the third quarter when Saunders entered the game for**

Varsity, O'Connor deliberately directed his kicks toward the young Varsity player rather than at the more experienced McKenzie. In addition, O'Connor kicked for good distance.

O'Connor also showed prowess in bucking and plunging. He often charged through the line for huge gains. Finally, O'Connor played a key role in rescuing his teammates. When an Argonaut half mishandled a punt, he frequently battled Varsity players to make the recovery. Dangerous work, but it prevented the Blues from obtaining good field position.

## 1915 HAMILTON TIGERS 13
## TORONTO ROWING AND ATHLETIC ASSOCIATION 7

The Argonauts' tremendous 1914 victory was followed by the most controversial game in Cup history. On Saturday, November 20, 1915, the Hamilton Tigers met the Toronto Rowing and Athletic Association to decide the national championship at Varsity Stadium, Toronto. The game was close and hard-fought. Unfortunately, to many the outcome of the game did not rest with the players but with Referee Ewart 'Reddy' Dixon. Dixon's numerous poor decisions caused a riot when the final whistle blew, and he was lucky to escape unharmed.

After Toronto surprisingly held a 4 to 0 lead into the second quarter, Referee Dixon stepped into the spotlight for the first of his many appearances. With the ball on the Toronto 30, Toronto's George Bickle rocketed the pigskin to the Hamilton 10-yard line. Toronto's wings quickly raced down the field, and slammed Sam Manson to the turf. Hamilton would have been buried deep in its own zone, but Dixon penalized Toronto for no yards. The call was questionable, and allowed Hamilton to scrimmage on the Toronto 30-yard line. From there, Hamilton scored its first point of the game.

In the third quarter Toronto widened the gap to 5 to 1, and then without warning the tide of the game turned in favour of Hamilton – thanks to Dixon. The Tigers desperately began to plunge the line, and soon forced the play from midfield to within the shadow of Toronto's goal posts. Scrimmaging on the Toronto 15-yard line, Hamilton gave the ball to Jack Erskine. Erskine cut around the end and picked his way toward the goal line. As he neared the end zone, Erskine was hit hard. The ball squirted free and rolled out of play behind the goal line, where Erskine lay sprawled. Toronto players were convinced that Hamilton would only get a single point. However, although out of position on the far side of the field when Erskine was tackled, Dixon improperly signalled a touchdown. The Toronto players' vehement protests were ignored and Dixon brought the ball out to the 35-yard line for the convert. The goal judge ruled Manson's convert good, but to the 1,500 spectators in the bleachers the ball had whistled wide.

Referee Dixon ran toward the goal judge, apparently to overrule him, then turned and allowed the point.

In the 1915 final between Hamilton Tigers and Toronto Rowing and Athletic Association, former Varsity star Ewart 'Reddy' Dixon caused a riot with his many controversial decisions as a referee.
(Canadian Football Hall of Fame & Museum)

Moments later Dixon made another controversial decision. Toronto stormed into Hamilton territory, where Bickle kicked the ball high to Hamilton's Manson. Manson allowed the ball to drop behind his goal line, and then watched it roll around until it rested at his feet. Meanwhile, Toronto tacklers gathered in the end zone ready to pounce on Manson. He stood over the ball gazing at the Toronto defenders, who were waiting patiently beyond the no yards zone. Snatching up the ball he darted cross-field for only about 20 feet before being slammed to the field. A rouge. Indeed, the boy at the scoreboard added another point to Toronto's score. But then came Dixon. To the amazement of the crowd, Dixon ruled no yards against Toronto, and he gave the Tigers possession on the Hamilton 45.

In the final quarter Dixon made two more controversial calls. After a dazzling punt return by Manson had given Hamilton possession on the Toronto 20-yard line, N. Lutz was given the ball. Lutz bucked the line, and squirted through. The Toronto players then stopped, awaiting a whistle that never blew. Lutz kept on running and charged into the Toronto end zone untouched.

Toronto was in shock. The players took Referee Dixon aside and vigorously complained that Hamilton had used illegal interference on the play. However, Dixon allowed the controversial score to stand.

With little time remaining Toronto mounted a drive which would have tied the score were it not for another suspect decision by Dixon. Using a series of creative plays, Toronto pushed into Hamilton territory. From there, a Toronto onside kick moved the ball closer to the Hamilton goal line. Another onside kick and the ball flew toward the Tigers goal line, Manson racing over to take it on the fly. But he slipped, the ball took an awkward bounce and rolled toward Dode Burkart, who had only to fall on the ball for an apparent touchdown. Again, there was no whistle. Hamilton dragged Burkart out of the end zone and when Dixon finally arrived on the scene he found the Toronto player lying on the 1-yard line. First down! The incensed Toronto players lost their composure and in three ensuing plays Toronto could not move the ball across the line.

Hamilton won the 1915 Cup 13 to 7. At Dixon's final whistle, the crowd poured onto the field seeking blood – Dixon's blood. Fans even cried, "Three cheers for Reddy Dixon, the best player on the Tiger team."

The former University of Toronto and Hamilton Tigers star (and Hamilton native) tried to get away, but the irate crowd surrounded him. Verbal insults were exchanged and according to those on the field, Dixon began to taunt the angry mob. Some fans reached their boiling point and were ready to pummel Dixon. Police had to use their batons freely to disperse the crowd and rescue him.

With many fans still in hot pursuit, Dixon was rushed to the relative sanctuary of the Toronto dressing room. Most of the Toronto players were content to leave Dixon alone. No one challenged him until Dixon arrogantly stated that there was no player nor anyone else who could show to his face where he had made an unfair decision. Crawford rose to his feet, stepped over to Dixon, and retorted, "You were the best man on the Tiger team, and if you don't like it you can lump it." Dixon simply stood silent realizing that Crawford was willing to back his words with his fists.

**The officiating of Dixon overshadowed the stellar play of Hamilton's Sam Manson. Although he struggled in the first few minutes of the game and was out-kicked, his strong play in the second half carried the Tigers to victory. In the second half Manson made several good runs and kicked with excellent judgment. After the game, Frank 'Shag' Shaugnessy, Ottawa's coach, remarked that Manson was the greatest player he had ever seen in a football uniform. He further stated, "They can talk about [Toronto's Hal] De Gruchy but he did not begin to show up like Manson. Sammy did practically the whole work behind the Tiger line, while De Gruchy had two able assistants. I think that Manson's generalship is responsible for the Tiger victory. Tigers have been a one-man team all season ..."**

Hamilton's 1915 victory was an exciting end to the first era of Grey Cup competition. From 1909 to 1915 the accomplishments of Canadian Football Hall of Fame Inductees Hugh Gall (Varsity and Parkdale), Smirle Lawson (Varsity and Argonauts), Ben Simpson (Hamilton Tigers), Bob Isbister Sr. (Tigers), and Ross Craig (Hamilton Tigers and Alerts) were exceptional, and their play helped to shape the Canadian brand of football. Unfortunately, Canadian football fans had to wait until 1920 to be treated to similar stellar performances. World War I brought a suspension of the game until 1918, and in 1919 there was little interest among the various league champions to proceed with playoffs.

## Chapter Three

# THE WEST STRUGGLES TO COMPETE
## 1920-1927

**A**fter a four-year hiatus, the Grey Cup championship resumed in 1920. The next eight years brought many changes in Canadian football. Two of the most significant occurred in 1921. First, the C.R.U. eliminated the centre scrim, and introduced the snap-back. As a result, the two players previously needed to support the third player in heeling the ball back to the quarter-back were eliminated, thereby reducing the number of players on each team from 14 to 12. The second significant change was the arrival of the West in the Grey Cup game. In 1921, the first western team challenged for the Grey Cup. The western teams were far inferior to the eastern, and they struggled in the games in which they appeared. Eastern critics believed that the western teams had no business challenging for the national title, and from 1920 to 1927 it was not uncommon for the Grey Cup to be an all-eastern final. Battle lines were drawn between the East and West in this period, and the western struggle to compete in the Grey Cup would not be resolved satisfactorily until after World War II.

## 1920 UNIVERSITY OF TORONTO 16
## TORONTO ARGONAUTS 3

The first Grey Cup game following World War I, played on Saturday, December 3, 1920, featured the Toronto Argonauts against the University of Toronto. With two of the most dominant teams in the first era of Canadian football once again playing for the title, the game promised to be a close contest. Under unfavourable weather and field conditions each team scored three times but Varsity's scores were worth more points so it won its fourth, and last, Grey Cup crown by a score of 16 to 3.

After falling behind 1 to 0, Varsity took the lead in the second quarter. Scrimmaging on the Argos' 50-yard line, Varsity's Westman and Carew crashed through the line for more than 20 yards. Then Varsity's Warren Snyder was given the ball. Snyder busted through centre, and into the Argo secondary. As he darted toward the Argo goal line, six different Argonaut tacklers had a chance to bring him to the turf, but Snyder squirmed away. Near the Argo goal line, he was met by another Argo tackler, threw himself sideways to protect the ball, and smashed over the goal line for a touchdown.

A legend of Canadian football, Harry Batstone made his first Grey Cup appearance with the Toronto Argonauts in 1920. (Canadian Football Hall of Fame & Museum)

The Argonauts then made the score 6 to 2 in the third quarter before a mistake ensured Varsity's victory. With Varsity in possession, Snyder kicked the ball to the Argos' Dunc Munro. While Munro attempted to catch the ball on the run, teammate Harry Batstone positioned himself several yards away, ready to take a pass. It never came.

Munro took his eyes off the ball, and it bounced off his arm. Jo-Jo Stirrett dribbled the loose ball toward the Argonaut end zone. Batstone gave chase, and overtook Stirrett as the ball crossed the Argo goal line, but was thrust aside as he went for the ball and Stirrett flopped on the ball for a touchdown.

In the fourth quarter, Varsity scored another touchdown on a clever run. The Blues marched the ball to the Argo 7-yard line, and from there the ball was handed to Red McKenzie. He could not find a hole, but just before Referee Ben Simpson whistled the play dead McKenzie reversed direction, scooted around the end, and scored.

Moments later, the Argos' Munro set up the game's last scoring chance when he galloped down the field for an electrifying 51-yard punt return. A few plays later a rouge ended the game 16 to 3.

Varsity's Joe Breen was the best player in the 1920 game. Although he did not score, his dazzling runbacks of Argo punts led Varsity to victory. Frequently Breen caught punts on the dead run, darting and crashing through the Argo tacklers at full speed. Very confident in his own ability, he never kicked the ball back to the Argos on Argo punts. Breen's runbacks convinced many critics that Breen was the best halfback in Canada.

## 1921 TORONTO ARGONAUTS 23 / EDMONTON ESKIMOS 0

In 1921, a team made history by issuing the first western challenge for the Grey Cup. The Edmonton Eskimos, the western champion, coveted the Dominion Championship. Accordingly, one month before the eastern playoffs were completed, Edmonton asked the C.R.U. to be allowed to contest for the Grey Cup. The C.R.U. did not object, but told Edmonton that it would have to wait until after the eastern playoffs were finished. The Eskimos did not like being required to wait, and withdrew. Two weeks later, Edmonton re-issued its challenge, and on December 3, 1921 became the first team from Western Canada to play in a Grey Cup game.

Edmonton's opponent was the Toronto Argonauts. Toronto was an extremely powerful club, undefeated in the regular season and playoffs, and outscored its opponents 226 to 55 in nine games. Edmonton stood little chance; the Argonauts destroyed the Eskimos 23 to 0.

Edmonton handed Toronto the Grey Cup title early in the first quarter. With the Eskimos lined up in punt formation deep in its own zone, Shieman snapped the ball back to Fraser. The snap was too high, and the ball whistled over Fraser's head. While Fraser recovered the ball, the Argos were given possession on the Edmonton 5-yard line due to loss of downs. On the next play, Shrimp Cochrane took the snap, worked around the end, and dove across the Eskimo goal line. 5 to 0.

**Lionel Conacher, Canada's greatest athlete of the first half century, led the Argonauts to Cup glory in 1921 against Edmonton Eskimos.** (Canadian Football Hall of Fame & Museum)

Another Edmonton error led to Lionel Conacher scoring on a 15-yard extension run. Recovering a misplayed punt on the Edmonton 15, Cochrane lateralled the ball to Harry Batstone, who lateralled to Britnell, who in turn lateralled to Conacher. The six-foot one inch, 185-pound Conacher steamed around the end, into Edmonton's end zone for the score.

Toronto increased its lead to 11 to 0 in the second quarter, and then Edmonton engineered its best drive of the game. A powerful ground attack led by Sheard, Fowler, and Yancey transferred play from deep inside Edmonton territory to the Toronto 25-yard line. Impressed with the Edmonton march, many spectators at Varsity Stadium roared on the Eskimos. On the next ground play Edmonton's Palmer, inspired by the fan support, burst through the Argonaut line for a major. The crowd's cheers soon turned to groans. Referee Simpson waved everyone back to the line of scrimmage. Edmonton was penalized for illegal interference, and thus the touchdown did not count. On the next play, Edmonton's drive ended when Toronto's Rommerill stripped the ball from an Edmonton carrier.

In the third quarter Conacher scored his second touchdown, taking a lateral and eluding every Edmonton tackler en route to paydirt. Batstone converted the score to give Toronto a 20 to 0 lead. Toronto continued to dominate, and following the touchdown added three more singles to close the scoring at 23 to 0.

The hero of the game was Toronto's Lionel Conacher. His running and kicking controlled the game. Often Conacher burst around the end of the Argo line to gain 30 and 40 yards, and he easily out-punted Edmonton's Fraser and Sheard. Conacher also received strong support from Harry Batstone and Shrimp Cochrane. Every time Toronto made an extension run, Batstone and Cochrane made sure that when the ball was tossed to Conacher, the latter would be at full speed. In addition, Batstone and Cochrane often drew Edmonton tacklers before feeding the ball to Conacher so that he would have a clear field of play. Conacher's all-round abilities, and help from Batstone and Cochrane, produced 15 of the 23 points scored by Toronto.

While football was Conacher's favourite sport, he was outstanding at hockey, baseball, lacrosse, and wrestling. From 1925 through 1937, Conacher starred in the National Hockey League. He played for four different N.H.L. teams, and won Stanley Cups with the Chicago Black Hawks and Montreal Maroons. In 1926, Conacher played Triple A baseball for the Toronto Maple Leafs, who won the Little World Series.

In 1950 he was named Canada's greatest male athlete of the first half-century. Four years later Conacher died after collecting a triple during a charity baseball game between Parliamentarians and the Press Corps.

Following the 1921 Grey Cup game, an Edmonton fan was involved in one of the strangest stories in Cup history. Gordon Winkler, an Edmonton lawyer and mine owner, had accompanied the Eskimos to Toronto. Winkler carried with him two suitcases which contained cans of a newly patented puncture curing compound for automobile tires. Not wanting to take these suitcases to a hotel, he stored them at the Union Station check room where he thought they would be safe. However, the suitcases were banged around. The compound leaked from one can and trickled through the suitcase. A parcel handler called the police. Alcohol, thought the police. Given that prohibition was in effect, the police staked-out the check room ready to arrest the owner of the suitcases.

When Winkler returned, the police surrounded him.

"Do you own those suitcases, young man?"

"I sure do," replied Winkler.

"Open them up," said an officer.

Winkler could not believe him. He briefly kidded with the officer, but quickly complied on seeing his angry face. While the police were confused by the cans' contents, they were going to arrest Winkler until he convinced them that anyone who gargled the contents of the cans would need a dynamite chaser.

## 1922 QUEEN'S UNIVERSITY 13
## EDMONTON ELKS 1

The West was not discouraged by its 1921 loss. The next year the Edmonton Elks travelled to Richardson Stadium, Kingston, Ontario for the second East versus West Grey Cup game. The eastern opponent was the Queen's University Golden Gaels. Edmonton was considered to be the more

Queen's University won three consecutive Cup titles largely due to Frank 'Pep' Leadlay, who also won two titles with Hamilton. (Canadian Football Hall of Fame & Museum)

experienced team, but most critics believed that Queen's was vastly superior. Queen's was fast, and it was led by two of the best players in Canadian football: Frank 'Pep' Leadlay, and Harry Batstone. Batstone, an accomplished hockey and baseball star, played a terrific game and, with support from Leadlay, led Queen's to its first of three consecutive titles on December 2, 1922.

In the first half, Queen's had difficulty scoring. Despite moving the ball well against the Edmonton defence, the team was unable to score because of errors. This kept Edmonton in the game, and before the end of the second quarter the Elks took the lead by scoring the first point by a western team in Grey Cup competition. The play which led to the score was a risky third down gamble. Scrimmaging from the Queen's 40-yard line, Edmonton needed 10 yards to retain possession. The ball was given to Curly Dorman, and he cleverly smashed through the line for the down. A few plays later, Jack Fraser tried his second drop-kick of the game. Similar to his first effort, the ball sailed wide of the posts. However, it reached the deadline to give Edmonton a 1 to 0 lead.

Billy Hughes, the Queen's coach, was extremely dissatisfied with the play of his team and during the intermission he gave his players a tongue-lashing. The coach's fiery speech sparked the Golden Gaels and in the second half Queen's controlled the game.

A kicking strategy propelled Queen's into a 2 to 1 lead in the third quarter, and then the turning point of the game occurred when Leadlay punted the ball to Edmonton's Brown from deep inside the Gael's territory. Brown circled under the ball, but could not catch it. Veale scooped up the loose ball for Queen's, and charged to the Edmonton 20 before being tackled. Three plays later, from the Edmonton 6 Johnny Evans handed the ball to Charlie Mundell, who barged through the line for a touchdown. Leadlay kicked the convert to make the score Queen's 8, Edmonton 1.

A few minutes later Queen's padded its lead by capitalizing on a penalty which left Edmonton one man short. Scrimmaging from the Edmonton 30-yard line, Queen's used three plays to gain 20 yards. Then Evans confused the Elks defence with a masterful fake. Evans motioned to lateral the ball one way, but changed direction and moved the ball the other way to Dave Harding. Edmonton players were caught out of position and Harding strolled into the Edmonton end zone for the game's last score: Queen's 13, Edmonton 1.

The stars of this game were Dave Harding and Harry Batstone. Throughout, Harding was brilliant on defence while Batstone excelled on offence.

Harding's tackles stopped many Edmonton running plays. Every time an Edmonton runner tried to bust through the Queen's line, Harding threw his body into the

Edmonton ball-carrier. Harding also contributed to the Queen's offensive game by combining with Batstone and Leadlay for long gains on end runs and extension plays. On some of these plays Harding scampered for gains of up to 30 yards.

Meanwhile Batstone's performance equalled his performance in the 1921 final. A sportswriter for the *Daily British Whig* reported: "Saturday's was probably the best game Harry Batstone has turned in for the Queen's team this year. He was here, there, and everywhere, and in the limelight more than in any other game this season." Batstone was the maestro orchestrating the Queen's passing attack. He would draw Edmonton tacklers toward him, and then show incredible daring by tossing the ball, basketball style, over the heads of the Edmonton players to nearby teammates. Batstone also gained many yards by plunging through the line or sprinting around the end, and by running back kicks.

## 1923 QUEEN'S UNIVERSITY 54
## REGINA ROUGHRIDERS 0

On December 1, 1923 Batstone was again at the centre of a Grey Cup victory. This time Queen's University defeated the Regina Roughriders. Regina was proud to represent the West in the Grey Cup, but after the game many wished the Roughriders had lost the western final. The Roughriders were humiliated 54 to 0. It was the largest margin of victory in a Dominion final since the Montreal Amateur Athletic Association defeated Peterborough 72 to 10 in the 1907 national senior football final.

The shellacking underscored the views of eastern football critics that the western style of Canadian football was greatly inferior to the eastern, and after the 1923 Grey Cup game rumours surfaced that Queen's deliberately ran up the score as a matter of protest at having to play a weaker western opponent. Queen's also resented competing in the first week of December because it was too close to examination time.

The outcome of the 1923 game was decided quickly. After taking a 1 to 0 lead, Queen's scored its first of a Grey Cup record nine touchdowns. Scrimmaging on the Queen's 10-yard line, Leadlay and Batstone combined for a thrilling 75-yard gain. Leadlay carried the ball for 20 yards, and then tossed it to Batstone. Regina tacklers were taken by surprise as Batstone sped past to the Regina 25-yard line. From there, Queen's gained 20 more yards, and then on third down from the Regina 5, Queen's faked a run through the line. The Regina defenders were again fooled. Batstone ran outside and shouted to quarterback Johnny Evans, "Gimme that ball!" Evans obliged and Batstone trotted around the end for the touchdown.

In the second quarter, Bill Campbell scored two touchdowns. The first came when Leadlay faked a lateral to Batstone, turned inside and handed the ball to Campbell. Regina defenders were dispersed all over the field and Campbell scored easily. Later in the quarter, he crossed when Regina's Peobles misplayed a Leadlay kick. The ball rolled into the Regina end zone where Campbell shoved Peobles aside, and fell on the ball.

In the third quarter, Evans recovered a blocked punt for a touchdown to give Queen's a 28 to 0 lead. Moments later, Batstone returned a punt 30 yards, and then burst through the Regina line for another score. The onslaught continued. 'Liz' Walker blitzed into the Regina backfield to intercept an errant Regina lateral and race downfield toward the Regina end zone. Five feet from the line, Regina's Brown dove, and wrapped his arms around Walker's ankles but, as he crashed to the turf, Walker reached out just across the goal line for the major.

On its next possession, Queen's scored again. Scrimmaging on its own 30-yard line, Queen's used eight plays to march 80 yards, including a 35-yard run by Batstone. Two plays later, Evans baffled Regina defenders with a faked extension run, and waltzed into the Regina end zone.

In the fourth quarter tempers flared. Following another long march by Queen's, a skirmish developed when Regina's Jerry Crapper high tackled Queen's Bud Thomas and threw a punch at him. This drew the Queen's Jack McKelvey into the melee, and he promptly punched Crapper. More blows were exchanged before the referees stopped the fight. Both Crapper and McKelvey were ordered off the field and penalized, while the ball was positioned on the Regina 10-yard line. Three plays later, Roy Reynolds stepped over fallen bodies for Queen's eighth touchdown. Leadlay added the extra point to make the score 49 to 0.

A few minutes later Queen's gained possession of the ball near the Regina 10. From there, Carl Quinn rambled into the end zone to finish the scoring in the game.

**The lop-sided game made heroes out of Batstone and Leadlay. They were a two-man show. W.J. Finlay of the *Manitoba Free Press* wrote: "They [Batstone and Leadlay] uncorked their daring end runs and long passes at full speed, faked kicks, and then ran the ball back, while they outguessed the Regina backfield by returning kicks with tacklers hanging on to them and gave an exhibition of skill with their hands and feet that western rugby had never seen."**

**Leadlay's punts were particularly impressive, easily out-distancing those of Regina's Scotty MacEachern. Leadlay's kicking produced four converts and three singles.**

**Batstone meanwhile was a running whirlwind. He could do no wrong. One eastern critic described his play as "the crowning performance of a remarkable season." Batstone scored two touchdowns, kicked two converts, and unofficially rushed for 182 yards in three quarters of play.**

# 1924 QUEEN'S UNIVERSITY 11 BALMY BEACH 3

The success of Queen's carried into the 1924 football season. Queen's finished the regular season undefeated, and played Balmy Beach in the eastern final. The winner of the game was expected to meet the Winnipeg Victorias, the western champion, but a day after the eastern final the Victorias told

the C.R.U. that it was unable to travel east because of dissension within the team. Winnipeg club executives wanted to travel east on one railroad, while the majority of the players wanted to use another. The club executive did not support the players and, when the players made their own arrangements, the club executive and the C.R.U. jointly announced that the players would not be recognized as representing the Winnipeg Victorias.

Then the executives and players settled their dispute and announced that the Victorias would travel east. Too late. Bobby Hewitson, Secretary of the C.R.U., stated that there no longer was a stadium in which to play. The C.R.U. had subsequently allowed Varsity Stadium in Toronto to be rented for the national junior championship. In addition, the C.R.U. had destroyed the Grey Cup game tickets.

Even if another stadium had been available, an East versus West Grey Cup would not have been played because Queen's, the eastern champion, announced it would not turn out. The university stated that the Grey Cup game would be too close to examination time, and that Queen's football equipment had been locked away for the rest of the year. Accordingly, the C.R.U. declared that on the strength of its victory in the eastern final, played November 29, Queen's was the 1924 champion.

The eastern final and eventual Grey Cup game was a thriller. After Queen's scored two singles in the first quarter, the Golden Gaels increased its lead on an unusual play. With the wind at the Beach backs and the ball on the Beach 1-yard line, everyone expected a punt. However, someone called a play for the quarterback – bizarre considering the Beach quarterback was not on the field but on the bench serving a penalty. When the ball was snapped from centre there was no one there, the ball dribbled into the end zone and Britton was smothered for a 2-point safety.

The teams then exchanged single points before heading into a wild third quarter. The Beach held Queen's in its own half of the field, so Queen's tried some risky plays to advance the ball. Once, a Leadlay toss to Chandler over a number of Beach players was deflected and Jimmy Keith of the Beach gathered it but fell awkwardly and was immediately tackled.

Moments later, the crowd was thrilled as Morris Hughes for the Beach launched a high punt into the wind – and then caught his own kick as the ball was blown back toward the line of scrimmage.

Britton then electrified the crowd as he broke tackle after tackle on

a punt return. The Beach was presented with an excellent opportunity to score, but a holding penalty against Alex Ponton on the runback resulted in Queen's getting possession on its own 30.

A few minutes later, Queen's brought the fans to their feet with the only scoring play of the quarter. With Beach in punting formation, Hughes took a high snap from centre while the Queen's defenders charged through the line. Hughes' kick was blocked. The ball flew directly into the arms of James Wright and with no one between him and the Beach end zone he easily scored.

In the fourth quarter, Queen's again had the crowd roaring when Chandler, Leadlay, and Brown combined on the longest kick return of the game. Chandler accepted a Beach punt while surrounded by would-be tacklers. Chandler wriggled past three opponents, then lateralled the ball to Leadlay. From the Queen's 20, Leadlay exploded down the sideline, escaping the clutches of many Beach players as he sprinted toward the Beach line. At midfield, 'Bub' Britton stood ready. Everyone expected a bone-crunching collision, when suddenly Leadlay cut up the middle of the field. Britton gave chase, and at the Beach 25 he began to overtake Leadlay. Leadlay realized he was tiring so he drew Britton to his right, while the Queen's Brown caught up to the play. Leadlay lateralled the ball to Brown, but Britton shoved Leadlay aside and made a spectacular shoe-string tackle on Brown. Three plays later, Referee Reg De Gruchy disallowed a Leadlay field goal by penalizing Queen's for holding. Queen's did not need the points, but after the game De Gruchy admitted that the holding penalty was a bad call.

Shortly thereafter, Queen's Chandler misplayed a Beach punt, and the ball bounced free. Ponton raced to the ball for the Beach, and with Queen's players surrounding him, dribbled toward the Queen's goal line. At the Queen's 20, Leadlay stepped ahead of Ponton. Leadlay pounced on the ball, and in turn was pounced on by Ponton. The ball was free again. Chandler eventually recovered for Queen's, but the officials ruled that the ball had been fumbled forward by Leadlay. This was an illegal forward pass under the C.R.U. rules, and therefore Beach was given possession on the Queen's 15-yard line. Three plays later, Britton lifted an onside kick into the Queen's end zone for a rouge.

Beach continued to threaten, and moments later was robbed of two points when Chandler ran a kick out of his own end zone. Just as Chandler crossed the goal line, he was knocked backward into the end zone. The

Beach celebrated a safety touch, but the officials ruled that Chandler was stopped at the 1. A minute later, the Beach scored a single to end the game Queen's 11, Balmy Beach 3.

**The stars of this game were Queen's Chandler and Leadlay. Replacing Batstone in the first quarter, Chandler played a sensational game. Chandler made a few mistakes, but he saved many situations. He was exceptional in eluding Beach tacklers to avoid being rouged.**

**Meanwhile Leadlay, without Batstone at his side, carried the majority of the Queen's backfield work. Any other player would have collapsed under this burden, but Leadlay handled the task with ease. He scored four of Queen's 11 points.**

## 1925 OTTAWA SENATORS 24
## WINNIPEG TAMMANY TIGERS 1

Queen's tried to earn its fourth consecutive Grey Cup berth in 1925. The team, on a 26-game winning streak, needed only one more win to defend its title. However, the Ottawa Senators were determined to end the run. The Senators dominated the eastern final, defeating Queen's 11 to 2. Queen's was dismayed by its defeat, but in sportsmanlike fashion sent a telegram wishing Ottawa the best of luck in the final. Ottawa did not need much luck. As reported in the *Ottawa Citizen* opponent Winnipeg Tammany Tigers was supposed to be "the greatest team that ever left the West in quest of the senior crown," but like every other western team it was no match for the eastern champion.

The Senators controlled the game from the opening kick-off and, midway through the first quarter after advancing the ball 45 yards in five plays, executed a brilliant onside kick. Charlie Lynch lifted the ball high and short into the Winnipeg end zone. Before the Winnipeg players could react, Lynch jumped high into the air to touch the ball, and thereby made it free for any Ottawa player. The ball landed at the feet of Charlie Connell, and he fell on it for the touchdown.

In the second quarter, the Senators scored four times. A single was followed by a touchdown on a 20-yard run around the right end. Connell swung wide while Edgar Mulroney carried the ball to the right. As the pair crossed the line of scrimmage Mulroney, who appeared ready to lateral the ball to Connell, suddenly tucked the ball under his arm, and sped past a bewildered Winnipeg defence for a touchdown.

Ottawa made the score 13 to 0 before Winnipeg scored its only point of the game in the third quarter. Then, in the fourth quarter, Ottawa ensured victory by capitalizing on a Winnipeg error. At the Winnipeg 5, a Winnipeg ball-carrier lost control of the leather and another Tiger recovered it. The officials ruled that the ball had been passed illegally forward so Ottawa was given possession. Two plays later Lynch took the snap for Ottawa, lateralled to Mulroney, who then pitched out to Jerry Ault, who in turn tossed the ball to Connell. With no one near him, Connell scooted around the end for an easy major.

Shortly thereafter, another Winnipeg turnover produced Ottawa's fourth touchdown when Don Young fell on a dribbled ball in the Winnipeg end zone. The Senators concluded the scoring with a single to make the final score Ottawa 24, Winnipeg 1.

**Ottawa, which had last won the Dominion title in 1902 seven years prior to the awarding of the Grey Cup, achieved this victory because of the great play of Charlie Connell and Charlie Lynch. Both excelled on offence and defence. Offensively, Lynch's generalship at quarterback was intelligent and creative, while Connell produced two touchdowns. Defensively, Lynch's tackling was as sharp as a sword, and he and Connell buried many Winnipeg ball-carriers for no gain.**

The play of Connell and Lynch and other Ottawa defenders enabled teammate Joe Tubman to produce one of the oddest moments in Cup history. On a Winnipeg punt, Tubman allowed the ball to plop into a thick puddle of mud. He retrieved the ball from the slop and, when he noticed that there were no Winnipeg players in his vicinity, wiped the ball clean on his thigh and then calmly booted the ball back to Winnipeg.

A University of Toronto ball carrier (light jersey) crosses the 55-yard line against Queen's University in a regular season game. Varsity lost the 1926 Cup to the Ottawa Senators. (City of Toronto Archives)

## 1926  OTTAWA SENATORS 10
## UNIVERSITY OF TORONTO 7

The muddy conditions under which the 1925 game was played were mild compared with the frigid weather in which the 1926 final was decided. For the second time in three years a western team did not travel east to challenge for the Cup. Regina Roughriders should have played the winner of

the eastern final, but the 'Riders announced that it would not challenge for the Cup because of the lateness of the season. Accordingly, the 1926 eastern final, played on December 4, became the 1926 Grey Cup game.

The temperature for the final between the Ottawa Senators and the University of Toronto was extremely cold. The soft and greasy Toronto Varsity Stadium field was transformed into a slippery sheet of ice, and during the game the freezing temperatures turned the ball into an oval cake of ice. Many fumbles resulted. One critic wrote: "It was a game in which each team did its utmost to hand the honours to the other."

The players accepted the conditions, but the fans did not. Prior to the game, a small riot broke out at the box office as many ticketholders demanded a return of their money. While some were accommodated the demand for a refund became so great that the box office was closed. Those who did receive a refund wished that they had not: the eastern final was a thrilling game which went down to the wire.

The excitement started from the opening kick-off. The Senators quickly established a 2 to 0 lead, and then Varsity threatened to score a touchdown. Ottawa's Joe Miller mishandled a Varsity punt, and the ball bounced to midfield where Varsity's Warren Snyder and 'Pug' Irwin dribbled the ball toward the Ottawa goal line with Miller and a half-a-dozen other Senators in hot pursuit. At the line, Miller raced ahead and, as Irwin desperately dove for the ball, kicked the ball into touch to prevent a Varsity score.

Varsity tied the game 2 to 2 before Ottawa moved back in front with a touchdown. A Varsity turnover gave Ottawa possession of the ball on the Varsity 10, and two plays later Charlie Lynch smashed through the centre of the line for the score.

In the second quarter the Senators made numerous mistakes which enabled Varsity to trim Ottawa's lead to 7 to 6. But in the next quarter, the Senators played aggressively to re-establish a 4-point lead. In this quarter Ottawa hammered Varsity players to the turf so hard that at one point penalties resulted in Ottawa playing three men short.

The hard hitting did not weaken Varsity's determination, and near the beginning of the fourth quarter the Blues had a chance to take the lead. With Ottawa in possession at the Varsity 20, the Senators tried an end run. Roos broke through the line for Varsity and knocked down a lateral from Lynch to Miller. Roos had no time to pick up the ball, so, with a clear path to the Ottawa end zone, he began a dribble. Toronto fans roared for a score but with only 12 yards to go Miller was able to avoid the calamity as he raced past Roos to recover the ball for the Senators.

Two plays later, Varsity seized a Senators fumble on the Ottawa 20, but Ottawa's defence held. Varsity obtained a single on a wide field goal attempt, and the game ended Ottawa 10, Varsity 7.

**The outstanding player of the 1926 game was Ottawa's Joe Miller. Despite the adverse conditions, he caught and kicked the ball with great precision. Miller was the offensive spark for the Senators, and his defensive play preserved Ottawa's**

**victory. Twice he halted dribbles which would have otherwise resulted in Varsity touchdowns. He scored five of Ottawa's 10 points.**

## 1927 BALMY BEACH 9
## HAMILTON TIGERS 6

The relations between East and West grew worse in 1927, and it was decided that the western champion would not challenge for the Cup. Thus for the second consecutive year the C.R.U. decided that the eastern final between the Big Four champion Hamilton Tigers, and the O.R.F.U. champion Balmy Beach would be the Grey Cup final. The game was fantastic, and it resulted in one of the greatest upsets in Cup history.

Most football critics who gathered to watch the 1927 final at Varsity Stadium on Saturday, November 26, 1927, did not give Balmy Beach much of a chance to defeat the Tigers. Although the O.R.F.U. was a senior football league, its teams were not considered to be very good. To make matters worse for the Beach, several of its better players were seriously injured and unable to play. Hamilton was made 10-point favourites, but the critics were stunned when the Beach defeated Hamilton 9 to 6.

The game was won and lost before most of the fans took their seats. For Beach, Alex Ponton kicked-off to Timmy Languay, who caught the ball deep in his own territory. Surrounded by Beach tacklers he tried to kick the ball back to the Beach but Ernie Crowhurst crossed in front of Languay, and blocked the kick. The ball bounced into the Hamilton end zone, where Languay hastily kicked it across the deadline to surrender the game's first point.

On the next play Hamilton's Jerry Timmis lost control of the football, the Beach recovering it on the Hamilton 20. From there, Beach gained eight yards in two plays. On third down the Tigers expected the Beach to kick, but Alex Ponton faked the punt and easily scooted around the right end for a touchdown to make the score 6 to 0.

Beach extended its lead to 9 to 0 before Hamilton threatened to end the Beach hopes of winning the Cup. In the third quarter Hamilton dominated the play, eventually getting a break by recovering a fumble on the Beach 25. On the next play Frank Leadlay dashed around the end for 15 yards. Three plays later, the Tigers lined up in kicking formation. The ball was on the far right side of the field. As Leadlay took the snap, he rolled-out in that direction, stopped to kick, then fooled everyone. Instead of kicking toward the posts, he lifted an onside kick toward the sideline. Hamilton's Tebor McKelvey caught the ball on the Beach 1-yard line, and he crossed for a touchdown: Balmy Beach 9, Hamilton 6.

In the last quarter, Hamilton desperately tried to manoeuvre into scoring position. However, the Balmy Beach defence held out. Then in the last minute of play Hamilton's Walker returned a punt to the Beach 35 to set up a game-tying field goal attempt. Leadlay's kick was straight but short.

Mansell 'Red' Moore returned the ball to the Beach 25, and two plays later the Beach celebrated its victory.

The most outstanding players in this Grey Cup game were Harry 'Yip' Foster and Mansell Moore of the Beach. Their brilliant catches, kicks, and punt returns throttled the Tigers in this game. Moore's punt-return performance was particularly spectacular. He frequently brought the crowd to its feet with punt returns of up to 30 yards. To one critic, Moore's play was one of the best seen in Canadian football in years. "Place the name of 'Red' Moore high on the wall in Fame's Hall," the critic wrote. "No backfielder, not even a [Lionel] Conacher or a [Harry] Batstone, ever played a better or possibly as good a game as the fiery-thatched Balmy Beach youngster did on Saturday. He was reckless, brilliant, and effective, and the Tigers couldn't stop him at all. Moore was the outstanding player on the field. He meant the difference between defeat and victory for his team, and how he came through is now a matter of history."

Umpire Joe O'Brien shared this view. After the game O'Brien said that Moore was one of the best players he had ever seen.

Meanwhile Foster's kicking kept Hamilton pinned deep in its own territory for most of the game. Foster easily out-kicked Hamilton's Frank Leadlay, and Foster showed great consistency in punting the ball high into the air to enable his outside wings to limit Hamilton runbacks. Foster's kicking produced three points.

The Beach 1927 Grey Cup victory ended an exciting era of Canadian football. The three wins by Queen's University from 1922 through 1924 showed how dominant University teams were in the early history of Canadian football. However, the University of Toronto's 1926 Cup appearance was the last made by a University team, and in 1936 the intercollegiate teams officially withdrew from Grey Cup competition.

The victories by Queen's and other eastern teams also showed the West that the eastern style of football was better than that of the West. The West struggled to gain recognition for its style of play, but ultimately the arrogant attitude of eastern football supporters led to much anger between the eastern and western football unions. Near the end of this era the West did not bother sending a team to the East to challenge for the Grey Cup. The West regrouped and began to build the football machines that would eventually capture the Grey Cup.

## Chapter Four

# REGINA ROUGHRIDERS UNABLE TO WIN CUP
## 1928-1934

n 1928 a western team returned to challenge for the Grey Cup. The Regina Roughriders was the most powerful western team ever assembled, and from 1928 to 1934 the Roughriders played in six Grey Cup games. But Regina won not one Cup. The strong eastern teams turned aside every Roughrider challenge for the national title during this period, and ensured that the Cup did not travel west.

This era of Canadian football was also highlighted by the introduction of the forward pass. In the 1929 Cup, Regina unveiled this new offensive weapon to the thrill of eastern football fans. The forward pass added a new dimension to the sport, and it immediately added controversy and confusion. According to Gordon Currie, author of *100 Years of Canadian Football,* "The poor referee [in the 1929 Grey Cup game] had considerable difficulty interpreting the still ill-defined rules under which the game was played and was repeatedly most confused when he had to change rule books at half-time."

The use of the forward pass by Regina was resented by eastern football representatives. A battle was waged over this weapon, and in the 1930 Grey Cup game the C.R.U. banned it. Bob Calder and Garry Andrews, in *Rider Pride,* described the reason for the ban as follows: "The 'Riders had caught the eastern officials off guard with their passing in 1929, and the C.R.U., fighting to discourage its use, ruled that the forward pass could not be used in the Grey Cup game unless both participating teams had utilized it during the season." Since Toronto Balmy Beach, the 1930 eastern champion, had not used the pass during the season, it could not be used in the 1930 game.

A year later the C.R.U. reversed its policy. After moving the convert scrimmage line from the 25-yard line to the 5-yard line, and deciding that the convert could be scored by a drop-kick, place-kick, run or pass, the C.R.U. endorsed the use of the forward pass for all leagues. The last-mentioned change immediately caused a stir among the eastern teams. Unfamiliar with the passing attack, eastern clubs scrambled to find specialized instruction on the use of the forward pass. In Montreal, Frank 'Shag' Shaugnessy invited Warren Stevens, a star quarterback from Syracuse University in New York, to instruct the McGill University quarterbacks. The Montreal Winged Wheelers were very impressed with Stevens' abilities, and secured his services. Montreal's decision was rewarded as Stevens led the Winged Wheelers to a Grey Cup title.

The forward pass made the Canadian game more exciting. However, the results of the Cup games from 1928 to 1934 were not affected by its use. In fact, footwear played a more prominent role in some of these games than did the forward pass.

## 1928 HAMILTON TIGERS 30 REGINA ROUGHRIDERS 0

Hamilton (striped jerseys) battle the Argonauts. Hamilton defeated Regina 30 to 0 to win the 1928 Cup. (City of Toronto Archives)

The first game of this period, played December 1, 1928, was between the Regina Roughriders and the Hamilton Tigers. Hamilton was a magnificent offensive machine, and it showed its prowess by mauling every opponent it faced. The Tigers outscored its 1928 opponents by a ratio of 9 points to 1, and thus Hamilton was expected to bury Regina. Hamilton amassed 22 first downs to Regina's five and easily defeated the Roughriders 30 to 0.

Hamilton quickly moved ahead following a Regina turnover. Regina's Fred Wilson and Jack Erskine made an error on a lateral, and Hamilton recovered the ball on the Regina 35. Five plays later, Brian Timmis, a former

Regina Roughrider, threw Regina tacklers aside and surged into the end zone from the Regina 10 to give Hamilton a 5 to 0 lead.

After increasing its lead to 7 to 0, Hamilton obtained the break which propelled it to overwhelming victory. Regina converted a third down gamble in the third quarter, and then Regina's Fritz Sandstrom lateralled the ball to Greg Grassick. Grassick was unable to control the ball and it bounced into the open field. A pride of Tigers raced to the loose ball, and Hamilton's Small dribbled downfield. As he tired, teammate Eddie Wright took over, dribbling into the Regina end zone where Jimmy Simpson fell on the ball for the major. Frank 'Pep' Leadlay kicked the convert to make the score Hamilton 13, Regina 0.

Hamilton scored two more touchdowns in the third quarter, and then Timmis closed the scoring in the final quarter when he hurdled over fallen Regina defenders and stormed into the Regina end zone.

**Despite the one-sided 30 to 0 victory, Regina gave a courageous display. Fritz Sandstrom was one of many Regina players who exemplified Regina's effort. In the second quarter, he split his head wide open tackling a hard-charging Leadlay. Blood oozed from the wound, but after having a bandage wrapped around his head, Sandstrom remained in the game. The injury did not affect Sandstrom as in the second half he continued to play a spirited and reckless game.**

**The hero of the 1928 Grey Cup game was Hamilton's Hawley 'Huck' Welch. He dominated the game with his tremendous punting, and easily kicked the ball further than the Regina kickers. Whenever Hamilton required a long kick, Welch provided one. In addition, Welch starred on punt returns. Often he combined with Leadlay for punt returns which brought the crowd to its feet. Welch finished the game with two singles.**

## 1929 HAMILTON TIGERS 14
## REGINA ROUGHRIDERS 3

Hawley Welch was in the spotlight again on November 30, 1929. For the second consecutive year the Regina Roughriders met the Hamilton Tigers in the Grey Cup game. Regina had a new weapon, the forward pass, in its arsenal, but still could not defeat the Tigers. Hamilton controlled the game with Welch's kicking and its powerful ground attack. The final score was Hamilton 14, Regina 3.

The first half was a struggle. Both teams had difficulty adjusting to an icy gale, and the score at the end of 30 minutes of play was Hamilton 2, Regina 1.

The most exciting play of the first half occurred in the second quarter following a blocked punt. Regina obtained possession and on the next play made history with the first forward pass thrown in a Grey Cup game. Regina's 'Jersey' Jack Campbell took the snap from centre, back pedalled a few steps, and then threw downfield. Hamilton's Simpson stepped in front of the intended receiver, to knock the ball down. However, according to the C.R.U. rules in 1929 the ball was still playable. A scramble ensued and Regina recovered the ball on the Hamilton 30.

The teams exchanged single points in the third quarter, and then Hamilton obtained the biggest break of the game when Regina's Brown mishandled a swirling Hamilton punt. Hamilton's Simpson recovered the ball and raced 40 yards for a touchdown.

Early in the fourth quarter a kicking duel produced an odd moment in Grey Cup history. Gibb accepted a Regina punt, and then lateralled the ball to Languay, who in turn kicked the ball back to Regina. It was clear that the ball would sail into the Regina end zone, so Referee Priestly charged toward the Regina goal line to be on top of the play. As Priestly watched the ball descend, he collided squarely with the goal post. Priestly collapsed to the field unconscious, while Regina's Saul Bloomfield was tackled for a rouge. The score was now Hamilton 10, Regina 3.

Hamilton scored three more singles before attempting its only forward pass of the game. Regina was taken by surprise, and Welch easily completed the pass to a wide-open Simpson. Simpson then lateralled to 'Cap' Fear, who trotted into the Regina end zone for a touchdown. However, the score was disallowed because Priestly ruled that the ball had been caught by Simpson within the Regina 25. According to the C.R.U. rules, this resulted in an illegal forward pass. Many spectators thought Priestly was wrong. They believed that Simpson had caught the ball on the Regina 35.

Many years after this game Hamilton coach Mike Rodden insisted that Welch, Simpson, and Fear had been robbed of scoring the first touchdown via the pass in Grey Cup history. Rodden said, "I've never charged that Umpire Priestly of Winnipeg was dishonest. But he called that touchdown back because he said it had been completed within the 25-yard line. Because of the snow, I don't know how he could even see the play."

Soon after, Welch hammered the ball across the deadline and the game ended Hamilton 14, Regina 3.

**For the second year in a row Hamilton's Hawley 'Huck' Welch was the most valuable player in the Grey Cup. Welch's kicking frequently kept Regina pinned in its own zone. This was especially important in the first half when Hamilton's offence only produced two points. Welch finished the game with six singles, two of which were scored while kicking into the icy gale.**

Brian Timmis guided Hamilton to Grey Cup victories in 1928, 1929 and 1932. (Canadian Football Hall of Fame & Museum)

The greatest individual performance in a Grey Cup game in this era occurred on December 6, 1930. Regina had again qualified, and this time it faced Balmy Beach. The forward pass was banned, and therefore Balmy Beach was favoured. However, Regina played an extremely good game, and only the heroic performance of Ted 'The Moaner' Reeve enabled Balmy Beach to win.

Beach dominated the first half. Sloppy play by Regina enabled Ab Box and Claude Harris to give the Beach a 5 to 0 lead. Then midway through the second quarter, Beach solidified its lead. Scrimmaging on the Beach 27-yard line, Frank Hendry broke through the line like a runaway train for a gain of 33 yards. A few plays later, Regina's Ken Traynor accepted a punt near his own goal line and was drilled. Traynor fumbled and Beach recovered the ball on the Regina 2-yard line. Three plays later, Bobby Reid crashed through the line for a touchdown.

Gay Kirkpatrick and Ab Box of Balmy Beach watch a referee unpile Beach and Regina Roughrider players in the 1930 Cup.
(Canadian Football Hall of Fame & Museum)

In the third quarter, Regina broke the shutout with a single. The score gave the team confidence, and in another three plays Regina defenders broke through the line of scrimmage to block a Harris punt. Regina recovered the ball on the Beach 20, and from there gained five yards on two plays. On the next play, Regina kicked the ball onside. Regina's Freddie Brown raced into the end zone, and then battled Dumy Mays for possession. A pile-up developed. Who was at the bottom? When the referees dispersed the pile of bodies, Brown was found clutching the ball tightly to his chest for a touchdown.

The momentum in the game was shifting, but a minute later a controversial decision took the steam out of the Regina attack. Bloomfield punted a high spiral into Beach territory where Mays allowed the ball to drop. The ball then took a wierd bounce toward the onrushing Regina players. Bloomfield quickly pounced on the ball, but he slid over the top of it. Then

Despite a seriously injured shoulder, Ted 'the Moaner' Reeve courageously led Balmy Beach to the 1930 championship.
(Canadian Football Hall of Fame & Museum)

Regina's Campbell scooped it up and shook off a number of Beach tacklers before being caught within the shadow of the Beach posts. However, Regina was penalized for an illegal forward pass, and the ball was moved back to the Beach 46. Visibly upset by the decision, the team was unable to take advantage of its field position.

In the final quarter Regina regained its composure. The 'Riders advanced the ball to the Beach 21, and threatened to take the lead. At this point, a lanky figure rose from the Beach bench, headgear in hand. There was a thunderous roar from the crowd, and Ted Reeve trotted onto the field. Reeve was not expected to play in this game due to injury, but Beach needed his brilliant defensive skills in order to maintain its lead. Reeve's presence was immediately felt as Regina was unable to gain a first down and was forced to punt.

Three plays later Regina's Saul Bloomfield accepted a Beach punt and tried to gallop down the field for a long return. He dodged a couple of tackles and appeared to be en route to a touchdown when at midfield Reeve hurled his body into Bloomfield's for a touchdown-saving tackle.

Soon Reeve was again the centre of attention. This time he broke through the line of scrimmage and blocked a Regina onside kick. The ball bounced to the Beach 48, and from there a group of Beach players dribbled it downfield. At the Regina 29-yard line, a Beach player flopped on the ball. A minute later Beach closed the scoring as Harris kicked the ball through the Regina end zone. The game ended Balmy Beach 11, Regina 6.

**The hero of the 1930 game was Ted Reeve. Despite seeing limited action, Reeve single-handedly preserved the Beach victory. In the fourth quarter, he entered the game risking further injury to a shoulder he had dislocated a week earlier, and courageously made two important tackles and blocked a punt. It was performances like this that enabled Reeve to be elected to the Canadian Football Hall of Fame on June 19, 1963.**

**Reeve was very modest about his heroics, and after the game credited Frank Hendry and Ross Trimble for the victory. According to Reeve, "Trimble's torn knee gave way early in the fray, but the big man held in there desperately for the greatest part of the distance to steady the kids on the line. Hendry started playing the game of his career and halfway through the first period cracked his collar-bone. Nobody knew that but himself until the match was over and he went right to the dying minutes of the contest without a rest or without one sign that he wanted relief."**

On December 5, 1931, the heroic performance of Ted Reeve in 1930 was succeeded by the heroic performance of Warren Stevens. After instructing the McGill University quarterbacks on the intricacies of the forward pass, Stevens remained in Canada to play for the Montreal Winged Wheelers. His passing led Montreal to the final where the Montreal passing attack unhorsed the Regina Roughriders 22 to 0. However, this game is not best remembered for Stevens' passing or the score but for the bizarre incidents which occurred off the field. Critical to the Montreal victory was the change in footwear the team made at half-time. This gave them added traction. Regina coach Al Ritchie after the game blamed himself for not having the proper footwear for his team, but as was later revealed he was not to blame. A mistake in delivery provided Montreal with the shoes which the Montreal players wore in the second half. Those shoes should have gone to the Regina dressing room!

In the first quarter a costly Regina error started Montreal on the road to victory. Scrimmaging from the 'Riders 37-yard line, Eddie 'Dynamite' James was greeted by a number of Wheelers, who forced a fumble. Montreal's Pete Jotkus and Henry 'Gab' Gabarino threw aside their blocks and began to dribble the ball toward the Regina goal line. At the 5, Jotkus scooped up the ball and carried it into the end zone for a touchdown. The major made the score Montreal 7, Regina 0.

In the second quarter, Montreal was presented with numerous opportunities to increase its lead, but was unable to capitalize. Then in the third quarter came the turning point. Regina was threatening to score having driven the ball from its own half to the Montreal 14-yard line in seven plays. James was then handed the ball, and he quickly forced his 190-pound frame through the line. But for the second time James could not control the ball. It rolled to the Montreal 3-yard line where Montreal's Wally Whitty recovered. Regina was devastated by the fumble, and for the remainder of the game never threatened to score.

The most spectacular play came near the end of the third quarter. Montreal had possession on the Regina 37 and Stevens took the snap. While the Regina defenders charged into the backfield and attempted to tackle the scrambling Stevens, Montreal's William 'Kennie' Grant sprinted for the Regina goal line. Eluding the clutches of several Regina defenders, Stevens threw the ball 45 yards to Grant. Grant made the reception three yards deep in the Regina end zone, and thereby scored the first touchdown via the forward pass in Grey Cup history.

In the final quarter, Huck Welch kicked a field goal

In 1931 Warren Stevens of the Montreal Winged Wheelers threw the first forward touchdown pass in Cup history. (Canadian Football Hall of Fame & Museum)

Warren Stevens.

for Montreal, and Whitty scored a 7-yard touchdown by accepting a lateral from Stevens and cutting a wide arc around the right end. Stevens converted the score on a play which baffled Regina. While Regina players had their arms upstretched in the hope of blocking the expected kick, Stevens faked the placement and scampered across the goal line untouched for the extra point. Regina had never been informed that a convert could be made by running the ball over the goal line!

**Montreal's Warren Stevens was the outstanding player of the 1931 game. On every offensive play Stevens stood out by either tossing the ball or running with it. His play selection throughout the game had the Regina defence guessing, and enabled him to engineer long drives. Stevens finished the game with 41 yards rushing, and 87 yards passing. He also threw an interception, and a touchdown.**

Although Stevens gave an outstanding individual performance, which was supported by teammates Gordon Perry, Huck Welch, and Tommy Burns, Montreal's victory rested with Regina coach Al Ritchie, manager Fred Wilson and player Gordon Barber. Combined, their fateful decisions regarding footwear cost Regina the 1931 Grey Cup game.

After the game, in an exclusive interview with *The Toronto Star*'s Lou Marsh, coach Ritchie lamented: "I pulled a boner.

"You know just as soon as we arrived here I hustled out to get my boys a practice on the field we were going to play upon. I couldn't get them on the actual battlefield at Montreal Stadium, but I had them on the practice field where ground conditions were about the same. I found that underneath the inch or so of snow the turf was still soft enough to give a cleat a grip. Good sharp cleats would be an advantage, I thought. My players agreed, and so I sent every one of their rugby boots out and had nice, long sharp cleats built on them. Shoemakers worked all night long to do them for me.

"Sixty-seven dollars those cleats cost me – and we would have been far better off without them. Sixty-seven dollars' worth of new cleats about ruined us," soliloquized Ritchie.

"[Molson Stadium] was just like a skating rink when it came time for the game. The long, sharp cleats our boys were shod with were worse than our old worn ones. They couldn't hold their feet at all on the icy spots."

"Fair for one as it was for the other," Marsh murmured to stir Ritchie on.

"Sure, but what happens," said Ritchie. "In the first half we begin to slide and skid and we had them to a 7 to 0 score … Then we go in at half-time … and half the Montreal team comes out in tennis sneakers and basket-ball shoes and beats the tar out of us. Makes a real team look like a set of monkeys because they can keep their feet and we can't … It's a crime that we have to go home beaten by 22 to 0 … "

Without Ritchie's knowledge, Barber and Wilson had made arrangements to obtain rubber-soled shoes. Calder and Andrews, in *Rider Pride*, described that: "During the previous evening, Barber, Desmond Grubb, and Greg Grassick were at the 'Riders hotel and, while the others went to bed, Barber wandered into a dance in the ballroom looking for excitement. Before going to bed, he stepped outside and found himself in a freezing snowstorm. He woke up Freddie Wilson, who made some telephone calls and arranged to have a set of canvas lacrosse shoes sent to the Roughrider dressing room. They never arrived, however, and the players were forced to wear the ill-suited cleats. When the Winged Wheelers took to the field, the Regina officials were stunned to see each player out-fitted in the lacrosse shoes. An errant delivery boy had taken them to the wrong quarters, and the delighted Wheelers … happily accepted the gift."

## 1932  HAMILTON TIGERS 25 / REGINA ROUGHRIDERS 6

A Hamilton player is tackled in the end zone by two Varsity Blues in the East final. One week later Hamilton won the 1932 Cup over Regina.
(City of Toronto Archives)

Regina made its fifth consecutive Grey Cup appearance on December 3, 1932. The Roughriders had the proper footwear for this game, but it did not matter as the powerful plunging barrage of the Hamilton Tigers stomped all over Regina 25 to 6.

Hamilton secured victory in the opening minutes of the first quarter. On the opening kick-off, Regina's Curt Schave was hit heavily as he ran back the kick. Schave fumbled, and Hamilton's Jimmy Simpson recovered to give Hamilton excellent field position. A few plays later the ball was advanced

to Regina's goal line area, and then Dinny Gardiner ran the ball around the end for a touchdown.

According to *Rider Pride*, this score should never have occurred. Regina had won the coin toss at the start of the game, and Regina coach Al Ritchie was going to elect to kick-off. However, Schave convinced Ritchie to change tactics. "[Schave] implored me to receive the kick-off," Ritchie later remembered. "He pointed out that the field was in fine condition and he said he felt like running and, oh my, how that boy could run. So I said, okay, we'll receive. Schave catches the ball and he starts up the field – he was a great runner that boy. Five, ten, fifteen, twenty yards he comes and then he's at midfield. Bang! somebody hits him. Pop! goes the ball from his arms. Thud! a Tiger grabs it …

"Well, I know we should have kicked off."

Hamilton extended its lead to 10 to 0, and then in the second quarter the Tigers capitalized on another Regina error. Scrimmaging near the 'Riders goal line, Regina's 'Augie' De Frate dropped back to pass. De Frate scanned the field and then threw the ball crossfield toward the sideline. But the ball hung in the air, allowing Ike Sutton to race into position for the interception. No one stood between Sutton and the Regina end zone, and he galloped across the goal line for Hamilton's second touchdown of the game.

The third quarter belonged to Hamilton's Brian Timmis. Playing in his last Grey Cup, the 10-year veteran of the Canadian gridiron and future Hall of Famer gave a magnificent performance which delighted the partisan Hamilton fans. In the first few minutes of the quarter, Timmis was particularly outstanding as he carried the ball on successive plunges from midfield to the Regina 32. Timmis then gained 12 more yards to set up a Gardiner field goal.

Hamilton's Jimmy Simpson scored a touchdown later in the quarter before Regina broke the shutout. Trailing 25 to 0 in the fourth quarter, Regina desperately threw the ball all over the field in an effort to manouevre into scoring position. Eventually the 'Riders scrimmaged on the Hamilton 1-yard line, and after six battering and bruising plays (with the assistance of penalties) De Frate squeezed into the end zone to end the scoring: Hamilton 25, Regina 6.

**Hamilton's victory was the result of the powerful running provided by Dave Sprague and Brian Timmis. Unofficially Timmis gained 105 yards rushing, and together they gained in excess of 200 yards. According to most observers, Timmis was the most important figure in Hamilton's victory, but for the second year in a row Regina coach Al Ritchie blamed Regina's loss on another factor.**

In a post-game interview, Ritchie leaned his thin form against a desk in the business office of the Hamilton Amateur Athletic Association Grounds and murmured sadly "Stagefright."

"We got off on the wrong foot when Schave fumbled on the first play and couldn't get the ball back till it was too late. I never saw a team so stagey before going into action, but I was sure the boys would be all right as soon as the preliminaries were over. They didn't come out of it, that's all."

In 1933 a new playoff format was temporarily introduced. Realizing that the standard of intercollegiate football was declining, the universities withdrew from the Grey Cup. Accordingly, to protect the interests of eastern Canadian football, the C.R.U. swiftly ruled that the western champion was required to play the Big Four champion to decide one of the finalists for the Grey Cup game. Winnipeg 'Pegs, tired after having already played two western playoff games, provided no match for the Big Four champion Toronto Argonauts. Considered the greatest football team ever assembled in Canada up to 1933, Toronto employed its razzle-dazzle end run tactics to perfection against Winnipeg, and sailed to a 13 to 0 victory. Then on December 9, 1933 Toronto defeated the Sarnia Imperials in a thrilling defensive struggle to capture the national crown.

The first half was dominated by the Imperials. Toronto's offence was stopped on every occasion, and only the terrific punting of Ab Box kept the score to Sarnia 1, Toronto 0.

Sarnia made the score 2 to 0, and as the third quarter of the game progressed it seemed that Toronto was headed to defeat. Suddenly, with eight minutes remaining in the third quarter, the momentum turned in favour of Toronto. With Sarnia ready to punt, Toronto's 'Tuffy' Griffiths charged through the line of scrimmage faster than the proverbial speeding bullet. He blocked the punt, and Toronto secured the ball on the Sarnia 35-yard line. On the next play, Jack Taylor sprinted around the end for 25 yards, and then Tommy Burns booted a field goal to give Toronto a 3 to 2 lead.

In the final quarter, two tremendous punts by Sarnia's Hugh 'Bummer' Stirling produced the tying score. Both teams played ferociously in an attempt to take the lead, but neither could get into scoring range. Then with five minutes remaining Toronto recovered a fumbled punt return on the Sarnia 52, and from there pushed the ball deeper into Sarnia territory. Eventually Toronto scrimmaged from the Sarnia 20-yard line, and Box scored a single.

In the last minute of play, Sarnia nearly snatched victory. Sarnia quarterback Rocky Parsaca threw a 25-yard pass to Norman Perry, who cut across the field and galloped down the sideline alone. Box dove at Perry's feet near the Toronto 45-yard line, but only managed to get a piece of Perry. Only at the Toronto 5 was Perry stopped. Sarnia smelled victory but Referee Jo-Jo Stirrett frantically waved his arms and ruled play dead at the Toronto 45 because Perry had stepped six inches out of bounds. According to the observers closest to the action the decision was accurate.

After the game, Perry recalled the play: "I don't know whether I stepped out or not. The officials said I did, and I was trying so hard to stay inside [the line] that I never noticed. Honestly, fellows, I don't know whether I stepped out."

From the Toronto 45, Sarnia was unable to gain any further ground, and Toronto hung on to win the 1933 Grey Cup game, 4 to 3.

**The most valuable player of the game was Toronto's Ab Box. Throughout the game, his punting prevented Sarnia from obtaining good field position. Even when subjected to a heavy rush, he managed to kick the ball far downfield. His defensive play was also instrumental in Toronto's victory. Often the last man between a Sarnia ball-carrier and the Toronto goal line, Box always made a touchdown-saving tackle. But for Box's tackles, Sarnia would have won the 1933 Grey Cup by a wide margin.**

Despite Box's heroic play, Toronto's 'Indian Summer' Frank Tindall believed that Sarnia only kept the game close because it had a definite edge in the footwear department. While Toronto players had problems with the icy field, Sarnia players were able to easily keep their balance. After the game Tindall described the Sarnia advantage: "You know we tried running shoes and then went back to cleats, but they held their feet much better than we did. I found out in the third quarter what the reason for that was. They had them filed across the top, making two points to every cleat instead of one. Those birds are what you would really call canny!"

# 1934 SARNIA IMPERIALS 20
REGINA ROUGHRIDERS 12

Regina returned to the Grey Cup game on November 24, 1934, and according to a Moose Jaw astrologer there were strong planetary influences in the universe which favoured a Regina victory. However, the eastern champion Sarnia Imperials had the 'stars' on its side in the national final. Led by Ormond Beach, Hugh Stirling, and Norman Perry the Imperials captured the Grey Cup by a score of 20 to 12.

Sarnia jumped in front 5 to 0 on the kicking of Stirling and Alex Hayes, before solidifying its lead with a touchdown early in the second quarter. With Regina in possession, Roughrider quarterback Ted Olson mishandled a snap. Sarnia recovered the ball on the Regina 40, and three plays later Beach avoided a strong Regina rush to complete a 35-yard pass to Stirling and move the ball close to the Regina posts. Then two plays later, Sarnia executed a perfect extension run. The ball was lateralled to Perry, and in turn to Gordie Patterson. No one could stop Patterson as the former University of Western Ontario Mustang steamed into the end zone.

Regina quickly answered this score after a bad snap on a third down punt gave the team possession on the Sarnia 6. Three plays later, Olson dove over the top of the line and into the end zone to make the score 11 to 5.

Late in the third quarter, Sarnia increased its lead with a play many western fans believed robbed Regina of a chance to win the 1934 Cup. Scrimmaging from near midfield, Sarnia's Stirling hammered the ball high into the gusty wind. Sarnia's outside wings raced down the field, and when Regina's Young caught the ball three Sarnia tacklers smashed into him.

The ball flew into the end zone where Sarnia's Johnny Manore quickly smothered it for a touchdown. Regina fans cursed the score, and in the press box western journalists, who had a clear view of the play, howled "No yards. No yards! That one won't go." The eastern journalists agreed, but on the field the referees felt that Young had been given the five yards required by the rules. The referees signalled touchdown, and Hayes kicked the convert to make the score Sarnia 17, Regina 5.

Regina reduced the gap to 17 to 12 in the fourth quarter when, on a third down gamble, Olson completed a 16-yard touchdown pass to Steve Adkins, who made a yard-high leap for a sparkling finger-tip catch. However, this was as close as Regina came to winning. Regina made many mistakes near the end of the game, and Sarnia closed the scoring with three unanswered singles.

**The best player in the 1934 Grey Cup game was Sarnia's Ormond Beach. A product of Kansas, Beach was all over the field defensively. On Regina's running plays, Beach hit the line with such force that Roughrider linemen were strewn across the gridiron. According to most observers it was the tackling of Beach which singlehandedly prevented Regina from winning the Grey Cup.**

Sarnia's 1934 victory ended the third era of Cup competition. From 1928 to 1934 the Regina Roughriders challenged the eastern football establishment six times, but could not take the Grey Cup west. Despite western teams playing progressively better football toward the end of the era, it remained clear that Canadian football was dominated by the eastern teams. However, Regina's efforts were a sign of things to come. The West was learning how to adapt its 'American' style of football to the eastern style of play, and in 1935 the West shocked the eastern Canadian football establishment by winning its first Grey Cup.

## Chapter Five

# THE GREY CUP GOES WEST
## 1935-1941

**A** new powerhouse emerged in 1935 to replace the Regina Roughriders as western Canadian champion. From 1935 to 1941, the Winnipeg 'Pegs, later to become the Winnipeg Blue Bombers, dominated western football, and competed in five Grey Cups. The 1935 Winnipeg team was the best ever to be sent east in pursuit of the Cup. Led by a group of talented American imports, Winnipeg took the Grey Cup west in 1935.

Winnipeg's upset stunned the eastern football establishment. For over four decades the eastern style of Canadian football played almost exclusively by Canadians had always been better, but now there was serious doubt concerning the superiority of their teams. The East wanted to maintain its superior position, and as a result of Winnipeg's 1935 victory a new round in the battle between the eastern and western unions was waged. Bending to the wishes of eastern Canadian football interests, the C.R.U. immediately implemented new import rules for all teams in Canada. In 1936, the C.R.U. decided that only American residents of Canada prior to January 1 of a year were eligible to play in games sanctioned by the C.R.U. The western teams, which featured many talented American players, ignored the absurd and restrictive rule. This led to sanctions against the western football teams, and in 1936 and 1940 only eastern teams were eligible to compete for the Grey Cup.

This obviously did not please the Canadian football fan. They wanted unity in the sport, and demanded to see the best football teams across Canada compete for the national title. They did not care about the C.R.U. rules or its internal politics. The tremendous enthusiasm for the East versus West Grey Cup games was best shown in 1941 when 19,065 people, a Grey Cup record at the time, jammed into Toronto's Varsity Stadium. Many fans were turned away at the gate, but most of them managed to find spots to watch the game by either climbing onto roof-tops or hanging out of windows of nearby buildings. Such overwhelming fan support eventually caused the Canadian football establishment to rethink its attitudes on import players in the Canadian game, and helped to bring peace to the warring eastern and western football unions.

Winnipeg's 1935 Grey Cup victory also brought a rapid movement toward professionalism in Canadian football. During this period it was not uncommon for western teams to provide free room and board to many of its highly-skilled and specialized American players. In some cases the American players were even paid a salary for playing. The eastern teams reacted to this by deciding to pay some of their better Canadian players. It was conceivable that if the eastern teams did not do so, then they would either move to the West or play in the United States where professionalism in football was rampant.

The changes to the Canadian game in this era were significant, and provided Canadian football with some of its greatest moments.

## 1935 WINNIPEG 'PEGS 18 HAMILTON TIGERS 12

The first Grey Cup game of this era was spectacular. On Saturday, December 7, 1935, the Winnipeg 'Pegs and the Hamilton Tigers met in Hamilton to decide the championship. Hamilton had stormed through the eastern play-offs, and was favoured to defeat the 'Pegs. However, Winnipeg received an incredible individual performance from Fritz 'Twinkle Toes' Hanson, and won 18 to 12.

In the first quarter, Winnipeg took the lead. Following a short punt by Hamilton's Huck Welch, Winnipeg's Russ Rebholz fired a pass for Bud Marquardt, who at full speed leapt high into the air. The Tiger defenders stood dumbfounded as Marquardt came down with the ball, and charged over the goal line for a touchdown.

The lead was reduced to 5 to 3 before Winnipeg scored another touchdown on the finest pass of the 1935 season. With the ball on the Hamilton 33, Winnipeg's Bob Fritz took the snap and quickly lateralled the ball to Rebholz. Rebholz shot around the end, while Tiger defenders shifted to

**Surrounded by Hamilton Tigers, a Winnipeg 'Peg smothers the ball in the 1935 Cup.**
(City of Toronto Archives)

stop the run. Suddenly, Rebholz stopped and faded back to pass. He kept dropping back and dropping back until he finally spotted Greg Kabat streaking through the centre of the field. Rebholz hit Kabat on the fly. With only one tackler to beat, Kabat cut across the field, shook off the Hamilton defender, and scored.

In the third quarter, a touchdown by Hamilton's Wilf Paterson and a single made the score Winnipeg 12, Hamilton 10. At this point, Hanson made one of the most memorable punt returns in Grey Cup history. Accepting a Welch punt at the Winnipeg 32, Hanson saw two Tiger tacklers anxiously waiting to sandwich him. Hanson sprinted to his left, wheeled, reversed his field, and then cut sharply straight ahead. Speeding straight down the middle of the field, Hanson had more difficulty evading his own men than Tiger tacklers, who seemed to be moving in slow motion. No Tiger laid a paw on Hanson and for the last 30 yards the closest player to him was teammate Kabat. After the game Frank 'Shag' Shaugnessy said that in 34 years of football he had never seen anything that equalled Hanson's magnificent dash.

Hanson's touchdown was the turning point of the game. Hamilton drew to within six points of Winnipeg, but in the last few minutes of the game the Tigers were unable to score the game-tying touchdown. Winnipeg's defence played extremely well, and ended Hamilton's last scoring threat when Hanson collected an onside kick in the Winnipeg end zone. Winnipeg 18, Hamilton 12.

**The outstanding player of the 1935 game was Fritz Hanson. Every journalist covering the game paid him the highest tributes. According to Lou Marsh, Hanson was the fastest man on a Canadian gridiron in over 30 years. Former Tiger players agreed, stating that he was probably the best football player since the era of Lionel Conacher. In comparing Conacher to Hanson, they noted that whereas Conacher ran the ball by speed and strength, Hanson made his runs with lightning speed and evasive skill. Hanson's display was innovative. M.J. Rodden wrote in *The Globe*: "How that man can go. He has the happy faculty of being able to reverse his field and he knows his way around in any company. He did things that were all wrong according to Canadian football ethics, and he got away with it." Throughout the game Hanson made many brilliant runs, returning kicks for over 300 yards, scoring a touchdown, and kicking a convert.**

Fritz Hanson soars across the field. He led the 'Pegs to the 1935 championship. (Canadian Football Hall of Fame & Museum)

Although Winnipeg won the 1935 Cup, it remained in the East. No one could find it! As he boarded the train homeward bound Joe Ryan, manager of the 'Pegs, stated: "It's probably down in Sarnia. We don't care very much if we ever get it, but I suppose it'll come along later."

## 1936 SARNIA IMPERIALS 26
## OTTAWA ROUGH RIDERS 20

In 1936 strife between eastern and western football officials prevented the West from winning its second Grey Cup. The C.R.U. strictly applied the rules it had adopted earlier in the year and, when the Regina Roughriders issued a challenge, five of Regina's American players were ruled ineligible.

Regina team officials, appalled with the C.R.U.'s decision, promptly withdrew their challenge. The Western Canada Rugby Football Union (the 'W.C.R.F.U.') immediately substituted Winnipeg as the western challenger for the Grey Cup, but after complaints from Regina and an urgent plea from Professor E.A. Hardy of Saskatoon, President of the C.R.U., the W.C.R.F.U. governors agreed that Regina should represent the West. However, the indecision displayed by Regina and the W.C.R.F.U. resulted in the C.R.U. neglecting to rent a site for an East versus West Grey Cup final. One could have been obtained, but when Regina demanded that the eastern champion guarantee 50 percent of Regina's expenses for the trip east, the C.R.U. rejected Regina's challenge and declared the 1936 eastern final, played on December 5, the Grey Cup game.

The two combatants for the championship were Sarnia Imperials and Ottawa Rough Riders. The game was played under ideal weather conditions, and the 1936 final was one of the best games in Grey Cup history. The teams played entertaining football for 60 minutes, the Imperials winning 26 to 20.

Early on it appeared that Sarnia would trounce Ottawa. A fumble gave Sarnia possession of the ball on the Ottawa 11-yard line, and two plays later Sarnia's Ormond Beach broke through the left side of the Ottawa line for a touchdown. Alex Hayes drop-kicked the convert to make the score 6 to 0.

A few minutes later Sarnia scored again. Scrimmaging on the Ottawa 42, Hayes accepted the snap from centre and ran toward the left end. At the line of scrimmage he lateralled the ball to Rocky Parsaca who gained 22 yards before tossing the sphere to Mike Hedgewick. The speedy Imperial halfback raced past the remaining Ottawa defenders for the touchdown.

Ottawa immediately answered this score. After moving the ball to the Sarnia 39, Arnie Morrison rolled right with teammates Tommy Daley and Andy Tommy following him closely. At the line of scrimmage Morrison fed the ball to Daley, who charged directly at Sarnia's 'Fat' Parsons. Daley appeared to have eluded the defender when Parsons grabbed Daley by the neck of his sweater and flung him to the turf. In mid-air Daley fired a lateral, basketball style, to Tommy. Tommy accepted the toss, and as Sarnia's Hayes moved across the field to make a touchdown-saving tackle, Tommy

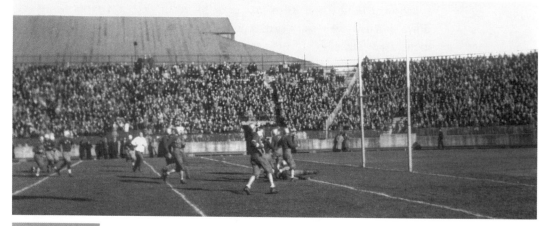

twirled. Hayes was left grasping the air, while Tommy sprinted into the end zone to complete the sparkling play.

In the second quarter Ottawa's Bernard 'Bunny' Wadsworth crossed into the Sarnia end zone to tie the game 12 to 12, but Sarnia soon regained its lead when Beach scored his second touchdown. Then, just before the end of the half Hedgewick scored his second major on an extension run, and Sarnia again led by 12 points: Sarnia 24, Ottawa 12.

Later with the score Sarnia 26, Ottawa 12, the Riders rallied to try to save the game. After scoring two singles in the fourth quarter, Ottawa engineered a six-play, 70-yard touchdown drive that featured a 33-yard run by Morrison. A few plays later, Morrison swept around the left end for a touchdown. Tiny Herman added the extra point: Sarnia 26, Ottawa 20.

With less than three minutes remaining, Ottawa battled to the Sarnia 11-yard line. From there, Ottawa desperately attempted to score. But on a third down gamble Sarnia's Hedgewick barely knocked away a touchdown pass intended for Joe Zelicovitz. Ottawa's last drive had failed, and Sarnia won the 1936 Dominion title.

The heroes of this game were Ottawa's George Arnold Morrison and Sarnia's Hugh 'Bummer' Stirling. Both players sparked their respective teams throughout the game.

Morrison, the 27-year-old quarterback, engineered one successful comeback in the first half, and nearly duplicated his feat in the second. He was instrumental on every offensive play as he either guided his team across the line, or crashed through the line himself. Ottawa fans were delighted that a lifetime suspension given to him by the C.R.U. in 1929 had been lifted. In an interview with Gordon Sinclair of *The Toronto Daily Star* after the game Morrison described the circumstances surrounding his suspension and subsequent reinstatement.

"It was 1929, the year of the big crash. Ottawa Rideau's were playing St. Thomas Yellow Jackets for the junior championship of Canada ... and losing. There were about 3,500 fans there and they thought the Ottawa boys were getting a raw deal from the officials. There was a lot of name calling even before we had a touchdown called back and you know how things get out of hand.

"There were just a few minutes to go so the crowd came out of the stands and [they] were standing there jeering when somebody touched off the spark that started guys swinging fists. Referee Harold Bailey was knocked flat, a lot of players were ganged and Mitchell Hepburn, who is now prime minister, had his fur coat ripped off. He was knocked down and trampled on and, of course, that makes a fellow sore."

"So you got the heave-ho?" inquired Sinclair.

"Yes ... they dropped me out for life ... I never socked anybody but I was captain of the squad so they dropped me out for life ... "

"Then what?" prodded Sinclair.

"Well, I was out in '30 but the next year I went to see Colonel Molson in Montreal, and some Ottawa friends pulled wires so I got back in."

"And you've played [football] since?"

"Yep," smiled Morrison.

Meanwhile, Stirling was everywhere from start to finish for Sarnia. Stirling kicked, broke-up passes, tackled, ran, and threw passes. To Charlie Conacher this brought back memories of the 1921 Grey Cup final in which Lionel Conacher single-handedly defeated the Edmonton Eskimos. Stirling's kicking was particularly important to Sarnia's victory. He once kicked the ball 80 yards, and rarely did he punt the ball under 45 yards. Stirling's great performances in this game and throughout his career were honoured when he was elected to the Canadian Football Hall of Fame in 1966.

## 1937 TORONTO ARGONAUTS 4
## WINNIPEG BLUE BOMBERS 3

Under the battle-cry "East is east, but West is best" the Winnipeg Blue Bombers challenged for the Grey Cup on December 11, 1937. Western fans remembered the 1935 victory by the 'Pegs, and were convinced that the Blue Bombers would destroy the Toronto Argonauts. But Toronto showed the western fans that the eastern style of Canadian football was still slightly superior to that of the western by defeating Winnipeg 4 to 3.

The Blue Bombers had a chance to blow the game open early in the first quarter. Toronto's Art West juggled a punt, and Winnipeg's Bob Fritz scooped up the loose ball in his own half. It appeared that no one would catch Fritz, but at the Toronto 15 Bob Isbister did the unexpected, diving for a touchdown-saving tackle. Three plays later, Winnipeg's Steve Olander scored a single.

In another few plays, Toronto received its largest break of the game. Winnipeg's Fritz Hanson was unable to control a Toronto punt, and Toronto's Bill Bryers recovered it. Toronto was in scoring position, and from a 45-degree angle Earl Selkirk split the uprights to make the score Toronto 3, Winnipeg 1.

After the game a dejected Hanson recalled his fateful fumble. "I lost the game for the Blue Bombers," he confessed. "I lost it when I fumbled in the first quarter. Those three points from placement which were scored three

plays later gave the darn Argos the championship. I played that ball wrong all the way on the punt."

To many fans, however, the turning point occurred near the end of the first quarter when Toronto's Bill Stukus was clobbered by Bud Marquardt. Stukus fumbled, and Winnipeg's Bill Ceretti collected the loose ball and raced into the Argonaut end zone. Jeff Nicklin hugged and kissed his team-mate as Referee Hec Creighton raised his arms aloft to signal a touchdown. But the touchdown did not count because Umpire Eddie Grant ruled that Stukus had been given no yards. The ruling was questionable, and it deprived Winnipeg of a Grey Cup victory.

With the score Toronto 4, Winnipeg 3, the Blue Bombers gathered its offensive arsenal for a final assault. But the Argonauts erected a defensive blockade which would have impressed John F. Kennedy. Winnipeg was unable to score, and when the final whistle sounded Toronto coach Lew Hayman reached down to pick up an object at his feet. Hayman kissed it. The rusty old horseshoe with protruding nails tasted good.

**Despite the loss, the best player of the game was Winnipeg's Bob Fritz. The 195-pound quarterback and coach was virtually unstoppable whenever he carried the ball. Even when Toronto knew that Fritz would carry the ball, he still managed to ram through the left side of the Toronto line for gains of five and seven yards. Fritz never gave up. With a face swollen and cut, and lips and eyes blackened, Fritz played himself into the frozen field in the last quarter.**

# 1938 TORONTO ARGONAUTS 30
# WINNIPEG BLUE BOMBERS 7

Western fans were not impressed with Toronto's 1937 victory. Accordingly when Winnipeg and Toronto met again on December 10, 1938, they expected another Winnipeg championship. But the western fans did not anticipate that Toronto's Alvin 'Buster' Red Storey would produce one of the greatest individual efforts in Grey Cup history and turn the 1938 national final into a 'Storey' to remember.

After Winnipeg had moved ahead 4 to 0, Toronto pulled into the lead in the second quarter. From the Toronto 54-yard line, Annis Stukus threw the ball far downfield to Art West. The fleet-footed Argonaut streaked past his coverage and caught Stukus' pass on the run. There was a clear field ahead of West, and he easily scored. Winnipeg then kicked a field goal, and in the third quarter Toronto's Teddy Morris prevented a Winnipeg touchdown when he recovered a dribbled ball on his own 8-yard line. The third quarter ended Winnipeg 7, Toronto 6, and the stage was set for an incredible final 15 minutes.

On the first play of the fourth quarter Toronto called an extension run which advanced the ball to the Winnipeg 28. From there Toronto ran the game-winning play. Morris ran the ball across the line of scrimmage, and then lateralled to Storey. Another extension run. However, as Storey moved crossfield he noticed that Winnipeg's defence had over-compensated in an effort to cover Toronto's outside runner. This left a gap immediately ahead of Storey. The lumbering redhead sharply cut toward the gap, weaved past a half-dozen Blue Bombers, and eventually staggered over the goal line.

Moments later, Storey scored again. After returning an interception to

**Two Winnipeg Blue Bombers go after the ball in the 1938 Cup against the Toronto Argonauts.** (City of Toronto Archives)

Toronto's Red Storey made the 1938 Cup memorable with three fourth-quarter touchdowns.
(Canadian Football Hall of Fame & Museum)

the Winnipeg 4, he converted a third down gamble by barging into the Winnipeg end zone.

Storey then stood in the spotlight when teammate Bob Isbister lateralled the ball to him at the Toronto 3-yard line. Winnipeg players were out of position and Storey sped downfield. Storey returned the ball more than 100 yards before being tackled by Art Stevenson. On the next play Bill Stukus faked a toss to Storey, and threw the ball to Bernie Thornton for a touchdown.

A few plays later, Storey scored an 11-yard touchdown. Storey's third touchdown was converted and the game ended Toronto 30, Winnipeg 7.

The hero of this game was number 64, Red Storey. The 200-pound native of Barrie, Ontario thrilled the Varsity Stadium crowd with his powerful runs. Essentially a part-time player, the 20-year-old rose from the bench, and injected life into the Argos by scoring a Grey Cup record three touchdowns in the fourth quarter. Storey's performance so inspired the 18,846 paying customers that when the game ended enthusiastic fans lifted Storey high on their shoulders and carried him off the field.

After the game Lew Hayman and Annis Stukus praised Storey. Hayman explained: "He was picking the spots out there today. That first touchdown of his was as pretty a piece of cutting-in as you could want to see."

Stukus stated, "I'm glad to see 'Red' go like that. He's always been a big help in keeping up the old spirit. When things weren't going right, he'd throw a sponge or a shoe at somebody in the shower and pretty soon we'd all be wise-cracking him. He can take a kidding, too. The guy, for some reason or other, takes a notion to hitch-hike up to Barrie on week-ends. He gets a ride for that."

Forty years after his great performance, Storey had fond memories of this game. "That day Art [West] was outside and I was inside and they double teamed him to shut-off our end run ... and that's how the fun started.

"[On my first touchdown] we saw they were double teaming West. I got the ball, saw Art West was in trouble and cut in. That was a 28-yard touchdown. It was one of those things ... every play in football is really an option, even if the playbook doesn't spell it out. On the second touchdown I intercepted a pass and went 40 yards to score. Art Stevenson had thrown the ball ... and I got it. The funny thing is, on that one and the other [touchdowns], everyone had a good shot at me. None of them was easy, is what I'm saying.

"The next touchdown I got was an 11-yard plunge over the middle. All told, I ran something like 190 yards in 12 minutes … On the third one, I guess it was a lot like the first one … they were watching West on the outside so the middle was there for me."

## 1939 WINNIPEG BLUE BOMBERS 8
## OTTAWA ROUGH RIDERS 7

Red Storey and the Toronto Argonauts did not qualify for the 1939 Grey Cup. Instead, the eastern champion was the Ottawa Rough Riders. Ottawa was an awesome team. The Rough Riders scored 207 points in three exhibition, six regular season, and three playoff games, while only allowing 51 points over the same number of games. Accordingly, Ottawa was expected to win. But the 1939 final, held on December 9, was not played under perfect conditions. Wet and cold weather during the week turned the gridiron rock-hard. In an effort to soften the turf the grounds crew poured 400 gallons of gasoline on the field and set it ablaze the day before the game. The fire did loosen the turf, but freezing temperatures on Friday night turned the gridiron back to its granite-like condition. A heavy snowfall on game day then blanketed the field to make the field conditions extremely slippery and the ball difficult to grasp. The powerful Rough Riders team did not play up to its potential in the sloppy conditions, and lost a squeaker to the Winnipeg Blue Bombers 8 to 7.

The Rough Riders started well when midway through the first quarter Andy Tommy scored a spectacular touchdown. With the ball on the Ottawa 48-yard line, Orville Burke completed a pass to Rick Perley. Perley cut upfield, and just before he was tackled lateralled the ball to Tommy. Tommy danced past three Winnipeg tacklers and then eluded Fritz Hanson to score the major. Winnipeg players protested that Tommy had stepped out of bounds at the Winnipeg 37, but a close examination of Tommy's footprints in the snow revealed that he had remained in the field of play. Tiny Herman kicked the convert, and Ottawa led 6 to 0.

However, the lead was short-lived. Winnipeg recovered a fumble on the Ottawa 10, and two plays later Andy Bieber strolled through the right side of the line for a 7-yard score. Greg Kabat then scored a single to tie the game 6 to 6.

The teams exchanged singles, and with but one minute and 10 seconds showing on the clock came the deciding score. Ottawa's Burke tried to make a shoe-string catch of a Winnipeg punt only to misplay the ball. Nicklin quickly recovered for Winnipeg to give his club possession on the Ottawa 34. A few plays later, Stevenson kicked the ball into the Ottawa end zone. Burke collected the ball, and hurriedly kicked it back to Winnipeg. The ball sliced off of Burke's foot, and sailed out of bounds at the Ottawa 8. From there, Stevenson blasted the ball into the stands to give Winnipeg an 8 to 7 victory.

The most valuable player in this game was Winnipeg's Fritz Hanson. A hero of the 1935 victory, Hanson again was the fuel that kept the Blue Bombers flying. On many punt returns Hanson evaded Ottawa tacklers just when it appeared that he would be stopped deep in his own territory. In addition, Hanson was featured in the Winnipeg passing and running attack. He completed the only successful Blue Bomber pass in the game, and he gained 126 yards rushing.

Ottawa (white jerseys) plays the Sarnia Imperials in the East final. A week later Winnipeg won the 1939 Cup by defeating Ottawa. (City of Toronto Archives)

## 1940    OTTAWA ROUGH RIDERS 8, BALMY BEACH 2
## OTTAWA ROUGH RIDERS 12, BALMY BEACH 5

Hanson did not get an opportunity to lead Winnipeg to a successful defence of its Grey Cup title in 1940 because a rule dispute prompted the C.R.U. to deny the western challenge for the Cup. Accordingly the 1940 final was an all-eastern affair, and for the only time in Cup history, the championship was decided by a two-game total point series.

The two challengers were the Ottawa Rough Riders and Balmy Beach. Despite being undefeated in the regular season, Balmy Beach, the champion of the inferior O.R.F.U., was given little chance to beat Ottawa. The Beach battled courageously but lost by a total score of 20 to 7.

Game 1 was played in a blizzard. Three inches of snow covered Toronto's Varsity Stadium field prior to the start and a further inch fell before the game ended. The snow caused each team much difficulty, and after 45 minutes of play the game was tied 2 to 2.

In the fourth quarter the Beach tired. This allowed Ottawa to take control. Dave Sprague finished an eight-play, 29-yard drive by accepting a lateral from Andy Tommy and charging into the Beach end zone. Orville Burke completed a pass to Rick Perley for the convert, and game 1 ended Ottawa 8, Balmy Beach 2.

Early in Game 2, Beach reduced Ottawa's lead to 8 to 7 when Bobby Porter busted through the left-centre of the line for a short touchdown run. The Rough Riders then added two singles to the score before sealing victory in the third quarter with a touchdown. The Beach had possession near its own 5, and on second down Porter dropped into the backfield. He had barely taken a couple of steps when the entire offensive line collapsed. Ottawa's Bernard Wadsworth and Tommy Daley slammed into Porter. The ball was jarred loose and Ottawa's Perley secured it. On the next play, a lateral on an extension run saw Daley break a tackle and race into the Beach end zone.

In the final quarter, Ottawa scored four singles to end the two-game series at Ottawa 20, Balmy Beach 7.

**The hero of this unique final was Ottawa's Dave Sprague. A veteran of Canadian football, Sprague gave a powerful running display which reminded many fans of his playing days with the Hamilton Tigers. Throughout the series Sprague punished Balmy Beach defenders with his hard-charging runs, which often left Beach tacklers sprawled in pain. In addition, in Game 1 he made two successive bone-crunching tackles on Frank Seymour which forced Seymour, who was considered the most talented Beach player, to the sideline. While Seymour eventually returned to the game, he was rendered ineffective by Sprague's tackles.**

Action from Game 1 of the two-game total point 1940 final between Ottawa Rough Riders (white jerseys) and Balmy Beach. (City of Toronto Archives)

**Sprague's performance was incredible considering that he played Game 1 with a seriously infected thigh. Shortly before game time *Ottawa Citizen* sportswriter Jack Koffman asked Sprague if he was healthy enough to play. Sprague answered, "The leg is bothering me, but I'll be able to go part of the time anyway." He played most of Game 1 and when the Rough Riders returned to Ottawa the leg was so bad that Sprague was immediately sent by team doctors to Ottawa's Civic Hospital for five days.**

**Sprague's last Grey Cup performance in 1940 in large part led to his induction into the Canadian Football Hall of Fame in 1963.**

Despite Sprague's retirement the Rough Riders qualified for its third consecutive Grey Cup game in 1941. With the general belief that this would be the last final during the War years, Ottawa and the Winnipeg Blue Bombers played a brilliant game on November 29, 1941. The teams waged war for 60 minutes, and turned the final into one of the best ever played.

Winnipeg opened the scoring with a field goal, and then Ottawa stormed ahead on an amazing punt recovery by Tony Golab. A high and short punt was allowed to bounce back toward the Ottawa kicker. Golab leaped high into the air to recover his own kick, and galloped down the sideline past a stunned Fritz Hanson for a touchdown.

In the second quarter Ottawa moved ahead 9 to 3 before Winnipeg tied the score. After Winnipeg's Bernie Thornton had a touchdown run called back because of an illegal forward pass, Winnipeg's Wayne Sheley set-up in punt formation. Awaiting the snap, he noticed that Ottawa defenders were bunching up to charge the kick. Sheley motioned to Bud Marquardt, and then called for the ball. As the Rough Riders charged the line of scrimmage Sheley faked the punt and completed a strike to Marquardt. The Winnipeg receiver shook a tackle, raced downfield, and at the Ottawa 5 Burke slammed him to the turf – but Marquardt no longer had the ball. Just before Burke's tackle, Marquardt had lateralled the ball to teammate Mel Wilson, who crossed for the score. McCance kicked the convert: Ottawa 9, Winnipeg 9.

*An Ottawa punt is nearly blocked by a Winnipeg Blue Bomber in the 1941 championship.*
*(City of Toronto Archives)*

In the third quarter Winnipeg regained the lead when Thornton broke through Ottawa's offensive line and hammered Burke. The ball floated into the air like a balloon. Marquardt pulled the ball down, and then soared 45 yards for a touchdown.

The Rough Riders answered this major with two field goals by George Fraser, and the game was again tied, 15 to 15. Next Winnipeg's Jim Lander

intercepted a Golab pass, and returned the ball to the Ottawa 36-yard line. Three plays later, McCance kicked his second field goal to give Winnipeg a 3-point lead.

Winnipeg hung on to this lead, and then at the midpoint of the last quarter the Blue Bombers faced a critical situation. With the ball on the Winnipeg 33 Hanson asked punter Lander if he was ready to kick. Gasping for air, Lander replied, "I'm so tired I can't even kick it over the line of scrimmage. You'd better try it." Hanson was not a good kicker, so he decided that Lander should fake the punt. The decision gave Ottawa an excellent opportunity to tie the game as Lander was grabbed and thrown to the turf short of the first down. However, Ottawa failed. From the Winnipeg 11-yard line Fraser missed a field goal. The ball reached the deadline, and the game ended Winnipeg 18, Ottawa 16.

**For the third time in this era the best player in the Grey Cup was Winnipeg's Fritz Hanson. The 150-pounder led Winnipeg to victory with a sparkling offensive performance. He always seemed to gain yards on running plays which looked likely to be stopped for a loss, and in the fourth quarter he shouldered the brunt of the Winnipeg attack after Sheley was injured. Hanson carried the ball 25 times for 66 yards.**

Despite the great individual performance produced by Hanson, Winnipeg's coach Reg Threlfall cited another reason for the Winnipeg victory. Threlfall displayed a five-cent notebook and two scratch-pads which contained all of Ottawa's plays. When asked to comment on how he got the plays, Threlfall described: "This scribbler I've had for years," he said, waving one of the pads. "When we played Ottawa two years ago in the final I made diagrams of all their plays.

"This pad," he continued, waving another, "has diagrams of the Ottawa plays noted by Bert Warwick [assistant coach of the Bombers] when he scouted the Ottawa versus Hamilton Tiger game last week in Ottawa.

"And this one," Threlfall waved the last pad, "I drew in the first quarter of the game today. Compare them – the plays are all the same!"

The pads helped Threlfall set his defence at crucial times in the game, and always put Winnipeg one step ahead of Ottawa.

The Grey Cup games from 1935 through 1941 showed that Canadian football was evolving. The game was no longer dominated by eastern teams; the three victories by Winnipeg indicated that the West was producing competitive football teams. Western players – for example Fritz Hanson, Greg Kabat, Chester McCance and Art Stevenson – proved that they were just as good as such eastern players as Ted Morris, Tony Golab, Hugh Stirling, Dave Sprague, Huck Welch, and Andy Tommy. However, the West would have to wait another decade before its teams were recognized by the majority of football fans as being equal to eastern teams. While World War II devastated western football as teams lost all their import stars and faced money shortages, it at the same time showed that the Grey Cup was a Canadian football institution. In contrast to World War I, the Grey Cup game was not suspended 'for the duration'.

## Chapter Six

# THE WAR YEARS
## 1942-1944

This chapter is dedicated to all of the
men and women who served in Canada's
armed forces during World War II

**W**e live in a privileged world and in a privileged country. I have not seen a World War and I have not been subjected to conscription. Yes, there was Vietnam, Afghanistan, the Falklands, Iran-Iraq, and Iraq again, but these conflicts pale in comparison to World War II. From 1939 to 1945 the world was on edge as young soldiers battled in Africa, Europe, and the Pacific.

There was gloom everywhere. No one knew what was in store. And in Canadian football it appeared that following the 1941 Grey Cup game all play would be suspended. But knowing how valuable the game was to the morale of Canadians, the military decided to organize football clubs. All across Canada, military bases formed teams in an effort to keep the spirit of Canadian football alive.

The military did an excellent job, and highly skilled teams were given the opportunity to challenge for the Grey Cup. Accordingly, for the only time in Cup history the champions from 1942 through 1944 were non-civilian teams.

## 1942 TORONTO R.C.A.F. HURRICANES 8
## WINNIPEG R.C.A.F. BOMBERS 5

The games during this period thrilled football fans, and reminded Canadians that there was more to life than war. This was very evident on December 5, 1942. While 12,455 frenzied football fans piled into Varsity Stadium, Toronto, thousands more huddled around radios in Canada and overseas to hear a condensed, delayed broadcast of the final. To the Canadian forces stationed in London, England the radio broadcast reminded them of home and made them feel at home. Reporter Scott Young of *The Globe and Mail* commented: "Some of the more nostalgic perched themselves on the backs of chairs, which they called 'bleachers', eating a variety of food, all of which they nick-named 'peanuts' for the occasion, while others sucked on small bottles which needed no nicknames – all trying to create the illusion of a sports atmosphere they have left behind for the duration, but certainly not forgotten."

The two teams in the first non-civilian Grey Cup game were the Winnipeg R.C.A.F. Bombers, and the Toronto R.C.A.F. Hurricanes. Winnipeg was led by former Blue Bombers Chester McCance and Wayne Sheley, while Toronto was captained by former Argonaut Bill Stukus, the best quarterback of the day. Stukus had enjoyed a terrific season in 1942, and before the game Hurricanes coach Lew Hayman told Stukus: "Give them the works. Shoot them wide and throw lots of passes." This was intended to take advantage of Stukus's experience and great passing ability. But in bitterly cold weather and on a field dotted with patches of ice, the strategy failed. Despite controlling the first half of the game, the Hurricanes only built a 2 to 0 lead.

A Toronto R.C.A.F. Hurricane eludes a Toronto Indian tackler. In 1942, the Hurricanes became the first non-civilian team to win the Cup. (City of Toronto Archives)

In the third quarter the Bombers took the lead. A fumble recovery by Jack Manners gave Winnipeg possession near midfield, and from there Sheley guided the Bombers to the Toronto 5-yard line. Then Sheley flung the ball deep into Toronto's end zone. Flight Lieutenant Eddie Thompson jumped and tried to knock the ball down for the Hurricanes, but he only managed to get his fingertips on the pass. The ball travelled through another pair of Hurricane hands and eventually settled in the arms of Winnipeg's AC2 Lloyd Boivin for a touchdown. The convert was blocked by Don Durno: Winnipeg 5, Toronto 2.

The Hurricanes answered immediately. Stukus, abandoning Hayman's game-plan, kept the ball on the ground. Relying on the running of AC2 Don Crowe and Johnny 'Pop' Poplowski, Stukus marched his forces into Winnipeg territory and with the ball on the Winnipeg 41 called a delayed buck. As Stukus dropped into the backfield, Poplowski and Crowe moved toward the line of scrimmage. There was a brief delay, and then Stukus handed the ball to Crowe. At the line, Toronto's Paul McGarry and Truck Langley opened a hole for Crowe. Winnipeg's OS Mel Wilson tried to plug the gap but AC2 Art Evans charged over from the short side of the Toronto line to force Wilson out of the way.

Crowe burst through and into the Winnipeg secondary. Winnipeg's safety man and tertiary defenders tried to stop Crowe. Now in full flight, Crowe barrelled over two Winnipeg tacklers en route to a magnificent 39-yard gain. Crowe explained the run. "There wasn't anything to it. Stukus called a delayed buck through centre, Evans swung out of the line, took out Wilson and the rest was easy."

On the next play, Poplowski rammed through the line for a touchdown.

The Hurricanes scored the only point of the fourth quarter, and the game ended Toronto 8, Winnipeg 5.

**For making all Canadians forget about the war for a few hours, all of the servicemen who played in this historic Grey Cup game were heroes. Every player gave a good effort, but the outstanding player was Toronto's Don Crowe. His hard-charging runs were instrumental in powering the Hurricanes to victory. Brilliant dashes on the slippery field set up six of Toronto's eight points, and prompted one sportswriter to comment that Crowe "... had a knack of using his football boots like snowshoes."**

## 1943 HAMILTON FLYING WILDCATS 23 WINNIPEG R.C.A.F. BOMBERS 14

The spirited victory by the Hurricanes in 1942 was followed by an inspirational Grey Cup win for the Hamilton Flying Wildcats on November 27, 1943. After defeating the R.C.A.F. Bombers 23 to 14 for the championship, former Hamilton Tiger player and Wildcats head coach Brian Timmis explained the significance of Hamilton's victory to Johnny Fitzgerald of the *Toronto Telegram*. "Last time I talked about winning the C.R.U. title, Johnny, I told you it wouldn't be the same as winning it in peace time, but I've changed my mind. This title is a title that has been won by the armed services, and the people who give them the arms to fight with. On my team are airmen, sailors, war workers and reserve army members, all doing a job for peace... . I'm prouder of this title than any of the three I won as a player. It's really a tribute to the services and the people who are backing them up."

The Wildcats won this game with an explosive first quarter. After moving the ball to the Winnipeg 30-yard line, Hamilton quarterback Joe Krol took the snap and rolled to his left. Winnipeg defenders shifted to stop Krol, when suddenly he cut back to the right, eluded three tacklers and threw the ball downfield. Doug Smith was wide open. He made the catch, and walked into the Winnipeg end zone. Krol converted to give Hamilton a 6 to 0 lead.

A few minutes later Winnipeg led for the only time. A Winnipeg single made the score 6 to 1, and then LAC Garnie Smith galloped around the right end for an 18-yard score. Chester McCance added the extra point: Winnipeg 7, Hamilton 6.

Hamilton was unimpressed by the Winnipeg score, and a pride of Wildcats soon burst through the line to confront Winnipeg punter Brian

**En route to paydirt in the 1943 final, a Winnipeg R.C.A.F. Bomber is pursued by the Hamilton Wildcats.** (City of Toronto Archives)

Quinn. Hamilton's Reg Bovaird got his hand on the ball, deflecting it skyward. While half-a-dozen players waited for the ball to come down, Hamilton's Jimmy Fumio climbed into the sky to snatch the ball. He then crashed to the ground for a touchdown.

Near the end of the quarter Hamilton scored again. Winnipeg's Dave Greenberg caught a punt in his own end zone, and promptly booted the ball back to Hamilton. Abe Zvonkin returned the kick to the Winnipeg 10, and three plays later Mel Lawson squirmed into the Winnipeg end zone.

In the third quarter, Hamilton made the score 21 to 7 on a field goal by Krol. Winnipeg responded with a long touchdown pass from Quinn to Corp. Dave Berry. McCance converted.

The Bombers were gaining momentum but five minutes into the fourth quarter Hamilton's defence held firm, preventing Winnipeg from scoring on three chances from the Hamilton 2.

Winnipeg eventually managed another single, only for Krol and Smith to reply with singles to make the final score Hamilton 23, Winnipeg 14.

**The most impressive players were Winnipeg's Ches McCance and Hamilton's Joe Krol. Appearing in his sixth Grey Cup, the big, powerful and aggressive McCance was a one-man gang for the Bombers. A threat every time he carried the ball, he often broke through the line for long gains. Up to four Hamilton tacklers were required to halt him.**

**While McCance's performance significantly contributed to Winnipeg's 14 points, Krol led the Wildcats to the championship. He was everywhere. On offence, defence, and special teams, Krol took the spotlight, scoring seven points, throwing a 30-yard touchdown, and setting up Hamilton's second touchdown with a 40-yard run. In addition, Krol ended Winnipeg scoring chances with spectacular tackles, especially on**

McCance. And he always gave Hamilton good field position by escaping Winnipeg tacklers on punt returns. Krol's performance was particularly outstanding considering he was shadowed throughout the game by Don Durno or Wally 'Chick' Chikowski.

The 1943 game was punishing on Joe Krol and the Wildcats. Accordingly, when the Halifax Navy issued a challenge for the Cup after Hamilton's victory, the Wildcats refused. Sam Manson, President of the Wildcats, stated in a telegram to Lt. Fred Cook of the Navy that many of the Hamilton players were "willing to [play], but after 13 games the boys are pretty well battered up."

## 1944 ST. HYACINTHE-DONNACONA NAVY 7
## HAMILTON WILDCATS 6

The Halifax Navy never contested for the Grey Cup. However on November 25, 1944 a team comprised primarily of navy war men captured the national title when the St. Hyacinthe-Donnacona Navy Combines, representing the Q.R.F.U., upset the defending champion Hamilton Wildcats.

For the last time in Grey Cup history, the game was an all-eastern final. A western team dearly would have wanted to participate, but the war effort in western Canada was so massive that there were neither enough players nor enough time to establish teams. This set up a Grey Cup final in which, for the only time, a team from the Q.R.F.U. participated. Underdogs St. Hyacinthe was, according to Red Burnett of *The Toronto Star*, a team which, "merely started out as a pick-up crew, a bunch of sailors who liked to muck it up on a football field and craved a little action." However, St. Hyacinthe exemplified the spirit of Canadian football. Throughout the season, several Combine players regularly travelled 80 miles (129 kilometres) – 40 (64.5) each way – to practices. Steve Levantis recalled those trips: "Rain or shine we piled into that truck, sang our way there and usually groaned all the way home. It was hell when the wind and rain moved in, but we loved it." The dedication shown by these players was rewarded as St. Hyacinthe squeaked past the Wildcats 7 to 6.

St. Hyacinthe opened the scoring with a single in the first quarter, and then extended its lead with a touchdown in the second quarter. With Hamilton in possession, Joe Krol sprinted across the line of scrimmage for a gain of 25 yards when he was hammered and Levantis recovered Krol's fumble on the Hamilton 39. Two plays later 'Dutch' Davey faded back to pass for St. Hyacinthe. Johnny Taylor was open in the flat, made the catch, paused, pivoted, and then dodged three Wildcat defenders en route to a 33-yard touchdown. The major gave St. Hyacinthe a 6 to 0 lead.

Hamilton pulled back in the fourth quarter. After applying constant pressure on St. Hyacinthe's offence, Krol returned a punt 15 yards to give the Wildcats possession on the St. Hyacinthe 45. From there Hamilton used three plays in scoring. In the most important play Krol charged around the end for an electrifying gain of 32 yards. On the next play Paul Miocinovich crashed over the Combines' goal line from three yards out. Krol converted to tie the game 6 to 6.

Both teams realized that the next point would win the game, and the

The 1944 champion, the St. Hyacinthe-Donnacona Navy Combines, was the only team from the Q.R.F.U. to win the Cup. (Canadian Football Hall of Fame & Museum)

Back row, left to right: W.O. J. Montague, P.O. G. Reid, W. Kydd (Asst. Coach), S. Segatore (Asst. Coach), F. Porter (Hon. President), Surg. Lt. Cdr. Lane, Lt. C. Ellis. Second row: P.O. G. Davey, O.S. M.McFall, Cook D. Kotavich, E.A./5 A. Sims, Cook J. Spicer, O.S. D. Campbell, C.P.O. L. Raymond. Third row: O.S. W. Patch, O.S. M. Baker, A.B. H. Chard, A.B. T. Bainbridge, Lt. I. Barclay, Lt. S. Abbot, A.B. J. Leonard, Bdsm. R. Swarbrick, A.B. P. Santucci (Co-Capt.). Fourth Row: Bdsm. R. Kirbyson, O.S. J. Taylor, O.S. J. Crncich, A.B. S. Levantis (Co-Capt.), A.B.J. Wedley, Lt. Cdr. A. Hurley. Front row: O.S. C. Ellis, Lt. W. Charron, A.B. D. Hiltz, K. Clarke (Mascot), P.O. O'Brien, A.B. Macleod, G. Brown (Coach).

tension on field and in the stands grew thick. Fans began to berate the St. Hyacinthe bench, which prompted some Combine players to climb into the stands. While fights broke out within the crowd, Davey moved play into Hamilton territory. With less than three minutes left, Davey hammered the ball into the Hamilton end zone. Hamilton's Gordon Miller was trapped and he had to boot the ball back to St. Hyacinthe. The kick sailed out of play at the Hamilton 15, and after another two plays Davey angled a high punt into Hamilton's end zone again. This time Hamilton's Ben Dyack caught the ball, to be rouged by Taylor for the game-winning point: St. Hyacinthe 7, Hamilton 6.

**St. Hyacinthe's Roy Kirbyson and Dutch Davey were the pick of the players. Kirbyson, wearing running shoes, was brilliant on kick returns. He caught the ball without error, and gained anywhere from five to 30 yards each time. Kirbyson's best efforts came in the third quarter when he returned the ball for 20, 25, and 35 yards in succession. His great runbacks throughout the game always gave St. Hyacinthe good field position.**

**Meanwhile Davey's masterful kicking was responsible for guiding St. Hyacinthe to victory as his long punts matched Krol's punts. In the fourth quarter, when Krol was forced to leave the game for 10 minutes, Davey kicked his team into scoring position and produced the game-winning point.**

While Kirbyson and Davey were proud to have guided St. Hyacinthe to a Grey Cup victory, the team believed it should not be crowned as Grey Cup champion because it had violated military service regulations, which stated that military teams were ineligible to compete against civilians during the war. Since Hamilton had some civilians on its team, the Combines believed that it should not have played Hamilton. The C.R.U. considered the concern raised by the Combines commander J. McFetrick, but determined that St. Hyacinthe's victory should stand. Accordingly, the C.R.U. passed a motion officially congratulating St. Hyacinthe on its victory.


World War II ended in 1945, and so did the military competition for the Cup. Although the 1942 through 1944 games were not the best in Grey Cup history, they showed that the spirit of Canadian football could not be interrupted by war. The Canadian armed forces did a tremendous job of keeping Canadian football alive during this period, and left Canadian football with brilliant memories.

The war years also left Canadian football with the Jeff Nicklin Memorial Trophy. Nicklin played football for the Winnipeg Blue Bombers prior to 1940, and was a very important ingredient in the Winnipeg Grey Cup champions in 1939. On March 24, 1945, Lt. Col. Jeff Nicklin was killed in action. A year later the officers and men of his paratroop battalion donated a trophy in his memory. Every year the war and Nicklin are remembered when the Trophy is awarded to the most outstanding player in the western division.

## Chapter Seven

# THE KING OF FOOTBALL

## 1945-1952

**W**ith the end of World War II in 1945, Canadian football evolved further. From 1945 through 1952 civilian football teams reorganized across Canada, and began to compete for the best football players. This competition renewed the movement toward professionalism in the Canadian game, and eventually led to the formation of the C.F.L. in 1958. The renewed professionalism also created new enthusiasm for the Canadian football fan and brought higher expectations for this era's Grey Cup games.

The increased excitement was highlighted in 1948 when Calgary Stampeder fans invaded Toronto for the final. The Calgarians, with their 10-gallon hats and fringed western outfits, turned Toronto into one big party, and transformed this game, and all those following, into a celebration of a Canadian sporting institution. For three days the Calgarians whooped and hollered, rode their horses and sang in the streets. To the staff of the Royal York Hotel the party atmosphere seemed like New Year's Eve.

The Calgarians also created havoc on game day. Fans supporting the two finalists blocked the major streets leading to Varsity Stadium in Toronto. While Calgary fans had taken over Toronto from Front to Bloor on Bay Street, Ottawa fans were in possession of Bloor Street from Yonge to St. George. Traffic was snarled for hours. Many missed the start of the game. Andy Lytle of *The Toronto Star* described the scene: "I left the office at twelve noon. I was going to be smart. I'd drive to a parking spot near the stadium and have a leisurely lunch at Chez Paree, Honey Dew or Murrays. What a hope! I was lucky to get into the park by one forty-five, lunchless ... I'd as soon drive across the continent as tackle that short Toronto trip again."

The 1949 and 1950 Cup games reflected the increased professionalism. Although poor field conditions prior to 1949 had caused no complaints, fans and teams were no longer willing to accept them. Everyone wanted the best players to compete on the best surface possible.

In 1949, C.R.U. and Toronto Varsity Stadium officials tried to turn a frozen gridiron into a playable surface. From goal line to goal line salt was sprinkled on the field. But the turf only became slippery and muddy. Tom Brook, Calgary's President was extremely displeased with the field conditions and stormed, "We can't do a thing about the weather but the C.R.U. or Varsity Stadium or whoever was responsible could have done something about the field. We had weather forecasts 36 hours in advance before snow started during the week, and it was certainly lack of foresight on somebody's part in not putting some sort of covering over the ground."

Warren Stevens, director of athletics for the University of Toronto, defended the field conditions, stating that there was little that could have been done. A tarpaulin covering was too expensive, and that would not have protected the field anyway.

Similar field conditions plagued the 1950 game. A heavy snowfall blanketed Varsity Stadium one day prior to the final, and it was decided to remove the snow. The bulldozers used to remove the snow left the field looking like it had just been strip-mined. There were huge holes all over the gridiron and when it rained on Cup day ponds developed on the field. One pond was six inches deep!

The wretched field conditions angered Jack Grogan, President of the Western Conference; the field was nothing short of a pig-sty and Grogan added, "There is no reason in the world why western teams and fans should travel 3,000 to 4,000 miles each year to see a shemozzle."

The argument over field conditions ballooned during half-time. In the press box, Calgary coach Les Lear stood toe-to-toe with Varsity athletic director Stevens. Words and fists exchanged and they had to be pried apart. Lear blamed Stevens for the messy field conditions. Stevens countered that the University was only a tenant, and that the stadium was owned by the government. No one was satisfied with this explanation and thus Stevens and C.R.U. officials were forced to answer more questions. The C.R.U. tried to pass the buck, saying it only rented the field from the University, and could hardly be held responsible for its condition.

Stevens replied: "We have to take all the criticism? It's the C.R.U.'s ball game. They rent the stadium. It's their baby. We don't know if we will be getting the Grey Cup game. Remember, Montreal wanted it changed to their city last year from Toronto. We had no suggestion and no pressure from the C.R.U. for a tarpaulin this year."

The C.R.U. eventually listened to the criticism and in 1951 purchased a tarpaulin for $12,000.

Despite the incidents surrounding the 1948, 1949, and 1950 Cup games, this period of Canadian football is best known for the greatest player in the game's history. Joe 'King' Krol, a veteran of two Cup games in the war years, led the Toronto Argonauts to five titles. Phenomenal in each Argonaut victory, he often single-handedly guided the championship. The heroic play of the 'King of Football' left everlasting memories on those who saw him play, and in 1963 he was inducted into the Canadian Football Hall of Fame.

## 1945 TORONTO ARGONAUTS 35
## WINNIPEG BLUE BOMBERS 0

The first game saw Krol weave his football magic. On Saturday, December 1, 1945 using wide-open, razzle-dazzle tactics, he led the Toronto Argonauts to a 35 to 0 victory against the Winnipeg Blue Bombers. The score left many western fans in shock. For years they believed that American football tactics of superb line plunging and accurate passing were superior to the wide-open style of play used by eastern teams. However, after the 1945 Grey Cup game, Winnipeg head coach Bert Warwick finally admitted, "I'm convinced; as far as I'm concerned from now on we'll have to play this wide-open game that they like in the East."

Toronto's Royal Copeland (No. 77) launches a deep pass in the 1945 Cup against the Winnipeg Blue Bombers. (City of Toronto Archives)

Bill Nairn, Winnipeg's line coach agreed. "We may as well accept it," he said. "We've got to play the type of football they play in the East. It was time the West stressed more end runs, and daring lateral passes such as Argos utilized."

Toronto's wide-open battle plans were unveiled early in the 1945 Grey Cup game. After advancing the ball to the Winnipeg 34, Toronto's Fred Doty and Doug Smylie combined for a spectacular touchdown. Doty burst through a huge hole for a gain of 25 yards, and then lateralled the ball to Smylie. There was no Blue Bomber defender as Smylie charged down the sideline for the score.

A few minutes later Krol combined with Billy Myers for a 45-yard touchdown pass. Toronto 12, Winnipeg 0.

In the third quarter Toronto scored two more majors. Royal Copeland scored the first when he swept off-tackle for 14 yards. Near the end of the quarter Krol completed a perfect pass to Smylie on the Winnipeg 3. There, Smylie turned and stumbled into the end zone. Dejected Winnipeg players stood rooted to the ground as Krol ran untouched into the end zone on the convert: Toronto 24, Winnipeg 0.

Krol's awesome play continued in the fourth quarter. He was all over the field, and soon intercepted a short pass thrown by Winnipeg's Harry Hood. Winnipeg players failed to react as Krol romped 60 yards downfield for another touchdown. He then converted the major by completing a pass to Frank Hickey.

**Touchdown Argos! The 1945 final score was Toronto 35, Winnipeg 0.** (City of Toronto Archives)

Chaos followed. Scrimmaging on its own 35, Toronto sent Myers through the line of scrimmage for one of the most electrifying runs in the history of Canadian football. As Krol settled back to take the snap, Myers stood motionless alongside him. Krol called for the ball, but it shot back to Myers! While Winnipeg tacklers charged Krol, Myers blasted through the line, bowling over a Winnipeg tackler. Another tackler was side-stepped. A third Winnipeg player tried to stop Myers but a quick change of speed left the player grasping air. No one else challenged as Myers sailed 75 yards to the line. At this point, the Varsity Stadium field turned into a sea of humanity. Fans charged onto the field to congratulate Myers and for five minutes they moved among the players and shook the goal posts. When control was restored, Toronto attempted the convert. However, when Myers took the snap he ran off the field to end the game 35 to 0. Myers explained he wanted the ball as his own special prize rather than have it kicked into the arms of a fan.

**The best player in this game was Joe Krol. Playing in his third Grey Cup Krol took charge of Toronto's forces. In all aspects of the game he led by example. Krol's running, passing, kicking, tackling, and blocking were outstanding. One of his best plays occurred on an extension run with Smylie and Myers. Krol was suppose to be the third man, but when Smylie found himself blanketed by a Winnipeg tackler, Krol rushed up and delivered a tremendous block which nearly lifted the defender out of the stadium. Former Argonaut Annis Stukus stated after the game: "Krol did everything except play the National Anthem on a piccolo." Krol finished the game throwing for two touchdowns and a convert, plus scoring seven points.**

## 1946 TORONTO ARGONAUTS 28 WINNIPEG BLUE BOMBERS 6

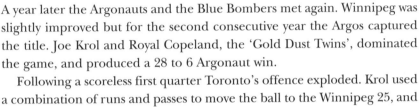

A year later the Argonauts and the Blue Bombers met again. Winnipeg was slightly improved but for the second consecutive year the Argos captured the title. Joe Krol and Royal Copeland, the 'Gold Dust Twins', dominated the game, and produced a 28 to 6 Argonaut win.

Following a scoreless first quarter Toronto's offence exploded. Krol used a combination of runs and passes to move the ball to the Winnipeg 25, and from there he zipped a bullet-like pass to Copeland. Copeland eluded Winnipeg's Walter Dobler, and sped into the end zone for the major.

In only three more plays Toronto scored again. Copeland, spotting Krol streaking down the middle of the field, threw him the ball on the Winnipeg 7, and Krol dodged two tacklers before crossing the Winnipeg goal line.

*From 1945 to 1952 Joe 'King' Krol dominated Canadian football and led the Argos to five championships. (Canadian Football Hall of Fame & Museum)*

The Argonauts returned to the attack. From the Winnipeg 40, Krol motioned to pass to Copeland. Just before releasing the ball Krol pulled his arm down. Winnipeg scrambled and this left Toronto's Ron Smylie open 20 yards downfield. The receiver crossed into the Winnipeg end zone untouched to make the score Toronto 16, Winnipeg 0.

Toronto extended its lead to 22 points in the third quarter. An amazing onside kick recovery by Copeland gave the Argos possession only two yards from Winnipeg's goal line, and on the next play Byron Karrys squeezed across. Then in the fourth quarter Toronto scored once more. Two plays after a 58-yard Krol pass to Leo Deadey, Krol scampered to his left. It appeared that Toronto had called an end run until Krol wheeled back to the right. Meanwhile, Copeland had sprinted into the Winnipeg end zone drawing a group of Winnipeg defenders and leaving Boris Tipoff uncovered. Krol laid a soft pass into Tipoff's arms for the touchdown. Krol then converted the major, and Toronto led 28 to 0.

With less than five minutes remaining in the game Dobler closed the scoring with a consolation touchdown, which he converted: Toronto 28, Winnipeg 6.

The heroes of the 1946 game were Toronto's Joe Krol and Royal Copeland. Not since the days of Frank Leadlay and Harry Batstone had two players so dominated a Grey Cup game. Both men were everywhere.

Offensively the 200-pound Krol was a one-man wrecking crew. With brilliant passing and excellent play selection, Krol navigated the Boatmen to victory. He completed seven of 13 passes for three touchdowns, scored one himself, set up a touchdown with an accurate onside kick, and booted three converts. In addition, Krol played a strong game on defence by making some hard-hitting tackles.

Winnipeg's assistant player-coach Martin Gainor said of Krol, "That Krol's terrific. He does everything but blow the whistle. He tosses touchdown passes, catches'em, converts'em, and punts'em a mile. Once I looked up and he's kicking off, then I hear crash and I look around and there's Krol burying the receiver."

Copeland also lauded Krol's performance. "Joe has no equal as a football player in my books," Copeland said, "and he could make anyone look good with his accurate passes. He is a perfect field general and the most completely relaxed athlete I have ever seen in action.

"Joe is also a wonderful guy when it comes to instilling confidence into his teammates and he just oozes with confidence himself. You just can't help get the fever. He is by far the greatest triple-threat player in Canadian football ... "

Like Krol, Copeland was an heroic performer on both sides of the field. Offensively, he did everything asked of him with brilliance. The blond bomber from North Bay, Ontario had the speed of a roadrunner, and jumped higher than a kangaroo. Copeland scored a touchdown, threw for another, and set up a third. On defence Copeland knocked down passes, and made important tackles. Early in the game he nailed Winnipeg's Harry Hood on the Toronto 10-yard line to keep Winnipeg from jumping into the lead.

Assessing Copeland's play, Gainor said, "... our defenders couldn't run with them, especially that Copeland. He doesn't run, he flies! Guess we should have equipped the tertiary with motor bikes."

When asked to compare Copeland with College, O.R.F.U., Big Four and U.S. professional football players, the experienced Krol said, "He is the greatest running half I have ever seen on a Canadian or American gridiron [and] the best in the game at getting into the open to receive passes, both through his terrific speed and ability to fake opponents out of position.

"Copeland does just about everything right. He's an outstanding blocker, a fine tackler and equally as good on pass defence as he is at receiving ..."

On November 27, 1947 Winnipeg tried to end Toronto's winning streak. For the third consecutive year Winnipeg and Toronto battled for the national title. Winnipeg played an exceptional game, but Krol was again dominant. In one of the greatest Cup games ever played a Winnipeg mistake in the last quarter allowed Krol to lift Toronto to a 10 to 9 victory.

The Blue Bombers opened the scoring following a fumble by Byron Karrys. Winnipeg gained possession of the ball on its own 38 and in nine plays drove 72 yards for a touchdown, when Bob Sandberg bounced off an Argo tackler and placed the nose of the ball across the Argo goal line.

On the first play of the second quarter Winnipeg's Don Hiney kicked a field goal to give the Blue Bombers a 9 to 0 lead. Toronto was struggling and at half-time trailed Winnipeg 9 to 1. However, the complexion of the game changed in the first few minutes of the third quarter. Toronto's Frankie Morris intercepted an erratic Winnipeg lateral, and then Krol sent Copeland far down the field. Two Bomber defenders got their signals crossed, allowing Krol to complete a long pass to Copeland, who skirted Winnipeg's last defender to score.

**Royal Copeland (catching the pass) scored the only Argo major of the 1947 Cup as the Argos again defeated the Blue Bombers for the third consecutive time.** (Canadian Football Hall of Fame & Museum)

Moments later Winnipeg lost an opportunity to seal a Grey Cup victory on one of the most controversial plays in Grey Cup history. Winnipeg had moved play into Toronto's half and set up in field goal formation. Winnipeg faked the kick. The ball was snapped to the kicker, Hiney, and he threw a short pass to Johnny Reagan. Securely tucking the ball under his arm, Reagan eluded one, two, three Toronto tacklers with brilliant swivel-hipped action, and ran into the Toronto end zone. But the referees did not signal a touchdown. Head linesman Bill 'Moose' Rogin had tooted his horn. Rogin conferred with Umpire Hec Creighton, and Rogin ruled that Reagan had received the ball behind the line of scrimmage. Under C.R.U. rules this meant that the pass was illegal.

The Winnipeg players were flabbergasted. They were certain that the play was legitimate. Reagan, commenting after the game and shaking his head said, "I'd bet my life I was over the line of scrimmage on the play. I turned around to see what was going on in our backfield and the ball came to me. I don't possibly see how I could have failed to have gone past the line of scrimmage. I'm certain I was well over."

Teammate Harry Hood agreed. After describing how he had rushed five yards forward on his blocking assignment on the play, Hood stated: "I could feel Johnny trying to push me out of the way. He must have been over the line of scrimmage because I was well over myself and he was right on my heels."

However, Rogin said, "Reagan was at least three yards behind his own line and possibly more when he made the catch."

Blue Bomber Bob Smith agreed. Walking up to Reagan in the dressing room, and looking him straight in the eye, Smith said, "Frankly, Johnny, I'm not sure you were over the line."

Toronto then scored two singles to tie the game 9 to 9, and with less than one minute remaining to play Winnipeg had possession. Two plays did not kill the clock, so Winnipeg huddled for third down. While Sandberg assessed Toronto's defensive formation, Toronto's Morris was sure that Winnipeg was planning a trick play because Sandberg was taking an unusually long time in the huddle.

Winnipeg set up in its V, kick formation, and Morris searched the line for a spot to break through and block the kick. He spotted that Winnipeg centre Mel Wilson had slightly shifted position. There was no way that on Wilson's angle he could snap the ball to the kicker.

A Winnipeg Blue Bomber tries to corral Joe Krol in the 1947 final. (Canadian Football Hall of Fame & Museum)

Morris kept his eyes on the ball. Sandberg called the snap and the ball shot back. But instead of going to Sandberg, the ball flew to Bert Iannone. Morris drilled Iannone. Another Argo followed, and then another. Within seconds a huge pile of bodies lay on top of Iannone. There was no gain and Toronto was awarded possession.

On the next play, Krol angled a punt toward the sideline. The ball struck 10 yards behind Winnipeg's goal line, and bounced into touch-in-goal. The single gave Toronto a 10 to 9 Grey Cup victory.

As Winnipeg players left the field, the post-mortem started. A Coroner's Inquest could have been established. Sandberg was asked: "Why did you gamble?"

A heart-broken Sandberg replied, "I took a look up at the scoreboard shortly before the play and it said there was three minutes to go. Since the score was tied, I felt we should try to hold the ball, that we had time to get the winning point ourselves. But the scoreboard was wrong and there wasn't any three minutes – there was only one minute."

Winnipeg coach Jack West was then asked if he blamed Sandberg for the loss. Confidently, he said no. "Sandberg realized that if the game went into overtime we would be no match for the Argos and their powerful reserve strength – it would be just postponing the inevitable. That play had worked for us before, it might have worked this time for a long gain. It was purely a gamble that lost."

**For the third consecutive year the hero of the game was Joe Krol. His skillful passing, fabulous running, and accurate kicking paved the road to Toronto's victory. He rushed five times for 18 yards, completed four of eight passes for 91 yards, and punted 10 times. However, Krol's best display came in running back kicks. In the fourth quarter, Krol returned three punts for over 70 yards. Finally, Krol was predominant in all of Toronto's scoring. He threw a 35-yard touchdown pass, kicked a convert, and scored four singles.**

## 1948 CALGARY STAMPEDERS 12
## OTTAWA ROUGH RIDERS 7

Krol and the Argonauts did not qualify for the Cup in 1948, and accordingly a new champion was crowned. On November 27 the Calgary Stampeders and the Ottawa Rough Riders battled for the Cup, and produced a wild game. The Stampeders used a couple of unusual plays to upset the Riders 12 to 7.

During the 1948 Cup, Bob Paffrath of the Rough Riders is mugged in the end zone. Calgary beat Ottawa 12 to 7. (City of Toronto Archives)

After Ottawa took a 1 to 0 lead, Calgary moved ahead just before the end of the second quarter. A 20-yard pass from Keith Spaith to Woody Strode gave Calgary possession on the Ottawa 14, and from there Calgary used the no longer legal 'sleeper' play. While Spaith fanned out his troops, Normie Hill was face down on the left sideline 'sleeping'. The Riders failed to notice Hill, and on the snap Spaith motioned to the left as Hill sprang to his feet and raced toward the Ottawa goal line. When Spaith threw the ball to Hill, Ottawa's Smylie hit Hill just as the Calgary player caught the pass.

The ball popped into the air but Hill watched the ball carefully, and grabbed it for the touchdown.

Everyone was impressed by the seemingly preplanned play. After the game, though, Spaith stated: "No, I didn't think it up. Norm did it sponta-neously. He does it quite a bit. The odd part of it is I never thought the ball would get to him because when I got it out from centre, it was caked with about a quarter-inch of mud. I just pitched it and prayed."

Ottawa regained the lead in the third quarter when Ottawa quarterback Bob Paffrath cut through the left side of the line for a major. Eric Chipper converted: Ottawa 7, Calgary 6.

The key moment came early in the fourth quarter on one of the strangest plays in the history of Canadian football. With Ottawa in possession on its own 38, Paffrath took the snap and stepped toward the line of scrimmage. On the left Pete Karpuk moved forward. Suddenly Paffrath pitched the ball to Karpuk but the pitch was wild, landing a few feet ahead of him. At that moment, three horns honked to indicate that there was a penalty on the play. The ball continued to roll. Karpuk looked at it. So did Calgary players and the referees. As Ottawa formed a huddle, Karpuk playfully kicked at the twirling ball before joining his teammates. At this point, Calgary's Strode waltzed up to the dancing sphere. Cautiously bending down, he looked at the nearby official, then picked up the ball. From a distance a Stampeder cried "Run!" Strode obeyed, charging downfield with a teammate to the Ottawa 15. On the very next play Pete Thodos galloped through a huge hole for the eventual game-winning touchdown. Fred Wilmot added the extra point to make the score Calgary 12, Ottawa 7.

After the game the wacky 'referees' touchdown was dissected. Everyone had an opinion about the strange turnover which led to the score. Sitting in a corner, hands hiding his face, Karpuk lamented, "I thought it was forward … I don't know."

Ottawa coach Billy Masters and Ottawa manager Jim McCaffrey stated, "it looked like a forward to us, but the officials ruled it was an offside lateral. We protested at the time because, to us, it was a grounded forward pass."

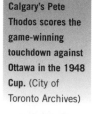

Calgary's Pete Thodos scores the game-winning touchdown against Ottawa in the 1948 Cup. (City of Toronto Archives)

In the Calgary dressing room a baffled Strode commented: "I looked at the ball on the ground. I bent down to pick up the ball and then I glanced right into the mouth of the referee. He didn't blow his whistle. That was the green light I was waiting for. That told me that the ball was alive because I wasn't familiar with the rule on a horn. But when that official moved out of my way, I figured it was time to start running."

Finally, Les Ferguson, Judge of Play, said "it was a lateral offside by about three to five yards. I was directly opposite the play on the far side of the field and it was definitely offside. There was no discussion among the officials."

Under C.R.U. rules at the time, the ball on an offside lateral was still playable.

**The top player in the 1948 game was Calgary's Chuck Anderson. Despite playing with a broken nose, and on the brink of exhaustion near the end of the game, Anderson was exceptional. His blocking, tackling, and open-field hits were all significant in Calgary's 12 to 7 win. In the fourth quarter, Anderson almost single-handedly prevented Ottawa from scoring. According to A.U. Chipman, President of the Winnipeg Blue Bombers, "Chuck Anderson was amazing. He was in on nearly every play."**

**Former gridiron great Lionel Conacher was also impressed. "Anderson's uncanny knack of getting a piece of practically every play that came at the Calgary line was magnificent to watch. Such superb playing has not been seen at Varsity Stadium in a long, long time."**

## 1949 MONTREAL ALOUETTES 28 CALGARY STAMPEDERS 15

Calgary unsuccessfully defended its crown on November 26, 1949. Led by quarterback Keith Spaith, Calgary met the Montreal Alouettes to decide who would be national champion. Field conditions were horrible. Calgary was unable to adjust to the conditions, and went down 28 to 15.

Montreal opened the scoring in the first quarter on a 75-yard touchdown march. The feature play of the drive was a 45-yard pass to Bob Cunningham. Then, Virgil Wagner culminated the drive by wriggling past Calgary defenders from four yards out.

On the ensuing kick-off Montreal recovered the ball when Calgary's Normie Hill was hammered by Glen Douglas. Four plays later, Frankie Filchock threw a deep touchdown pass to Cunningham to make the score Montreal 11, Calgary 0.

Calgary then picked up the pace, scoring a single and a converted touchdown. The major came from Harry Hood on a 14-yard run around Montreal's right end.

Montreal soon retaliated. With the ball on his own 39, Spaith called a delayed long pass. Sugarfoot Anderson sped down the field but before Spaith could unwind his throwing arm, Montreal's Herb Trawick slammed into Spaith from behind to pop the ball loose. Trawick secured it, shook off Hood, and motored into the Calgary end zone.

In the third quarter a controversial penalty set up another Montreal major. Filchock threw a long pass to Wagner only for Rod Pantages to climb into the air for the interception. Calgary celebrated until Judge of Play Jimmy Simpson penalized Pantages for interference. The Calgary coaching staff was outraged. After the game Calgary coach Les Lear recalled the decision: "It stunk." Simpson overheard and he and Lear almost got into a fight. The pair were separated, and then referee Hec Creighton gave his opinion on the penalty. "I was too far away to see actually what happened, but Jimmy ruled that Pantages kept backing into Wagner as the latter kept pulling away to get the pass, which was high. Jimmy said the interference went on perhaps for about ten yards."

Four plays later, Wagner smashed into the end zone for a 1-yard touchdown. Chester McCance kicked the convert: Montreal 23, Calgary 7.

On the next play another weird and memorable Grey Cup moment surfaced. As McCance lined up for the kick-off, a drunken fan wandered onto the field, swaggered over to Pantages, and appeared to give him advice on how to return the ball. While the fan continued with his instructions, McCance kicked the ball. Pantages caught the kick, as a referee pushed the fan to the turf. Pantages, using the fan's advice, fought off five Montreal tacklers for a 47-yard return.

A few minutes later Montreal kicked a field goal and Calgary scored a safety. Then Anderson recovered a loose ball, and rambled down the field for a Calgary touchdown. In the last few minutes McCance and Fred Kijek kicked singles for the Alouettes, to end the game Montreal 28, Calgary 15.

**Montreal's Frankie Filchock was the hero of the game. His passing was deadly, his generalship perfect, and his defensive play amazing. Filchock completed 12 of 20 passes for 210 yards, and prompted one writer to suggest that he was the greatest passer Canadian football had ever seen. The same journalist also suggested that with the exception of Sammy Baugh of the Washington Redskins and Otto Graham of the Cleveland Browns, Filchock was the best quarterback of his era.**

Defensively, Filchock was all over the gridiron. He knocked down many passes, and made three interceptions. In addition, he stopped two potential Calgary touchdown drives.

## 1950 TORONTO ARGONAUTS 13
## WINNIPEG BLUE BOMBERS 0

In 1950, it was Joe Krol's turn to shine again. On a muddy Varsity Stadium he led Toronto Argonauts to a 13 to 0 victory against the Winnipeg Blue Bombers. The game, played on November 25, was not remembered, though, for Krol's heroics. Instead, the 'Mud Bowl' is recalled for the apparent near drowning of a Winnipeg player.

After Krol guided Toronto to a 4 to 0 lead, Winnipeg's Robert Porter 'Buddy' Tinsley was found motionless in a deep puddle. Fans screamed as they believed that Tinsley was drowning. Referee Hec Creighton rolled the 260-pound man onto his back. Tinsley's limp arm crashed like a soggy log into the puddle to send water almost two feet into the air. Fans continued to scream, but Tinsley escaped from the puddle unharmed.

Forty years later Tinsley recalled the incident. "I was in a lot of pain because I went into the game with a charley horse and I was bandaged from mid-calf to the top of my thigh. I'd just got hit where the leg hurt most. My leg went numb, but I wasn't unconscious. I was mad."

Before the first half ended Volpe kicked a 16-yard field goal to give Toronto a 7 to 0 lead.

The Argonauts sealed its victory with a touchdown in the third quarter. Jake Dunlap blocked a punt, and teammate Arnie Stocks recovered the ball. Six plays later, Al Dekdebrun snuck over the right guard for the major. Krol completed the scoring with a single: Toronto 13, Winnipeg 0.

Toronto's Joe Krol (No. 55) sloshes across the field in the Mud Bowl. Toronto defeated the Winnipeg Blue Bombers 13 to 0. (CFL Photos)

Toronto's Al Dekdebrun and Joe Krol shared the honours. Dekdebrun called a perfect game as he utilized plays suited to the muddy conditions. Dekdebrun called many counters, traps, and reverses to allow his runners to get plenty of traction. In addition Dekdebrun, unlike Jack Jacobs, the Winnipeg quarterback, never mishandled the ball. When some reporters inquired how he managed to handle the muddy and gooey ball, he explained that he had taped filed-down thumb tacks to his throwing hand to get a better grip.

Meanwhile Krol dominated the game with his tremendous punting. Krol also produced the game's best play when, after mishandling a snap, he scampered for 15 yards without the benefit of blocking. The run set up a field goal which helped propel Toronto to victory.

## 1951 OTTAWA ROUGH RIDERS 21
## SASKATCHEWAN ROUGHRIDERS 14

A year later the Ottawa Rough Riders and the Saskatchewan Roughriders challenged for Lord Grey's mug. Unlike the two previous games, the field was in excellent condition. However, no balls could be found! While Governor-General Viscount Alexander awaited the ceremonial kick-off referees scurried around. Twelve footballs were eventually located but during the game all were kicked into the stands. When the last ball disappeared the public address announcer successfully appealed for its return and the game, played November 24 at Varsity Stadium, was completed with only one football.

Saskatchewan would have preferred that all of the balls had been lost. The western Riders entered the game decimated by injuries. In addition its best player, Bob Sandberg, had been ruled ineligible to play by the C.R.U. Ottawa took advantage of Saskatchewan's problems to win 21 to 14.

Saskatchewan held a 2 to 0 lead before Ottawa broke the game open on a spectacular run. Scrimmaging on the Ottawa 40, Ottawa quarterback Tom O'Malley faked a hand-off to Benny MacDonnell. As MacDonnell charged into the line, O'Malley bootlegged. This pulled Saskatchewan's Jack Wedley and Roy Wright closer to the scrimmage line. The flat zone was left wide open. As Saskatchewan defenders tried to stop the apparent plunge into the line, O'Malley gave the ball to Howie Turner. The resulting run gained 68 yards.

After the game Turner said, "They didn't even see the ball until I was 20 yards past the line of scrimmage. Their left end was looking the other way when I passed him. The faking fooled them completely."

On the next play MacDonnell barged through the line for a touchdown.

Early in the second quarter Ottawa scored another major. John Wagoner recovered a fumble, and from the Saskatchewan 29 O'Malley avoided a rush to pass to Alton Baldwin, who dragged two tacklers over the goal line for the score. Bob Gain converted to give Ottawa a 12 to 2 lead.

In the third quarter with the score 13 to 2, Ottawa scored its third touchdown. Scrimmaging on the Ottawa 45, O'Malley sent Pete Karpuk in motion.

A group of Ottawa Rough Riders tackle a lonely Regina Roughrider in the 1951 Cup.
(Canadian Football Hall of Fame & Museum)

The receiver ran wide right before cutting sharply down the field. Karpuk out-raced Del Wardien and made an over-the-shoulder catch en route to a 65-yard major.

Saskatchewan battled back in the fourth quarter. Trailing 20 to 2, Glenn Dobbs threw a touchdown pass to John Nix. Three minutes later, Sully Glasser ran off-tackle and barged through the line for another touchdown. Only six points now separated the teams, but Ottawa's defence held out, stymying a Saskatchewan sleeper play before an O'Malley single closed the scoring at Ottawa 21, Saskatchewan 14.

The hero of this game was the 1948 'goat', Pete Karpuk. In the first quarter, his punt returns ruined Saskatchewan's battle plans, and in the third quarter his long touchdown reception gave Ottawa its winning score. Karpuk finished with a touchdown and 175 all-purpose yards. After the game Saskatchewan coach Harry 'Blackjack' Smith said, "Karpuk hurt us most. Karpuk was terrific."

Although Karpuk and his Ottawa teammates played a great game, Bob Kramer, a Saskatchewan executive, believed that Ottawa's hero of the game was the Saskatchewan head coach! As described in *Rider Pride*, Kramer explained:

> The night before the Grey Cup game, I called together the officials of the Big Four and explained that with our injury situation we wouldn't be able to provide much of a game. I asked for permission to use Bob Sandberg. They said there was no way they'd allow that: rules were rules. So I got up, said 'To hell with ya, I'm going to dress Sandberg anyway,' went out, slammed the door, and was about at the elevator when [Jim] McCaffrey, President of the Rough Riders, came after me to come back and talk some more. Finally, they agreed that we could play Sandberg with no protest in the game ... Anyway, I got up early that next morning, the morning of the game, and I went out to where we had the team at the Seaway Motel. I got a hold of Clair Warner, the President, and I said 'Now don't you say a damned word about this. Don't tell a soul. You get Sandberg dressed and get him into that game.' ... I went

down to the game … and Sandberg was still sitting on the bench. Smith hadn't brought him in yet. So I went down to the dressing room at the half and got a hold of Smith and he says, 'Well, I'm sorry, Mr. Kramer, the score's not so good yet,' so I jumped up and I said, 'Why haven't you played Sandberg?' He says, 'Well, I am going to play him when we're down.' So I said, 'What the hell is twenty-two to two?'

… he never did play him … After it was over, I went back to the dressing room, … and I went over to Smith and he says, 'Well, I'm sorry,' and I says, 'Well, you should be. You can pack your suitcases, and head for home as fast as you can. We could have won that game with Sandberg in the line-up.'

## 1952 TORONTO ARGONAUTS 21
## EDMONTON ESKIMOS 11

Kramer's theory was never tested as on November 29, 1952 the Edmonton Eskimos and the Toronto Argonauts clashed for the national title. This game was historic because for the first time the Grey Cup was televised. CBLT which showed the game live, estimated that 700,000 people watched the game within its viewing area. The picture was clear, but during the third quarter a microwave receiver used at the station to pick up the signals from the mobile unit at Varsity Stadium in Toronto failed. While the television announcer continued to describe the game a repairman climbed 300 feet up a tower to repair the receiver. Twenty-nine minutes later the telecast was restored, and viewers were able to watch the exciting conclusion of the game.

The Eskimos opened the scoring late in the first quarter, when Normie 'the China Clipper' Kwong scooted around the end for a 5-yard touchdown. The Argos quickly answered in the second quarter as Nobby Wirkowski wriggled across the Edmonton goal line for a touchdown. Red Ettinger kicked the convert and Toronto led 6 to 5.

The Wirkowski major sparked Toronto. Ettinger scored a field goal, and then Billy Bass barged into the Edmonton end zone for another touchdown.

Toronto appeared headed for easy victory, but in the third quarter the Eskimos trimmed Toronto's lead. Employing a double-wing formation, quarterback Claude Arnold advanced the Eskimos to the Toronto 10. From there Kwong followed the blocking of Rollie Prather and Mario DeMarco for his second touchdown.

In the last quarter the assault continued. Edmonton was foiled on one scoring chance and then Arnold drove the Eskimos to the Toronto 17. Trapped behind the line of scrimmage, Arnold avoided a sack with a short screen pass. But the ball came loose and Toronto's Art Scullion recovered.

A deflated Edmonton made another error with Toronto gaining possession on the Edmonton 36. On the next play, Wirkowski called a "three thirty-two across, ends cross." Wirkowski later explained the play. "Three signified it was a pass. Thirty-two meant that it came off a run – it was a play

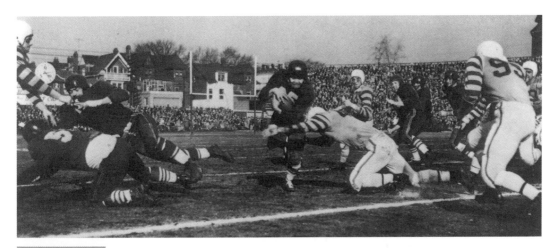

action pass, one fake outside, one fake inside. Ends cross meant that ends criss-crossed. Al Bruno, the primary receiver, went down about 10 and then cut left to right, and [Zeke] O'Connor cut from right to left about five yards underneath him as a decoy."

As the play unfolded, Wirkowski executing his fakes to Bass and to Doug Pyzer, Edmonton defenders Rollie Miles and Frank Filchock got their own signals crossed. Both covered Bruno, leaving O'Connor wide open. Wirkowski completed the pass to O'Connor, and the receiver pranced into the end zone for a touchdown. Ettinger added the extra point to close the scoring at Toronto 21, Edmonton 11.

**The star of this game was Toronto's Nobby Wirkowski. Although he completed only eight of 19 passes, the average yards gained per pass was 29.4. This was much better than the 14.3 yards per pass of Claude Arnold. In addition, Wirkowski scored a touchdown and threw for another. For his performance Wirkowski was awarded the game ball.**

Toronto's 1952 victory ended a fabulous stage in Canadian football. Joe Krol helped Toronto win this game, and led the Argos to four other championships. His dominance on offence, defence and special teams was unmatched. While players like Garney Henley, Jackie Parker, Russ Jackson and Ron Lancaster would later become Canadian football legends, they were not as great as 'King' Krol. Krol was the finest player ever in Canadian football: his tremendous abilities generated much excitement which continued into the next era of Canadian football.

## Chapter Eight

# PARKER 3, ETCHEVERRY 0
## 1953-1956

From 1953 to 1956 Canadian football experienced tremendous changes. With the end of the Argos' and Joe Krol's domination of the game, two other Canadian football legends stood in the spotlight. In the West a youthful John Dickerson 'Jackie' Parker led the Edmonton Eskimos to three successive Grey Cup appearances, while in the East an experienced Sam 'the Rifle' Etcheverry guided the Montreal Alouettes to three national finals in a row. The Edmonton versus Montreal finals were electrifying.

There was also much excitement off of the field. The C.R.U. negotiated major television contracts, and began to honour the best player throughout Canada with the Schenley award. Canadian football began to look more like a modern professional sport. The larger western and eastern teams recognized the changes, and accordingly on January 22, 1956 the Big Four and the Western Inter-Provincial Football Union decided to distance themselves from the C.R.U. by forming the Canadian Football Council (the 'C.F.C.'). The purpose of the C.F.C. was to administer and represent professional football interests in Canada. G. Sydney Halter was named the first commissioner, and under his leadership national negotiation lists were introduced and the value of a touchdown was increased from 5 to 6 points. It quickly became apparent that the C.F.C. could not function under the rigid and primarily amateur structure of the C.R.U. Two years later the C.F.C. withdrew from the C.R.U. and became the Canadian Football League.

## 1953  HAMILTON TIGER-CATS 12
## WINNIPEG BLUE BOMBERS 6

The first Cup game was played between the Hamilton Tiger-Cats and the Winnipeg Blue Bombers on November 28, 1953. Winnipeg was not expected

CASEY

KUSSEROW

The critical play of the 1953 final as Hamilton's Lou Kusserow buries his shoulder into the abdomen of Winnipeg's Tom Casey. (Canadian Football Hall of Fame & Museum)

to provide Hamilton with much of a challenge for the national title since it had endured a gruelling six-game playoff schedule en route to the Cup game, but Winnipeg surprised the Tiger-Cats. The Blue Bombers showed few signs of playoff fatigue with a courageous game which was not decided until the final whistle.

The Tiger-Cats roared into the lead following an exchange of punts early in the first quarter. A controversial decision assisted Hamilton on an eight-play, 54-yard touchdown drive which was culminated by Ed Songin on a 1-yard quarterback sneak. On the drive, Hamilton's Bernie Custis had fumbled the ball out of bounds. Under C.R.U. rules this should have resulted in a 10-yard penalty against Hamilton, but the officials ruled that Custis had stepped out of bounds before he lost the ball. According to Joe Krol this decision was incorrect. "The play took place right in front of where several Argos and myself were sitting and we all agree that Custis was in bounds when the ball popped out of his arms ..." If the referees had seen what Krol and his teammates had seen, it is unlikely that Hamilton would have scored the touchdown.

Over the next few minutes and into the second quarter the teams traded turnovers until Lou Kusserow intercepted an errant lateral thrown by Winnipeg's Bud Korchak, and returned the ball to the Winnipeg 21. The turnover presented Hamilton with a glorious scoring chance, but the Tiger-Cats squandered it when Tip Logan missed a field goal.

The missed kick ignited the Blue Bombers and before the end of the half Winnipeg threatened to tie the game. 'Indian' Jack Jacobs completed a 54-yard pass to Neill Armstrong, and then tried to throw a touchdown pass to Bud Grant, but Hamilton's Vito Ragazzo intercepted the pass to end the half, Hamilton 6, Winnipeg 0.

The Blue Bombers tied the game midway through the third quarter. Scrimmaging on the Hamilton 50, Winnipeg used five plays to take the ball to the Hamilton 1. From there Gerry James crashed into the end zone. Korchak added the convert.

Four plays later, Hamilton re-established its 6-point lead. Hamilton moved play to the Winnipeg 53, and from there Songin threw his best pass of the 1953 season. While Songin rolled out to his left, Ragazzo sprinted straight down the field then cut into the flat, and Songin delivered a rainbow pass. The lone Winnipeg defender, Geoff Crain, gambled on intercepting the ball, but missed. Ragazzo caught the pass, and rambled the remaining 30 yards for a touchdown. Logan kicked the extra point: Hamilton 12, Winnipeg 6.

The Blue Bombers desperately tried to tie the game again. However, in the fourth quarter a potential touchdown drive was thwarted when a reception made by Winnipeg's Tom Casey was ruled incomplete because teammate Andy Sokol had deflected the ball while it was en route to Casey. The ruling took the starch out of Winnipeg's offence until, with less than six minutes remaining, Jacobs engineered a spectacular drive. Sacked for a 12-yard loss close to his own posts Jacobs used a series of pass plays, including a rarely used tackle-eligible play, to move the Bombers to the Hamilton 4. The referee informed Jacobs that there was time for one more play, but Jacobs did not hear him because of the roar of the crowd.

On the snap of the ball Jacobs quickly dropped back to pass while Armstrong and Casey ran their pass routes. The only Hamilton defender near Armstrong and Casey was Kusserow. Kusserow could not cover both receivers, so he gambled that Jacobs would throw the ball to Casey. He was right.

Feeling the pressure from Hamilton's rush, Jacob's ignored Armstrong and gunned the ball to Casey. At the same instant, Casey reached up to grab the ball. Kusserow stuck his shoulder into Casey's abdomen and the ball fell incomplete on the Hamilton 1-yard line as the clock ran out. Accordingly, Hamilton won the 1953 Cup by a 12 to 6 score.

After the game the incompletion was reviewed. Winnipeg claimed that Kusserow interfered with Casey and that there should have been a penalty. "I'm positive I was interfered with," a dejected Casey told a room full of reporters. "I was hit before I could touch the ball."

Meanwhile, Kusserow said, "Perhaps I did interfere. I don't know. I made my move just as Jacobs started to throw and I hit Casey just as the ball hit him. It was either him or me."

Game footage, however, clearly showed that Kusserow had not interfered. The hit was perfectly timed.

Jacobs was also put under a microscope, and he later wrote: "I didn't know that was the last play, that time had run out. I missed the referee's signal, busy thinking about what plays to call I guess …

"I faked to [Gerry] James and threw to Casey, who was what is called the 'swing' halfback. That means he is in motion after or just a little before the ball comes out, swinging wide on the weak side.

"I had to throw quickly because someone [Bob Garside] was in on me. Whoever it was hit my arm just as I threw and it blooped the ball up in the air. I thought Kusserow was going to intercept it."

**The most valuable player of the game was Lou Kusserow who gave an excellent performance on both offence and defence. But in a losing cause Jack Jacobs was the best player on the field. Jacobs was a study in coolness and concentration. After**

being ridiculed for Winnipeg's 1950 Grey Cup loss, Jacobs wanted to show Canadian football fans that he was an excellent quarterback. He did that by completing 31 of 48 passes for over 350 yards against a brilliant Hamilton defence.

Everyone praised Jacobs' performance. Winnipeg coach George Trafton said: "I think Jacobs called a good ball game and also played a helluva game himself. I think he proved to you easterners that he is the best passer in Canada."

Frankie Gnup, an ex-Big Four player and coach, agreed with Trafton. Gnup said of Jacobs: "He's the greatest in Canada, there's no argument about that."

## 1954 EDMONTON ESKIMOS 26 MONTREAL ALOUETTES 25

Over the next three years Jackie Parker and Sam Etcheverry dominated the Grey Cup as the Eskimos and Alouettes met in the national final. On November 27, 1954, the Eskimos entered the Grey Cup as vast underdogs. Labelled a 'two-dollar football team', Edmonton was given little chance of defeating the Alouettes. However, Montreal was unable to prevent a last quarter surge by Edmonton, and lost 26 to 25.

Edmonton started this exciting game with a touchdown. After marching the ball to the Montreal 3, Rollie Miles accepted a pitch-out and moved to his left. Miles wanted to throw, but was unable to find a receiver. Soon a swarm of Alouette defenders trapped him 25 yards behind the line of scrimmage. A sack appeared imminent when suddenly Bob Dean levelled Montreal's Herb Trawick. The block gave Miles additional time and he threw the ball to Earl Lindley for a touchdown.

A few minutes later Montreal scored on a record-setting touchdown pass.

Chuck Hunsinger was the 'goat' of the 1954 Cup but here he stumbles into the end zone to give the Alouettes the lead over Edmonton. (Canadian Football Hall of Fame & Museum)

Scrimmaging on the Montreal 20, Sam Etcheverry gunned a short pass to Red O'Quinn. While the pass was high, O'Quinn reached up to make an over-the-head, one-handed catch. Edmonton defenders, amazed by the circus-like reception, stood frozen admiring the grab. This allowed O'Quinn to race away for a 90-yard touchdown.

In another ten plays, the Eskimos scored again. After moving the ball 85 yards Bernie Faloney ran a quarterback sneak from the Montreal 1. Faloney's initial attempt was stopped, but with a shove from Normie Kwong, Faloney squirmed into the end zone.

Edmonton's Jackie 'Spaghetti Legs' Parker straight-arms an Alouette. In the 1954 final Parker scored the game-winning touchdown.
(Canadian Football Hall of Fame & Museum)

Edmonton held a 14 to 6 lead early in the second quarter when Montreal took charge of the game. Etcheverry engineered a 12-play, 100-yard drive which resulted in another spectacular touchdown for O'Quinn. A few minutes later Etcheverry assembled an 11-play, 90-yard touchdown series. This time Chuck Hunsinger scored the major on a pitch-out. Ray Poole converted the touchdown to give Montreal an 18 to 14 lead.

Montreal scored the only point of the third quarter and showed no signs of losing its lead in the fourth. Etcheverry started with two successful passes and two running plays, and then threw the ball to Joey Pal. Pal cut in over the middle, raced past his defender and caught Etcheverry's pass for a 14-yard touchdown.

The Alouettes soon had the opportunity to put the game out of reach. An interception by Bruce Coulter allowed Montreal to drive the ball to the Edmonton 7. With a third down and four yards to go, a successful field goal would have increased Montreal's lead to 14 points, but Montreal coach Doug 'Peahead' Walker decided to take a chance. The gamble failed, and sparked the Eskimos.

Taking possession on its own 25, Edmonton stormed downfield. A risky third down play put the ball on the Montreal 27, and three plays later Glenn Lippman exploited a gaping hole for a 14-yard major. The convert made the score Montreal 25, Edmonton 20.

Montreal was still in no danger and with little time remaining advanced the ball to the Edmonton 10. On the next play the Alouettes lost the 1954 championship on one of the most memorable and controversial turnovers in Cup history. Hunsinger was given the ball, and he proceeded left with Trawick and Poole in front blocking. But Hunsinger was caught from behind. Spinning back to the 20 he flipped a basketball-style shovel pass to Poole. The ball bounced twice before settling into the hands of Parker, and he headed downfield for a touchdown.

After the game Parker described the score. "I saw our linebacker Ted Tully and defensive end Rollie Prather had a back trapped behind the line of scrimmage. I was playing right outside defensive halfback and started to float right to be able to get the angle and be ready for what looked like a possible end run. As soon as I saw Tully and Prather just about had him, I came up fast to try to help make sure he was going to be thrown for a loss and wasn't going to wiggle away.

"Tully grabbed Hunsinger by the leg and Prather hit him hard higher up. Hunsinger had the ball out in front of him with both hands and it looked like when Tully hit him it squirted away. The ball bounced right in front of me … My first intention was to fall on it. But there wasn't anybody else there, so I followed the ball, and when it took a little hop, I picked it up … I hesitated for just a split-second and somebody hollered 'Go, Jackie, go!'

"I just took off out there, heading on a line for the corner of the field and the goal line … I felt I was home free when I had about 20 yards to go and I sneaked a quick look over my shoulder. Etcheverry had stopped his pursuit and then I really began to worry. I'd figured they'd call the play back … I dog-trotted the last 10 yards afraid to look around again to see if they called it back. When I did look around, after crossing the goal line, the official had his arms up and I knew that no matter what happened in the next couple of minutes, we'd won the Grey Cup."

Meanwhile Montreal players and other field-level observers believed that Parker's touchdown should have been nullified. They insisted that Hunsinger's toss was an incomplete pass. Hunsinger agreed. Bitterly, with tears in his eyes, Hunsinger told a crowded Montreal dressing room, "It wasn't a fumble or a lateral. It was a forward pass. It lost the game for us, but the play should have been called back because of an incomplete pass."

Referee Hap Shouldice, who made the ultimate decision, saw the play differently. "It was clearly a fumble and not a forward pass. That ball left him as he was being thrown for a loss behind the line of scrimmage …"

Bob Dean converted the touchdown, and shortly thereafter the game ended Edmonton 26, Montreal 25.

**In this exciting Grey Cup game three players stood in the spotlight. For Montreal, Red O'Quinn was phenomenal setting the record for the most receptions and yards receiving in a Grey Cup game by catching 13 passes for an incredible 316 yards! In addition he scored two touchdowns.**

**Edmonton's Eagle Keys played courageously. The 29-year-old, six-foot three, 220-pound centre, unbelievably played most of the game with a broken leg. Carried from the field in the first quarter in extreme pain, he remained on the bench. Keys was then reinserted into the line-up, and continued to play until the pain in his leg grew so severe that tears swelled in his eyes. Edmonton coach Frank 'Pop' Ivy was very impressed by Keys' play, and stated that his performance "took a lot of courage and intestinal fortitude." Ivy added, "I'm mighty proud of Eagle."**

**Top man of the game was Jackie Parker, whose 95-yard record-setting fumble return for the game-winning touchdown was the game's most important play. Parker also contributed to Edmonton's victory in many other ways. After Montreal took an 11-point lead in the fourth quarter, Parker scrambled for a 14-yard gain which set up Edmonton's first touchdown of the fourth quarter. That play was intended to be a pass, but Parker did not have the strength to throw the ball because of a badly injured shoulder. The shoulder hampered Parker on offence for most of the game, but on defence he used it to stop Montreal runners. In great pain he courageously continued to play.**

The heroics of Parker were again featured on November 26, 1955 when the Eskimos met the Alouettes at Empire Stadium, Vancouver. This was the first Grey Cup ever played west of Ontario and a then Cup record crowd of 39,417 fans turned out. The tremendous crowd inspired both teams with many Cup records being set as Edmonton defeated Montreal 34 to 19.

After Montreal took an early 1 to 0 lead on a missed field goal, the Eskimos scored the game's first touchdown on a 12-play, 85-yard drive. The feature player in the drive was Normie Kwong. Kwong prevented a Montreal touchdown by alertly recovering a dribbled fumble, and then he barged into the end zone for a 1-yard major. The Alouettes answered this score with a 1-yard touchdown of its own. Using a mixture of strong running and good passing plays, Etcheverry drove Montreal to the Edmonton 1, from where Pat Abbruzzi plunged into the end zone. Bud Korchak converted to give Montreal a 7 to 6 lead.

In the last minute of the first quarter, Montreal extended its lead. After Montreal's Jim Miller recovered a fumble on the Edmonton 42, Etcheverry threw a long pass to Hal Patterson. Patterson caught the pass behind defender Bob Heydenfeldt, and in a couple of strides crossed the Edmonton goal line.

A turnover led to Edmonton's next score. With Montreal threatening to produce another touchdown, Etcheverry lost possession on the Edmonton 29. Four plays later, Edmonton's Johnny Bright took a reverse hand-off from Parker, broke numerous Montreal tackles around the right end, and scored a spectacular touchdown.

Montreal's Joey Pal breaks up a pass intended for Edmonton's Johnny Bright in the 1955 Cup. (Canadian Football Hall of Fame & Museum)

Montreal soon drove the ball to the Edmonton 15. Facing a second down and inches, Edmonton stacked the line, expecting a run, but Etcheverry foxed the Eskimos with a pass over the head of Parker and into the arms of Patterson for an easy major.

Before the end of the first half, Edmonton scored the game's sixth touchdown. From the Montreal 15 Parker threw a short pass to Heydenfeldt. The receiver caught the ball 10 yards downfield, and curved into the end zone for the touchdown. Bob Dean kicked his third convert to make the score Montreal 19, Edmonton 18.

The tide of the game turned in favour of the Eskimos in the third quarter. The Eskimos drove the ball to the Montreal 1 and from there Kwong charged through the line for the eventual game-winning touchdown.

Montreal's defence could not halt Edmonton's offence, and shortly thereafter Edmonton marched the ball from its own 13 to the Montreal 3 using only one pass play, and no less than 11 punishing ground plays. Then Bright bustled into the end zone.

The Alouettes still had a chance to win and appeared poised to score another touchdown when Etcheverry marched his gridiron gladiators 67 yards to the Edmonton 21. However, on the next play Parker stepped in front of Montreal's Jim Miller and intercepted an Etcheverry pass. The fans realized that Montreal would not now come back to win the 1955 Grey Cup. According to Edmonton's Rollie Miles, "That pass had TD written all over it, but when Jackie took it I think it broke the Als' heart."

Edmonton's Dean closed the scoring with a single and a field goal. The single resulted from a hilarious play in which a young fan scooped up a missed field goal in the Montreal end zone and disappeared into the stands. The final score was Edmonton 34, Montreal 19.

The pick of the crop for the second consecutive year was Jackie Parker. In only his second year of Canadian football Parker played with the experience of a veteran as he guided the Edmonton offence using a variety of plays and deceptive tactics to march his club repeatedly down the field. On many occasions, fakes on hand-offs confused both the Alouette defenders and referees. After the game Normie Kwong recalled an incident in which he plunged through the line on a fake hand-off, while Parker shot around the end. Kwong was tackled on the play, and the referee was ready to blow his whistle until Kwong pointed to Parker. Kwong said, "The official looked at me, and I looked at him, and he ran away. That was all there was to it."

Parker's deceptiveness allowed him to run and to pass freely. He finished the game completing eight of 16 passes for 128 yards, and running the ball six times for 69 yards. Everyone was impressed by Parker's offensive play. "That Jackie Parker sure called a great game," commented Montreal's Pat Abbruzzi. "Parker seemed to come up with the right call all day. On second down when yardage was needed to hold onto the ball, he always made a perfect call to get that first down."

Montreal's Johnny Williams added, "Where are those guys who said that Parker couldn't pass? That guy is a good passer. He can't throw as well as Sam [Etcheverry] but he sure keeps the defence honest by throwing that old pigskin when you least expect it."

Parker also played well defensively. In the second half he batted down many passes and made hard-hitting tackles on Montreal receivers. The best defensive play came in the third quarter when he intercepted an Etcheverry pass deep in Edmonton's territory.

Normie Kwong and Sam Etcheverry were also stellar in this game. Each player established Grey Cup records as Kwong carried the ball 30 times for 145 yards, while Etcheverry completed 30 of 39 passes for 508 yards.

On November 24, 1956, Montreal and Edmonton again met in the Grey Cup final. Despite Edmonton's previous two victories, Montreal was favoured to finally defeat the Eskimos. Montreal was still guided by the masterful Sam Etcheverry, while Edmonton had Canadian quarterback Don Getty. The critics expected Getty to collapse under the pressures of a final, but the future premier of Alberta played a tremendous game and led the Eskimos to a third consecutive title.

The first half was a see-saw battle. Hal 'The Prince' Patterson put Montreal into the lead with a touchdown, and then Johnny Bright and Getty scored majors to put Edmonton ahead. Soon Montreal regained the lead as Patterson scored again on the most spectacular pass of the game. From the Edmonton 38, Etcheverry threw to Patterson, who was sprinting into the Edmonton end zone. Oscar Kruger was stride-for-stride with Patterson. Patterson deflected the ball, and then a mesmerized Kruger could only watch Patterson's aerial gymnastics as he stretched to grab the twirling sphere and crashed to the turf for the score.

Parker scored on a 10-yard pass before the end of the second quarter, but once again Montreal regained the lead when Etcheverry snuck into the Edmonton end zone early in the third quarter: Montreal 20, Edmonton 19.

The Eskimos tied the score. Then came the criticial moment. Montreal's Joey Pal fumbled a punt deep in his own zone, and two plays later Bright raced 16 yards for a touchdown.

The turnover and subsequent touchdown unnerved Montreal. Etcheverry was shaky; within minutes he threw two interceptions which led to Edmonton scores. The first resulted in a Joe Mobra field goal, while the second ended in a Getty touchdown.

In the fourth quarter Parker scored again. A few minutes later, Montreal's Abbruzzi scored a touchdown: Edmonton 44, Montreal 27.

**The football splits the uprights during the 1956 championship. Edmonton defeated the Alouettes for its third consecutive title.** (Canadian Football Hall of Fame & Museum)

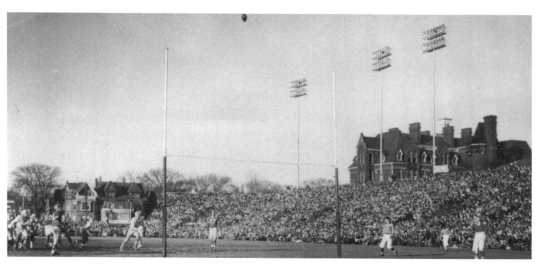

With less than five minutes remaining, Edmonton was headed for victory. Montreal desperately tried to make the score more respectable, but in the dying minutes failed on a third down gamble on its own 23, giving Edmonton excellent field position. While Edmonton coach Frank 'Pop' Ivy instructed Getty to run out the clock, Parker convinced Getty to go for another touchdown. Two plays later Parker ran wide, skidding into the Montreal end zone for his third touchdown of the game. At this point the fans swarmed onto the field. Parker was mobbed and the ball disappeared. Another could not be found, so the officials declared the game over. It was later revealed that another ball was available for the convert attempt, but C.R.U. Secretary Harry McBrien stated that the sideline officials could not get the ball through the mob and onto the field. Accordingly the game ended Edmonton 50, Montreal 27.

**Don Getty and Jackie Parker were the outstanding players. The Montreal-born and Toronto-raised Getty handled the ball well and he mixed his plays with the skill of a veteran quarterback. Whenever Montreal stacked the line of scrimmage in an effort to stop Edmonton's inside running plays, Getty called end runs to spread out the Montreal defensive line. With Montreal's defensive line spread out, Getty would send Johnny Bright through the middle. This mixture of ground plays was responsible for Edmonton's victory and allowed Bright to rush for a Grey Cup record of 171 yards.**

**After the game Edmonton coach Frank Ivy and Parker praised Getty's performance. Ivy said, "He did a tremendous job. He called a tremendous game. I didn't send in a play." Parker added, "Don is a great football player. He proved it under the pressure at Varsity Stadium. He called the plays, make no mistake about that, and he called them well. When we got off to a slow start in the game, Don kept as cool as a julep when a lot of young players might have pressed too hard."**

**Getty completed seven of 16 passes for 104 yards, ran three times for 14 yards, and scored two touchdowns.**

**Meanwhile, Parker was a defensive and offensive spark for the Eskimos. Whenever Edmonton needed yardage Parker was given the ball. Parker carried the pigskin 19 times for 115 yards, caught two passes for 26 yards, scored three touchdowns, and kicked a single. His three majors tied a Grey Cup record, and his 19 points set a Grey Cup record, which was broken two years later.**

The 1956 game ended another exhilarating stage in Canadian football. The professionalism of the sport was solidified and attendance at games across Canada increased. Jackie Parker and Sam Etcheverry dominated this brief period and combined to produce some of the greatest national finals ever played. Parker's guidance of the Eskimos to three consecutive titles over Etcheverry and the Alouettes was a sign of the future excitement that would be seen in Canadian football. Edmonton and Montreal later presented additional spectacular Grey Cup games, and eventually the Eskimos assembled the greatest dynasty in the history of the game. However, before this occurred Hamilton Tiger-Cats came to dominate Canadian football, and Ron Lancaster, Russ Jackson, Garney Henley, and Tony Gabriel would become heroes of the game.

## Chapter Nine

# KING OF THE JUNGLE
## 1957-1967

From 1957 through 1967 Hamilton Tiger-Cats dominated Canadian football. Led by a punishing defence and a sparkling offence, the Tiger-Cats mauled opponent after opponent. In 11 years, the Tiger-Cats made no less than nine Grey Cup appearances and won four titles.

Hamilton's dominance was somewhat overshadowed by many unique and bizarre situations. As in the period from 1945 to 1952 weather conditions plagued the championship games. In 1959 a heavy snowfall a few days prior to the game left the west end of Toronto's C.N.E. Stadium saturated with water and prompted one reporter to describe the game as 'The Battle of the Bog', while in 1965 a 35- to 50-mile-per-hour (56- to 80-kilometre-per-hour) westerly wind resulted in the 'Wind Bowl'. The worst weather conditions ever at a Grey Cup also occurred in this period. In 1962 a thick fog rolled over C.N.E. Stadium and forced the suspension of the game. Many people criticized Commissioner G. Sydney Halter for allowing the game to start but television network contracts, fan inconvenience, and weather reports compelled Halter to proceed with the game. In addition this era featured the first and only overtime game in Cup history, the premature end to a Cup game after a mob of fans rioted late in the fourth quarter, and the most controversial tackle in a Grey Cup game.

## 1957 HAMILTON TIGER-CATS 32
## WINNIPEG BLUE BOMBERS 7

However, these years are best remembered for the oddest incident in the history of the sport. In the 1957 Cup game, played on November 30, a fan wandered along the sideline and tripped Hamilton's Ray 'Bibbles' Bawel as the Hamilton defender roared down the field for a potential touchdown. Bawel scrambled to his feet ready to challenge the tripper but the fan, dressed in a trench coat and wearing a black Ivy League style cap faded into the crowded background, walked in front of the Hamilton bench, crossed it, and disappeared through an exit. Who was this mysterious tripper? Speculation grew. In the press box, a Winnipeg reporter said, "It looks like a Winnipeg bookmaker … He looks familiar, but I can't identify him."

Following the game C.R.U. secretary Harry McBrien announced that the spectator involved was a prominent Toronto lawyer. "Inquiries were made at his home, but his wife answered 'I know nothing about it – my husband left for Windsor after the game'," McBrien said.

The tripper was David Humphrey (later Mr. Justice Humphrey of the Ontario Court General Division). Thirty-five years after the game, Humphrey recalled what had prompted him to trip Bawel. Humphrey described that he had encountered on the sideline a man who had been a jury foreman in a criminal proceeding in which Humphrey was representing the accused. Because the accused was convicted and sentenced to death, Humphrey held a grudge against the foreman. Accordingly, Humphrey grew so angry that he had to do something. Instead of taking out his anger on the former jury foreman, Humphrey tripped Bawel.

The tripping incident did not play a large factor in the 1957 final, but provided much hilarity to an otherwise lop-sided game. The Tiger-Cats out-played the Winnipeg Blue Bombers and roared to a 32 to 7 victory.

Hamilton's dominance in the 1957 game was displayed on the four-teenth play of the first quarter. With Winnipeg in possession on its own 38, quarterback Kenny Ploen called a double left formation-58 pitch. Dennis Mendyk received a lateral from Ploen, and gained 12 yards when he was clobbered from behind by Cookie Gilchrist. The impact knocked the ball out of Mendyk's arms, and into Bawel's. With no Winnipeg players between him and the Winnipeg goal line, Bawel had no trouble in scoring.

**First quarter action from the 1957 final as a Hamilton Tiger-Cat tippy-toes down the sideline.**
(Hamilton Public Library Archives)

Hamilton quarterback Bernie Faloney then engineered a 5-play, 46-yard touchdown drive. From the Winnipeg 2 Faloney followed excellent blocking into the end zone to make the score Hamilton 13, Winnipeg 0.

Two critical mistakes then cost the Blue Bombers the Grey Cup. After marching the ball to the Hamilton 12 in the second quarter, Ploen threw an end zone pass to Ernie 'Alabama' Pitts. The wobbly pass enabled Bawel to intercept. "That interception solidified confidence in our pass defence strategy," beamed Hamilton coach Jim Trimble, "and I wasn't worried after that."

In the third quarter Winnipeg again took the ball to the Hamilton 12. This time it was handed to Gerry 'Kid Dynamite' James. James gained four yards, only to be destroyed by Ralph Goldston and Bawel. James fumbled. Hamilton recovered. James later confessed, "I feel that fumble early in the third quarter was the turning point in the game. I was going for a first down when two Tiger-Cats hit me. Someone hit my elbow and the ball was jarred loose … I'm not trying to make excuses. I should have held onto the ball, but early in the game my hand was stepped on and broken."

Winnipeg never threatened to score again until late in the game.

On the first play of the fourth quarter Hamilton's Gerry McDougall blasted over left tackle to score a touchdown, then Gilchrist charged over left tackle for another six points. This was followed by lawyer Humphrey's trip of Bawel's interception return. The Tiger-Cats demanded a touchdown, but referee Paul Dojack decided to move the ball half the distance to the goal line because "Bawel was obviously trapped by two Blue Bombers converging on him." No harm done. Only two plays later, Gilchrist scored from 16 yards out. Steve Oneschuk converted and Hamilton led 32 to 0.

Near the end Winnipeg broke the shutout. From the Hamilton 15, Canadian quarterback Barry Roseborough withstood a tremendous Hamilton rush to complete a short hook pass to Mendyk, who tossed aside Hamilton tacklers and scored. Ploen's extra point closed the game at Hamilton 32, Winnipeg 7.

**The outstanding player was Ray Bawel; he was all over the field. Whenever Winnipeg's offence pressed, he emerged to either knock down a crucial pass, make a touchdown-saving interception or pounce on a fumble. The fumble recovery in the first quarter which he returned for a touchdown set the tone for the game.**

**Bawel's performance was truly remarkable considering that two months before the Cup game his career appeared to be over. He had been released by the Philadelphia Eagles and was ready to retire. However, Trimble, who had coached Bawel in Philadelphia, knew that he still had something to contribute to football. Accordingly Bawel was brought to the Tiger-Cats, and showed he could dominate the most important game of the season.**

Winnipeg's John
Varone (No. 85)
watches Jimmy Van
Pelt throw a touch-
down pass in the
1958 Cup against
Hamilton.
(Canadian Football
Hall of Fame &
Museum)

## 1958 WINNIPEG BLUE BOMBERS 35
## HAMILTON TIGER-CATS 28

In 1958 Canadian football took its last step in the process of evolving into
a professional sport. The newly formed Canadian Football League wrestled
control of the Grey Cup from the C.R.U. and promptly decided that amateur teams could no longer challenge for the trophy. This was a remarkable
departure for the first Grey Cup champions were amateur teams such as
the University of Toronto and Queen's University. However, the step taken
by the C.F.L. was proper. By 1958 the university teams had long since stopped
competing for the Grey Cup, and the other amateur teams were no longer
able to compete with the professionals.

In celebration of this final evolution, the first C.F.L. Grey Cup championship game, played on November 29 at Vancouver's Empire Stadium, was
spectacular. Hamilton, led by veteran quarterback Bernie Faloney, was
expected to romp over Winnipeg and retain its title. Yet Winnipeg's rookie
quarterback James Sutton Van Pelt had other ideas. Playing the game of his
life, he scored a then Grey Cup record 22 points to lead the Blue Bombers
to an upset 35 to 28 victory.

The early stages were all Hamilton. On its first offensive series Gerry
McDougall bolted around the right end for a nine-yard touchdown, and
two minutes later Ralph Goldston returned a fumble for another major.

Winnipeg responded decisively. Following Goldston's touchdown, the
Bombers moved the ball into Hamilton territory, from where Van Pelt
called the 'Lewis Special'. Van Pelt handed-off the snap to Leo 'the Lincoln
Locomotive' Lewis. The Winnipeg back headed right, then wheeled left.
Meanwhile as Van Pelt sprinted down the sideline, Hamilton's Vince Scott
dove at Lewis. But before Scott could tackle him, Lewis threw the ball to

Van Pelt. The Winnipeg quarterback shifted past a Tiger-Cat defender and scampered across the Hamilton goal line.

Van Pelt then kicked two field goals to make the score Hamilton 14, Winnipeg 13. This closeness caused much bitter play on the field. Eventually Hamilton lost its composure. Goldston made a rough tackle on Lewis and was ejected. While Goldston denied any unnecessary roughness, Lewis confirmed that Goldston had punched him. "He just slugged me. He was lying under me and just clubbed me with his fist like this." (Lewis jabbed upward with his knuckles.)

Hamilton head coach Jim Trimble refused to accept Goldston's ejection. During the half-time intermission Trimble confronted Judge of Play Paul Dojack underneath the stands.

"I saw him slugging the other player," Dojack said to Trimble.

"Did you actually see Goldston do any slugging?" Trimble prodded.

"Yes, I did," said Dojack as he turned away.

"Are you so concerned you're going to walk off," demanded Trimble. "Did you ever play football … in a big game … a Grey Cup game?"

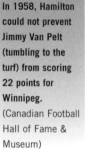

In 1958, Hamilton could not prevent Jimmy Van Pelt (tumbling to the turf) from scoring 22 points for Winnipeg.
(Canadian Football Hall of Fame & Museum)

Dojack stopped and replied, "I took that into consideration, but I saw Goldston slugging Lewis."

As though he could not really believe what Dojack had said, Trimble asked once more, "Did you see him hit that boy?"

When Dojack again said yes, Trimble hesitated, took a deep breath and walked across the field toward the Hamilton dressing room. Still unsatisfied with Dojack's ruling, Trimble lodged a protest with the C.F.L.

The Tiger-Cats should have focused its energy on the game rather than

on Goldston's ejection. Distracted, and with only eight seconds remaining in the second quarter, Hamilton committed a costly error. Instead of running out the clock Cam Fraser was instructed to punt. The snap sailed over Fraser's head, bouncing into the Hamilton end zone where Norm Rauhaus recovered it for a touchdown.

Early in the third quarter Faloney completed a touchdown pass to Ronnie Howell to put Hamilton back into the lead. But, after recovering a fumble on the Hamilton 33, Winnipeg's Charlie Shepard plunged over centre for a 1-yard major. The Tiger-Cats continued to claw into Winnipeg territory, and soon moved ahead again. From the Winnipeg 34 Faloney faked a hand-off to McDougall and faded back to pass. When Howell streaked behind the Winnipeg coverage Faloney passed the ball to him for his second major of the game. Steve Oneschuk converted the touchdown and Hamilton led 28 to 27.

Two minutes and 59 seconds later, Van Pelt sealed Winnipeg's victory by completing a 24-yard pass to Ploen, and on the next play sneaking into the end zone. Shortly thereafter, Shepard kicked a single to end the game Winnipeg 35, Hamilton 28.

**The hero of the game was Jimmy Van Pelt. The 23-year-old native of Chicago, cool as a cucumber, handled his offensive tasks like a veteran, and called a game which produced the most out of his players. "Van Pelt called a tremendous game," beamed head coach Bud Grant. "We sent in a few plays, but most of them were Jimmy's calls."**

**Every time Winnipeg's offence touched the ball it was Van Pelt who made Winnipeg look dangerous. The former University of Michigan star completed nine of 17 passes, ran the ball four times for 28 yards, and caught a pass for 20 yards. Van Pelt was also responsible for kicking field goals and converts. When the game ended he had scored two touchdowns, two field goals, and four converts. The 22 points were a single game individual scoring record which stood until 1977 when Don Sweet scored 23 points for the Montreal Alouettes.**

## 1959 WINNIPEG BLUE BOMBERS 21
## HAMILTON TIGER-CATS 7

On November 28, 1959 Winnipeg and Hamilton met for the third consecutive time. The Tiger-Cats dearly wanted revenge for 1958 but Hamilton was no match for the lighter and quicker Blue Bombers. Winnipeg wore down the heavy Hamilton defence, and scored 18 points in the fourth quarter to repeat as Grey Cup champion by a score of 21 to 7.

After falling behind 3 to 0 on a Gerry James field goal in the first quarter, the Tiger-Cats moved into the lead on three scoring plays. The first occurred in the second quarter when Winnipeg was forced to punt from deep in its own territory. Hamilton's Vince Scott burst past Winnipeg's blockers and hurled his body in front of a Charlie Shepard punt. The ball struck Scott in the chest, and bounced into the Winnipeg end zone. Scott flopped on the ball, and the Tiger-Cat fans roared touchdown. However, in the muddy west end of C.N.E. Stadium in Toronto the pigskin squirted free, and Winnipeg's Jack Delveaux pounced on it to surrender a single.

The single point did not satisfy Hamilton's President Jake Gaudaur, who demanded that Hamilton be awarded a touchdown. Gaudaur claimed, "As long as you have momentary possession of the ball behind the goal line, it's a touchdown. That's according to the rules."

Scott and Referee Paul Dojack disagreed with Gaudaur. Scott confessed that he never had possession of the ball: "I blocked the kick with my chest. Then I fell on the ball in the end zone, but both the ball and myself kept sliding, and it got away from me."

Similarly, Dojack stated, "Scott didn't have the ball at all. It went right past him."

In the third quarter Steve Oneschuk kicked two field goals to make the score Hamilton 7, Winnipeg 3. Winnipeg then scored a single before the critical moment occurred. With Hamilton in possession in its own half, Winnipeg's Roger Savoie hammered McDougall. The Hamilton ball carrier fumbled, and Buddy Tinsley made the recovery. On the next play, Winnipeg set up the game-winning major.

Just before Winnipeg quarterback Kenny Ploen took to the field, coach Bud Grant pulled him aside. Winnipeg spotter Joe Zaleski had advised Grant that the inexperienced Len Chandler had replaced the veteran Ralph Goldston in the Hamilton secondary. This was the message Grant relayed to Ploen.

As Winnipeg emerged from its huddle, Hamilton lineman John Barrow sensed that Winnipeg was going for the bomb. Barrow called back to Chandler, "Look out for the pass." Chandler nodded. At the snap Farrell

Funston sprinted downfield, and Chandler picked him up. Funston cut in a few strides, cut out a few strides, and then cut in again. Chandler was still with him. Then Funston burst toward the left goal post, Chandler on his heels, while Ploen unloaded the ball. Funston, realizing the pass would be short, turned back. Chandler turned too, but instead of being on the inside of Funston, he was on the outside of the receiver. The pair battled for the ball. Chandler fell, while Funston caught the ball on the Hamilton 2. From there, Shepard scampered into the end zone.

Over the next few minutes, Shepard kicked three singles, and Ploen threw the ball to Pitts for a 33-yard touchdown. James added the convert. Ten seconds later Winnipeg was the winner, 21 to 7.

The most valuable player of the 1959 final was Winnipeg's Charlie Shepard. The 26-year-old import from North Texas State College and the Pittsburgh Steelers was awesome. His punting and quick kicking on second down in the fourth quarter was Winnipeg's greatest offensive weapon. Against a team which employed Canada's best long-range kicker in Cam Fraser, Shepard easily surpassed him. In three of the four quarters Shepard's kicking was solely responsible for keeping Hamilton penned in its own half of the field.

Shepard also contributed significantly to Winnipeg's ground attack. He led all Winnipeg rushers with 54 yards in 16 carries.

While Shepard performed heroically on the field, fans in the stands performed heroics when they were involved in the hottest play of the game. According to *Montreal Gazette* sportswriter Vern DeGeer, a ruckus occurred during Shepard's blocked punt in the second quarter. Apparently a sportsman had bought a new trench coat for the final. Finding it warm in the stands, he decided to shed the coat and hold it in his lap. Fine, except that the coat contained a book of wooden matches. As Vince Scott reached for the ball in the end zone, the matches ignited and the coat caught fire. Dozens of fans who rallied to put out the flames were unable to douse them until the coat resembled a burnt pancake.

## 1960 OTTAWA ROUGH RIDERS 16 EDMONTON ESKIMOS 6

Hot plays continued in Grey Cup competition in 1960 when the Ottawa Rough Riders faced the Edmonton Eskimos. Edmonton was no match for the larger Rough Riders, with Ottawa winning 16 to 6. But this Grey Cup game was remembered less for the sparkling plays than the mob which swarmed the field and tried to pull down the goal posts with 41 seconds remaining in the game. Immediately Referee Seymour Wilson huddled with Ottawa's Bob Smith and Russ Jackson, and Edmonton's Rollie Miles. They agreed that Jackson would run a couple of quarterback sneaks to kill the clock. However during their conversation a teen-ager raced onto the field, scooped up the football, and blazed toward the Ottawa end zone.

The mob roared its approval, prompting Commissioner Halter to dispatch Harry McBrien onto the field. While the public address announcer pleaded in vain for the fans to leave the field, McBrien advised Referee Wilson that Halter had ordered that the game be concluded. Given the message the players rushed off the gridiron.

Ottawa's domination in this Grey Cup game was established early in the first quarter. Edmonton's Miles tried to return an Ottawa punt when he was levelled by Angelo 'King Kong' Mosca. Miles dropped to the turf like a cement-block dropped from the top of the CN Tower, and he fumbled the ball. Ottawa's Gilles Archambault recovered it, and five plays later Gary Schreider kicked a field goal.

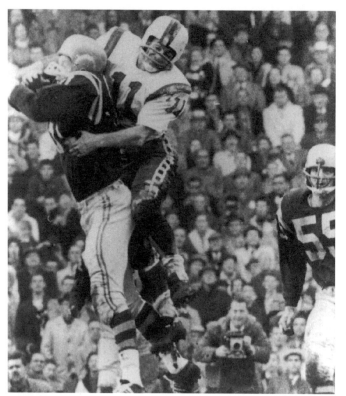

Ron Stewart (No. 11) of Ottawa makes a sparkling defensive play against Edmonton. Stewart was the 1960 game's outstanding player. (Canadian Football Hall of Fame & Museum)

Midway through the second quarter Edmonton scored its only points. With the ball on the Edmonton 47, Jim Letcavits was sent over the middle. When he broke into the clear Jackie Parker threw him the ball. The Edmonton receiver broke free of two Rider defenders, and got by Schreider for a touchdown.

It only took Ottawa five plays to regain the lead. Scrimmaging from its own 37, Ottawa moved the ball to the Edmonton 32. On the next play Jackson bootlegged, a masterful fake. While most of the Ottawa backs ran to the right, Jackson drifted left. Then Jackson heaved the ball 32 yards to Bill Sowalski for a touchdown to make the score Ottawa 9, Edmonton 6.

Sowalski described the touchdown. "I'm supposed to go down and out on the play," he said. "But I told Russ that the defensive man was turning with me every time. I thought we could make it straight down. That's the way it happened. Russ threw a strike into the end zone and the Edmonton man was miles away."

In the third quarter Ottawa tried to extend its lead when the Riders punted the ball into the Edmonton end zone, where Edmonton's Joe-Bob Smith lost control of the ball and Ottawa's Jim Reynolds fell on it. Ottawa celebrated but the officials penalized Reynolds for no yards.

The critical moment of the game came midway in the fourth quarter on a third down punt by Ottawa's Jim Conroy. Edmonton's Smith returned the ball to the Edmonton 2 where he was sandwiched by Reynolds and Lou Bruce. A fumble enabled Kaye Vaughan to pounce on the loose ball for his first touchdown in 14 years of competitive football! Afterwards Vaughan smiled, "It was a great thrill scoring. I didn't jump up and down, but I sure was happy. I was coming downfield with Bruce, concentrating on hitting Smith. Lou hit him and the ball came bouncing out at me … I saw it, grabbed it, and slid home."

Schreider converted. A few minutes later the mob ended the game at Ottawa 16, Edmonton 6.

Although Ottawa's Ron Stewart was selected as the game's most valuable player for his dazzling punt returns, many football critics believed that teammate Lou Bruce was the best player. His rushing of quarterback Jackie Parker was extremely effective in neutralizing Edmonton's offensive attack. Whenever Parker tried to roll out

Bruce, playing with his knee heavily bandaged and well-braced, prevented Parker from gaining the outside. In addition, Bruce's jarring hit on Joe-Bob Smith allowed Vaughan to score Ottawa's insurance touchdown in the fourth quarter.

## 1961 WINNIPEG BLUE BOMBERS 21
## HAMILTON TIGER-CATS 14

A year later the Hamilton Tiger-Cats and the Winnipeg Blue Bombers returned to the Grey Cup. In an exciting game, played on December 2, 1961, they battled into overtime. Winnipeg scored the only points during the two 10-minute overtime halves, thus winning the Cup, 21 to 14.

Hamilton opened with a spectacular pass-and-run. Scrimmaging from the Hamilton 20, quarterback Bernie Faloney threw an 8-yard pass to Paul Dekker. Dekker escaped a pair of Winnipeg tacklers, then sped downfield to score a record-tying 90-yard touchdown. After the game, Winnipeg defensive end Norm Rauhaus described what happened on the play. "[Baz] Nagle was playing Dekker man-to-man and I was deep. I had a hunch it [the pass] might be to him even before Faloney threw and I started over. But I moved up a little too far and didn't have a good angle on him and he broke the tackle."

A Winnipeg single made the score Hamilton 7, Winnipeg 1, and then near the end of the second quarter Hamilton threatened to score another major. A long pass to Gerry McDougall and a pass interference penalty gave Hamilton possession only a yard out. On the last play of the quarter Faloney lost control of the ball as he handed off to one of his running backs. Bombers piled on the ball, and Hamilton squandered a glorious scoring chance.

*Winnipeg's Kenny Ploen (No. 11) cuts across the 50-yard line in the 1961 Cup.*
*(Canadian Football Hall of Fame & Museum)*

In the third quarter Winnipeg closed the gap to three with a field goal before Hamilton scored its second touchdown. At the Winnipeg 37, Faloney threw a short pass to Ralph Goldston, who shook off Winnipeg's Nick Miller for the major. Then Winnipeg kicked another field goal to end the third quarter at Hamilton 14, Winnipeg 7.

The Blue Bombers took control of the 1961 Grey Cup game in the final quarter. Winnipeg pinned Hamilton deep in its own zone, and then embarked on the game's wildest drive. After gaining 13 yards, Winnipeg lost 20. On the next play, Ploen combined with Funston for 33 yards. The ball was now on the Hamilton 5, and after three plays, James blasted into the end zone. The major was converted: Hamilton 14, Winnipeg 14.

The game remained tied until the second overtime period. Quarter-backing changes by Winnipeg in the first period caused the Hamilton defence to believe that Winnipeg had abandoned the passing attack. The Tiger-Cats were surprised, then, when Ploen fired a deep pass to Ernie Pitts to put Winnipeg in scoring position. A few plays later Ploen again dropped back to pass. Unable to find a receiver, he shot around the right end, at the line of scrimmage shifting left to avoid Hamilton's Zeno Karcz and Don Caraway. George Druxman then flattened another Hamilton defender to leave Don Sutherin as the only Tiger-Cat between Ploen and the Hamilton goal line. Sutherin put his shoulder into Ploen, but the Winnipeg quarter-back bounced away from Sutherin to score. Shortly after James kicked the convert, the game ended at Winnipeg 21, Hamilton 14.

**The offensive heroes in this 80-minute battle were Winnipeg's Gerry James and Kenny Ploen. James was the game's highest scorer as he collected two field goals, two converts, and a touchdown. Meanwhile, Ploen was voted the game's most valuable player. He featured in every Winnipeg drive, and in overtime led the Bombers to the Grey Cup.**

## 1962 WINNIPEG BLUE BOMBERS 28
## HAMILTON TIGER-CATS 27

Winnipeg defended its 1961 championship against Hamilton in the 1962 Fog Bowl. Despite atrocious conditions both teams played superb football in the best Grey Cup game that people never saw. ABC's Jim McKay was ecstatic about the game: "This is the greatest football spectacle of them all.

I've not seen hitting as hard as this in any game … what a pity the fog had to spoil it."

Eventually Commissioner Halter halted the game to consult the weather office and team officials. Advised that the fog would not dissipate, Hamilton – one point down – demanded that a new game be played the next week, while Winnipeg wanted the game to continue. Halter was not satisfied with the options presented to him by the teams, and thus at 5:31 of the fourth quarter he halted the game until the following day. At a press conference Halter declared: "If play is started Sunday it will be finished regardless of the weather. But if it is impossible to start, I intend to recommend to the Canadian Football League Executive that the game remain unfinished and declared no contest." Under relatively clear skies and before a sparse crowd of 15,000 fans the game was completed on Sunday, December 2. The Blue Bombers held onto the lead it had secured prior to the postponement and won 28 to 27.

The Tiger-Cats opened the scoring midway through the first quarter when Garney Henley roared through the line. From the Hamilton 36, he weaved all the way down the field for a breathtaking 74-yard touchdown.

At the start of the second quarter, Winnipeg surged ahead. Leo Lewis bounced off Hamilton's Pete Neumann and swept into the end zone to culminate an 83-yard drive. Gerry James added the extra point to make the score Winnipeg 7, Hamilton 6.

At this point, fog began to roll over C.N.E. Stadium. Winnipeg then advanced the ball to the Hamilton 17. On the second play Lewis took a hand-off and threw a touchdown pass to Charlie Shepard.

Hamilton came back, with Joe Zuger leading the Tiger-Cats to its second touchdown as he completed two passes and ran twice to move the ball to the Winnipeg 3. From there, Bobby Kuntz crashed into the end zone. Then Hamilton recovered a fumble on the Winnipeg 18, and on the next play Henley accepted the ball from Zuger on a reverse. While Henley looped around from the left side, teammate Hal Patterson threw a bone-jarring block to open the right side of the field. Henley followed the block, and stormed across the Winnipeg goal line.

In only four more plays Winnipeg answered Henley's touchdown with the third of its own. Passes moved the ball to the Hamilton 35, and from there Winnipeg coach Bud Grant instructed quarterback Hal Ledyard to call a special flea-flicker play. Ledyard completed a short pass to Farrell Funston, who lured Hamilton's John Barrow toward him. As Barrow came to tackle Funston, Lewis charged out of the backfield and accepted a lateral from Funston. The fleet-footed back avoided Henley and raced down the field for the score.

Back came Hamilton. A 53-yard pass to Henley moved the ball to the Winnipeg 15. Seconds later Zuger combined with Dave Viti for another converted touchdown which made the score Hamilton 26, Winnipeg 21. The see-saw contest continued with Lewis returning the ensuing kick-off

64 yards, and five plays later Shepard smashing into the end zone. James booted the convert to give Winnipeg a two-point lead.

Hamilton then missed a glorious opportunity. A long march moved Hamilton from its own 37 to the Winnipeg 23. From there, Sutherin was instructed to kick a field goal. His effort was wide, and Winnipeg's Ron 'Pepe' Latourelle conceded a single point.

In the fourth quarter Sutherin missed another field goal. Then Winnipeg pushed play into the Hamilton zone. It was now getting more and more difficult to see, so when the electronic scoreboard disappeared it was decided that the game should be halted.

The following day Hamilton desperately tried to move ahead. Back-up Hamilton pivot Frank Cosentino repeatedly took the Tiger-Cats into scoring position. Each time a penalty or poor judgment ruined the chances. On the last play of the game, Zuger tried to punt the ball into the Winnipeg end zone. The ball landed short, and Winnipeg retained its title by a single point, 28 to 27.

**The outstanding player was Leo Lewis. Offensively, the 29-year-old animal husbandry graduate from Lincoln College was a terror. In every Winnipeg touchdown Lewis was the key player. Aside from scoring two of the four Winnipeg majors, he threw a touchdown pass to Shepard, and made a 16-yard reception to set up the other. His 1962 performance was his best in Grey Cup competition, and according to Winnipeg coach Bud Grant, the Blue Bombers would have lost without him.**

**Another heroic performer in this game was Garney Henley. On both offence and defence Henley played a sensational game. He was all over the field knocking down passes and making tackles, and was Hamilton's only offensive threat. Whenever Hamilton scored Henley was involved. Henley gained 99 yards rushing, 118 yards passing, and scored two touchdowns.**

## 1963 HAMILTON TIGER-CATS 21
## B.C. LIONS 10

Henley and the Tiger-Cats returned to the Grey Cup on November 30, 1963. This time Hamilton's opponent was the British Columbia Lions. B.C. wanted to make its first championship appearance memorable, but a controversial 'late' tackle on B.C.'s best player ended the Lions' chances of winning. The tackle was so devastating that after the game it was analyzed in more detail

**B.C.'s Willie 'The Wisp' Fleming (No. 15) was injured in the 1963 final when Hamilton's Mosca (No. 68) applied a controversial tackle.** (Canadian Football Hall of Fame & Museum)

than the John F. Kennedy assassination. While most fans and reporters accused Hamilton's Angelo Mosca of deliberately attempting to injure B.C.'s Willie 'The Wisp' Fleming, Fleming said, "I don't remember much of the play. I know I didn't see Mosca coming." Meanwhile Mosca explained, "Willie was running along the sideline and [Gene Ceppetelli] tackled him. He was still moving and the whistle hadn't blown. I was afraid he would slip [Gene's] tackle and get away – that's Willie's style – so I hit him. I drove my helmet against his chest and head. That's all there was to it."

C.F.L. Commissioner Halter also gave his view of the tackle. He said, "It looked to me as if the officials had it covered. It looked like a borderline case. I am practically certain that it was in the field of play and it appeared that Mosca had committed himself before Fleming was stopped." Still photographs and the game film revealed that the hit was clean, but it left Fleming with a concussion. He was forced to leave the game, and he took with him the Lions' chances for Grey Cup glory.

After a scoreless first quarter in which Hamilton was unable to convert a third down from the B.C. 3, Hamilton coach Ralph Sazio huddled with his offence. Distressed with his club's performance, he told his players, "Look, those guys on defence are playing their hearts out. They keep getting you the ball, and what are you doing? Not a thing. It's about time you settled down."

The short, fiery speech ignited the Tiger-Cats. Scrimmaging from the Hamilton 22-yard line in the first few minutes of the second quarter, Faloney used a mixture of runs and passes to drive Hamilton 88 yards in 10 plays.

The drive culminated in Faloney rolling out and throwing a short touch-down pass to Willie Bethea.

On the ensuing series Mosca made the bone-crunching tackle on Fleming, and B.C.'s Peter Kempf kicked a field goal. A Henley catch for a 41-yard gain then gave Hamilton possession on the B.C. 15, and two plays later Art Baker blasted into the B.C. end zone. Sazio labelled Baker's touchdown: "After that [score] I was sure we were home free."

The play that clinched Hamilton's victory occurred on the opening series of the third quarter. The Tiger-Cats called a pass play in which Hal Patterson was the primary receiver. On the snap of the ball, Patterson shot downfield. He looked at defender Neal Beaumont, and then glanced at defender Shafer. Meanwhile Hamilton's Dave Viti ran a hook pattern in front of Beaumont to hold the B.C. player short. At this point, Hamilton's Tommy Grant cut across the field. As Viti and Grant continued their pat-terns, Patterson slipped behind Shafer. Faloney, with plenty of pass protec-tion, threw the ball when Patterson broke into the clear. Patterson made the catch behind B.C.'s defence and sprinted down the field untouched. It was Patterson's fifth career touchdown in Grey Cup competition, breaking the previous record held by Hamilton trainer Jimmy Simpson. While Simpson congratulated Patterson, Don Sutherin converted the touchdown to make the score Hamilton 21, B.C. 3.

In the fourth quarter Hamilton wasted a lot of time before B.C. scored the game's final points. Two spectacular catches by Greg Findlay helped move the Lions to the Hamilton 5, from where Joe Kapp fired a deep end zone pass to Mack Burton. At the deadline, Burton leaped to make the touchdown reception. Sutherin disputed the score: " ... oh, how I hated to give up that touchdown ... It doesn't matter I guess but I hated to give them one ... Burton caught the ball in bounds ... but when he came down ... his heel was over the line. It should not have counted." Kempf added the extra point, and a minute later the game ended Hamilton 21, B.C. 10.

**The best player was Hamilton's Bernie Faloney. The veteran quarterback played an outstanding game, and his running and passing frequently electrified the crowd. Faloney's signal calling was deliberate. He picked apart B.C.'s defence piece by piece, and frequently exploited its deep secondary. Faloney completed 13 of 20 passes for a total of 261 yards, and two touchdowns. He also gained 54 yards on nine rushes.**

**After the game, B.C.'s assistant coach Jim Champion was left nearly speechless by Faloney's performance. "Faloney beat us," Champion admitted. "They played well. There's no denying it. We contained their running attack fairly well. But the passing ..." Champion looked at his feet and his voice trailed off.**

# 1964 
### B.C. LIONS 34
### HAMILTON TIGER-CATS 24

The Lions avenged its 1963 loss to the Tiger-Cats on November 28, 1964. With vivid memories of Mosca's hit on Fleming, the Lions played a spirited and emotional game. The brilliant Bill Munsey and Joe Kapp led the Lions to a 34 to 24 victory.

Midway through the first quarter B.C. jumped into the lead. Two plays after Fleming had caught a 33-yard pass, Bob Swift climbed a mountain of bodies for a major.

Punishing blocking along the scrimmage line in the 1964 Cup between B.C. (light jerseys) and Hamilton. (Canadian Football Hall of Fame & Museum)

At the start of the second quarter B.C. widened its 7 to 0 lead on a play which was labelled the vital moment of the game. Kapp guided the Lions to the Hamilton 8-yard line, and from there B.C. coach Dave Skrien instructed Peter Kempf to kick a field goal. However the holder, Pete Ohler, was unable to control a high snap from centre Jesse Williams. On the line of scrimmage B.C.'s Jim Carphin looked for a signal from the referee. When he did not see one, he realized something was wrong in the backfield and ran into the Hamilton end zone. Ohler scrambled to recover the ball, then threw to Carphin for an unexpected touchdown. Many people believed that the play had been planned, and Carphin later explained, "That wasn't exactly a broken play touchdown. Peter and I have an understanding that he'll throw to me in the event of a bad snap. My normal job is to block, then release to cover in case of a wide placement."

The touchdown gave B.C. a 13-point lead, and forced the Tiger-Cats to take more risks. Hamilton's risky play ultimately led to defeat.

The Tiger-Cats were able to reduce B.C.'s lead by only one point before, five plays later, the Lions scored its third touchdown. From the Hamilton 46 Kapp called a '44 Flag Trap.' Kapp handed the ball to Fleming, who moved toward the left guard position. As Hamilton defenders closed in Fleming changed direction and accelerated, cutting in and out of the heavy traffic at the line of scrimmage. An excellent block downfield from teammate Sonny Homer gave Fleming more room, and he scored.

Five plays into the third quarter the Tiger-Cats rallied to get back into the game. Three battering ground plays had gained 18 yards, and then Faloney called an extension run. B.C. thought that Faloney had called an option pass, so defenders Paul Seale and Norm Fieldgate moved toward the line of scrimmage to ensure that Faloney would not cross it. Faloney had no intention of running or passing, and as Seale and Fieldgate moved closer to him, the Hamilton pivot lateralled to Johnny Counts. B.C. defenders were taken by surprise, and Counts charged down the sideline for a touchdown. Don Sutherin converted the score leaving Hamilton behind by a score of 20 to 8.

Hamilton continued to gain confidence, but with eight minutes gone in the third quarter Kapp produced another touchdown to seal the Lions' victory. B.C. advanced the ball to the Hamilton 18 and from there Munsey stormed through the left side of the line. Munsey broke the tackle of Hamilton's John Barrow, and then carried Dick Cohee into the end zone. As Lions' tackle Gus Kasapis later expressed it, "I think we broke [Hamilton's] spirit then. They thought they could run against us but when we came right back it killed them."

**A B.C. Lion dives over the line in the 1964 game.**
(Hamilton Public Library Archives)

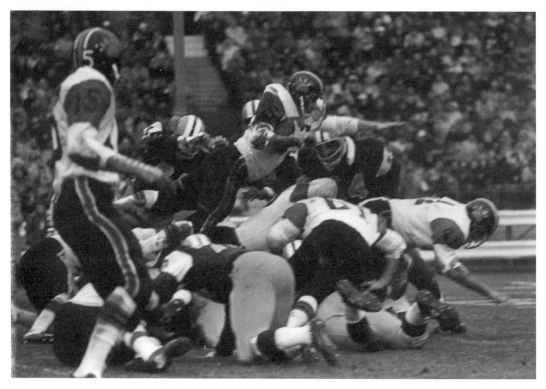

On the last play of the third quarter a disastrous lateral drove another nail into the Hamilton coffin. Faloney pitched low to Counts. The Hamilton back was unable to grab the ball, allowing B.C.'s Dick Fouts to kick it to Munsey. Munsey scooped up the ball, and raced 65 yards for another touchdown. After the game, Sazio stated, "I felt the play that really broke our backs in Saturday's Grey Cup game was the final play of the third quarter. At the time we were on B.C.'s 35-yard line and driving for a touchdown and, in spite of the fact we trailed 27-8, we were still very much in the game. Then Bernie Faloney tried a long lateral to Johnny Counts and it was fumbled. If there was a turning point in the game that was it."

In the Hamilton dressing room Counts described the play. "It was down here," said the disconsolate Tiger-Cat rookie, brushing his hands across his shins. "I managed to grab the ball after I dropped it, but somebody jumped on my back and the ball squirted loose."

Meanwhile Munsey explained: "Dick Fouts kicked the ball ahead and I was able to get it before Counts could recover. [Fouts] made a great play on it."

In the fourth quarter the Tiger-Cats made the score respectable. Faloney threw a 12-yard touchdown pass to Tommy Grant, and then a single and safety took the score to B.C. 34, Hamilton 17. With less than five minutes remaining Faloney again drove the Tiger-Cats to paydirt. From the B.C. 8 he finished a 7-play, 43-yard drive with a touchdown pass to Stan Crisson. Sutherin converted the touchdown to make the final score B.C. 34, Hamilton 24.

**The outstanding player of the 1964 Grey Cup game was B.C.'s Bill Munsey. The 23-year-old native of Uniontown, Pennsylvania and graduate of the University of Minnesota gave a tremendous two-way performance. Substituting for the injured Bob Swift on offence Munsey, who had been used exclusively as a defensive back all season, played like a first-string running back. He carried the ball seven times for 54 yards, and scored a touchdown. On defence Munsey excelled in making bone-crunching tackles. In addition Munsey scored a second touchdown on a fumble recovery.**

**Munsey received much praise for his performance from his teammates. Tom Brown yelled, "Munsey, Fantastic!" Pete Ohler shouted, "Munsey's the hero." Paul Seale added, "People just don't realize how great this man is."**

**Hamilton's best player was Bernie Faloney. In his seventh and last Cup the legendary Faloney kept Hamilton's spirit alive even when the Tiger-Cats fell behind by 26 points. Faloney completed 18 of 33 passes for 239 yards and two touchdowns, and he ran 11 times for 57 yards. Faloney's 1964 performance helped him set all-time Cup records for most touchdown passes thrown (8), most passes completed (92), most passes thrown (169), and most yards passing (1,369).**

## 1965 HAMILTON TIGER-CATS 22 WINNIPEG BLUE BOMBERS 16

B.C.'s thrilling 1964 Grey Cup victory was followed by the wild and wacky 1965 Wind Bowl between the Tiger-Cats and the Winnipeg Blue Bombers. A violent westerly wind off Lake Ontario and over C.N.E. Stadium on

November 27 led to special ground rules being adopted for the game. C.F.L. officials, referees, and team representatives agreed that greater emphasis would be given to C.F.L. Rule 10, Section 6, Article 5. This allowed referees the discretion to ignore the 'no yards' regulation on short kicks where players had no opportunity to allow the punt returner the mandatory five yards, and it was agreed that when a team punted into the wind the ball would automatically be whistled dead when coming into contact with the punt returner. In addition, the windy conditions caused 50 of the 60 minutes to be played in the east end of the field, and led the Bombers to surrender three safety touches. Those safety touches were critical as Hamilton defeated Winnipeg 22 to 16.

After taking a 1 to 0 lead on the opening kick-off, the Tiger-Cats extended its lead on the strength of the play of Dick Cohee. Cohee shook a tackler for a 32-yard gain, and two plays later broke two more tackles to score a touchdown.

Winnipeg then conceded the first of the safeties before reducing Hamilton's lead in the second quarter. Interference and roughing-the-passer penalties gave Winnipeg possession on the Hamilton 6, and from there Art Perkins spun past Hamilton's Herb Paterra for a major.

The special ground rules then enabled the Bombers to move ahead. Hamilton's Joe Zuger was forced to punt from inside his own end zone, and he launched the ball high and short into the wind. As Winnipeg's Dick Wozney circled under the ball near the Hamilton 22, Zuger charged down the field in an attempt to recover the kick. They collided and the ball dropped to the turf where Hamilton recovered. However, under the pregame agreement the ball was awarded to the Bombers. Two plays later, Leo

Hamilton's John Barrow (No. 61) sets his sights on Winnipeg's Leo Lewis (No. 29) in the 1965 Cup. (Canadian Football Hall of Fame & Museum)

Lewis barged through the line for a 5-yard touchdown.

The Tiger-Cats broke the game open in the third quarter. With the ball on the Hamilton 41, Zuger led his squad to the line. Winnipeg deployed its 62 Regular defensive set in which the front foursome allowed a gap in the middle for linebackers Al Miller and Paul Robson to fill, and halfback Ed Ulmer moved in tight on the outside left. This configuration was effective on inside running plays, but this time Zuger called for a pass. As Willie Bethea charged out of the backfield Winnipeg's Phil Minnick moved up to cover him. Minnick expected Bethea to run a short full-back pattern, and so when Bethea continued straight down the field Minnick fell behind. Zuger completed a pass to an unattended Bethea. At the Winnipeg 5 Henry Janzen was unable to stop Bethea.

Next, the wind caused the game's strangest play. Punting the ball high into the air, Ulmer watched in amazement as the ball was blown back toward him. Ulmer hesitated, allowing Hamilton's John Barrow to grab it. Promptly, Barrow turned and galloped into the Winnipeg end zone. The Hamilton fans hollered touchdown, but the referees ruled that the ball was dead by contact.

A few minutes later Winnipeg conceded two more safeties to make the score Hamilton 21, Winnipeg 13. Many arm-chair quarterbacks questioned the strategy, but Winnipeg coach Bud Grant explained: "We really didn't have any choice. We thought it was better to give up six points than a possible 21. Under the same circumstances, we'd have done the same thing all over again."

The Tiger-Cats scored once more before the end of the quarter on an incredible play by Zuger. While standing in punt formation, he watched the snap sail over his head, then scrambled to collect the ball at his own 35, as a squadron of Bomber tacklers descended upon him. Miraculously evading the tacklers, Zuger slammed the ball into the Winnipeg end zone, where Winnipeg's Cooper was rouged. The single according to Winnipeg's Herb Gray was the most important point of the game. Gray said, "That was the big play of the game for me. If we had trapped him, I think we might have pulled it out."

In the fourth quarter, Winnipeg was only able to score a field goal. Hamilton's defence was superb, and late in the game the Tiger-Cats halted a Winnipeg third down gamble on the Hamilton 31 to ensure its 22 to 16 victory.

**The dominant player in this Grey Cup game was Hamilton's John Barrow. On many occasions Barrow burst into the Winnipeg backfield to tackle Winnipeg's quarterback or running back for a loss. No one could stop the marauding 29-year-old lineman, and after the game Bud Grant said, "I thought Barrow played an outstanding game. But does he ever play any other way?" Barrow collected 42 of 52 M.V.P. votes cast by the media, and thereby was named the game's most valuable player.**

Canadian football fans were given a break from seeing the Hamilton Tiger-Cats in the 1966 Grey Cup. Guided by Russ Jackson, the Schenley award winner as the most outstanding player, the Ottawa Rough Riders eliminated the Tiger-Cats from playoff contention. Meanwhile in the West the Saskatchewan Roughriders qualified for the Grey Cup game to set up an Ottawa versus Saskatchewan final. Ottawa was expected to win, but on November 26 Ron Lancaster and George Reed played an incredible game to lift Saskatchewan to its first Grey Cup title, 29 to 14.

Ottawa seemed headed to victory from the opening kick-off. Jackson fired a deep pass to Whitman Tucker and the Ottawa receiver caught the ball behind coverage. Saskatchewan's Dale West and Larry Dumelie gave chase, but were unable to halt Tucker, who scored a 61-yard touchdown.

A few minutes later, Saskatchewan capitalized on a controversial interception which West returned to the Ottawa 9. Jackson had passed to Ted Watkins, but the receiver was knocked down by Dumelie and West was able to intercept. There was no penalty on the play, although Dumelie indicated that he had expected to be fingered for pass interference. "It was strictly an accident. We were both going for the ball," Dumelie said. "But I fully expected I would be called after my feet got tangled with Watkins'."

Two plays later Lancaster executed a beautiful play which fooled Ottawa's defence. In the huddle Jim Worden convinced Lancaster that he could get clear deep in the Ottawa end zone. Thus Lancaster faked a hand-off to Reed, and threw to Worden. The Ottawa defence bought the fake and Worden was all alone to catch the touchdown pass. Saskatchewan players celebrated the score and Worden said to Lancaster, "See, ... I told you I could beat him deep."

Ottawa (dark jerseys) tries to get away from its posts in the 1966 championship. Saskatchewan won 29 to 11. (Canadian Football Hall of Fame & Museum)

After another Ottawa turnover Saskatchewan scored its second touchdown. A long pass to Ed Buchanan moved the ball to the Ottawa 19, and in another two plays Alan Ford was sent into the Ottawa end zone on a flag pattern. Defender Bob O'Billovich stood between Lancaster and Ford, and appeared to be in a good position to intercept Lancaster's pass. However, the hard and low pass slipped through O'Billovich's hands and Ford, while falling, made the touchdown catch.

Following the game Lancaster conceded that Ford's touchdown may have been lucky. Ninety-nine out of 100 times, Lancaster suggested, O'Billovich would have had the ball. He added, "I didn't even see O'Billovich when I threw the ball. It's one of those things which happens about once in a season. You're glad when it goes your way."

Meanwhile O'Billovich moaned, "I should have had it. It just swished through my hands. What hurts is that it sailed right to their intended receiver. I've seen the same play dozens of times and the ball would shoot off the ground."

Ottawa responded to this score immediately. On the first play following the ensuing kick-off Tucker streaked behind West. Jackson eluded a tackler in the backfield, rolled-out, and threw long. Tucker grabbed the pass on the Saskatchewan 40, and romped to the Saskatchewan end zone. Moe Racine added the extra point to bring the score to Saskatchewan 14, Ottawa 13.

Ottawa tied the score, but in the third quarter the turning point of the game occurred. On second down from the Saskatchewan 33 Lancaster threw a short pass to Worden. While Ottawa corner Mike Blum intercepted the pass, Worden was sent sprawling to the ground. The officials ruled that Gene Gaines had interfered with Worden, and accordingly Saskatchewan retained possession.

Ottawa coach Frank Clair was incensed. He violently protested the decision, and Worden's comments after the game indicated that Clair's protest was valid. In the crowded Saskatchewan dressing room Worden said, "Don't print this, but I took a dive on the play and it worked. I could see he had a chance for the interception but I guess I made it look like interference."

Meanwhile Clair emphasized that the decision cost Ottawa the game. "If it hadn't been for that call we would have had the ball with first down on their 40. Instead, they kept it and dominated the third quarter."

On the first play of the fourth quarter Saskatchewan scored the eventual game-winning touchdown. From the Ottawa 5 Lancaster threw a very risky pass to Hugh Campbell, who was surrounded by O'Billovich, Joe Poirier and Gaines. The ball came in low, and Poirier and Campbell went for it simultaneously. Poirier came up with the ball, but the referees had already signalled touchdown. It was a good call, Poirier later admitted. "I got a hand on the ball, but I was a little too late."

Saskatchewan sealed its victory when Reed scampered 31 yards to produce the game's sixth touchdown. The run was brilliantly executed from start to finish. Lancaster had noticed that Ottawa linebacker Ken Lehmann was drifting outside his normal position and leaving a gap down the centre of the field. Lancaster decided to exploit this gap by giving the ball to Reed, with Jack Abendschan, Al Benecick and Ted Urness providing perfect blocking to spring Reed free.

Later in the quarter Alan Ford kicked a single to close the game's scoring: Saskatchewan 29, Ottawa 14.

**Ron Lancaster and George Reed were the best players in Saskatchewan's first Grey Cup victory. Lancaster, the ex-Ottawa Rough Rider, performed fantastically. He**

was in complete control, dispersing Ottawa's defence early with his passing attack, and then shifting to a grinding ground assault in the second half when Ottawa's front line began to tire.

Ottawa defender Jim Conroy was awed by Lancaster's tactical brilliance. "Man did Ronnie ever call a great game," Conroy said. "He went at us around the ends, and, when we closed that off, he moved to the middle. Then he went back to the ends. He was terrific."

Meanwhile Reed was a huge factor in Saskatchewan's second half success. Whenever Saskatchewan needed a first down to retain possession Reed was called upon to get the necessary yardage. Despite an ache in his right ankle and a kink in his shoulder, Reed was the game's leading rusher. He gained 133 yards in 23 carries, and scored a touchdown.

## 1967 HAMILTON TIGER-CATS 24 / SASKATCHEWAN ROUGHRIDERS 1

The Tiger-Cats returned to the Grey Cup game on December 2, 1967. It was Canada's 100th birthday, and Ottawa was expected to again represent the East in the national final. However, Hamilton's defence was magnificent in the eastern playoffs. Ottawa's offence scored only three points against Hamilton in the two-game eastern final, and lost the series 37 to 3.

Hamilton's opponent was the Saskatchewan Roughriders. Saskatchewan was still led by Ron Lancaster and George Reed, but they could not duplicate their 1966 heroics. The Tiger-Cats, who entered the Grey Cup game having not allowed an opposing offensive touchdown in its last five games, shut down Lancaster and Reed, and preserved its incredible streak, 24 to 1.

A trio of Hamilton Tiger-Cats halt Saskatchewan's George Reed (No. 34) in the 1967 final. (Canadian Football Hall of Fame & Museum)

**The 1992 Calgary Stampeders hoist the Grey Cup.** (Photo by John E. Sokolowski)

**The outstanding offensive player in the 1985 Cup was B.C.'s quarterback Roy Dewalt.** (CFL Photos)

**Another perfect spiral is thrown by Saskatchewan's Ron Lancaster (No. 23) in the 1972 Cup against the Hamilton Tiger-Cats.**
(Canadian Football Hall of Fame & Museum)

1981: Neil Lumsden (No. 32) throws a block for Edmonton teammate Warren Moon. (CFL Photos)

Hamilton's Dieter Brock stumbles into the end zone in the 1984 Cup. (CFL Photos)

**Glen Suitor (No. 27) and Dave Ridgway (No. 36) celebrate Saskatchewan's 1989 Grey Cup triumph.** (Photo by John E. Sokolowski)

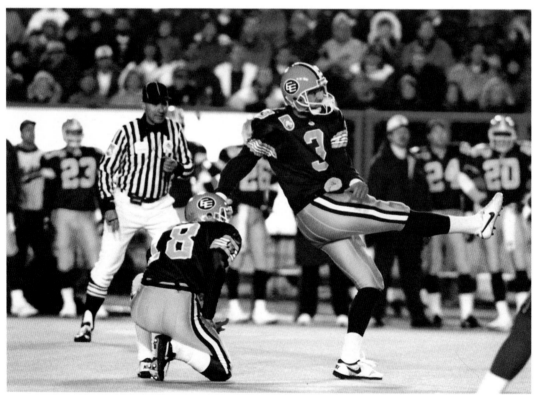

**Edmonton's Sean Fleming (No. 3) kicked six field goals in the 1993 Cup.** (Photo by John E. Sokolowski)

**Hamilton's Garney Henley (No. 26) watches a Saskatchewan Roughrider close in for a tackle in the 1967 final.** (Canadian Football Hall of Fame & Museum)

**Argonaut stars Doug Flutie (left) and Mike 'Pinball' Clemons dash through the snow in the 1996 'Snowdown in Steeltown.'** (Photo by John E. Sokolowski)

Calgary's David 'Sponge' Sapunjis (No. 25) is hit by Winnipeg's Andrew Thomas in 1992. (Photo by John E. Sokolowski)

There goes Toronto's Raghib 'Rocket' Ismail (No. 25) on another kick return. In 1991 the 'Rocket' returned four kick-offs for 183 yards. (Photo by John E. Sokolowski)

**A group of Winnipeg Blue Bombers prepare to tackle Edmonton's Henry Williams (No. 2) in the 1990 Cup.** (Photo by Art Martin)

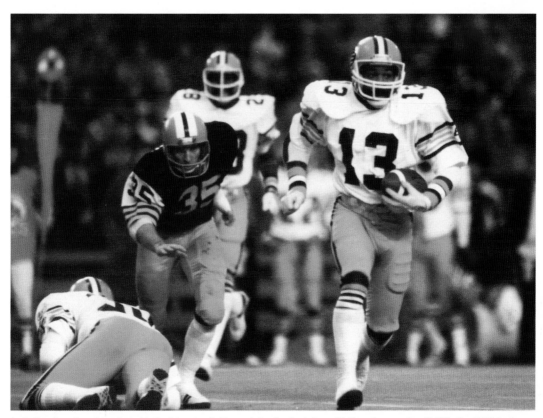

**A six-time Grey Cup champion with the Edmonton Eskimos, defensive back Larry Highbaugh races downfield in the 1980 final.**
(CFL Photos)

The B.C. Lions swarm teammate Lui Passaglia during 1994 victory celebrations. (Photo by John E. Sokolowski)

In 1984, Willard Reaves (No. 33) scored two Grey Cup majors for Winnipeg as the Blue Bombers blasted the Tiger-Cats. (CFL Photos)

The M.V.P. in the 1967 Cup, Hamilton's Joe Zuger, drops back to pass. (Canadian Football Hall of Fame & Museum)

The Tiger-Cats opened the scoring on a nine-play, 85-yard touchdown drive. The key play was an incomplete pass to Hamilton's Fleming which resulted in a pass interference penalty to Saskatchewan's Bob Kosid. The penalty upset Fleming because it robbed him of a sure touchdown, but on the next play Joe Zuger exploited a large opening in the centre of the field to score a touchdown.

It appeared that Saskatchewan would tie the score following the ensuing kick-off as its offence looked sharp. However, Ed Buchanan dropped a sure touchdown pass. More than 20 years after the game, Saskatchewan's Wayne Shaw and Ted Urness agreed that this error was vital. They said that some Saskatchewan players were demoralized by the lost opportunity to have scored a touchdown.

Saskatchewan made the score 7 to 1, but midway through the second quarter Hamilton widened its lead. Scrimmaging from the Hamilton 33, Zuger dropped back to pass. Saskatchewan blitzed, and this left Hamilton receiver Ted Watkins in a one-on-one situation with defender Larry Dumelie. As Watkins breezed past Dumelie, Zuger fired Watkins the ball. Saskatchewan's Bruce Bennett and Ted Duchinski gave chase, yet they could not prevent the 72-yard touchdown.

Hamilton then added four singles before scoring the game's last points. Midway through the fourth quarter, with Saskatchewan in possession on its own 51, Lancaster called an audible. On the snap of the ball, Buchanan moved toward the line, and Lancaster suddenly pitched the ball to him. Buchanan, who had missed the audible, was surprised by the toss. He was unable to catch the ball, and this allowed Hamilton's Billy Ray Locklin to recover and sprint downfield for the touchdown which made the final score Hamilton 24, Saskatchewan 1.

Joe Zuger was the star of the game. A quarterback subjected to much criticism during the regular season, he showed the critics that he could produce in the big game. Zuger executed coach Ralph Sazio's game plan perfectly. Throughout the game, Zuger kept Hamilton's offence moving, and never allowed Saskatchewan to obtain excellent field position. The ball was thrown with authority: he completed eight of 20 passes for a total of 164 yards.

In addition to his quarterback duties, Zuger handled Hamilton's punting, averaging 44.7 yards per kick. This was seven yards per kick more than that of Saskatchewan's Alan Ford. Finally, Zuger figured in most of Hamilton's scoring. He

**scored one touchdown, threw for another and kicked three singles. This was accomplished despite Zuger playing with a broken nose, and having blood streaming down his face after his first-quarter touchdown.**

The play of Joe Zuger, John Barrow, Bernie Faloney, Garney Henley and other Tiger-Cats dominated Canadian football from 1957 through 1967. The other eastern division teams were relatively powerless to dethrone the Tiger-Cats as eastern division champion during most of this period, while Hamilton's Grey Cup opponents also had difficulty handling them. Hamilton's defence during this period was the best ever assembled in Canadian football, and its play resulted in the wall of the Canadian Football Hall of Fame being graced with many of the Tiger-Cats who played for these great Hamilton teams. Barrow, Faloney, Zuger, and Henley, along with Angelo Mosca, Tommy Joe Coffey, Cookie Gilchrist, Don Sutherin, Hal Patterson, Vince Scott and Tommy Grant all contributed to Hamilton's nine Grey Cup appearances in this era and were deservedly inducted into the Hall. While the Tiger-Cats enjoyed some Grey Cup success in the 1970s and 1980s, the Hamilton franchise has never been as dominant as it was in this exciting time.

## Chapter Ten

# END OF THE ROAD
## 1968-1977

**M**any great players and great teams have competed for the Grey Cup, and their exploits are etched deep in the memories of Canadian football fans. From 1968 to 1977 some of the finest Cup memories were produced as legendary players sought to guide their teams to glory. Sadly for many of these legends the games in which they competed during this period marked their last Cup appearances as players. For the Ottawa Rough Riders, Canadian-born quarterback Russ Jackson made his farewell in outstanding fashion. Chosen as the C.F.L.'s most outstanding player in 1969, Jackson guided his gridiron gladiators to Cup victory. For the Saskatchewan Roughriders, Ron Lancaster competed in his last Cup in 1976. Lancaster had been chosen the league's outstanding player that year, but he was unable to duplicate Jackson's 1969 feat. Saskatchewan suffered a heart-breaking Cup loss to Ottawa, 23 to 20. Other heroes who ended their playing careers included Angelo Mosca, Tommy Joe Coffey, Garney Henley, Jackie Parker, and George Reed.

## 1968 OTTAWA ROUGH RIDERS 24
## CALGARY STAMPEDERS 21

The first Grey Cup game in this era, played November 30, 1968, established a level of play which was later seen in the 1976 and 1977 games. For the first time in 19 years the Calgary Stampeders qualified for the final as it swept the Saskatchewan Roughriders two games to none to capture the western division crown. However, the Calgary victories were costly as its best running back Dave Cranmer was injured. This allowed Calgary's opponent, the Ottawa Rough Riders, to concentrate on stopping Calgary's passing attack. Ottawa's defence played well and its offence, led by Hamilton native Russ Jackson and Vic Washington, guided the Rough Riders to a 24 to 21 victory.

Ottawa threatened to storm into a huge lead in the first quarter but three times Don Sutherin missed field goals. Then Ottawa's Wayne Giardino blocked a Calgary punt. The ball bounced into the Calgary end zone where Ted Woods smothered the ball to surrender a single.

After Sutherin had kicked a field goal to give Ottawa a 4 to 0 lead in the second quarter, Peter Liske put the Stampeders ahead. Calgary moved the ball to the Ottawa 1, and two plays later Liske dove across the Ottawa goal line.

A few minutes later, Calgary scored again. The Stampeders advanced the ball to the Ottawa 21, and from there Liske called a break-out and up pattern. Calgary's Terry 'the Flea' Evanshen streaked behind Ottawa's Billy Van Burkleo and caught Liske's pass for a touchdown.

In the third quarter, came 'the' moment. With the ball on the Ottawa 48 Calgary set up in punt formation. However, Calgary's Ron Stewart was unable to get his punt away as Gene Gaines and Ken Lehmann broke across the line of scrimmage. Stewart tried to escape but Ottawa's Jim Cain tackled him on the Calgary 52.

After the game Stewart was still in shock over the play. "I'd like to know what happened myself," he said. "I saw Lehmann busting in on me and thought he might block it, so I turned away from him. I hoped I did the right thing. Then somebody else got me. That Lehmann got in there so quickly he must have lined up offside."

The play inspired Ottawa and, nine plays later, Russ Jackson went over from 1 yard out. Sutherin converted the major to make the score Calgary 14, Ottawa 11.

On the second play of the fourth quarter the Rough Riders took the lead on a still-standing Grey Cup record run. Scrimmaging on the Ottawa 30, the Riders came to the line in a triple flanker left set. Jay Roberts, Ottawa's tight end, lined up on the left, Bo Scott was the middle flanker, Whitman Tucker the wide flanker and Vic Washington the lone running back. On the snap Washington sprinted left, and Jackson flipped him the ball. Ottawa players executed their blocks downfield, and suddenly Washington dropped the ball. Calgary's defence froze while, magically, the ball bounced back to Washington. Ottawa's Tom Benyon then erased a Calgary defender to spring Washington free. The fleet-footed Ottawa back sprinted down the sideline and out-raced Calgary's Jerry Keeling for an 80-yard score.

After the game, Washington described the play, "I took the pitch-out. I was looking to get behind my blockers when the ball bobbled right through my hands. The ball hit the ground ... but bounced back in my arms. I got a block from [Tom Benyon] and ... the Calgary players froze on the play. It gave me an opening and I was gone."

Washington concluded, "All I could think, as I ran, was I hope I don't get a cramp!"

Ottawa then capitalized on a blocked Calgary field goal. The Rough Riders used three plays to move the ball to the Ottawa 40, and then Jackson called an 'Adkins Across'. In the huddle Jackson reminded Margene Adkins to go deep and not to slow down. When the ball was snapped, Roberts and Ottawa's Ron Stewart moved across the scrimmage line to gain attention. As Calgary shifted to pick up all the Ottawa receivers, Adkins crossed the field from right to left. Calgary's Keeling was caught out of position, and when Jackson threw, the receiver had a clear path to the end zone.

In the last few minutes of the game an exchange of turnovers gave Calgary the ball on the Ottawa 17. A few plays later Liske threw a short touchdown pass to Evanshen. The score was converted. With 1:32 remaining and Ottawa three points in the lead, Calgary's Art Froese was instructed to try an onside kick. As he moved toward the ball he collided with referee Paul Dojack, who was clearly out of position. The collision upset the timing of the play, and thus Tom Schuette was able to secure the short kick-off without being pressured by Calgary players. Ottawa then ran out the clock to capture the 1968 Grey Cup, 24 to 21.

**The player of the game in this exciting final was Ottawa's Vic Washington. Every time he touched the ball the 22-year-old rookie speedster from Wyoming University electrified the crowd. In the fourth quarter he made a brilliant run which sealed Ottawa's victory. Washington concluded the game with 128 yards on 13 carries, and 25 yards on three pass receptions. He also scored a major. When asked to assess Washington's contribution, Ottawa coach Frank Clair was almost speechless. Clair simply said, "Washington played a great game."**

On November 30, 1969 it was Russ Jackson who played a great game. The Ottawa Rough Riders had qualified for its second consecutive Grey Cup game, and this time faced the western champion Saskatchewan Roughriders for the national title. This was Jackson's final game as a player, and he took charge to ensure that it was his most memorable. Jackson played brilliantly in guiding Ottawa to a 29 to 11 victory.

Saskatchewan jumped into the lead midway through the first quarter when Ottawa's Billy Van Burkleo had difficulty on a third down punt. Van Burkleo's feet slipped out from under him, and he crashed to the gridiron. With no chance to get up and kick, Van Burkleo tried to toss the ball to teammate Jim Mankins. However, Saskatchewan's Ken Reed knocked the ball from Van Burkleo's grasp and recovered it on the Ottawa 31. In another two plays Ron Lancaster fired the ball to Alan Ford for a 28-yard touchdown.

A 2-point safety made the score 9 to 0 before Ottawa got on the board. Jackson guided his club to the Saskatchewan 11-yard line early in the second quarter, and from there spotted the seldom-used Jay Roberts streaking for the Saskatchewan goal line on a look-in pattern. Saskatchewan's Wally Dempsey was draped all over Roberts, but Jackson fired the ball anyway. Roberts made a spectacular catch on the Saskatchewan 4 and then bulled across the goal line with several Green Rider defenders on his back.

Next Ottawa capitalized on a Saskatchewan turnover deep in Ottawa's half. On second down and 10, Jackson came to the line recognizing that Saskatchewan was going to blitz. He hollered, "Stew! It's a blitz! Get open!" On the snap Ron Stewart faked a pass block to the outside, held for a three count, and then manoeuvred into the right flat. Meanwhile Saskatchewan's Wayne Shaw penetrated the Ottawa offensive line and headed toward Jackson.

**Gene Gaines (No. 22) of the Ottawa Rough Riders returns the ball against Saskatchewan in the 1969 final.**
(CFL Photos)

Jackson pumped once to Mankins on the outside, then looped a short screen pass to Stewart. Shaw grazed the ball but was unable to change its direction. On making the reception Stewart followed excellent blocking provided by guards Tom Schuette and Roger Perdrix and tackle Dave Braggins en route to an 80-yard touchdown. The score was the deciding moment of the game. Afterward Saskatchewan's George Reed disgustedly said, "I fumbled and instead of getting a big jump on them, they came back and Jackson throws that screen to Stewart and he goes all the way to score. I think it gave them the lift they needed."

Saskatchewan's chance of winning was further crushed in the third quarter when Reed collected a pass and thundered toward the Ottawa end zone. A score was likely until at the Ottawa 7 Joe Poirier knocked Reed off-balance and Barry Ardern drove him to the turf.

Poirier later described his touchdown-saving dive: "We were in a five-four and we were able to shut them off from their outside running thank God. But you have given something away. You had to expect something from Lancaster. He's such a smart quarterback. So we were willing to give up the short zone. But [I] was lucky to get to Reed on that one. Just lucky."

After two successful plays Jack Abendschan missed a field goal to make the score Ottawa 14, Saskatchewan 10.

Following another Saskatchewan single, Ottawa received a break to seal victory. Saskatchewan's Bob Kosid mishandled a punt, and Dan Dever recovered the ball on the Saskatchewan 27-yard line. Two plays later, Jackson rolled to the right, avoided defender Ed McQuarters, then scrambled to his left. He encountered another group of tacklers, but again managed to scramble away. Finally Jackson spotted Mankins in the end zone, and fired him a touchdown pass.

Following the game McQuarters was still shaking his head at Jackson's tremendous effort. He could not believe that the Ottawa quarterback had eluded him. "I had him and he ducked," McQuarters said. "There were others that had him too but he just ducked and was gone. I don't know how [he did it], he just did."

Meanwhile Jackson said, "I was going to the right when I saw a guy come at me. Somehow he missed and I reversed my direction. Then, bang, six points."

Early in the fourth quarter Jackson produced another Ottawa major. From the Saskatchewan 32 he called for a screen pass to Stewart. Jackson hung onto the ball as long as possible, and while being hammered by Shaw and McQuarters completed the pass to his back. Stewart obtained excellent blocking as he sprinted downfield for the score. After the game Shaw was still bewildered by the touchdown: "[Jackson] had the ball when I hit him. I couldn't figure out why he didn't have the ball when he hit the ground."

Sutherin converted and then scored a single to close the game at Ottawa 29, Saskatchewan 11.

**The brightest star of the 1969 game was Russ Jackson. Cautious in the first quarter, Jackson slowly unveiled a range of successful plays against Saskatchewan's**

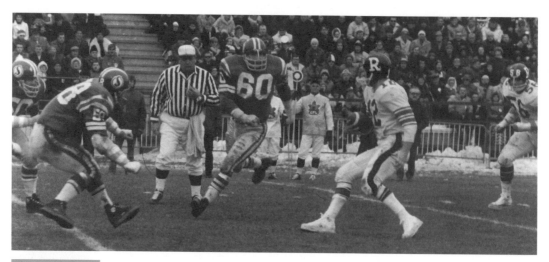

Scrambling from
the pocket, Ottawa's
Russ Jackson
(No. 12) looks for
an opening in the
1969 Cup. (CFL
Photos)

blitzing defence. In the second quarter Jackson launched his attack, mixing a powerful ground attack with a selective aerial assault. This play selection kept Saskatchewan's defence off-balance for most of the game.

Jackson's brilliant scrambling ability was another highlight. Whenever it appeared that the Saskatchewan defenders were going to nail him for a loss, he always managed to get away. Jackson's two touchdown passes to Stewart and the one to Mankins resulted from his marvellous scrambling ability.

Jackson finished the game completing 13 of 22 passes for 254 yards, four touchdowns and no interceptions. He also gained 31 yards on five rushes. This performance earned him the selection as the game's outstanding player, and much praise from ex-teammate Ron Lancaster. Lancaster was happy for Jackson, realizing that it was Jackson's last. "He just went out in an unbelievable way. For most of us the end comes when they throw you out, boo you out or your body gives out. He goes out with everything – there's nothing left for him to win."

## 1970 MONTREAL ALOUETTES 23
CALGARY STAMPEDERS 10

With the departure of Jackson, Ottawa did not make the playoffs in 1970, and thus the door was wide open for a new eastern champion to be crowned. The Montreal Alouettes, who finished behind Hamilton Tiger-Cats and Toronto Argonauts, seized the opportunity made available by Ottawa's last-place finish, and upset both Hamilton and Toronto to represent the East. Meanwhile, in the western division, Saskatchewan Roughriders and Calgary Stampeders battled in an exciting western final. Each team won a game in the best of three series, and then took the deciding game to the last play. Saskatchewan was leading 14 to 12, when Calgary's Larry Robinson lined up for a field goal. The snow-covered surface did not make his task any easier. His aim was good and Calgary headed to the Grey Cup.

On the strength of Calgary's dramatic win in the western final, it was anticipated that the Cup, played November 28, would be Calgary bound.

But Montreal had other plans. In balmy 46 degree Fahrenheit (8 degree Celsius) weather the Alouettes upset the Stampeders 23 to 10.

There was no early indication that Calgary would lose as in the first quarter the Alouettes made two errors which led to Calgary opening the scoring. Shortly after Calgary's Frank Andruski had intercepted a pass, Montreal's Bob Storey misplayed a punt. This allowed Brian Marcil to recover the ball on the Montreal 15. Three plays later, Hugh McKinnis swept left, received an outstanding block from wingback Dave Cranmer, and scored a 6-yard touchdown.

However, Montreal quickly responded. On the ensuing series Montreal quarterback Jesse Sonny Wade engineered a 10-play, 73-yard series for a major. On the Calgary 10 Montreal's Moses Denson made an incredible play. Denson took a handoff, and was immediately plastered by Calgary's Terry Wilson. But Denson refused to go down. While Wilson continued to pull at Denson, the Montreal back tossed the ball to Ted Alflen for a touchdown. Calgary coach Jim Duncan was amazed by the score, and later deemed it to be the key moment of the game.

Wilson described the play. "I guess I was the only person in the park who didn't see the touchdown. I hit [Denson] good. He didn't go down. I had him by the legs and when he stayed up I tried to grab for whatever I could. He maintained fantastic balance."

Wilson added, "It's one of those things you'd like to get another chance at. I'd tackle him high the next time. I was just thinking of stopping the first down and he was stopped. It was a big play for them."

The clubs then exchanged field goals before the Alouettes took control in the third quarter. Al Phaneuf intercepted a stray pass, and on the next

play Bruce Van Ness passed to Terry Evanshen to give the Alouettes possession on the Calgary 7. From there Wade called a 36-Slant R Reverse Left. As Wade took the snap and dropped back for what looked like a pass, Alflen, Peter Dalla Riva and Van Ness scampered into the secondary to loosen right corner linebacker Jim Furlong, right cornerback Gig Perez, and right safety Robinson. On the line of scrimmage left tackle Ed George and left guard Pierre Desjardins held their pass blocks for a count of three,

Montreal's Sonny Wade (No. 14) reaches for the ball. Montreal captured the 1970 Cup by defeating Calgary 23 to 10. (CFL Photos)

and then slipped out ready to block downfield.

Meanwhile, in the backfield Tom Pullen slowly began to run toward Wade. Just as Wade was belted by John Helton, Pullen accepted a hand-off, stormed across the line of scrimmage, and at the 5-yard line leapt high into the air, bounced off a tackler and skipped over the goal line.

In the fourth quarter Montreal closed the game's scoring with another touchdown on a 9-play, 65-yard drive. The touchdown play came when Wade, noticing a large opening in the Calgary defence, called an automatic 92. As Wade later described, "I had called for what we refer to as a toss-trap. We fake a toss to Van Ness going wide, and hand-off to Moses going straight up the middle. But as I looked over their defence at the line of scrimmage, I saw they were stacked in the middle and that [Garry] Lefebvre had only single coverage on the right side."

Lefebvre, who barely heard the audible, ran a post pattern, and Wade delivered the ball to him for a touchdown. George Springate, a member of the Quebec Legislative Assembly, added the extra point, and five minutes later the game ended at Montreal 23, Calgary 10.

**Instrumental in Montreal's victory was quarterback Sonny Wade. A product of Emory & Henry College in Emory, Virginia, and a draft pick of the Philadelphia Eagles, Wade remained cool and collected throughout the final. He operated Montreal's offence with the deftness of a surgeon, and dissected the Calgary defence piece by piece. Wade did not waste much time with routine drop-backs. Rather, he called many play action passes which yielded much yardage on short passes to Terry Evanshen and to backs coming out of the backfield. His calling of signals earned him the honour of being selected as the game's most outstanding player. Wade's final statistics were 16 of 33 passes completed for 157 yards, three interceptions, and a touchdown.**

Montreal's 1970 victory exemplified the spirit of this Canadian football institution more than any other Grey Cup win. After the game Bruce Van Ness explained how the game impressed him. "You just can't imagine it. I think it started building way back on Thursday. When you come from the States you know the Super Bowl and the big college games, but these only involve the sports fans. Sure there are millions of them down there, but it's nothing like this.

"Up here, the whole country gets involved."

## 1971 CALGARY STAMPEDERS 14
## TORONTO ARGONAUTS 11

A year later the whole country celebrated the first Grey Cup game to be played on artificial turf. At Vancouver's Empire Stadium on November 28, 1971, Calgary Stampeders and Toronto Argonauts battled to end long Cup droughts. Calgary had not won since 1948, while Toronto had been shut out since 1952. Led by Joe Theismann and Leon 'X-ray' McQuay, Toronto believed that the Argos' drought would end. However, on a rain-soaked gridiron, Calgary's swift defensive line so dominated the game that Toronto's offence obtained few scoring chances. Near the end of the game McQuay committed the most memorable turnover in Argonaut Cup history. His fumble on the Calgary 11 gave Calgary a 14 to 11 victory.

In the third quarter of the 1971 final, Toronto's Roger Scales (No. 51) scores a touchdown against Calgary.
(Canadian Football Hall of Fame & Museum)

The Stampeders opened the scoring midway through the first quarter. After a controversial ruling allowed Calgary to retain possession of the ball, Calgary's Jerry Keeling moved the Stampeders to the Toronto 11. From there Keeling completed a pass to Herman Harrison for a touchdown.

In the second quarter, Toronto kicked a field goal, and then Calgary scored its second touchdown with the assistance of another controversial call after Rudy Linterman had fumbled on a 40-yard gain and Toronto had recovered. Referees ruled that Linterman had been tackled before losing the ball. Toronto's bench went wild, but Hap Shouldice, supervisor of C.F.L. officials in the East, confirmed that the ruling was correct. Two plays later Jesse Mims scooted into the Toronto end zone.

Toronto's special teams gave the Argonauts momentum in the third quarter. Calgary's Jim Sillye was unable to control a Zenon Andrusyshyn punt. Joe Vijuk scooped up the ball, then wrestled Sillye for possession, and flipped the ball to Roger Scales.

The Argo offensive guard encountered no resistance in his 38-yard run for a touchdown. Ivan MacMillan converted and then kicked a single to make the score Calgary 14, Toronto 11.

With 3:10 remaining in the game Toronto's Dick Thornton presented the Argonauts with a glorious chance to win. Thornton intercepted a poor Keeling pass and returned the ball 55 yards to the Calgary 11. McQuay then committed his memorable fumble. On second down and six, Theismann handed the ball to the fleet-footed back. McQuay headed left, then cut toward the middle. His feet slipped out from under him, he fell elbows first to the turf and the ball sprung loose. Calgary's Reggie Holmes made the recovery.

After the game McQuay described the play. "Hell, it was an end sweep left and I was closed off wide," he angrily murmured, "so I tried to cut and I slipped and my right elbow hit the ground and it just popped up. It was real wet and it just popped up."

Wayne Harris gave the Calgary viewpoint. "It looked pretty likely to us that they'd go to Leon McQuay because that had been their pattern all year. They hadn't been using Bill Symons much...we'd been handling their passing pretty well, especially in that close, where we switch to man-to-man coverage. So we were looking to McQuay."

Larry Robinson continued: "He lost his footing when he tried to cut back inside … and I helped him fall. The ball came out from under his arm as he went down and [we] recovered. That was the game right there."

Toronto had a chance to get the ball back, but three plays later the Argos' Harry Abofs booted a Calgary punt out of bounds. According to then section 9, Article 3 of the C.F.L. Rule Book, "When the ball is kicked out of bounds, it shall belong to the opposite team, subject to the penalty applicable on the kick-off." Calgary was given possession, and the game ended Calgary 14, Toronto 11.

The outstanding player of the 1971 game was Calgary's Wayne Harris. He roamed all over the gridiron and frequently stopped outside and inside runs. He was particularly effective in preventing Toronto's sweeps by either punishing the ball carrier with a solid tackle or stripping the blocking. In addition, Harris made an important fumble recovery in the fourth quarter.

Harris received a lot of praise for his play. Calgary coach Jim Duncan: "Wayne Harris is the greatest. It was a defensive struggle; our whole defence played well, but Wayne is the greatest. He came out to cut off those sweeps and they didn't know where he was coming from."

Harris finished the game with five tackles and three assists.

# 1972 HAMILTON TIGER-CATS 13
# SASKATCHEWAN ROUGHRIDERS 10

On December 3, 1972 the 60th Grey Cup provided Canadian football fans with another exciting finish. For the entire game Hamilton Tiger-Cats and Saskatchewan Roughriders engaged in a colossal defensive struggle in front of 33,993 fans at Hamilton's Ivor Wynne Stadium. The teams were deadlocked at 10 but on the last play of the game Ian 'the Burlington Boot' Sunter lifted Hamilton to victory.

For Saskatchewan, Sunter's last play heroics were reminiscent of the western final. In the fourth quarter of that game Saskatchewan erased a 10-point lead held by the Winnipeg Blue Bombers to tie the game 24 to 24. Then, on the last play Jack Abendschan attempted a 23-yard field goal. The kick was wide, but Winnipeg was forced to punt the ball back to Saskatchewan. Lancaster collected the kick and promptly booted the ball back into the end zone. Winnipeg's Paul Williams grabbed it, and again kicked the ball back to Saskatchewan to avoid the single. However, Williams' kick resulted in a no-yards penalty to the Bombers, and Abendschan was given a chance to kick another field goal. This time the effort was good and Saskatchewan qualified for the 1972 Grey Cup.

The Tiger-Cats opened the scoring in the first quarter as five plays after Hamilton's Al Brenner intercepted a Ron Lancaster pass, quarterback Chuck Ealey threw a 15-yarder to Dave Fleming. The game film showed that Fleming made the catch while out-of-bounds, but afterwards a gregarious Fleming stated, "My feet came down in bounds. There was no question so far as I was concerned."

Chuck Ealey (No. 16) marched the Hamilton Tiger-Cats past the Saskatchewan Roughriders to capture the 1972 title. (Canadian Football Hall of Fame & Museum)

A few minutes later, Hamilton's Bobby Krouse blocked a Saskatchewan punt and Sunter kicked a field goal to make the score Hamilton 10, Saskatchewan 0.

The Roughriders trimmed Hamilton's lead on the ensuing series. Runs by George Reed and passes to Alan Ford and Gord Barwell helped to move Saskatchewan to the Hamilton 8, and from there Lancaster completed a touchdown pass to rookie Tom Campana.

A Hamilton touchdown was nullified due to offside, then the Roughriders tied the score. From the Hamilton 13 Abendschan booted a field goal to make the score 10 to 10.

The third and fourth quarters featured a defensive struggle. Both teams prevented the offences from threatening until late in the fourth quarter when Lancaster made a 31-yard pass to Bob Pearce which gave Saskatchewan possession on the Hamilton 48. However, Lancaster was unable to take advantage of the field position and Pearce punted the ball to the Hamilton 15.

1:51 remained. Ealey was instructed to take the Tiger-Cats into field goal range. Ealey relied on his passing attack; three tosses to Tony Gabriel gained 54 yards. Then Ealey called a 64 Dice Drift. All of the receivers went out on hook patterns, with Garney Henley playing off the line. Ealey threw to Henley, who made a spectacular one-handed catch on the Saskatchewan 26.

As Ealey ran one more play, Hamilton coach Jerry Williams asked his punter Billy Van Burkleo if he could guarantee punting the ball out of the end zone. Van Burkleo replied, "I think it could be difficult."

Williams then summoned Sunter to his side. "You think you can make it?"

"Sure," Sunter said confidently.

"Okay," Williams replied. "Go in there and do your best. If you miss we'll beat them in overtime."

Hamilton lost a yard, and with a mere 13 seconds showing on the clock Sunter trotted onto the field. He passed Ealey, who said, "Take it easy. We got a lot of confidence in you. Let's make this last kick a happy one."

Hamilton set up in field goal formation and Henley turned to Sunter. "Take your time. Up and easy, kick it through the posts." When the ball was snapped back to Henley, Sunter lowered his head and gave the oval a soccer-style kick. The ball split the uprights as Henley shouted "Atta baby!" The final score was Hamilton 13, Saskatchewan 10.

**The hero of the game, as voted by the Football Reporters of Canada, was Chuck Ealey. Snubbed by every team in the United States in the 1972 college draft, the 22-year-old from Toledo, Ohio played with the poise of a veteran. Throughout the game Ealey refused to panic, and performed better whenever the pressure grew. This was evident in the latter stages of the fourth quarter when he coolly marched his team into range for the winning field goal. Ealey completed 18 of 29 passes for 291 yards, and ran nine times for 63 yards.**

**According to Saskatchewan coach Dave Skrien it was Ealey's scrambling ability that was the main difference in the game. "It's hard to say whether we played poorly**

inside or they played well ... but we couldn't contain Ealey. The game was just like I figured it would be before it started. They played an all-round good game and Ealey came up with the big plays."

Ian Sunter and Garney Henley were also stars. Sunter scored seven points, including the game-winning field goal, and was selected as the game's outstanding Canadian performer.

Meanwhile Henley's exceptional performance on both offence and defence silenced the critics who had suggested that his 1972 Schenley selection as the most outstanding player in Canada over Winnipeg's Mack Herron had been a sentimental gesture. Henley's spectacular 15-yard reception with less than 30 seconds left in regulation time was a key to helping Hamilton win the Grey Cup. He made seven receptions for a total of 98 yards. For the legendary Henley this performance was memorable because the 1972 game was his last appearance as a player in a national final. He retired in 1975 after 16 seasons and on June 30, 1979 was elected into the Canadian Football Hall of Fame.

## 1973 OTTAWA ROUGH RIDERS 22 EDMONTON ESKIMOS 18

Edmonton's Tom Wilkinson hands the ball off to Roy Bell in the 1973 Cup. (CFL Photos)

In 1973 there was more excitement as clubs battled toward the Grey Cup. The Ottawa Rough Riders won the thrilling eastern championship, while the Edmonton Eskimos came from behind in the last minute of its final to capture the western crown.

Despite Edmonton's electrifying victory in the western final, Ottawa was favoured to win. The Rider defence played aggressively in a brutal display which left Edmonton quarterbacks Tom Wilkinson and Bruce Lemmerman seeking medical attention. Ottawa won 22 to 18.

Edmonton opened the scoring on its first drive of the game. After Wilkinson was illegally levelled by Wayne Smith, the Eskimos advanced the ball to the Ottawa 29. From there Wilkinson handed the ball to Roy Bell, who used excellent blocks from Larry Watkins, Willie Martin and Calvin Harrell and blasted through a gaping hole for a touchdown.

A few minutes later Ottawa obtained possession on the Edmonton 38. Ottawa quarterback

Rick Cassata took advantage of the field position with a deep pass to Rhome Nixon. Nixon blazed behind defender Billy Cooper and scored easily. After the game Cassata described the touchdown. "The Edmonton defence expected a running play. I looked up and saw Cooper move the wrong way. That's when I decided to throw to Rhome Nixon. I didn't exploit Cooper on purpose because of his [pulled hamstring], but it fit the situation."

An Edmonton field goal and an Ottawa safety touch then brought the score to Edmonton 10, Ottawa 9 and with time running out in the first half it appeared that the score would not change. But with only 28 seconds remaining and Ottawa facing a third down and one, the Riders gambled. Cassata fooled the Edmonton defence with a long pass to Nixon which put the ball on the Edmonton 38. From there, Gerry Organ booted a field goal.

This field goal demoralized Edmonton, and in the third quarter the Eskimos struggled. Then, midway through the quarter, Cassata engineered a powerful drive of four plays which sealed Ottawa's victory. After moving the play to the Edmonton 18, Cassata handed the ball to Jim Evenson. Evenson rambled to the Edmonton 3, and then tossed aside defenders Dick Dupuis, Larry Highbaugh and John Farlinger for the score.

For Ottawa coach Jack Gotta, Evenson's touchdown was the game's turning point. "It was an important seven-pointer for us," Gotta explained, "but more than that it was the physical aspect of it. It made the other members of the team realize we were taking over."

In 1973, Rick Cassatta (No. 16) got excellent pass protection from his offensive line as Ottawa triumphed over Edmonton 22 to 18. (CFL Photos)

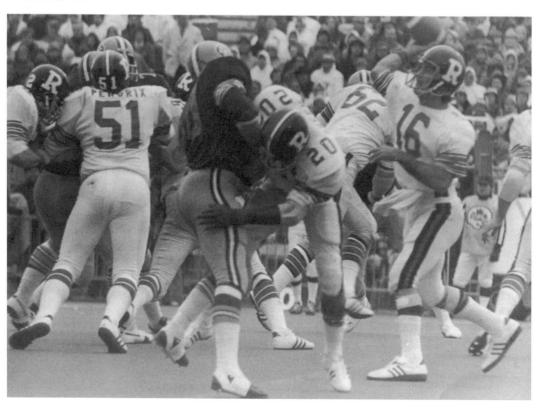

In the fourth quarter Organ added another field goal to make the score Ottawa 22, Edmonton 10. The game was out of reach but the Eskimos continued to battle. Garry Lefebvre kicked a single, and then with seven seconds remaining in the game he caught a 4-yard touchdown pass from Wilkinson. Dave Cutler added the convert to end the game Ottawa 22, Edmonton 18.

The M.V.P. was Ottawa's Charles Brandon. Playing both ways, Brandon was stellar throughout the final. Offensively, it was his key block which helped to spring Evenson free for Ottawa's third quarter touchdown. In addition, Brandon contributed to Cassata's pass protection, and opened other holes for running backs Art Green and Evenson. Defensively Brandon was solid as a rock. He made excellent plays to shorten Edmonton ground gains and to induce losses. To one observer Brandon appeared to have been in on 90 percent of Ottawa's tackles.

Jack Gotta was very happy that Brandon was chosen. He said, "That guy never complains, never moans or bitches. I think his real talent has never really been brought forward because coaches like me just have to use him at so many positions."

Ottawa's Al Marcelin said, "That award couldn't have gone to a more deserving player. The guy was only the greatest football player on the field."

The outstanding Canadian in the game was Edmonton's Garry Lefebvre. Although he had much difficulty punting the ball, his offensive and defensive play stood in the spotlight. Lefebvre scored seven points on the strength of an 85-yard punt and a touchdown. Defensively he shadowed Ottawa's Rhome Nixon and Terry Wellesley extremely well. His coverage was so good that during the game he killed two Ottawa scoring threats with timely interceptions.

## 1974 MONTREAL ALOUETTES 20 EDMONTON ESKIMOS 7

On November 24, 1974, the Eskimos returned to the Cup with the help of another western final victory which was not sealed until the last minute. Trailing by 11 points, the Saskatchewan Roughriders struck for a late touchdown. Then, Saskatchewan tried an onside kick. However, Edmonton's Tyrone Walls smothered the short kick-off to ensure a 31 to 27 Edmonton victory.

Edmonton's Grey Cup opponent was the Montreal Alouettes. Guided by head coach Marv Levy and the talented Johnny 'Ordinary Superstar' Rodgers the Alouettes were favoured to beat Edmonton on a windswept and wet Empire Stadium field in Vancouver. Montreal's defence contained Edmonton's offence and the Alouettes easily won 20 to 7.

Edmonton's only points of the game came early in the first quarter. Scrimmaging from the Edmonton 48, Tom Wilkinson directed a 10-play, 62-yard touchdown drive. Passes to George McGowan and Garry Lefebvre and a roughing penalty helped move the ball to the Montreal 8 and from there Wilkinson threw a pass to Calvin Harrell for the score.

On the ensuing series Montreal missed a field goal, and then at 3:29 of the second quarter Levy made the most crucial decision of the game by replacing starting quarterback Jimmy Jones with Sonny Wade.

The switch sparked the Alouettes. Don Sweet scored a single, and shortly afterwards Phil Price returned a fumble to the Edmonton 8. From there a pass interference penalty against Larry Highbaugh kept Montreal's chance for a touchdown alive, and on the next play Larry Sherrer swept wide right for a major.

Dick Harris followed by intercepting a pass to give the Alouettes possession on the Edmonton 29. Montreal gained 19 yards, and Sweet kicked a field goal to end the first half at Montreal 11, Edmonton 7.

In the second half Edmonton's offence was completely ineffective. An injury to Wilkinson in the first quarter had weakened his passing and every time he went long he underthrew his receivers. Meanwhile Edmonton's defence kept on conceding penalties. The Alouettes continually moved the ball into scoring range and Sweet kicked three field goals to provide Montreal with a 20 to 7 victory.

The three players who starred in Montreal's victory were Sonny Wade, Don Sweet, and Junior 'Hawaiian Punch' Ah You. Coming off the bench to replace Jimmy Jones, Wade took control of the game. He utilized a variety of running and passing plays to keep Edmonton off-balance for nearly 45 minutes.

While the other quarterbacks in the game seemed to have trouble throwing, Wade reared back and fired at will. On many occasions, Wade courageously threw the ball into crowded groups of Edmonton defenders. It was this passing which guided Montreal to victory. Wade completed 10 of 25 passes for 139 yards and three times his passes resulted in Edmonton pass interference penalties that ultimately led to Montreal scores. Wade also fulfilled his punting duties extremely well. Even with a rain-soaked football Wade produced his best punting performance of the season. In nine punts, he averaged 41.6 yards per kick.

Sweet was the game's outstanding Canadian player. A native of Vancouver, Sweet attended Washington State University on a baseball scholarship and had no intention of playing college football until WSU's head coach spotted him kicking placements during a physical education class. The Alouettes were glad that Sweet decided to try his foot at football because his kicking provided the margin of victory in the 1974 Grey Cup. Sweet was responsible for 14 of Montreal's 20 points on four field goals, a rouge, and a convert; his four field goals beat the record of George Fraser, who kicked three for the Ottawa Rough Riders in the 1941 game.

The defensive player of the game was Ah You. At six-feet three inches, the Samoan was a one-man gang for Montreal. In the first quarter his relentless pursuit of Edmonton quarterback Tom Wilkinson resulted in a crushing blow which forced Wilkinson from the game. Later, Ah You slammed into Edmonton's Roy Bell, causing a fumble. Montreal recovered the ball, and a few plays later the Alouettes scored its only touchdown.

Touchdowns were again rare in the 1975 Grey Cup game. For the second consecutive year, Montreal Alouettes and Edmonton Eskimos battled for Lord Grey's silver. The game was played in Calgary's McMahon Stadium on November 23, and as expected the temperature was frigid, so low that more than 15 years later Bruce Lemmerman said that he could still feel the cold from that game coursing through his veins.

"After we'd been out there about five minutes trying to warm up, I turned to one of the guys and said we might as well go in, this is a waste of time," Lemmerman remembered. "The temperature was down to about minus 25 degrees. There was no way we were going to get warm. I remember the big long tubes along the sidelines with the hot air blowing in. The players were sitting on them. You hated to get up and go on the field. I carried a charcoal handwarmer the entire game."

However, the temperature did not prevent Natia Stooshnoff from warming up the crowd as she streaked onto the field during the national anthem. Clad only in a flimsy slip, Natia danced across the turf. The police were reluctant to cause a commotion during the anthem, and it was only after the anthem had been completed that Natia was apprehended. As for the game, Edmonton defeated Montreal 9 to 8.

Montreal opened the scoring on its first possession. Starting on the Edmonton 48, Montreal pivot Jimmy Jones utilized Joe Petty, Johnny Rodgers and Larry Smith to move the Alouettes to the Edmonton 27. From there, Sweet comfortably kicked a field goal.

A few minutes later, Jones again found Petty and Smith to march Montreal into scoring position. At the Edmonton 40 Sweet launched a rocket through the uprights: Montreal 6, Edmonton 0.

In the second quarter Tom Wilkinson moved Edmonton into field goal range. Cutler easily cut Montreal's lead in half. Montreal's offence roared back, and long gains by Peter Dalla Riva and Smith again advanced Montreal into Edmonton territory. Sweet was instructed to try another field goal, but this time he missed. Larry Highbaugh conceded a single, and at half-time the Alouettes held a 7 to 3 lead.

The turning point of the game came very early in the third quarter when Montreal advanced the ball to the Edmonton 4 following a fumble recovery. Faced with a third down and goal situation, Montreal players expected Sweet to go for a field goal, but Montreal's head coach Marv Levy decided to gamble. The decision was a mistake. Rodgers, struggling to control a pitch-out, was eventually forced out of bounds by John Farlinger three yards short.

After the game, Levy took the criticism as he explained: "At that point in the game, I didn't want to give up field position. If we had gone for the field goal we would have had to kick-off to them into the wind."

Edmonton soon launched its best offensive drive of the game. Scrimmaging on the Edmonton 35, Bruce Lemmerman completed passes to George McGowan and Stu Lang to move the Eskimos to the Montreal 18. From there, Cutler booted his second field goal to close the gap to a point, 7 to 6. Then on the last play of the third quarter Cutler kicked a 52-yard field goal.

In the fourth quarter Montreal had difficulty moving the ball against Edmonton's defence, and eventually the Eskimos scrimmaged from the Montreal 40. Cutler was dispatched onto the field for what appeared to be another field goal attempt, but Cutler had different instructions. Cutler merely booted the ball out of play at the Montreal 23. He later explained: "That's all we wanted to do, although I should have kicked it a bit further. I knew I couldn't have made the field goal because my kicks are so high and the wind would have held it up. We just wanted to pin Montreal in their own zone."

He added: "I don't mind kicking the ball out of bounds like that and having a missed field goal on my record. I'm just out here to do a job. If they ask me to try a 100-yarder, I'll do it. In fact if it would help the team, I'd kick the ball behind me."

At this point, Sonny Wade replaced Jones as Montreal's quarterback. The switch gave Montreal confidence and in less than two minutes Wade moved Montreal to the Edmonton 11. From there, Sweet attempted the potential game-winning field goal in the final minute. However, Jones had extreme difficulty fielding the snap. He placed the ball down sideways and Sweet's kick sailed wide and across the deadline for a single.

Forty-five seconds later the game ended Edmonton 9, Montreal 8.

After the game Montreal centre Wayne Conrad, Jones and Sweet gave their versions of the fateful kick. "As far as I know, when it left my hands it was spiralling back okay," Conrad explained. "I can't watch it; as soon as I let it go I have to get my head up to block. But it felt all right. Obviously there was a breakdown but, look, it takes three of us to make this goddam thing go and you got to blame all of us when something like this happens."

Jones: "It wasn't a clean exchange, the timing was a little disrupted. The ball was cold and there was a tail to the snap because of the wind. I did not have full control of it. As it was, it just missed, it almost hit the crossbar."

Meanwhile a displeased Sweet said, "There were complications. I'd rather wait until I see the film to find the breakdown. But the ball wasn't there. It just wasn't there. You have 1.3 seconds from snap to kick and there's no time for a stutter step. It flashed through my mind to wait but you can't. I don't like to pass the buck because as a pro you should get it done."

Then he added, "It's a shame, but things happen for a reason, as the Lord says."

**The three stars in this cliff-hanger were Dave Cutler, and Montreal's Lewis Cook and Steve Ferrughelli. Cutler scored all of Edmonton's points with three very impressive long range field goals. He was chosen as the game's outstanding Canadian.**

**The best defensive player in the game was Cook. Along with teammate Gordon**

Judges, Cook prevented Edmonton from sustaining a passing attack. Whenever Edmonton tried long passes, Cook either knocked them down or intercepted them.

Ferrughelli was chosen as the game's outstanding player. In a losing cause he did everything possible to lead the Alouettes to victory. On 15 carries he gained 85 yards, and on two receptions, 20 yards.

The heroic efforts provided by Cutler, Cook, and Ferrughelli exemplified the spirit of the Grey Cup, as did the 68 oil workers who unofficially set a record for distance travelled to a Grey Cup game. Stationed in the Northwest Territories, they chose to travel to Calgary via Montreal and Edmonton – nearly 11,000 kilometres (6,800 miles) – to participate in celebrating Canada's football institution.

## 1976 OTTAWA ROUGH RIDERS 23
## SASKATCHEWAN ROUGHRIDERS 20

Trailing 20 to 16 in the fourth quarter, Ottawa shocked Saskatchewan in 1976 with Clements' 24-yard touchdown pass to Gabriel (arm raised).
(Canadian Football Hall of Fame & Museum)

The low-scoring 1975 result was followed by one of the most exciting games in Grey Cup history. The Saskatchewan Roughriders perilously clung to a four-point lead against the Ottawa Rough Riders as time was running out. Saskatchewan had just prevented Ottawa from converting a third down within the Saskatchewan 2-yard line. When it appeared that Saskatchewan would win, Tony Gabriel caught the most memorable touchdown pass in Ottawa history to lift Ottawa to a 23 to 20 victory.

In the first quarter Ottawa jumped into a 3 to 0 lead on a Gerry Organ field goal, and then York University graduate Bill Hatanaka electrified the crowd with one of the longest punt returns in Grey Cup competition for a touchdown. A Saskatchewan punt bounced toward the sideline as the Ottawa bench hollered "no yards!" Saskatchewan defenders hesitated and in this instant Hatanaka stepped up to grab the ball. Hatanaka eased past a few frozen Saskatchewan defenders and charged toward the Saskatchewan end zone. Downfield, Ottawa's Mark Kosmos levelled another Saskatchewan player. Hatanaka shook off Ted Provost, so only punter Bob Macoritti remained. At the Saskatchewan 25 Macoritti lunged at Hatanaka, but the Ottawa returner accelerated to complete a 79-yard touchdown return.

After the game a jubilant Hatanaka commented: "I saw our line hold up their offensive linemen, and I knew I could get a good runback if I got past the first wave of tacklers. One guy infringed on the no-yards area and once I got by him I headed to my left because I knew our blocking was set up that way.

"I made a pretty good move on one guy … and once I got by him I started thinking maybe this is it. About halfway down the field I saw the kicker and he had a perfect angle on me. But I still thought I had a chance because I knew that most kickers aren't all that hot at tackling.

"Basically, I just tried to keep a smooth stride. I knew there were a couple of guys chasing me and I was feeling the pressure from them as well as the pressure of fatigue. So I kept telling myself, 'Keep your stride … one, two, three, four …' Yeah I was counting and breathing deeply. Like a long distance runner. I was happy when it was over."

In the second quarter Saskatchewan attacked Ottawa's 10 to 0 lead. First, after Saskatchewan advanced the ball to the Ottawa 5, a third down gamble was stopped. But Ottawa's offence was unable to take advantage of the stellar play of its defence and a few minutes later Macoritti kicked a field goal. Then Lancaster drove Saskatchewan to the Ottawa 15. From there Lancaster threw to Steve Mazurak. The receiver made a spectacular leaping catch on the Ottawa 5 and sprinted across the field parallel to the Ottawa goal line. He soon spotted an opening and cut sharply toward the goal line for the score.

Before the end of the quarter Saskatchewan scored again. Provost intercepted Tom Clements. On the next play Lancaster completed a pass to Bob Richardson, who kept Rod Woodward, Peter Crepin and Peter Stenerson at bay to score a touchdown. Macoritti kicked the extra point, so the half ended Saskatchewan 17, Ottawa 10.

Saskatchewan widened the lead to 10 before Ottawa mounted its comeback. Organ kicked a field goal, and then tried to inspire his team with a 52-yard run on a fake punt. After the game, Organ was asked if the fake had been pre-planned. "I thought about it at halftime," Organ recalled. "I talked about it with Kosmos … I told him I thought they weren't rushing me on my punts. I told him I thought I could run with the ball.

"I didn't plan it that way on that particular play, though. After I caught the ball, I had every intention of punting, but I took a step forward, looked up, saw that nobody was rushing me, and decided to take off. Naturally, I was primarily concerned with getting the first down. But Kosmos put a good block on [Rhett] Dawson and I just turned on the after-burners," Organ chuckled. "By the time I was finished, I was out of gas. I don't think I could have run another foot."

Ottawa was unable to capitalize on Organ's run, but early in the fourth quarter Organ kicked another field goal to give Ottawa an opportunity to win the 1976 Cup. Four points separated the teams.

With less than four minutes remaining, Clements drove Ottawa to within one yard and 15 inches of the Saskatchewan goal line only for Saskatchewan defensive tackle Frank Landy to push off an Ottawa blocker to halt the drive. Three plays later Saskatchewan punted and, with 44 seconds left in the game, Ottawa embarked on the game-winning drive. Ottawa moved the ball to the Saskatchewan 24. Clements waved off a play from the bench to call a "Rob I, fake 34, tight end flag."

The 'Rob' instructed Gabriel to line-up on the right side of the Ottawa line, the 'I' indicated the backfield formation, and '34' meant that the third man in the 'I', the fullback, was to carry the ball through the number four hole, the space between the right guard and tackle, in the line. Meanwhile the 'tight end flag' indicated that Gabriel was to streak downfield and cut to the flag.

Gabriel ran his pattern. Saskatchewan safety Provost moved in to cover Gabriel, but then Gabriel dipped his left shoulder and inclined his head. Provost bought the fake and Gabriel was behind the coverage. Clements threw and Gabriel snatched the ball from the sky for the touchdown. While armchair critics blamed Provost, Saskatchewan coach John Payne rightly concluded, "Gabriel ran a super route to make the big catch. I won't fault Provost or anyone else on our club. Gabriel simply came up with a real gem."

Organ converted the touchdown and 20 seconds later Ottawa celebrated its ninth Grey Cup victory.

**For Saskatchewan's Ron Lancaster, the bitterness of defeat was extreme. Despite completing 22 of 35 passes for 263 yards and two touchdowns, the 38-year-old Canadian football veteran was unable to provide Saskatchewan with its second national title. The 1976 Grey Cup game was Lancaster's fifth and last as a player, and in 1982 his outstanding 19-year C.F.L. career was remembered when he was inducted into the Hall of Fame.**

**Tom Clements and Tony Gabriel gained the laurels for the victory. Clements, the 23-year-old quarterback was an inspiration to his Ottawa teammates. Although many of his drives were stalled by dropped passes and unnecessary penalties, Clements never let adversity affect his performance. Even after failing on the third down gamble from inside the Saskatchewan 2 late in the game, he kept his composure to engineer the game-winning drive.**

Clements finished by completing 11 of 25 passes for 174 yards and a touchdown, and ran five times for 37 yards. This performance earned him the selection as the outstanding player.

Meanwhile Gabriel, a native of Burlington, Ontario, was the top Canadian. His clutch performance in the dying minutes clinched Ottawa's victory. Describing Gabriel's performance, Saskatchewan tight end Bob Richardson said, "Tony Gabriel – the guy's unreal. I knew that [fourth quarter touchdown] pass was going to Gabriel. Everybody did and he still caught it."

Gabriel caught seven passes for 124 yards and one touchdown.

## 1977 MONTREAL ALOUETTES 41 EDMONTON ESKIMOS 6

Ottawa's 1976 Grey Cup victory was followed by a Montreal Cup triumph. The Alouettes qualified for the 1977 Cup, played on November 27, by defeating Ottawa 21 to 18 in the eastern final. Montreal then battled the western champion Edmonton Eskimos. Field conditions were extremely poor. A heavy snowfall struck Montreal's Olympic Stadium the night before the game and hastily the grounds crew cleared the snow. However, the field was still wet, and overnight sub-zero temperatures turned the turf into a sheet of ice. The grounds crew then spread salt pellets and while the ice did melt a slimy chemical solution was left behind. The very treacherous footing turned the 1977 final into an unpredictable fight.

Realizing that footwear could be the difference and recalling the 1931 Grey Cup game in which similar conditions faced the combatants, Montreal players fired staples into the soles of their shoes. Thus Montreal players had the better traction and together with a record-setting performance by Don Sweet the Alouettes won the 1977 final 41 to 6.

Early moments were dominated by turnovers. After Sonny Wade fumbled a snap on the Edmonton 1, an interception by Montreal's Dick Harris led to the opening score. A long pass to Bob Gaddis and runs by John O'Leary put the Alouettes in scoring position. Sweet kicked a field goal.

A few minutes later Montreal capitalized on two more Edmonton turnovers. On each occasion Montreal moved the ball into scoring range and Sweet booted field goals. Then Sweet scored a single to give Montreal a 10 to 0 lead.

At the end of the second quarter and at the beginning of the third, the kickers continued to produce points. Edmonton's Dave Cutler kicked two field goals, and Sweet added another to make the score Montreal 13, Edmonton 6. At this point the Alouettes took charge. Following Sweet's fifth field goal Wade turned an interception by Tony Proudfoot into a touchdown. Wade moved Montreal to the Edmonton 7, and two plays later Wade fired a pass to Peter Dalla Riva. Dalla Riva sheltered the ball with his body to make a touchdown reception.

Near the end of the quarter, Randy Rhino returned a punt 52 yards to give Montreal possession on the Edmonton 10 and to set up Wade for a

Sonny Wade (No. 14) of Montreal completed 22 of 40 passes against Edmonton to become the 1977 Cup M.V.P.
(Canadian Football Hall of Fame & Museum)

screen pass to O'Leary and a major. Edmonton protested the score, and later Montreal's centre Wayne Conrad admitted that the touchdown should not have stood because he had clipped Edmonton's Dan Kepley. When referee Bill Dell was questioned about the clip that his crew missed, Dell responded, "It's possible [we missed the infraction], but I don't feel that's the fault of the officials. That is simply a great case for a sixth official. The referee is in the backfield with the quarterback. The line umpire is at the line and the other official on that side is downfield with the deep receivers. The others are also in their positions on the other side of the field. When a play like that develops and then they throw a screen pass, we have a blind spot in that particular area. Mechanically everything was done correctly."

At the beginning of the fourth quarter Montreal's Vernon Perry made a spectacular interception, returning the ball to the Edmonton 7. Wade immediately threw a short pass to Gaddis for a touchdown. Sweet converted, then kicked a single before closing the scoring with a 16-yard field goal. It was Sweet's sixth placement of the game and enabled him to set two individual Grey Cup scoring records.

The six field goals were the most ever kicked by one player, and the sixth field goal gave Sweet 23 points to break the record of 22 established by Jimmy Van Pelt in 1958. The 1977 final was the finest moment in Sweet's football career, and accordingly he was selected as the game's outstanding Canadian.

The best defensive player in the game was Montreal's Glen Weir. He was all over Edmonton quarterbacks and backfielders, and often ruined Eskimo offensive attacks. Weir's hard hitting and relentless effort enabled him to record two sacks and two fumble recoveries.

Meanwhile the outstanding player of the game was Sonny Wade. For the third time in his illustrious career Wade guided the Alouettes to victory by calling an excellent mixture of running and passing plays. Wade masterfully avoided Edmonton's pass rush and effectively used the roll out to either scamper across the line of scrimmage or to complete a pass. Wade finished the game completing 22 of 40 passes for 340 yards.

In addition Wade's punting was tremendous. His long and high kicks gave Edmonton runners little chance for good returns, and held them to an average return of four yards per kick.

Montreal head coach Marv Levy paid the highest praise to Wade. "Sonny Wade is now unquestionably the premier quarterback in Canada."

Montreal's powerful 1977 Grey Cup win ended perhaps the most exciting era in Canadian football history. Over a period of 10 years Hall of Fame members and Canadian football legends Tommy Joe Coffey, Jim Corrigall, Terry Evanshen, Wayne Harris, John Helton, Garney Henley, Russ Jackson, Jerry Keeling, Ron Lancaster, Marv Luster, Ellison Kelly, Ed McQuarters, Angelo Mosca, George Reed, Ron Stewart, Whit Tucker and Gene Gaines thrilled Grey Cup crowds with their heroic performances. In this period all competed in their last Grey Cup games and more than any other group of Canadian football legends they exemplified the spirit of the Canadian game. These players represented the golden age of Canadian football, and since their departure there have been very few players who have managed to generate their spirit and equal their accomplishments. While more recent Cup games have produced many memorable moments, they have showcased few legends. Canadian football awaits another player to reproduce the heroics displayed by Russ Jackson, Garney Henley and Ron Lancaster.

## Chapter Eleven

# THE EDMONTON ESKIMO DYNASTY
## 1978-1982

**T**he greatest dynasty in Grey Cup history has been the Edmonton Eskimos from 1978 through 1982. The Eskimos defeated every eastern team to win five consecutive titles. The building of this dynasty began immediately after Edmonton's humiliating defeat in the 1977 game. Edmonton recruited talented young stars such as Warren Moon and Tom Scott, and it was emphasized to veterans Tom Wilkinson, Dave Fennell, and Dan Kepley that it was their responsibility to provide team leadership.

## 1978 EDMONTON ESKIMOS 20
## MONTREAL ALOUETTES 13

The mixture of new talent with the veterans was a potent elixir and its powerful impact on Canadian football was felt with the commencement of the 1978 regular season. The Eskimos compiled 10 wins, 4 losses, and 2 ties and then came from behind to defeat the Calgary Stampeders 26 to 13 in the western final. Meanwhile the Montreal Alouettes defeated the Ottawa Rough Riders 21 to 16 in the eastern final to set up a re-match of the 1977 Ice Bowl. Montreal was expected to repeat as Grey Cup champion, but Edmonton was determined to take the Cup west. The 1978 Grey Cup game, played on November 26 at Toronto's C.N.E. Stadium, was a defensive struggle which Edmonton won 20 to 13.

One of the key plays in the game occurred midway through the first quarter. The Eskimos, with a 3 to 0 lead, had moved the ball to the Montreal 15. Another field goal attempt? The Eskimos called a trick play instead. As Edmonton lined up, Tom Scott stood momentarily behind kicker Dave Cutler and holder Tom Wilkinson. This was the normal routine for Scott, awaiting instructions from Wilkinson as to which side of the line required support. Scott was told to line up on the left, but he did not remain there

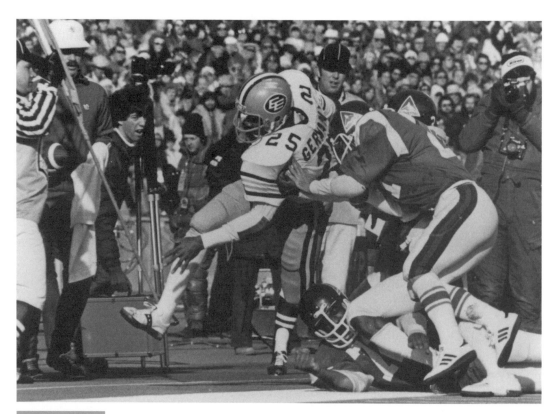

long. While Wilkinson shouted his cadence, Scott stepped back from the line and galloped toward him. Centre Bob Howes snapped the ball back to Wilkinson. Cutler motioned to kick, but at the last moment Wilkinson, from his knees, flipped the ball to a racing Scott who obtained a first down. Two plays later – a Jim Germany touchdown.

After the game reporters hounded Edmonton head coach Hugh Campbell for an explanation of the fake field goal. None of them recalled seeing the Eskimos practice the play, and thus *The Globe and Mail*'s Scott Young asked "Did you practice it a lot to make it work so slick?"

"We worked it once this week," Campbell replied.

"Was that in the closed practice the Eskimos held here the day they arrived?"

"No," grinned Campbell. "We worked it in the dark early in the week, in Edmonton. There were reporters there but we got them down to the other end of the field, nobody watching, and we ran it once with the whole team. That's all, except a few times with the three guys immediately involved."

Campbell was then asked where he got the idea for the play. "You have to use creative thinking when you're a head coach, and I have quite an imagination," Campbell replied. After a brief pause he added, "Actually, I saw it on the halftime highlights on Monday Night [N.F.L.] Football. I think the Seattle Seahawks used it."

Following the Germany touchdown the game turned into a kicking duel and before the end of the second quarter the Alouettes scored a field goal, while Edmonton claimed a field goal and single. The Eskimos added another field goal in the third quarter, and then Montreal attempted to come back.

With Edmonton in possession near its own 10, Montreal's defence exploded across the line on the snap of the ball. Distracted by the Montreal rush, Germany misjudged a hand-off from Wilkinson. Gordon Judges recovered the ball and two plays later Joe Barnes followed the blocking of Pat Bonnett to score a touchdown.

After the game Campbell and the Edmonton players agreed that this fumble was a key to the game. "We had been doing a lot of things, particularly defensively, that were pretty good," Campbell said mildly. "Then we gave them the ball on our own 10-yard line. That ignited their fire. If we hadn't made that one mistake I doubt that they would have scored against us in the second half."

Wilkinson concurred. "Had we not fumbled on that last play of the third quarter, we would have beaten them easily. I just played it too conservatively, too cautiously, trying to protect the 14-point lead. One of the Montreal guys came too quickly and as I reached out my arm with the ball to hand it off, he knocked it out of my hand."

Halfway through the last quarter Montreal's Vernon Perry intercepted a pass to give the Alouettes possession on the Edmonton 31. Sonny Wade replaced Barnes at quarterback, but was unable to move his club. On third down, Don Sweet kicked a field goal to make the score Edmonton 17, Montreal 13.

The Alouettes continued to attack. With less than two minutes remaining Edmonton's Larry Highbaugh made the defensive play of the game. Wade threw a bomb to Bob Gaddis, and as the ball arrived Highbaugh leaped into the air, stuck out his left hand and plucked the ball back to earth, incomplete.

A minute later Cutler kicked another field goal and then Montreal engineered its last desperate drive. Wade marched the Alouettes to the Edmonton 27, and from there he tried to throw a touchdown pass. But Edmonton stormed into the Montreal backfield. With little time to pass, Wade in desperation flipped a lateral to offensive tackle Bill Kahl-Winter. Startled, Kahl-Winter dropped the ball. Edmonton gained possession and won, 20 to 13.

**The most valuable player in this Grey Cup game was Edmonton's Tom Wilkinson. The gritty gridiron veteran ripped the Alouette defence apart. Utilizing a short passing game, Wilkinson retained possession of the ball for Edmonton and frequently had Montreal defenders scrambling all over the field.**

**Praising Wilkinson's performance, Montreal defensive tackle Glen Weir said, "Wilkie's a smart, smart quarterback. I just wish he hadn't lost all that weight and had retired a year ago. He just kept plunking away at us in the first quarter. He kept [Montreal's defence] on the field for a long time. There's not much you can do to prevent those short passes. Going into the game we felt we had pretty well everything covered, but obviously we missed something."**

Wilkinson finished the game completing 15 of 25 passes for 111 yards, and running three times for nine yards.

The outstanding Canadian player of the game was Edmonton's Angelo Santucci. A graduate of Hamilton's Westdale Collegiate and St. Mary's University in Halifax, Santucci was not expected to get much playing time but when Don Warrington was injured in the first quarter Hugh Campbell inserted Santucci into the line-up. Immediately, the young Canadian had an impact. Wilkinson successfully utilized Santucci's abilities in both the running and passing attacks to further exploit Montreal's defence and keep them scrambling. Santucci gained 25 yards on five receptions, and 30 yards on six carries.

Edmonton's Dave Fennell was the defensive star of the game. Together with Dan Kepley, Fennell was everywhere, harassing the Montreal quarterbacks or hammering the Montreal ball carriers. So often was Fennell in the Montreal backfield that Barnes and Wade thought that he was the thirteenth man on the field for the Alouettes.

Edmonton was delighted with its victory, but after the game Wilkinson and Kepley horrified Grey Cup custodians. As the pair carried the Cup from the field, each holding a handle of the precious silverware, they were accosted by overly exuberant and highly intoxicated fans. Suddenly, Wilkinson went to the turf. Then Kepley went down. The trophy struck the ground hard and broke in two. C.F.L. officials were shocked but as Wilkinson later said there was nothing any of them could do: "The fans almost hit as hard as the Alouettes."

## 1979  EDMONTON ESKIMOS 17
MONTREAL ALOUETTES 9

The trophy was repaired for the 1979 classic and for the third year in a row the finalists were Edmonton Eskimos and Montreal Alouettes. With the game being played in Montreal, on November 25, the Alouettes hoped that its home-field advantage would give it another Grey Cup title. However, Edmonton – vividly remembering its 41 to 6 defeat in 1977 at Olympic Stadium – demanded revenge. Edmonton's defence played brilliantly, and the team won its second consecutive Grey Cup championship, 17 to 9.

The Eskimos opened the scoring midway through the first quarter. After Jim Germany rushed for seven yards to move Edmonton to the Montreal 43, Tom Wilkinson decided to go to the air. Montreal's defence forced Wilkinson to scramble but he was still able to spot Waddell Smith frantically waving his arms near the left side line. Smith made the catch, and steamed downfield. Realizing that he would score easily Smith waved bye-bye to the nearest Montreal defender Jim Marshall just before crossing the goal line.

After the game a smiling Smith described the touchdown: "I just ran two yards and turned. Their whole secondary over-rotated. They thought their line was going to sack Wilkie and ran in to help them. Wilkie, with all that experience though, got away and spotted me open. It was nothing from then on."

Montreal then scored two field goals prior to halftime, and another in the third quarter to take a brief 9 to 7 lead. Only six plays after Montreal's third field goal Warren Moon threw a 33-yard touchdown pass to Tom Scott on a post-corner pattern.

"I was working against Larry Uteck and we'd set him up in the first half with a lot of inside patterns toward the goalposts," Scott recounted after the game. "This time, I faked another of them. Uteck went for it and then I veered out toward the sidelines – a flag. Uteck was hurrying across a bit late, and Warren dropped the ball right into my hands." A Dave Cutler field goal made the score Edmonton 17, Montreal 9. There was still plenty of time remaining for the Alouettes to at least tie the game, and with two minutes to play it appeared that Montreal would send the game to overtime. However, a controversial clipping penalty against Montreal's Gerry Dattilio robbed Montreal's Keith Baker of a spectacular 85-yard touchdown on a punt return and preserved Edmonton's victory. Although television replays did not conclusively show that Dattilio had clipped Edmonton's Pete Lavorato, there was no doubt in the Edmonton player's mind that he had been illegally blocked. He stated, "I don't want to badmouth Montreal, but they have nothing to complain about. I was clipped. [Dattilio] got me from behind. I would have been able to tackle [Baker] if I wasn't blocked from the back.

"And if I hadn't tackled him, I definitely would have been able to turn him inside where one of my teammates would have gotten him. The clip allowed him to run to the outside, all the way to the end zone. It was just a dumb play the way I look at it," Lavorato continued. "How else can you

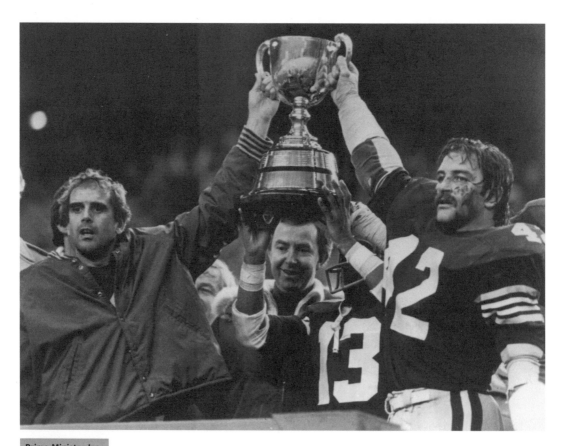

describe it? Well, on second thought, maybe Montreal figured there was nothing to lose, so they hit me from behind."

Despite Edmonton's victory all three stars came from the Alouettes. Don Sweet's three field goals earned him the selection as the game's outstanding Canadian, while teammate Tom Cousineau was picked as top defender. Cousineau was a tower of strength, the main reason why the explosive Edmonton offence was defused for the majority of the game. Cousineau punished every Edmonton ball carrier with his thunderous hits and made a key interception to end an Edmonton drive in the second quarter.

Germany termed Cousineau's performance "great", and added, "He earns every nickel he's paid. I've never played against a more punishing tackler."

Finally, the game's outstanding offensive player was David Green. Spearheading the Montreal attack, whenever the Alouettes were in danger Green single-handedly got them out. " ... Green is the complete back, isn't he?" Germany later said, "He runs outside and inside, he catches passes and he blocks. What more can the man do?"

On the day, Green gained 142 yards on 21 carries, and 30 yards on four receptions.

Montreal was unable to qualify for the 1980 final. The team deteriorated, and thus the Hamilton Tiger-Cats re-emerged as the eastern division champion. However, Hamilton, which finished the regular season with 8 wins, 7 losses, and 1 tie was no match for the powerful Eskimos. Edmonton outscored the Winnipeg Blue Bombers 34 to 24 in the western final, and then demolished Hamilton 48 to 10, on November 23, to capture another Cup.

The Eskimos put the game out of the reach of the Tiger-Cats early. After moving ahead 3 to 0, Warren Moon marched Edmonton 94 yards for a touchdown. A key play in the drive occurred when Moon unleashed a 55-yard bomb to Danny Buggs which put the ball on the Hamilton 1. On the next play, Jim Germany smashed through the line for the score.

Hamilton's Bernie Ruoff then kicked two field goals before Edmonton scored another major. Moon brilliantly utilized his scrambling ability to drive Edmonton to the Hamilton 1, and from there Germany charged into the end zone.

Shortly afterwards, Edmonton's Joe Holliman intercepted a David Marler pass to start another Edmonton scoring drive. Moon advanced the ball to the Edmonton 35, and then he came to the line ready to throw a short pass. However, Moon noticed that Hamilton's secondary was in man-to-man coverage. Moon audibled for a bomb.

Brian Kelly sprinted past Hamilton's David Shaw, and at the Hamilton 35 hauled in Moon's pass. Shaw gave chase, but Kelly easily outdistanced him for the score.

A dejected Shaw described Kelly's touchdown. "It was just a bad read on my part. I studied films on the receivers all last week and Kelly always cut to the inside. It was a nice move."

Meanwhile Kelly explained: "About the middle of the first quarter I figured I could go deep and I told Warren. When the right time came up he called the play and it worked. I just ran straight down … I just ran by the guy."

After Hamilton had made the score Edmonton 24, Hamilton 10, Edmonton buried the Tiger-Cats. Edmonton faked a punt in the third quarter, which led to a 48-yard gain by Neil Lumsden, and three plays later Moon passed to Scott for a 19-yard touchdown.

Then at the beginning of the fourth quarter, Edmonton embarked on its fifth touchdown drive. Moon flung the ball all over the field, and eventually he threw another short touchdown pass to Scott.

With Edmonton leading 41 to 10, the Tiger-Cats attempted to make the score look respectable. However, Hamilton's offence was unable to muster an attack, and near the end of the game Hamilton surrendered the ball to Edmonton on the Tiger-Cat 23-yard line. Three plays later, Tom Wilkinson (Moon's substitute) threw a third touchdown pass to Scott, giving him the record for most touchdowns received in a Cup.

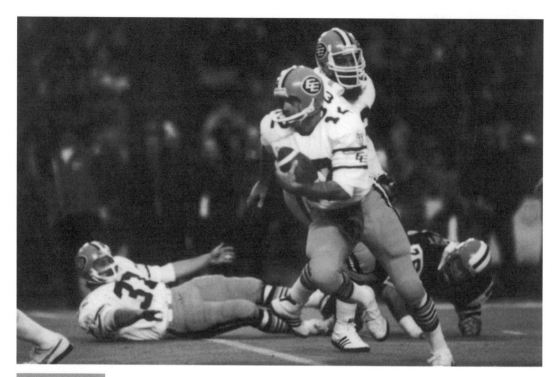

Taking charge in the 1980 final, Edmonton's Tom Wilkinson (No. 12) gains ground against the Hamilton Tiger-Cats. (CFL Photos)

When Wilkinson was asked if he deliberately threw that major to Scott to establish the record, the quarterback replied, "I was trying to spread the passes around when I came in at first, but at the end, yeah, I was going to Scottie. Actually, on the touchdown play, I was hoping to go underneath to Neil Lumsden. He was covered so I went to the secondary receiver, Scottie."

Cutler converted, and the game ended Edmonton 48, Hamilton 10.

The most brilliant player for Edmonton was Warren Moon. He made something happen every time. His passing game had Hamilton's secondary completely baffled, and when he could not find a receiver open, Moon confidently scrambled through gaping holes.

Hamilton defender Wayne Smith described Moon's performance best. "He was the star of the show. Our job was to contain him. And although I thought we put lots of pressure on him, he was able to elude us."

Moon's play in the 1980 game was perhaps his finest moment in a brief but illustrious C.F.L. career. He completed 21 of 33 passes for 398 yards, threw three touchdown passes, and ran seven times for 71 yards.

Another offensive star for Edmonton was Tom Scott. According to many fans, the 1980 final was a game of pitch-and-catch between Moon and Scott. The diminutive slotback seemed to be everywhere on the Exhibition Stadium turf, and on the day he caught 12 passes for 174 yards and three touchdowns.

After the game, Moon said of Scott, "I don't think there is a person in the league who can cover him one-on-one. When they blitz as much as Hamilton did today, they're going to leave people open one-on-one and it's my job to see it and hit him."

The last hero of the game was Edmonton's Dale Potter. A native of Ottawa and graduate of Hillcrest High School and the University of Ottawa, the six-foot, two-inch,

220-pound linebacker played fantastically. Throughout, he was a thorn in the side of the Tiger-Cats. Potter rushed Hamilton quarterbacks vigorously and often he dropped back into the secondary to cover potential receivers.

Potter's spectacular play earned him the selection as the game's outstanding Canadian player and the game's best defensive player. For the man who was credited with six tackles and three knockdowns, the awards were well deserved.

Dan Kepley: "Dale is the damnedest linebacker I know. He is the most consistent, unselfish, inspirational player we have on our club. He deserves these awards, just like he has deserved others."

## 1981 EDMONTON ESKIMOS 26
## OTTAWA ROUGH RIDERS 23

A year later the Eskimos returned to the Grey Cup ready to capture an unprecedented fourth consecutive title. To many western fans an Edmonton victory was assured well before the 1981 final. Canadian football had developed to a stage where the eastern teams were abysmal in comparison. In earlier years eastern teams and fans protested against having to play inferior western opponents, but now the tables were turned. However, unlike the times when the C.R.U. would listen to the eastern protests, Canadian football was now a professional sport and the C.F.L. was unable to arbitrarily change the playoff format to eliminate an East versus West Grey Cup final. Accordingly, when the 5 and 11 Ottawa Rough Riders won the eastern title on the strength of a 102-yard touchdown pass-and-run by Pat Stoqua, Ottawa was entitled to compete for the Grey Cup.

Ottawa entered the game as 22-point underdogs, but on November 22, 1981 the Rough Riders almost produced the greatest upset in Grey Cup history. Courageous Ottawa battled Edmonton to the final second before succumbing to the mighty Eskimos 26 to 23 in one of the best Cup games ever played.

Ottawa opened the scoring on its first possession. Quarterback Julius Caesar Watts drove his troops 62 yards to the Edmonton 27, and from there Gerry Organ gave the Riders a 3 to 0 lead.

Organ added another field goal, and then Ottawa surged further ahead with a touchdown when an interference penalty gave Ottawa possession on the Edmonton 5. Three plays later Jim Reid rammed into the end zone.

Ottawa continued to play brilliantly and early in the second quarter an interception by John Glassford created another scoring chance. From the Edmonton 38 Watts scrambled for 19 yards, and on the next play Sam Platt broke several tackles to score a touchdown. Organ kicked the convert, and Ottawa amazingly led 20 to 0.

At this point Tom Wilkinson took over at quarterback from a struggling Warren Moon. The change sparked Edmonton's offence, but it was able to score only one point before the end of the half.

In the third quarter Moon was reinserted at the helm of the Edmonton offence and he quickly engineered an Eskimos touchdown. A battering ground attack moved the ball to the Ottawa 2, and from there Jim Germany stormed across the Ottawa goal line.

Two plays later, disaster struck Ottawa's Grey Cup hopes. Edmonton blitzed Watts, who was drilled by Dan Kepley and James 'Quick' Parker. The ball came loose, and Dale Potter recovered on the Ottawa 3. A few plays later Moon scored, Dave Cutler kicked a convert and Edmonton trailed by only five points.

Midway through the fourth quarter Ottawa re-established a comfortable lead with a field goal, but minutes later Moon masterfully guided Edmonton downfield for another touchdown. Passes to Tom Scott, Marco Cyncar and Neil Lumsden moved the ball to the Ottawa 2 and from there Moon dove into the end zone. Edmonton tied the score on a 2-point conversion. Moon escaped a rush from Ottawa's Greg Marshall and completed a pass to Cyncar in the Ottawa end zone.

With time running out a controversial call destroyed Ottawa's dreams of winning the Grey Cup. From the Ottawa 33, Watts threw a 20-yarder to Tony Gabriel in the left flat as Edmonton's Gary Hayes shoved Gabriel and grabbed his jersey. The nearest official, Maury Mulhern, threw his penalty flag, while Gabriel made the catch and was tackled.

**The Edmonton Eskimos won the Cup in 1981, but Ottawa's J.C. Watts (No. 6) was the game's M.V.P.** (CFL Photos)

Ottawa fans cheered the reception, but soon they booed as the referee announced: "Penalty Ottawa and Edmonton. Pass interference." The penalty erased the gain, and shortly thereafter Edmonton moved the ball to the Ottawa 20 where Cutler kicked the game-winning field goal.

After the game Ottawa players blamed Mulhern's decision for Ottawa's 26 to 23 defeat. Gabriel, the victim of Hayes' blatant interference said, "I

had position ... he was over my back ... the call should have been against him. They called interference on him and then the officials went and had a conference and decided it was double interference – but I had inside position ... does the call make sense?"

Gabriel added, "If it was offensive pass interference they should have dropped the flag right away, not waited until I caught the ball ..."

Ottawa defensive tackle Mike Raines was infuriated. "A gutless call – a cop out," Raines boomed in the Ottawa clubhouse. "Here's a man [Gabriel] who's barely able to stand up. The defensive back pushes him off twice. Hell, I'd rather that Edmonton had blown us out of the park than have a call like that which cost us the game."

He continued, "There's no such thing as double pass interference. The official has to have the guts to call it one way or the other. I could accept it easier if the guy had only called interference on Tony. I've played in the league for seven years now and officiating has always been a problem. Something has to be done about them. They've got to run clinics or something for those guys. It's a shame the way it is and what's worse, it just cost me $5,000."

Raines concluded, "It was a gutless call. The officials were intimidated by the crowd and the Eskimos."

Under Rule 4 Section 3 Articles 1 and 2, and Rule 6 Section 4 Article 8(a) the double pass interference call was legitimate. Thus Ottawa's John Glassford was correct in disagreeing with his teammates when he said: "The officiating? It didn't lose the game for us. We lost the game ourselves."

**Despite the heart-breaking loss Ottawa's J.C. Watts was named the game's outstanding offensive player. For most of the game, especially the first 30 minutes, Watts had the Edmonton defence rattled with his passing and running. Watts was allowed to roam freely and was always able to execute the big play. Watts finished the game completing 16 of 29 passes for 204 yards, and he rushed the ball five times for 29 yards.**

**Ottawa's Glassford and Edmonton's Neil Lumsden excelled at their positions and accordingly Glassford was selected as the game's outstanding defensive player, while Lumsden was selected as the top Canadian.**

**However, the real stars in this game were Ottawa's Tony Gabriel and Edmonton's Tom Wilkinson. In their last Cup game these two Canadian football legends electrified the crowd and exemplified the spirit of the Grey Cup. Despite suffering from partially torn ligaments in his left knee and playing with a knee-brace, Gabriel was Ottawa's leading receiver with six catches for 76 yards.**

**Wilkinson's performance in the second quarter relaxed the Eskimos and showed Moon that Ottawa's defence could be solved. Wilkinson completed 10 of 13 passes for 80 yards, but his largest contribution came off the field. During the intermission Wilkinson gave a heart-felt pep talk which more than any individual player's performance in the 1981 Grey Cup game lifted Edmonton to victory.**

**"Tom reminded us who this season was for," said Edmonton defensive end David Boone, referring to former teammate Don Warrington, who was killed in a car accident**

a few months after the 1980 season had ended. "The last thing [Wilkinson] said before the second half was 'Give'er', which is what Don always said."

Inspired by Wilkinson's brief speech the Eskimos outscored Ottawa 25 to 3 in the last 30 minutes to win.

The contributions to Canadian football made by Gabriel and Wilkinson were recognized as each was inducted into the Canadian Football Hall of Fame.

## 1982 EDMONTON ESKIMOS 32
## TORONTO ARGONAUTS 16

On November 28, 1982 Edmonton won its fifth consecutive national title, this time against the rejuvenated Toronto Argonauts. After completing the 1981 season at 2 and 14 the Argonauts cleared decks and hired coaches Bob O'Billovich and Darrell 'Mouse' Davis. These two introduced the feared run-and-shoot offence to Canadian football, and gave Toronto a good chance of winning its first Cup in 30 years. However, Toronto missed out. Knowing that head coach Hugh Campbell was retiring from Canadian football and heading to the Los Angeles Express of the United States Football League, Edmonton destroyed Toronto 32 to 16.

The first half was wild. Edmonton jumped into a 3 to 0 lead, and then Toronto quarterback Condredge Holloway combined with Emanuel Tolbert for a spectacular touchdown. From the Toronto 24 Holloway escaped an Edmonton blitz and hit Tolbert with a short pass. Immediately, Dan Ferrone levelled Edmonton defender Larry Highbaugh and Tolbert was loose. The fleet-footed receiver then bounced off Dan Kepley and watched as teammate Terry Greer blazed across the field to make a thrilling block on another potential Edmonton tackler. Eighty-four yards later, Tolbert crossed the Edmonton goal line.

Warren Moon led Edmonton's reply. The ball was driven deep into Toronto's half of the field, and on the first play of the second quarter Moon rolled to his left, got outside Toronto's containment, and threw a touchdown pass to Brian Kelly.

Toronto answered this score quickly. Taking possession on the Toronto 28, Holloway engineered a 10-play touchdown series by utilizing his superb athletic ability. Holloway ran the ball four times for 30 yards, and on the last play avoided Edmonton's Tom Tuinei and threw to Greer for a touchdown. Dean Dorsey converted, so Toronto led 14 to 10.

Yet again the lead changed hands. Moon threw a deep pass to Kelly. Toronto's Darrell Wilson slipped on the play, and Kelly easily caught the pass to score. Before the end of the half, Edmonton moved the ball to the Toronto 22, enabling Dave Cutler to kick his second field goal and to give Edmonton a 20 to 14 lead.

Early in the third quarter Toronto's hard-hitting defence recovered an Edmonton fumble on its own 7, but on the next play the offence committed a turnover. Attempting to gain good yardage quickly, Holloway called

for a swing pass. Cedric Minter went in motion to create the classic imbalance of the run-and-shoot by having five receivers running patterns on the left side of the field. On the snap, Minter curled around and raced down the sideline. Holloway rolled left and then completed a pass to Minter. However, just beyond the Toronto 40-yard line Highbaugh jolted the Argonaut receiver. Minter straightened up, enabling Edmonton's Gary Hayes to reach in from behind Minter to strip the ball from his arms. Dan Kepley recovered the loose ball and advanced to the Toronto 34.

"That was the pivotal play," Argo head coach O'Billovich later recalled. "We had a big gain. If we had gone in to score, we would have been back on top. Instead, they took it in and scored."

Edmonton defender Hayes agreed that the fumble was vital. "I tried to jump and get the ball, but it just barely went over my finger tips. Right away, I was chasing [Minter]. I saw him try to fake Larry Highbaugh out. I came in from behind. Larry hit him and I think he was going down. I saw the ball under his [right] arm, and I was going for it. That's what we're always taught – let the first man make the tackle and let the second go for the ball. I brought my right hand up and kind of punched his arm."

Nine plays later on a third down gamble, Neil Lumsden bashed past John Pointer and dove over the goal line for a 2-yard major.

In the final quarter Edmonton's defence dominated. The Eskimo offence was always given good field position, and Cutler booted two more field goals. Toronto then closed the scoring when Hank Ilesic was forced to kick the ball across his own deadline. The 2-point safety brought the final score to Edmonton 32, Toronto 16.

In Edmonton's fifth consecutive Grey Cup victory the man of the game was Warren Moon. Playing very much as he did in the 1980 Grey Cup, Moon brilliantly guided the Eskimo offence using the passing game. In the second half, when the weather conditions worsened, Moon switched to a potent ground attack which ran the Argonauts out of C.N.E. Stadium. Moon finished with 21 completions in 33 passes for 319 yards. He was also the game's leading rusher (91 yards on nine carries).

Moon's play earned him the selection as the game's outstanding player and praise from Hugh Campbell. "What can you say about perfection?", Campbell said. "He ran, he passed, he did everything. In my book, no quarterback has so many strengths as Moon. I remember Russ Jackson for his toughness and his intelligence, Ron Lancaster for his intelligence and poise. Moon has all that and other qualities besides. Moon's performance was as good as I've seen in a Grey Cup game. He's got to be the No. 1 quarterback in football, tied with [the Pittsburgh Steelers'] Terry Bradshaw or [the San Francisco 49ers'] Joe Montana."

The game's other star was Dave Fennell. Together with David Boone, Fennell was instrumental in limiting the track-meet atmosphere Condredge Holloway and the Argonauts wanted to introduce. Constantly pressuring Holloway, Fennell helped Edmonton record seven quarterback sacks. Fennell was credited with 2½ of these sacks and barely missed five others.

Fennell's performance reminded many fans of Dale Potter's performance in the 1980 game. He was selected the game's outstanding defensive player and the game's outstanding Canadian.

A two-time Grey Cup M.V.P., Warren Moon (No. 1) lifted Edmonton to its fifth consecutive title in 1982. (CFL Photos)

Edmonton's five consecutive Grey Cup victories were an incredible feat. No other team in Canadian football history had ever won more than three in

a row and since 1982 no other team has won back-to-back championships.

However, Canadian football has changed dramatically since the Edmonton dynasty. In today's Canadian game players such as Tom Wilkinson, Warren Moon, Jim Germany, Tom Scott, Brian Kelly, Dave Cutler, Dale Potter, Dave Fennell and Dan Kepley, who were all key players in helping Edmonton win its Grey Cups, would very rarely remain on the same team for more than a few years. While many Canadian football fans have criticized this lack of continuity, the switching around of players like Matt Dunigan, Damon Allen, Doug Flutie and Danny Barrett has created more excitement and unpredictability in the C.F.L. These players and many others have produced some of the most spectacular Grey Cup games, including the greatest in history.

## Chapter Twelve

# HEADING TOWARD GREATNESS
## 1983-1988

**B**etween 1983 and 1988 Canadian football was turned upside down. The Edmonton Eskimo dynasty ended in 1983, and over the next several years every C.F.L. team made a determined effort to win the Grey Cup. The Toronto Argonauts, the Winnipeg Blue Bombers, the British Columbia Lions and the Hamilton Tiger-Cats all ended droughts.

While the Grey Cup games were spectacular, they were overshadowed by criticism of the C.F.L. The game in eastern Canada had been deteriorating prior to 1983 and had come under close scrutiny. The better western teams demanded that the playoff structure be changed to allow an extra western team into the playoffs if the western division's fourth place team compiled a better record than the eastern division's third place team. The C.F.L. eventually succumbed to the demands of the West, and thus in 1986 the fourth place Calgary Stampeders were awarded a playoff berth instead of the third place Montreal Alouettes.

Although the change in the playoff format was justifiable, its effect was disastrous on the league. The Montreal franchise, which had been experiencing organizational and financial troubles, could not afford to miss the 1986 playoffs. C.F.L. fans in Montreal lost interest in the Canadian game, and a year later the Alouettes folded. This left the East division with only three teams while the West division had five. Accordingly, the C.F.L. moved Winnipeg into the East. More criticism. Only in the C.F.L. was a team from a western city playing in a league's East division.

However, the critics should have concentrated less on geography and more on the play because these years brought two of the most exciting Grey Cup games of all time.

The 1983 Cup game was played between the Toronto Argonauts and the B.C. Lions on November 27. Toronto, making its second consecutive appearance, was looking to end a 31-year championship drought. However, football pundits were uncertain if Toronto could beat the Lions. The Argonauts encountered considerable difficulty with the Hamilton Tiger-Cats in the eastern final and barely won a high-scoring game as Cedric Minter plunged into the Hamilton end zone with only 27 seconds left to make the final score Toronto 41, Hamilton 36.

In the western final the Lions scored three touchdowns in the fourth quarter to maul the Winnipeg Blue Bombers 39 to 21. The Lions' explosive performance was expected to continue in the Grey Cup and to lead it to victory in the friendly confines of B.C. Place. However, Toronto's defence held up and another last quarter major by Minter gave the Argos an 18 to 17 victory.

After both teams started cautiously, the Lions opened the scoring late in the first quarter. Facing second down and short from the Toronto 47, B.C. quarterback Roy Dewalt surprised the Argos by throwing a bomb. Leroy Paul was unable to cover the shifty 'Swervin' Mervyn Fernandez, and the B.C. receiver made an over-the-shoulder catch for a touchdown.

**Joe Barnes (arm extended) came off of the bench in the 1983 final to lead the Argos to its first title in 30 years.**
(CFL Photos)

Midway through the second quarter Toronto retaliated. Quarterback Condredge Holloway drove Toronto to the B.C. 14, and from there dumped a screen pass to Jan Carinci. Toronto offensive guard Mike Hameluck and

offensive tackle John Malinosky anchored a blocking wall ahead of Carinci as he sprinted into the B.C. end zone.

The Lions soon scored again. A 24-yard pass to Fernandez took B.C. to the Toronto 20, and on the next play Dewalt threw successfully to John Henry White. Lui Passaglia converted, and before the end of the half he added a field goal to give B.C. a 17 to 7 lead.

In the third quarter Toronto began to take control of the game. The defence intercepted two passes and recovered a fumble to provide the Argos with three field goal opportunities. However, Hank Ilesic was unable to capitalize on the chances and Toronto entered the fourth quarter trailing 17 to 9.

Ilesic was displeased with his poor kicking effort, and thus switched shoes on his left foot.

"I was having problems with my other one, not the kicking shoe," Ilesic explained. "I was slipping and that was causing me to reach for the ball. I had [equipment manager] Jeff Howe go back into the dressing room and bring me my old shoe."

Changing footwear worked. Toronto marched the ball into B.C. territory, and from the B.C. 43 Ilesic split the uprights to make the score B.C. 17, Toronto 12.

For the next few minutes neither team threatened. Then, with less than five minutes remaining the Lions defence collapsed. With Toronto in possession on its own 53 back-up quarterback Joe Barnes called a 90 series play. This meant that he was going to take a three-step drop and fire rapidly to the first open receiver. On this play, though, the first such receiver, Paul Pearson, did not get the ball. Although Barnes blazed a pass to Pearson, B.C. halfback Mel Byrd levelled the Argonaut just as the ball arrived. The ball flew out of Pearson's grasp, but miraculously into the arms of Emanuel Tolbert for a first down.

"There's no time to think in that situation, you just react," Tolbert later explained. "It popped up and I grabbed it. I don't really remember too much else about it."

Two plays later Pearson made a twisting circus-like catch on the B.C. 5. From there Barnes rolled out to the left, and looped a short pass to Cedric Minter for a major.

Minter recalled the play. "They had a rover [Kevin Konar] on me and he got kind of caught up on the inside. I just went into the flat and backed into the end zone. The ball seemed to hang up there forever. Everything stopped. I didn't see anybody else or even hear anything."

Toronto's 2-point conversion attempt failed, leaving the score Toronto 18, B.C. 17, and the Lions still had a chance to win. But Toronto's defence prevented B.C. from getting into scoring range, and so after 31 years the Argos won another Grey Cup.

**In a losing effort B.C.'s Rick Klassen played an outstanding game. On many occasions, together with Ruben Vaughan and Mack Moore, he burst into the Toronto**

backfield to pressure or sack Argo quarterbacks. For his effort Klassen was chosen the game's top Canadian.

The game's outstanding defensive player was Carl Brazley. Released by the Ottawa Rough Riders and the Buffalo Bills in 1983, Brazley brought his talents to the Argos. Brazley was never far from the ball. He had his receivers covered like a blanket, and made an interception and a fumble recovery. In addition, Brazley ran back punts and kick-offs.

And then there was Joe Barnes. Replacing an ailing Condredge Holloway in the second half, the 32-year-old Texan was able to get Toronto's sluggish offence untracked. He spread the Lions' defence wide with his scrambling ability and threw the ball sharply. The Lions could not prevent Barnes from marching the Argos down-field and eventually he was able to lead Toronto to victory.

"He changed the whole tempo of the ball game," Lions' defensive tackle Moore later said. "When he came into the game, he got Toronto's offensive line excited and they started coming off the ball. Then Barnes found a couple of soft spots in our defence and he went to work on them. He was the difference."

Barnes completed 14 of 24 passes for 175 yards, and ran three times for 36 yards to become the star.

## 1984 WINNIPEG BLUE BOMBERS 47 HAMILTON TIGER-CATS 17

Toronto's hopes of repeating a year later were quashed in the low-scoring 1984 eastern final. The Hamilton Tiger-Cats, led by Dieter Brock, forced Toronto to overtime and upset the Boatmen 14 to 13. Meanwhile in the western final the Winnipeg Blue Bombers soared to victory. Winnipeg quarterback Tom Clements and receiver James Murphy were incredible in that game as Winnipeg easily outscored the B.C. Lions 31 to 14. On the strength of this victory Winnipeg was expected to demolish Hamilton. On the other hand, with the game-day temperature at minus 11 degrees Celsius (12 degrees Fahrenheit) and Edmonton's Commonwealth Stadium frozen solid many believed that the Tiger-Cats would upset the Bombers. Winnipeg did have difficulties in the early going, but Hamilton's defence was unable to prevent Clements from winning his second Grey Cup title as the Bombers blasted Hamilton 47 to 17 in the Tundra Bowl.

The Tiger-Cats started ferociously. Scrimmaging from its own 16, Hamilton marched the ball downfield in nine plays. Passes of 40 and 11 yards to Rocky DiPietro put Hamilton into scoring position, and then from the Winnipeg 15 Brock found a huge hole for a touchdown.

Three minutes later Felix Wright intercepted a Clements pass to put Hamilton in scoring position again. The Tiger-Cats advanced the ball to the Winnipeg 7, and from there Brock passed to DiPietro for a major. Bernie Ruoff converted and Hamilton led 14 to 0.

The turning point of the game occurred midway through the second quarter. With Hamilton leading 17 to 6, Brock floated a poor pass toward

Winnipeg's Tom Clements (No. 2) looks into the backfield after accepting a snap from centre in the 1984 Cup. Winnipeg crushed the Hamilton Tiger-Cats 47 to 17. (CFL Photos)

Rufus Crawford from deep inside Hamilton territory. Winnipeg's David Shaw intercepted and four plays later Willard Reaves blasted through the line for a touchdown. Shaw described his interception: "We were in cover three. That's when we have three men deep and I have the responsibility of covering the deep half. I got the slotback and the running back. What I did was kinda bait Dieter. He thought I was playing man-to-man. I came up on Ron Johnson and Dieter felt Rufus would be open. But my responsibility was really to cover Rufus. Dieter threw the ball up, but it really didn't have any zip on it. I might have made the play, but it would have been a knockdown."

Winnipeg on its next possession took the lead. Clements guided the Bombers close to the Hamilton goal line, and then fired a pass to Joe Poplawski. Two Hamilton defenders could not stop him from scoring.

Thirty-six seconds later, the Bombers produced another major. Winnipeg's Tyrone Jones levelled Brock and forced a fumble. Stan Mikawos collected the loose ball, to be escorted by a squadron of teammates to the end zone.

After the game, Brock said, "Yeah, that [fumble] was a big mistake … a breakdown in the blocking. We've had some of those this year. But I don't blame the guys. All year long, there have been so many changes we didn't have the same people together long enough to become a unit."

Trevor Kennerd converted the score, and shortly thereafter he kicked his third field goal to make the halftime score Winnipeg 30, Hamilton 17.

Hamilton's offence disappeared in the second half and Winnipeg was able to pad its lead. Kennerd added another field goal in the third quarter, and in the fourth Reaves and Jeff Boyd scored converted touchdowns to end the game Winnipeg 47, Hamilton 17.

The game's outstanding offensive player was Tom Clements. He mixed his plays with the skills of an alchemist and often exploited the short flats by forcing the Hamilton linebackers to cover the Winnipeg receivers which left its running backs uncovered. Clements finished the game completing 20 of 29 passes for 281 yards, and scoring a touchdown.

Sean Kehoe also played brilliantly for the Blue Bombers. A graduate of the University of Alberta, Kehoe played the best game of his C.F.L. career. Two pass receptions by Kehoe led to Winnipeg's first score, and later in the game Kehoe contributed to Reaves' first touchdown by making a key reception which took the ball to the Hamilton 3. Kehoe then made another key catch a few plays prior to Poplawski's touchdown. Finally, just before half-time, Kehoe returned a punt 30 yards to set up another Winnipeg score. After the game Hamilton's Rufus Crawford said, "The main thing that killed us today were those little passes to Kehoe. We tried playing a linebacker against him on that play, but they simply couldn't stay with him."

Tom Clements added, "Sean came through with some big runs and played a great game for us."

Kehoe was the game's leading rusher with 89 yards on 12 carries. He also caught five passes for 47 yards, and was selected as the game's outstanding Canadian.

The third hero of the game and the game's outstanding defensive player was Winnipeg's Tyrone Jones. He was all over Hamilton's Dieter Brock, and forced the fumble which led to Stan Mikawos' touchdown. In addition he recorded four quarterback sacks and was credited with seven unassisted tackles.

# 1985 B.C. LIONS 37
HAMILTON TIGER-CATS 24

Hamilton sought to avenge its 1984 defeat against its 1985 opponent, the B.C. Lions. However, B.C. was extremely explosive. The Lions whipped the defending champion Bombers 42 to 22 in the western final, and then blasted the Tiger-Cats 37 to 24 to capture its second Grey Cup title.

B.C. started strongly, and on its second possession produced the opening score. Scrimmaging from the B.C. 26, quarterback Roy Dewalt threw a long pass to Ned Armour. The pass was slightly short but Armour outmuscled Less Browne to make the catch. Browne then tripped and Armour, the former San Diego State track star, raced downfield for a touchdown.

After the game Browne lamented, "I had my hand on that ball but it was the wrong hand and [the ball] popped into his hands."

B.C. increased its lead to 13 to 0 and then in the second quarter Hamilton's Grover Covington recovered a fumble to give the Tiger-Cats possession on the B.C. 49. Another three plays, and Hamilton's Ron Ingram made a spectacular leaping catch to score a 33-yard major.

Hamilton scored again. From inside his territory quarterback Ken Hobart electrified the crowd with a 61-yard dash, and a few plays later Johnny Shepherd dove over the B.C. defensive line to score from one yard out. Bernie Ruoff kicked the convert and Hamilton led 14 to 13.

The opening score in 1985 as B.C.'s Ned Armour (No. 8) wards off Hamilton's Less Browne (No. 15). (CFL Photos)

Hamilton looked to hold this lead until halftime, but near the end of the second quarter came a vital moment. With B.C. in punt formation Hamilton's Mitchell Price broke through the line and headed toward Lui Passaglia. Forced to run, Passaglia smartly gained 12 yards to give B.C. a first down. On the next play Dewalt combined with Armour for his second touchdown.

B.C. head coach Don Matthews later exulted: "That [run by Passaglia] saved us ... it took the momentum away from Hamilton."

With the score B.C. 29, Hamilton 17, the Lions sealed the victory on one of the most bizarre plays in Grey Cup history. From the B.C. 44, Dewalt gunned a deep pass to Jim Sandusky. The ball was off target, but Hamilton's Paul Bennett stuck a hand into the air and deflected the ball directly into Sandusky's arms. Unsurprised by his good fortune, Sandusky headed for paydirt without breaking a stride.

"I was in shock," Hamilton's Donovan Rose, who was five feet from the reception, later said, "I couldn't believe it because I didn't think he had any chance at all to catch the ball. I guess it was fate."

Bennett agreed. "That was sad. I had three fingers up. The ball just changed direction when I touched it. I heard the cheering but I didn't know what was up until I saw Sandusky scooting for the goal line."

Near the end of the game Hamilton's Steve Stapler scored a converted touchdown and Passaglia added a single to end the game B.C. 37, Hamilton 24.

**The two stars of the game were B.C.'s Roy Dewalt and Lui Passaglia. Dewalt's quarterbacking was amazing. His passing was sharp and snappy, and his play calling alert. Throughout the game, the 29-year-old pivot confused the Hamilton defence with his play selection and this allowed him to throw three touchdowns.**

**"I never expected this kind of game," lamented Hamilton middle linebacker Ben Zambiasi afterward. "We stopped them but we got beat on three big plays and that really surprises me. Dewalt couldn't have thrown those balls better. We've survived in the past on forcing turnovers on defence but Dewalt never gave us a chance."**

Dewalt completed 14 of 28 passes for 394 yards, and was named the game's outstanding offensive player.

Passaglia, a 10-year C.F.L. veteran, gave an excellent kicking performance. He averaged 41.2 yards per punt, and booted five field goals, three converts, and a single. His most important contribution to B.C.'s victory was his 12-yard run. It inspired his teammates, and disheartened the Tiger-Cats. A dejected Al Bruno later said, "There is no doubt that Passaglia changed the momentum of the game with that play. On that one play he could have been the player of the game ... He made one helluva move to get out of there." Passaglia was chosen the game's outstanding Canadian.

## 1986 HAMILTON TIGER-CATS 39 EDMONTON ESKIMOS 15

A year later, Hamilton gained its third consecutive opportunity to win the Grey Cup. After trailing by 26 points in the two-game total points eastern final, Hamilton and Mike Kerrigan engineered an incredible comeback. With a C.F.L. playoff record 35 of 47 passes for 364 yards in the second game, he led Hamilton to a 59 to 56 total point victory against the Toronto Argonauts.

The Tiger-Cats' momentum carried over into the 1986 Cup on November 30. Hamilton completely outplayed the western champion Edmonton Eskimos in the final, 39 to 15.

Hamilton roared to victory early in the first quarter with the assistance of some excellent work by its defence. Grover Covington forced Edmonton quarterback Matt Dunigan to fumble and on the next play Kerrigan threw a 39-yard touchdown to Steve Stapler.

A few minutes later Hamilton's Mark Streeter blocked an Edmonton punt, and Jim Rockford recovered the ball in the Eskimos' end zone for a touchdown. Paul Osbaldiston added the convert and then kicked five consecutive field goals to make the half-time score Hamilton 29, Edmonton 0.

In the third quarter Hamilton increased its huge lead on its first possession. Scrimmaging from the Hamilton 32, Kerrigan engineered a six-play drive culminating in a 44-yard touchdown pass to Ingram.

At last Edmonton scored its first points of the game. After surrendering the ball on the Hamilton 11 due to a failed third down gamble, Larry Wruck blocked an Osbaldiston punt to give the Eskimos possession on the Hamilton 37. From there Edmonton moved the ball 31 yards and then back-up quarterback Damon Allen rolled out and steamed into the Hamilton end zone.

Hamilton's defence continued to play extremely well. It stopped another Edmonton third down gamble deep in its own zone, and prevented Edmonton from scoring until late in the fourth quarter when Brian Kelly caught an 11-yard touchdown pass from Allen. With 24 seconds left in the game Osbaldiston tied a Grey Cup record with his sixth field goal to end the game Hamilton 39, Edmonton 15.

Hamilton's Mike Kerrigan instructs his teammates during the 1986 final. (Photo by Art Martin)

Although Paul Osbaldiston scored 21 points in this Grey Cup game and was selected as the game's outstanding Canadian, the game's most outstanding offensive player was Hamilton quarterback Mike Kerrigan. A product of Northwestern University and a cast-off of the New England Patriots, Kerrigan mercilessly ripped apart Edmonton's secondary. The Eskimos had expected that Kerrigan would use a lot of short passes, but instead he exploited Edmonton's deep zones. Kerrigan completed 15 of 32 passes for 304 yards and two touchdowns.

Defensively, the single most-destructive player on the field was 30-year-old Grover Covington. Together with Mike Walker, David Sauve and Mitchell Price, Covington controlled the game. He recorded three sacks, recovered one fumble, and created three turnovers. For his effort Covington was selected as the game's outstanding defensive player.

## 1987 EDMONTON ESKIMOS 38
TORONTO ARGONAUTS 36

On November 29, 1987 Canadian football celebrated its 75th Grey Cup game. Every C.F.L. team wanted to be involved, but only the Edmonton Eskimos and the Toronto Argonauts qualified. Edmonton had blasted B.C. 31 to 5 in the western final, while Toronto had sailed past Winnipeg 19 to 3 in the eastern final. Edmonton and Toronto were evenly matched teams and they combined to produce one of the most thrilling Cup games in history. The teams traded touchdowns and field goals until eventually Edmonton's Jerry Kauric kicked a last-minute field goal to give the Eskimos a 38 to 36 victory.

The first scoring play of the 75th classic was unbelievable. Toronto's Lance Chomyc missed his second field goal of the game, and Edmonton's Henry 'Gizmo' Williams collected the ball five yards deep in his own end zone. Argo tacklers charged toward Williams, and he raced to his right. With tacklers mirroring his move, Williams shifted into overdrive, blazing around the corner and speeding down the sideline to leave a group of would-be tacklers stranded. Near midfield Williams slanted in a long diagonal to the opposite side of the field. Soon the only man between Williams and the Toronto end zone was Chomyc. The Toronto kicker chugged across the field to try to cut off Williams, but the Edmonton runner sprinted past and set a Grey Cup record for the longest uninterrupted touchdown run, 115 yards.

Over the next few minutes the teams exchanged field goals, and then from the Toronto 49 Gilbert Renfroe threw a 61-yard touchdown pass to Gill 'The Thrill' Fenerty.

Toronto's Darnell Clash soon afterwards intercepted a Matt Dunigan pass which led to another Argo score. Renfroe moved the ball 73 yards in nine plays to the Edmonton 5, and from there Fenerty followed the blocking of guard Randy Ambrosie and offensive tackle Kelvin Pruenster to put Toronto ahead 16 to 10. Chomyc converted Fenerty's touchdown, and then Doug 'Tank' Landry increased the Argos' lead when he recovered a Dunigan fumble and roared 54 yards for a touchdown.

Toronto appeared to be in charge until with less than two minutes remaining in the second quarter Edmonton blocked a punt and obtained possession on the Toronto 39. A few plays later substitute Edmonton pivot Damon Allen completed a touchdown pass to Marco Cyncar. Kauric added the extra point and the half ended Toronto 24, Edmonton 17.

Toronto held on to a 27 to 21 lead through the third quarter, but on the first play of the fourth quarter Allen threw 15 yards to Brian Kelly for a major and Kauric converted to give Edmonton a one-point lead. However, eight plays later Chomyc kicked a 32-yard field goal to put Toronto ahead again. Back and forth moved the lead, Edmonton rebounding with a 17-yard touchdown on a bootleg by Allen. Then Danny Barrett marched the ball to the Edmonton 25 from where he burst through a gaping hole for a touchdown.

After the game Barrett described his touchdown. "I told the guys if they could hold their blocks for an extra half second or so that I figured I could score," Barrett said. "They did and after that it was just a matter of not getting too excited and tripping over my own feet."

Toronto's 2-point convert attempt failed, and a few minutes later Kauric kicked the game-winning field goal with 45 seconds remaining. *Ottawa Citizen* reporter Earl McRae asked, "Jerry, the pressure; how did you deal with the pressure on the big kick?"

"The pressure was there," Kauric softly replied, "but I went in knowing I had to make it. We were behind, this was the one. The snap was there, the pin placement was there, I made it."

**Record-setter: On a missed Toronto field goal, Henry Williams of the Edmonton Eskimos thrilled the 1987 Cup crowd with a 115-yard touch-down return.** (Photo by John E. Sokolowski)

McRae: "What were the last words you heard before you went out to kick the field goal?"

"You won't believe it," Kauric explained. "Coach [Joe] Faragalli said, 'Son, there's no pressure on this one'."

Despite Kauric's game-winning field goal, the hero of Edmonton's 38 to 36 triumph was Damon Allen. Replacing the injured Matt Dunigan in the second quarter Allen, the younger brother of National Football League star Marcus Allen, put on one of the greatest quarterbacking performances of all the Grey Cups by dismantling Toronto's defence. He was the picture of professionalism and never panicked. In the latter stages of the fourth quarter, Allen maintained his composure and coolly marched the Eskimos into Toronto territory for the game-winning field goal.

Allen completed 15 of 20 passes, the highest passing percentage in Grey Cup history, for 255 yards and he ran six times for 46 yards.

After the game, Toronto's Doug Landry said, "[Allen] was the man. We took away [wide receivers] Brian Kelly and Stephen Jones. They were not a factor, but Allen made the difference."

The game's other offensive star, and the most valuable Canadian, was Edmonton's Milson Jones. He was a workhorse, and often rammed through the Toronto defence to gain valuable yardage. In the fourth quarter, Jones broke three tackles for 14 yards and set up Kauric's final field goal. Jones finished the game gaining 76 yards on nine carries.

The last Grey Cup game of this period was as thrilling as the 1987 final. On November 27, 1988 the Winnipeg Blue Bombers and the B.C. Lions battled ferociously for the title. The teams were tied entering the fourth quarter, and then Trevor Kennerd gave Winnipeg a 3-point lead. Winnipeg's defence was playing brilliantly and held off two last-minute B.C. offensive thrusts to win the game 22 to 21.

After falling behind 1 to 0, the Lions jumped into the lead midway through the first quarter. Starting on the B.C. 35, Matt Dunigan advanced the ball to the Winnipeg 14, and from there Anthony Cherry rambled into the Winnipeg end zone for a touchdown.

Two field goals by Kennerd tied the game. In the second quarter B.C. retook the lead by keeping the ball primarily on the ground, gaining 48 yards in five plays to put the ball on the Winnipeg 26. Two plays later, Dunigan threw the ball to David Williams, who streaked across the middle for a major.

Winnipeg answered this score immediately. The Bombers swiftly moved play to the B.C. 35 where James Murphy told quarterback Sean Salisbury, "I can beat those guys on the post." Salisbury nodded and on the next play he completed a pass to Murphy. B.C.'s Rick Ryan and Andre Francis converged only to collide with each other rather than with Murphy, who sprinted across the B.C. goal line untouched.

" ... We had an in-route called," Murphy later explained, "and I just broke into the seam about 18 yards downfield. I could see I had a lot of room, so I just started running ..."

B.C.'s Lui Passaglia missed a 41-yard field goal and the half ended with B.C. 15, Winnipeg 14.

B.C. extended its lead by three early in the third quarter and then, facing a third down on its own 21, B.C. coach Larry Donovan made one of the worst decisions in Grey Cup history. Needing 1½ yards, Donovan gambled. Dunigan was instructed to carry the ball, but Winnipeg's Michael Gray slammed violently into him and held him short of the first down. Three plays later Kennerd kicked a field goal to make the score B.C. 18, Winnipeg 17.

After the game, Winnipeg linebacker James 'Wild' West said, "I was shocked when they went for it at their own [21]-yard line. They needed more than a yard. It was at least a yard-and-a-half. They figured they could run on us. We thought that was a big insult. The really stupid part was that they tried a quarterback sneak. Man, that was dumb. As soon as we stopped them, I knew we'd win."

Donovan: "I was told [by assistant coach Adam Rita] that we only needed a yard. If I'd known it was more I wouldn't have gone for it, [but] I made the decision. I have to live with that."

Winnipeg's defence produced two more brilliant plays, first blocking a Passaglia field goal, and then cornerback Rod Hill intercepting an errant pass and returning the ball to the B.C. 26. The interception resulted in a single point, and the teams entered the final quarter tied 18 to 18.

Early in the fourth quarter the teams exchanged singles before Winnipeg's Bob Cameron took charge. His punting drove B.C. back into its own zone and, with less than five minutes to play, B.C. was forced to scrimmage from under its own goal posts. The B.C. offence was unable to move the ball, and on third down Passaglia punted. The kick was good, but a no-yards penalty against the Lions gave Winnipeg possession on the B.C. 27. Kennerd kicked his fourth field goal on the third play following to give Winnipeg a 3-point lead.

The Lions then marched the ball downfield but at the Winnipeg 7 Gray made the defensive play of the game. As Dunigan tried to force a line-drive pass to Jan Carinci, Gray flung his arm skyward. He deflected the ball, and at the 3-yard line Winnipeg's Bennie Thompson batted the ball up in the air for Gray to pluck it from the sky for the interception.

Dunigan lamented, "It was an over-under play for us. Jan Carinci was the receiver underneath and he was open. I threw a strike. It was going to be for a touchdown. I was going for the win and that play was a touchdown. But I sure didn't expect that pass to be tipped and then intercepted."

Gray also did not expect the interception. "This would never happen again," he said. "Never. If you had to sketch out the perfect scenario, this would be it. I still can't believe it happened."

Cameron later conceded a 2-point safety to close the scoring at Winnipeg 22, B.C. 21.

The game's outstanding offensive player was Winnipeg's James Murphy. Every time Winnipeg mounted a sustained scoring attack Murphy was involved. In the first quarter, his 71-yard reception resulted in Winnipeg's only touchdown of the game. Murphy finished the game with five receptions for 165 yards.

Another offensive star for Winnipeg was Bob Cameron. Despite kicking into a strong 40-60 kilometre-per-hour (25-37 miles-per-hour) wind for half of the game Cameron produced one of the best punting performances ever seen in a Grey Cup. He averaged 41 yards per kick, and was selected as the game's outstanding Canadian. According to Winnipeg's Michael Gray it was an award Cameron richly deserved. "Bob was consistent for us all year," Gray said. "He should have been our most valuable player because he kept us out of trouble. That's what he did today. That's why he's the best punter in the league."

The third star was Gray. The anchor of Winnipeg's defensive line, he was key to the two biggest defensive plays of the game. In the third quarter he stuffed Dunigan to prevent a third down conversion at the B.C. 20, while in the fourth quarter he intercepted a Dunigan pass on the Winnipeg 3 to preserve Winnipeg's victory. For his efforts, Gray was selected as the game's most outstanding defensive player.

Defensive tackle Michael Gray thrusts the ball skyward. In the 1988 final Gray's outstanding defensive play propelled Winnipeg to a thrilling 22 to 21 victory against B.C. (Photo by John E. Sokolowski)

The excitement generated by the Grey Cup games in this period, especially the 1987 and 1988 games, was much needed for Canadian football. The C.F.L. was perplexed by the collapse of the Montreal franchise and seemed unable to promote a game which only a decade before had been extremely popular. The media had lost confidence in the game, but the players and many fans were still unwilling to give up on one of Canada's greatest sport institutions. Loyal fans continued to support the game, and they would soon be rewarded as Canadian football headed toward greatness following the 1988 Grey Cup game. In 1989 came the finest of all Grey Cups, and with the arrival of new stars and a fresh direction following the appointment of Larry Smith as Commissioner in 1992, the C.F.L. expanded for the first time into the United States.

## Chapter Thirteen

# GREATNESS AND BEYOND

## 1989-1996

T he most recent years in the history of Canadian football have been filled with both anxiety and excitement. While many football critics have proclaimed week after week that the C.F.L. would soon go the way of the dinosaur, the level of play on Canadian football fields has been electrifying. The 1989 Grey Cup game was the greatest ever played, and the excitement generated by that game was sustained in the other Cup games from 1990 through 1996. The spectacular play of Kent Austin, Tony Champion, Tom Burgess, Raghib 'Rocket' Ismail, Matt Dunigan, Doug Flutie, David Sapunjis, Damon Allen and Lui Passaglia provided an impetus for expansion of the Canadian brand of football into the United States, and showed that the Grey Cup championship could still be one of the greatest sports institutions in North America.

## 1989 SASKATCHEWAN ROUGHRIDERS 43 HAMILTON TIGER-CATS 40

The 1989 classic featured Hamilton Tiger-Cats and Saskatchewan Roughriders. Each team had upset favoured playoff opponents en route to the final, and thus it was impossible for the massive crowd at Toronto's Skydome on Sunday, November 26 to predict the outcome. The teams were evenly matched and it was not until the final seconds that a winner was decided, as from the Hamilton 26, Dave Ridgway kicked the most memorable field goal in Grey Cup history to give Saskatchewan a thrilling 43 to 40 victory.

The early part of the first quarter was dominated by the Tiger-Cats. Hamilton kicker Paul Osbaldiston, presented with two field goal opportunities, easily gave Hamilton a 6 to 0 lead. Then after Saskatchewan scored a single, Hamilton quarterback Mike Kerrigan's brilliant aerial assault drove the Tiger-Cats 65 yards in 7 plays, a drive capped by a touchdown pass to Tony Champion. The Hamilton receiver ran to the corner of the Saskatchewan end zone, fended-off Harry Skipper and made the reception.

In the second quarter the teams combined for five touchdowns. Early on, Saskatchewan reduced Hamilton's 13 to 1 lead through quarterback Kent Austin. Three passes moved the ball to the Hamilton 5, with Austin completing a touchdown pass to Ray Elgaard.

A minute later Hamilton scored its second touchdown. With the ball near the Saskatchewan 30, Kerrigan read a Roughrider blitz perfectly. While Saskatchewan defenders poured through the line, Kerrigan quickly tossed a short pass to Derrick McAdoo, who caught the ball over the middle and raced into the Saskatchewan end zone.

This touchdown was immediately followed by an equally spectacular major. On the next play from scrimmage, Austin threw a deep pass to Jeff Fairholm. Hamilton defender Will Lewis was stride-for-stride with him, but as the ball arrived Fairholm gained the inside position. Lewis tried to knock Fairholm down yet Fairholm, stumbling and nearly falling on his face, made the catch. He then shook free of Lewis and bolted into the Hamilton end zone on a 76-yard pass-and-run.

The Tiger-Cats bounced back. Relying on the running of McAdoo, Kerrigan marched Hamilton 70 yards in eight plays. Then from the Saskatchewan 1 McAdoo plunged across the goal line to complete the drive.

Saskatchewan scored the final points of the first half on its next series. With Hamilton receiver Earl Winfield substituting for the injured Lance Shields at cornerback, Austin exploited Winfield's area for several completions. Saskatchewan moved play to the Hamilton 5, and from there Austin threw a touchdown pass to Don Narcisse. Ridgway converted the major, and the half ended Hamilton 27, Saskatchewan 22.

In the third quarter the combatants exchanged field goals before Saskatchewan narrowed the Hamilton lead. Osbaldiston had to leap high into the air to corral a Rae Robirtis snap in the Hamilton end zone and the Hamilton kicker was compelled to concede a safety.

Saskatchewan charged ahead. Two plays after the safety, Narcisse zig-zagged across the field for a gain of 52 yards. Then Hamilton's Sonny Gordon was penalized for pass interference in the Hamilton end zone. This gave Saskatchewan possession on the Hamilton 1 and from there Tim McCray dove across the goal line.

In the fourth quarter two field goals by Ridgway, and a field goal by Osbaldiston took the score to Saskatchewan 40, Hamilton 33. Less than two minutes remained in the game, and Hamilton desperately sought a touchdown to keep alive its hopes of winning the national title. Scrimmaging at the Hamilton 35, Kerrigan engineered another long drive. A pass interference penalty against Saskatchewan's Steve Wiggins put the ball on the Saskatchewan 11, and three plays later Kerrigan threw the ball to Champion.

Hamilton's Tony Champion makes an acrobatic catch to tie the 1989 Cup 40 to 40. Saskatchewan won 43 to 40. (Photo by Art Martin)

The ball was high, but Champion maintained his concentration, spun, stretched and made the most spectacular touchdown reception of all Grey Cups as he dove backwards in midair. Osbaldiston kicked the extra point and the game was tied 40 to 40!

Overtime loomed. However, there was just enough time for Saskatchewan to move the ball into scoring range. Utilizing a hurry-up offence, Austin completed passes to Elgaard and to Mark Guy, and Saskatchewan had possession on the Hamilton 26. With less than 10 seconds on the clock, Saskatchewan attempted a 33-yard field goal. While Hamilton called a time out to plot its strategy, Ridgway and Glen Suitor chatted. "I went to Glen and told him to talk to me about something other than football," Ridgway said later. "The kick was the last thing I wanted to talk about at that time. So, we talked about camping. I've never been camping, so he said he would take me and let the bears eat me. I started to laugh … It settled me down, but as soon as we lined up I was nervous again."

Ridgway took a deep breath, and prepared to kick. As he waited for the snap a thought flashed through Ridgway's mind: "I said [to myself] don't hit the upright and have it go for nothing. If I missed I wanted it to go far enough that it would go at least deep enough to force them to try to punt it back out."

Ridgway didn't have to worry. He accurately drilled the ball between the uprights, and Saskatchewan won the game 43 to 40.

After the game a jubilant Ridgway told reporters, "I was just glad to see it go through."

This incredible game produced many heroes. For Hamilton receiver Tony Champion was brilliant, despite playing most of the game with broken ribs. Whenever the Tiger-Cats needed a big play, Champion provided it. He caught eight passes for 106 yards, including the magnificent late fourth quarter touchdown. If Hamilton had won the 1989 Grey Cup game, then Champion would have been chosen the game's outstanding offensive player.

Instead the honour went to Saskatchewan quarterback Kent Austin. A native of Nantick, Mississippi, the 26-year-old quarterback surgically dissected Hamilton's defensive secondary. Once Austin found a groove in the second quarter, Hamilton was unable to stop the Saskatchewan aerial attack. Austin was brilliant throughout the game, and his skills shone brightly in the final 44 seconds when he drove Saskatchewan 56 yards to set up Ridgway's game-winning field goal. Austin finished the game completing 26 of 41 passes for 474 yards.

Dave Ridgway and Chuck Klingbeil also stood out for their performances. Ridgway performed remarkably under pressure, and kicked four converts and four field goals. Accordingly, he was chosen the game's outstanding Canadian. Klingbeil was the game's outstanding defensive player. He recorded three sacks, including one which resulted in a 20-yard loss, and had two unassisted tackles.

## 1990 WINNIPEG BLUE BOMBERS 50 EDMONTON ESKIMOS 11

The excitement generated by Saskatchewan's 1989 Grey Cup victory continued through the 1990 C.F.L. season and playoffs. Led by Tom Burgess, the Winnipeg team was determined to reclaim the Grey Cup. Winnipeg compiled a 12 and 6 regular season record, and then disposed of the Toronto Argonauts in a thrilling eastern final. With less than 30 seconds remaining in a tied game, Burgess scrambled for 31 yards. This put Winnipeg on the Toronto 32, and from there Trevor Kennerd kicked the game-winning field goal.

Edmonton Eskimos and Calgary Stampeders battled in the western final. Calgary desperately wanted to end its 19-year absence from the Grey Cup, but Edmonton quarterback Tracy Ham did not co-operate. Ham compiled 441 passing yards, and easily sent Edmonton to the final in a 43 to 23 victory.

Edmonton's impressive win made it the favourite. However, Winnipeg's defence gave a stellar performance in the final. Ham was defused, and the Bombers soared to a 50 to 11 Grey Cup title.

The Winnipeg defence established itself early in the first quarter. After Ham marched Edmonton to the Winnipeg 20, linebacker Greg Battle ended an Edmonton attack with a sparkling interception. Battle picked off a touchdown pass intended for Keith Wright, and then returned the ball to the Edmonton 43. The turnover ignited the Winnipeg offence, and moments later Kennerd kicked a field goal to open the scoring.

After one more play another turnover gave Winnipeg possession in Edmonton territory. Winnipeg took the ball to the Edmonton 11 with

In the 1990 final, Tom Burgess passed for 286 yards and led Winnipeg to a 50 to 11 victory against the Eskimos. (Photo by John E. Sokolowski)

Burgess then throwing a beautiful rainbow to the deep corner of the Edmonton end zone where Lee Hull made the reception.

In the second quarter Winnipeg's defence continued to dominate. On every Edmonton possession, it prevented the Eskimos from scoring a touchdown. Edmonton was forced to rely on the kicking of Ray Macoritti, who managed a single and a field goal to make the half-time score Winnipeg 10, Edmonton 4.

At the start of the third quarter Edmonton appeared poised to take the lead. Ham utilized his ground attack to move the ball downfield, but following a 6-yard run by Blake Marshall, Winnipeg forced the most critical error of the game. Using the hurry-up offence, Ham threw a pass to Michael Soles. The Edmonton receiver was open until Battle suddenly climbed over Soles for the interception. Soles fell, leaving Battle with a 32-yard touchdown return. The score was ironic as after the game Battle explained that if Edmonton had not used the hurry-up offence, he would not have been on the field. "I was hurt. I was tired. My wrist hurt and I felt like I had turf toe. I was trying to get off the field, but the Eskimos went without a huddle. I had to get up and go after it. I was lucky. The pass went right into my hands and all I had to do was run it into the end zone. I guess you could say it was a big play."

Winnipeg scored again. A 55-yard reception by Perry Tuttle gave Winnipeg excellent field position, then Tuttle stretched out to grab another pass for a touchdown. The onslaught continued. Edmonton's offence was unable to control the ball and after another Eskimo fumble, Winnipeg gained possession on the Edmonton 18 when David Williams was stripped of the ball on a punt return. From there, Burgess flipped a centre-screen pass to Warren Hudson and he smashed through the Edmonton secondary for a touchdown.

Before the end of the third quarter the Bombers scored another major. An interference penalty to Edmonton's Keith Gooch put Winnipeg on the Edmonton 2, and two plays later Hudson dove over the goal line. Kennerd kicked his fifth convert, and Winnipeg led 38 to 4.

Edmonton finally cut into Winnipeg's insurmountable lead in the fourth quarter. Scrimmaging from the Edmonton 35, Ham pieced together a good march which took the ball deep into Winnipeg's half. Then with the ball on the Winnipeg 20, he zipped a pass through the hands of defender Less Browne to Larry Willis for a touchdown. This was Edmonton's last scoring chance of the game.

The Bombers controlled the remainder of the quarter and, following a safety and field goal, Winnipeg closed the scoring with its sixth touchdown. From inside Winnipeg territory, back-up quarterback Danny McManus completed a 15-yard pass to Rick House. Edmonton's sloppy coverage allowed House to gallop downfield for a major. Kennerd added the extra point, and the game ended Winnipeg 50, Edmonton 11.

**The game's outstanding player was Winnipeg quarterback Tom Burgess. Acquired from Saskatchewan Roughriders following the 1989 season, Burgess skilfully utilized the short passing attack frequently to move Winnipeg into scoring position. In addition Burgess did not hesitate to run with the ball when necessary. Edmonton was surprised by Burgess's scrambling, and more than anything else this was the major factor in keeping Edmonton's defence bewildered. On the day, Burgess completed 18 of 31 passes for 286 yards and three touchdowns, and he ran seven times for 26 yards.**

**Another offensive star was Winnipeg's Warren Hudson. A product of the Oshawa Hawkeyes in Ontario, the 6-foot-2, 225-pound back surprised many with his play. The Eskimo defence frequently ignored Hudson, and accordingly he was able to make receptions for large gains. In the third quarter, Hudson stood prominently in the spotlight as he scored two touchdowns in five minutes. Hudson rushed the ball four times for seven yards and caught four passes for 66 yards. As a result he was selected as the game's outstanding Canadian.**

**The game's biggest star was Winnipeg linebacker Greg Battle. In the first quarter his goal-line interception set the tone for the game. Then, in the third quarter his interception and touchdown return took the spirit out of the Eskimos. Battle was a one-man wrecking crew and along with his interceptions he made a fumble recovery and was credited with four initial tackles. Battle was chosen the game's best defensive player, and according to teammate James 'Wild' West it was an award Battle deserved. "That dude is awesome," West said. "He had a great game and really set the tone for our defence."**

## 1991 TORONTO ARGONAUTS 36
## CALGARY STAMPEDERS 21

Less than a year later, a new ownership group which included Wayne Gretzky and John Candy purchased the Toronto Argonauts. For years Canadian football had lacked direction in its corporate offices and boardrooms. Financial troubles loomed throughout the league, and the Canadian game had disappeared from the front page headlines. However, with the involvement of Gretzky and Candy the game instantaneously moved back to the forefront. The new Argonaut ownership wanted to revitalize the league, and provided leadership when it signed highly touted American college star Raghib 'Rocket' Ismail. A graduate of Notre Dame, the Rocket was a speedster. In an instant he could thrill football fans with long dashes on punt and kick-off returns.

The involvement of Gretzky and Candy was reflected in the exciting play during the C.F.L.'s 1991 regular season. While rookies Ismail and B.C.'s Jon Volpe dazzled C.F.L. supporters from coast-to-coast with their running, B.C. quarterback Doug Flutie excited the fans game after game en route to breaking Warren Moon's single season passing records for attempts, completions and yards. With the performances of Ismail, Volpe, and Flutie drawing rave reviews it was anticipated that the Argonauts and B.C. Lions would be headed for a showdown in the 79th Grey Cup championship, played Sunday, November 24. However, while the Argonauts easily captured the eastern title, the Lions were unable to advance in the western playoffs. Led by veteran quarterback Danny Barrett the Calgary Stampeders eliminated the Lions 43 to 41, and then disposed of the Edmonton Eskimos 38 to 36 to capture the western title.

Despite the thrilling victories produced by the Stampeders, the Argonauts were favoured to win the 1991 Grey Cup. Yet, there were doubts surrounding the health of Toronto quarterback Matt Dunigan. Dunigan had broken a collar bone during the regular season, and he re-injured it during the eastern final. Without his leadership, it was believed that Toronto would lose. But Dunigan played one of the most inspirational games in Canadian football history, and guided Toronto to a thrilling 36 to 21 victory.

The opening score occurred on Calgary's first possession. With Barrett dropping back to pass, Toronto cornerback Ed Berry carefully positioned himself in the Argos' defensive secondary. Accordingly when Barrett tried to complete a pass to a receiver in Berry's zone, the Toronto defender was able to intercept the pass. The field ahead of Berry was clear, and he scooted down the sideline for a 50-yard touchdown return.

After Toronto took an 8 to 0 lead, Calgary scored its first touchdown. Scrimmaging from his own 33-yard line Barrett, with the assistance of a pass interference penalty, drove the Stampeders to the Toronto 1, and from there he plunged into the end zone.

In the second quarter an exchange of field goals took the score to Toronto 11, Calgary 10. Then, Ismail tried to increase the Toronto lead. Accepting a punt from Calgary's Jerry Kauric, he blasted down the field for 67 yards only to be mauled by a Stampeder. The ball came loose, and Calgary recovered.

In the third quarter Ismail continued to display his brilliant kick-return ability, but Toronto was unable to capitalize on the field positions he provided. Instead Calgary's Mark McLoughlin gave the Stampeders the lead.

With the score Calgary 14, Toronto 12 many onlookers began to wonder if Toronto head coach Adam Rita would replace Dunigan. The Toronto quarterback was struggling, yet Rita decided to leave him in. Rita's confidence was rewarded, as late in the quarter Dunigan provided the game's turning point. Scrimmaging from the Calgary 48-yard line following a short punt, Dunigan accepted the snap, turned to his right and faked a hand-off to Mike 'Pinball' Clemons. While Clemons surged forward, Dunigan faded to the right. He spotted a wide-open Darrell K. Smith, and fired the ball to the receiver for a touchdown.

Calgary head coach Wally Buono recalled the play: "We were in zone coverage and, on a play like that, the corner and safety have to squeeze in. They didn't close as hard as they had to and the ball was caught."

The touchdown inspired the Argos. On the first play of the fourth quarter Reggie Pleasant halted a Calgary attack with an interception, returning the ball to the Calgary 12 for Lance Chomyc to put over a field goal to give Toronto a 22 to 14 lead.

An unnecessary penalty taken by Ismail eventually led to Calgary gaining possession on the Toronto 31. From there, Barrett completed an 18-yard pass to David Sapunjis, and then Barrett combined with Allen Pitts for a 13-yard touchdown heave. McLoughlin converted to reduce Toronto's lead to a point, but on the next play Toronto increased the margin.

Toronto huddled on the sideline and prepared its kick-return strategy. "In the huddle everyone was saying they were going to get me a big return," Ismail later explained. "They say that a lot of times, but this time was different. This time they said it with eyes that went right into the soul."

McLoughlin kicked a squibbler toward Ismail, and as he bent down to retrieve the ball Toronto blockers erased every Calgary player on the field. An enormous hole developed down the middle and the Rocket blasted into it. In seconds Ismail emerged on the far sideline untouched. No one was

Toronto's Matt Dunigan (No. 16) played the entire 1991 Cup with a severely injured collar bone. Here, Dunigan courageously tested the shoulder against Calgary on a quarterback sneak.
(Photo by John E. Sokolowski)

near him as he sprinted down the field for a then record-setting 87-yard kick-off return. After the game Ismail recalled the dash: "I picked [the ball] up, looked up and took a couple of steps and broke to the middle. There was a gaping hole there, but one Stampeder [Errol Tucker] was standing there. I cut to the right and he fell, or whatever. I cut to the sidelines and I saw their kicker and someone else trying to get the angle on me. But I knew I was going to score. I looked around and held the ball up and said, 'Yeah, yeah, I can't believe I'm doing this'."

On the ensuing kick-off, Toronto ensured victory. Keyvan Jenkins misplayed Chomyc's kick, the ball bouncing off his body toward onrushing Argos. Keith Castello recovered it on the Calgary 36, and on the next play Paul Masotti made a spectacular acrobatic catch to provide Toronto with another touchdown. Chomyc converted for the final score, and 10 minutes later the game ended Toronto 36, Calgary 21.

Despite Calgary's loss Danny Barrett and David Sapunjis were two of the game's better performers. Barrett completed 34 of 56 passes, both Grey Cup records, for 377 yards, while Sapunjis earned the selection as the game's outstanding Canadian. Whenever Barrett needed a key reception he looked for Sapunjis. The slotback finished the game with four catches for 45 yards, and he ran the ball twice for 27 yards.

The outstanding offensive player was Toronto's Ismail. The Rocket, who had earlier in the week lost the C.F.L.'s most outstanding rookie award to B.C.'s Jon Volpe, proved that he was one of the league's premier performers. His punt and kick-off returns sparkled and directly led to Toronto's victory. According to Sapunjis, "Rocket was here to play and he came up big … He came to win a championship and helped his team more than anyone else on the field."

Ismail finished the game with 261 all-purpose yards, and a touchdown.

Unofficially, the game's most valuable player was Matt Dunigan. While his statistics were not awesome, his performance was courageous as he played the entire game with a badly injured shoulder. After the game the pain was so severe that tears filled his eyes.

Sportswriters could not believe that Toronto would use such an unhealthy player in the most important game of the year but Adam Rita explained: "What was at stake really? A football game. But there was also a man's pride and dignity at stake. Matt had a lot to prove and I could feel he felt that from day one."

Rita admitted that he thought about removing Dunigan, "But Matt said, 'My arm feels like a rag, but coach I'm finishing it.' In that situation you've got to listen. You've got to believe. That's how heroes are made."

On November 29, 1992 the Grey Cup game produced more Canadian football heroes. Matt Dunigan was signed by the Winnipeg Blue Bombers, and overnight the Bombers became a contender. The Argonauts collapsed without his leadership, and Winnipeg easily qualified for the 1992 Grey Cup final.

In the West, Doug Flutie brought his passing talents to the Calgary Stampeders. With an established corps of excellent receivers, Flutie again emerged as the best quarterback in Canadian football. He guided the Stampeders through the tough western division, and set up what was expected to be a classic Grey Cup quarterback showdown by leading Calgary to a 23 to 22 overtime victory against the Edmonton Eskimos in the western final. But the showdown never took place. While Flutie nearly broke every Grey Cup passing record, Dunigan was unable to solve Calgary's defence and the Stampeders easily defeated the Bombers 24 to 10.

Flutie set the tone for the game on the opening play. Dropping back, he completed a 39-yard pass to Derrick Crawford. He then moved the Stampeders deeper into Winnipeg territory where Mark McLoughlin booted a 37-yard field goal.

Calgary made the score 4 to 0, and then at 10:58 of the quarter Flutie served notice to Winnipeg that the Grey Cup was bound for Calgary. Scrimmaging at the Winnipeg 35, Flutie instructed David Sapunjis to line-up on the left of the ball. Winnipeg blitzed which left Sapunjis in one-on-

Former Heisman trophy winner Doug Flutie (No. 20) throws while on the run during the 1992 final. Flutie was selected the game's M.V.P. as Calgary defeated Winnipeg 24 to 10. (CFL Photos)

one coverage with Winnipeg linebacker Lorenza Baker. While Flutie eluded the rush, Sapunjis broke into the clear near the left sideline. Flutie threw him the ball and Sapunjis made the reception for a touchdown.

Sapunjis described the play: "[It's] called Lucky 721; the seven is for a deep route for me. The idea is, when a linebacker is covering me one-on-one, we're going to go deep. We felt that when they had their linebackers on our receivers like that, we would get open. It was a mismatch. Doug threw the ball up in the air and I got under it."

Winnipeg's offence continued to sputter with Dunigan at the helm. In the second quarter the Stampeders produced the only points with long drives of 75 and 67 yards respectively ending in McLoughlin field goals. The half ended Calgary 17, Winnipeg 0.

Both teams were held off the scoreboard in the third quarter, but at the start of the final quarter Flutie ensured Calgary's Grey Cup victory. Starting from the Winnipeg 54, Flutie guided Calgary to the 15 in five plays. Then he threw a touchdown to Allen Pitts. McLoughlin kicked the convert, and Calgary led 24 to 0.

At this point Dunigan was replaced by Danny McManus. McManus had better success against Calgary's solid defence and midway through the fourth quarter he provided the Bombers with an opportunity to break the shutout. McManus directed the Bombers to the Calgary 40 for Troy Westwood to kick a field goal and make the score Calgary 24, Winnipeg 3.

Calgary was content to protect its huge lead. Four minutes were eaten off the clock before Winnipeg scored again. From the Winnipeg 47 McManus engineered a 3-play touchdown drive which ended in a 27-yard pass to Gerald Alphin. Westwood added the extra point, and the game ended Calgary 24, Winnipeg 10.

**For Calgary quarterback Doug Flutie the victory was extremely satisfying. The 5-foot-9, 170-pounder was the game's outstanding player. A product of Boston College and a former Heisman Trophy winner, Flutie brilliantly used his half roll to the right and left to stay ahead of Winnipeg's blitzing defence. At times he miraculously escaped the Winnipeg rush and finished the game completing 33 of 49 passes for 480 yards and two touchdowns. In addition, he rushed four times for 20 yards.**

**After the game, Calgary head coach Wally Buono praised the performance of his diminutive quarterback. "The scheme was there. Doug always understood the scheme and what he had to do. He's a complete quarterback. Last week he killed Edmonton with his running. Today, he was a surgeon, destroying you with the pass."**

**The other leading offensive player was Calgary slotback David Sapunjis. For the second consecutive year Sapunjis, a graduate of the University of Western Ontario, used his deceptive speed and great hands to earn the selection as the game's outstanding Canadian. He was one of Flutie's favourite targets, catching seven passes for 85 yards and a touchdown.**

Despite the outstanding play of Flutie and Sapunjis, Calgary's Stu 'the Fireman' Laird offered another explanation for the Stampeders' victory.

Late in the regular season Laird discovered a card picturing a Grey Cup ring with the words 'Calgary Stampeders'. Inspired by the card, Laird had some more printed and he distributed them to his teammates. The Calgary players embraced the card. Said Laird: "I got them printed up after [a regular season game against] Edmonton and it was a way to stay focused. I carried it during games, and any time I needed something to get me pumped up, to get me inspired, I'd reach into my sock [where I kept the card] and looked at the picture of the Grey Cup ring." The inspiration was just what Laird and his teammates needed as the Stampeders delivered the Grey Cup back to Calgary for the first time in 21 years.

## 1993 EDMONTON ESKIMOS 33
## WINNIPEG BLUE BOMBERS 23

In 1993, Calgary was poised to repeat. Doug Flutie continued to dominate Canadian football and Calgary was the best team in the western division. However, the Edmonton Eskimos had its sights set on a Grey Cup championship and while the Stampeders became embroiled in a battle with the league over a late-season change to the western playoff format, the Eskimos prepared for the playoffs without distraction. The Eskimos destroyed the Saskatchewan Roughriders 51 to 13 in one of the two western semi-final games, and then a week later on a snow-covered McMahon Stadium field in Calgary the Eskimos slipped past the Stampeders 29 to 15 to capture the western title. In the East, Winnipeg Blue Bombers anticipated its fourth eastern title in six years. Despite playing without star quarterback Matt Dunigan for much of the season, the Bombers finished first and then disposed of the Hamilton Tiger-Cats 20 to 19 in the eastern final.

Winnipeg's narrow victory convinced many that the Bombers stood little chance of defeating the Eskimos in the Grey Cup. Edmonton, the overwhelming favourite, guided by quarterback Damon Allen, won the 1993 final, played on November 28, 33 to 23.

For Winnipeg fans the game was lost in the first quarter. With the Bombers in punt formation midway through the quarter Nick Benjamin snapped the ball over the head of kicker Bob Cameron. Cameron chased the bouncing ball deep in his own zone, grabbed it and then swung around to punt. However, Edmonton's special team leader Bruce Dickson blocked the kick and teammate Morris Lolar recovered the ball on the Winnipeg 4. On the next play Lucius Floyd burst into the end zone for a touchdown.

Two plays later Winnipeg committed another costly turnover. Blaise Bryant was unable to secure the the ensuing kick-off, allowing Edmonton's Trent Brown to recover it on the Winnipeg 26. From there Edmonton gained 24 yards in four plays and then Allen rolled-out and completed a short touchdown pass to Jim Sandusky.

A few minutes later, Don Murphy intercepted a Sam Garza pass in

Rushing for 90 yards on 14 carries and completing 17 passes for 226 yards, Damon Allen won his second Grey Cup M.V.P. award. The final score in the 1993 game was Edmonton 33, Winnipeg 23. (Photo by John E. Sokolowski)

Winnipeg territory for Sean Fleming to kick a field goal from 41 yards out to make the score Edmonton 17, Winnipeg 0.

After changing ends Edmonton extended its lead to 21 to 0 before Winnipeg got on the scoreboard. Scrimmaging from the Winnipeg 35 Garza engineered a 75-yard drive in 11 plays. He moved the Bombers to the Edmonton 3, and from there pitched the ball to Michael Richardson. The powerful back motored around the end and scored.

In the last 2:30 of the quarter the teams traded field goals to make the half-time score Edmonton 24, Winnipeg 10.

In the third quarter the Bombers lost an opportunity to cut the Edmonton lead in half. With Edmonton in possession, Allen slipped on the turf. Believing that no one had touched him, Allen scrambled to his feet but in so doing lost the ball. Winnipeg linebacker Paul Randolph recovered it and he charged downfield. However, the officials declared that Allen had been touched while on the ground by Winnipeg's Loyd Lewis, and thus the play was dead before Randolph's recovery. Winnipeg was outraged. Afterward a disappointed Randolph explained, "They blew the whistle when I was already 20 yards downfield. That's just a judgment call by the official. That would have been a big emotional lift for us."

The play later proved to be critical as Winnipeg recovered a fumble on the Edmonton 35, and Garza scored a major. If Randolph's recovery had stood, the game would have been tied 24 to 24. Instead, the teams entered the fourth quarter with Edmonton leading 24 to 17.

The teams exchanged field goals early on. Then Winnipeg made another critical mistake. With the ball near the Winnipeg 35, Garza attempted to spark his team by scrambling for yardage. However, he lost the ball, and Edmonton capitalized on the turnover by scoring a field goal.

The 10-point deficit made the Bombers nervous. Winnipeg players pressed too hard to reduce the lead, with David Williams missing a sure touchdown pass deep in the Edmonton end zone. Winnipeg was compelled to kick a field goal from the Edmonton 32. With only six seconds left in the game, Edmonton scored three more points to close the scoring: Edmonton 33, Winnipeg 23.

Edmonton's 1993 Grey Cup victory rested on the shoulders of quarterback Damon Allen and placekicker Sean Fleming. Duplicating his 1987 Grey Cup heroics Allen, a 30-year-old, eight-year C.F.L. veteran, proved that he was a passing and running threat. He mixed pin-point passing masterfully with gutsy running and thus Winnipeg's defence was kept off balance throughout the game. Allen completed 17 of 29 passes for 226 yards and a touchdown, and he was the game's leading rusher with 90 yards gained on 14 carries. The performance earned Allen the selection as the game's outstanding player. According to Winnipeg head coach Cal Murphy, and his Edmonton counterpart Ron Lancaster, Allen deserved the award.

"I really thought when we kicked that field goal [with less than 3 minutes remaining in the fourth quarter] that we could hold them, but I give full credit to Damon for getting them out of there," said Murphy after the game. "He did a heck of a job of doing it. Did he get the outstanding player award? Well, he played pretty outstanding."

Lancaster commented: "Damon did what he had to do to win. When he had to complete a pass on the final drive, he did. When he had to run out of trouble, he did. After all he's been through, he deserved the Grey Cup victory and he deserved the M.V.P."

For Fleming the 1993 Grey Cup game was the finest moment in his young C.F.L. career. After an outstanding time at the University of Wyoming, the 23-year-old native of Burnaby, British Columbia had tremendous difficulty adjusting to professional football. There were doubts that he would survive his second C.F.L. season, but his kicking improved throughout the year. He continued to gain confidence, and in the Grey Cup he booted six field goals, two converts, and a single to earn the selection as the game's most outstanding Canadian.

# 1994 B.C. LIONS 26
## BALTIMORE FOOTBALL CLUB 23

A year later another Canadian-born kicker stood in the Grey Cup spotlight. With the Baltimore Football Club making the first appearance by an American-based franchise, B.C.'s Lui Passaglia showed that despite the enormous difference in population Canadian-born and Canadian-trained players could be as good as American-born and American-trained players. Inspired by a raucous hometown crowd, Passaglia was able to clear his mind of an earlier missed field goal attempt and split the uprights with no time showing on the clock to give the Lions a memorable 26 to 23 victory. It was a championship which many football critics did not expect B.C. to win. They believed that Baltimore, comprised completely of American players, had greater depth, and was accordingly a better team.

The critics initially seemed to be right as Baltimore dominated the first half of the 1994 game, played on November 27. After B.C. had taken an early 3 to 0 lead, Baltimore began to control the play. Guided by quarterback

Tracy Ham, Baltimore displayed its offensive prowess with a 7-play, 59-yard touchdown drive midway through the second quarter. From the B.C. 1, Baltimore's Mike Pringle capped the drive as he swept off left tackle for the score.

Less than a minute later Baltimore scored again. B.C. pivot Kent Austin threw an errant pass which Baltimore linebacker Alvin Walton intercepted. Walton then flipped the ball to teammate Karl Anthony, and Anthony steamed 36 yards for the major: Baltimore 14, B.C. 3.

The Lions answered the defensive touchdown with a defensive touch-down of its own. B.C. pushed Baltimore back to its own 7 then B.C.'s Charles Gordon intercepted a Ham pass on the Baltimore 17. Gordon immediately headed toward the Baltimore end zone for the major.

With the score Baltimore 20, B.C. 10, B.C. produced the game's turning point. The Lions were stalled at the Baltimore 27. Passaglia lined up for a field goal. However the Lions faked the attempt. Darren Flutie took the snap, sprang to his feet, and set off to his right. Baltimore was taken by sur-prise and Flutie gained 17 yards. Three plays later, back-up quarterback Danny McManus stumbled into the end zone for a touchdown.

Flutie described his important fake. "It changed the whole momentum of the game. From there [confidence] spread throughout the team and we took off.

"Jody Allen, our special teams coach, made the call. He said I had to put the ball down on the tee, let them rush and then haul ass around the corner. I got to the corner and no one was there, so I got to the 10."

Passaglia proceeded to kick two field goals to give B.C. a 23 to 20 advan-tage. A few minutes later Baltimore threatened to regain the lead. Baltimore had moved the ball to the B.C. 10, and on second down Ham sprinted toward the Lions' goal line. It appeared that he would score as he stretched out to place the ball across the plane of the line. But before he could do so B.C. free safety Tom Europe knocked the ball out of Ham's grasp. The ball bounced away from the B.C. goal line, and B.C.'s Tony Collier recovered it.

Baltimore players were incensed. They believed that Ham had scored, and after the game Ham dejectedly said: "All I know is that I broke the plane of the goal line. I fumbled but not until after I broke the plane. You don't have to break the back of the line, just the front. I threw my arm out in a calculated effort to break the plane. I fumbled after that. It should have been a touchdown."

Baltimore's Donald Igwebuike did, however, tie the game to set up the dramatic ending. The Lions then drove the ball to the Baltimore 37 with the assistance of a controversial reception by Ray Alexander, and Passaglia was instructed to kick a field goal. Everyone expected Passaglia to put the Lions ahead, but the attempt sailed wide. While Baltimore returned the ball to its own 5, it was forced to punt three plays later. B.C. was once again in position for a field goal. The Lions moved the ball to the Baltimore 38, and on the last play of the game Passaglia made no mistake with a field goal.

B.C.'s Darren Flutie (No. 82) gains 17 yards on a fake field goal in the third quarter of the 1994 Cup. B.C. defeated the Baltimore Football Club 26 to 23. (Photo by John E. Sokolowski)

Lion players smothered Passaglia at midfield, and as Passaglia later said: "[After missing the first field goal] I had this feeling like I was on my way to hell and now I'm on my way to heaven, riding on a cloud."

Although Baltimore's Karl Anthony was chosen as the game's most valuable player, the real stars of the 1994 game were Lui Passaglia and Sean Millington. Millington was a powerful offensive force, and came up with big plays whenever the Lions needed them. Earlier in Grey Cup week B.C. coach Dave Ritchie had said: "Millington can play with any import in this league". Millington proved his coach right. The Vancouver native and graduate of Simon Fraser University was the game's second leading rusher, gaining 85 yards on 13 carries.

Passaglia performed heroically under intense pressure. Despite missing a field goal with two minutes left he displayed cool professionalism as he kicked the game-winning points. The 19-year C.F.L. veteran scored 14 of B.C.'s 26 points and was chosen the game's outstanding Canadian player.

## 1995 BALTIMORE STALLIONS 37
## CALGARY STAMPEDERS 20

On November 19, 1995 the Baltimore Stallions obtained another chance to take the Grey Cup to the United States. This time Baltimore's opponent was the Calgary Stampeders. Notwithstanding a mid-season injury to star quarterback Doug Flutie, Calgary, riding the arm of back-up pivot Jeff Garcia, was still a powerhouse. Calgary finished the season with an outstanding 15 and 3 win/loss record and it easily disposed of arch-rival Edmonton Eskimos

37 to 4 in the North Division final. (As a side note the C.F.L. realigned its divisions in 1995 for the purpose of setting up a guaranteed Canada versus United States final. While the North Division was comprised of the eight Canadian-based teams, the South Division was made up of the five U.S.-based teams. These divisions only lasted one year.) But Flutie and his team-mates were outplayed in the Cup. The Stallions dominated all aspects of the game and captured the prize that had eluded it the year before. In 1995 the Baltimore Stallions became the first, and perhaps last, team based in the United States to win the Grey Cup.

Baltimore's special teams gave Calgary early warning that the Cup was headed south. Calgary was forced to punt on its first possession, and Tony Martino drove the ball to Baltimore's Chris Wright. Wright accepted the kick on his own 28-yard line, and with an 85 kilometres per hour (53 miles per hour) wind at his back he flew down the field. Stampeder tacklers were unable to corral the fleet-footed Wright, who raced 82 yards for a spectac-ular, record-breaking touchdown. Baltimore 7, Calgary 0.

Following two Mark McLoughlin field goals the Stampeders took the lead in the first minute of the second quarter. From the Baltimore 3 Flutie threw a touchdown pass to Marvin Pope: Calgary 13, Baltimore 7.

The Stallions reduced Calgary's six-point lead to three, and then half-way through the quarter Baltimore's special teams produced another big play. With Calgary in punt formation Baltimore defender O.J. Brigance beat his blocker and charged toward Martino. As Martino kicked the ball, Brigance lunged forward and stretched out his arms to block the kick, and teammate Alvin Walton scooped up the loose ball on the Calgary 5 and dove into the end zone.

Baltimore dominated the remainder of the first half.

Early in the third quarter the Stallions held a 24 to 13 lead, but the Stampeders were far from being defeated. From the Calgary 35-yard line, Flutie engineered a time-consuming 11-play drive which culminated in the Calgary quarterback sneaking into the Baltimore end zone from a yard out.

The momentum seemed to be shifting, yet on Baltimore's next posses-sion quarterback Tracy Ham answered Flutie's major with a touchdown of his own. After moving the ball 79 yards on eight plays, Ham dropped back to pass on second down and nine to go from the Calgary 13. While the Stampeder secondary covered Ham's receivers Baltimore's offensive line erected a fortress around their quarterback. Ham surveyed the field and even-tually sprinted from the protection of his pocket into the Calgary end zone.

The Stampeders tried to fight back. But at 6:25 of the final quarter Baltimore defensive back Charles Anthony shattered Calgary's hopes of win-ning the Cup. Deep inside Baltimore territory, Anthony intercepted a long Flutie pass intended for Calgary slotback Allen Pitts. From then on the Stallions kicked two field goals and the game ended: Baltimore 37, Calgary 20.

**Although Calgary's David Sapunjis was chosen the outstanding Canadian player, the hero of the game was Baltimore quarterback Tracy Ham. Subjected to a barrage**

of negative criticism by the media, Ham proved that he could win the big game. Ham exploited the talents of his offence by smartly mixing his passing and ground attacks. Calgary's defence was never permitted to get comfortable. Ham finished the game completing 17 of 29 passes for 213 yards and two touchdowns. Ham also ran the ball seven times for 24 yards and one touchdown.

Notwithstanding the fact that Ham's statistics were not spectacular, Baltimore head coach Don Matthews praised his quarterback. "Tracy Ham called every single play today. Every one. And he called a great, great game."

Near the end of the third quarter of the 1995 final Tracy Ham (No. 8) scored a 13-yard touchdown to give Baltimore a 31 to 20 lead over Calgary. (Photo by John E. Sokolowski)

But Matthews was also quick to add that the victory was a team effort. After declaring that the 1995 Grey Cup final was a dream game, Matthews said: "You win championships by making big plays. Our offence, our defence, our special teams; they all made big plays."

## 1996 TORONTO ARGONAUTS 43 EDMONTON ESKIMOS 37

Following Baltimore's historic Grey Cup victory in 1995 much uncertainty surrounded the C.F.L. A decision by the National Football League to allow the N.F.L.'s Cleveland Browns to move to Baltimore triggered the death of the C.F.L.'s expansion into the States. The defending Grey Cup champion was forced to move, and eventually the Stallions resettled in Montreal to revive the defunct Montreal Alouettes. The four other American-based teams folded.

The C.F.L. attempted to deflect the criticism resulting from the expansion failure, and became 'Radically Canadian'. The league did an excellent job of marketing itself, but throughout the 1996 regular season negativism surrounded the Ottawa Rough Riders and B.C. Lions. Accordingly, fans largely abandoned both franchises and the league was forced to give them financial aid. Notwithstanding the problems faced by Ottawa and B.C., the league forged ahead and on Sunday, November 24 produced a brilliant 1996 Grey Cup final.

Fans were given a preview of what to expect in the final during the eastern and western division finals. In the West the Edmonton Eskimos overcame blizzard conditions to defeat the powerful Calgary Stampeders. Edmonton's Sean Fleming booted five field goals as he led Edmonton to a 15 to 12 last-minute victory. In the eastern final Mike 'Pinball' Clemons returned the opening kick-off 90 yards for a major against the Montreal Alouettes. The touchdown ignited the Argos and Toronto easily sailed to victory. After the game Clemons described the major: "It was excellence of execution. It opened up like the Red Sea, and I felt like Moses."

The big play by Clemons and the blizzard in Calgary were a prelude to the Cup game itself. Billed as the 'Showdown in Steeltown', the final will be remembered as the 'Snowdown in Steeltown'. A snowstorm slammed Hamilton's Ivor Wynne Stadium and blanketed the field. Everyone expected the conditions would hamper the scoring and slow down Toronto quarterback Doug Flutie, but the snow and 40 kilometre-per-hour (25 mile-per-hour) winds did neither. The game was action-packed from start to finish and eventually the Argos produced a 43 to 37 victory.

In the first quarter the game belonged to Edmonton. After it took a 2 to 0 lead on a safety touch, pivot Danny McManus combined with 'Downtown' Eddie Brown for one of the most spectacular touchdown catches in Grey Cup history. McManus threw a deep sideline pass to Brown, who was in bump-and-run coverage. Brown eluded his defender but the ball in turn eluded him and was headed to the turf. Somehow Brown retained his concentration and kicked the ball back into his hands for an amazing shoestring catch and outraced the stunned Argonaut defender for a 64-yard touchdown: Edmonton 9, Toronto 0.

Spectacular plays continued in the second quarter. With Toronto trailing 9 to 3, Argo punt returner Jimmy 'the Jet' Cunningham electrified the crowd. Accepting a Glenn Harper punt at the Toronto 30, Cunningham zoomed up the middle of the field, got by Blake Dermott and then watched as Donald Smith eliminated Harper with a devastating block. No other Edmonton player could get close to the Jet, who slid into the Eskimo end zone to celebrate his 80-yard touchdown return.

Following a Toronto field goal, McManus produced another thrilling score. This time he threaded the needle between two Argo defenders with a pass to Jim Sandusky. While the Argo defenders crashed to the ground, Sandusky scooted 75 yards down the field to give Edmonton a 16 to 13 lead.

On the ensuing series, Toronto regained the lead. Starting on the Toronto 35, Doug Flutie marched the Argos to the Edmonton 2 on six plays. From there, Flutie handed the ball to Robert Drummond, who smashed into the end zone.

Mike Vanderjagt converted and on the next play Henry 'Gizmo' Williams set a Grey Cup record. Taking Toronto's kick-off at the Edmonton 19, Williams charged straight ahead and set up his blockers. He then cut to the right and sped across the snow-covered field and down the right sideline.

Soon Vanderjagt was the only defender in sight. A desperate diving tackle failed. Williams was untouched and he scored a 91-yard touchdown.

Doug Flutie quickly responded to Williams' score. Utilizing Drummond and Clemons, Flutie moved Toronto to the Edmonton 10. Flutie dropped back to pass but found the field wide open ahead of him, so he tucked the ball under his arm and sprinted into the Edmonton end zone. The second quarter ended on a missed field goal attempt by Edmonton's Fleming: Toronto 27, Edmonton 23.

Over the next 20 minutes the Argos extended its lead to 33 to 23. Then at the mid-point of the fourth quarter, Edmonton's Eric Blount collected a pitch-out in the Edmonton backfield and picked his way into the Toronto end zone for a 5-yard major, and six minutes later Vanderjagt collected his fifth field goal to give Toronto a six-point margin.

Edmonton still had plenty of time but only two plays after the Vanderjagt field goal came the only turnover of the game. From the Edmonton 40 McManus fired a pass to Darren Flutie. Flutie slipped and the ball bounced off his chest into the arms of Toronto defender Adrion Smith. Immedi-

The scoring parade continued when Toronto's Jimmy 'the Jet' Cunningham (No. 86) took flight on an 80-yard punt return in the 1996 championship.
(Photo by John E. Sokolowski)

ately Smith and a group of Argos charged toward the Edmonton end zone for the game's eighth touchdown.

A little more than a minute remained and it appeared that the Grey Cup was headed to Toronto. But Edmonton did not give up. McManus used eight plays to drive his team from near his own 40 to the Toronto 6. Two plays later McManus completed a touchdown pass to Mark Tobert.

Edmonton then attempted an onside kick. Toronto was ready for the play, recovering the ball. Nine seconds later the 84th Grey Cup game ended.

**This exciting game produced many stars. Edmonton's Danny McManus, Eddie Brown and Henry Williams were outstanding. For Toronto, Paul Masotti, Robert Drummond and Jimmy Cunningham shone brightly. But the biggest stars and heroes of the game were Mike Vanderjagt and Doug Flutie.**

**Vanderjagt is a native of Oakville, Ontario. While his counterpart missed**

three field goals, Vanderjagt kicked five, without a miss. Toronto head coach Don Matthews was elated with Vanderjagt's effort, and he was relieved that Vanderjagt had reported to the 1996 training camp. After having been cut by the Argos in 1994 and 1995, he had contemplated not trying out for Toronto in 1996.

The other hero, Doug Flutie, had been labelled as a 'fair-weather' quarterback. Thus he entered the game determined to silence his critics. Two days after winning his fifth league M.V.P. award, Flutie weaved his football magic and played 'Flutie-ball' whenever possible. He utilized his offensive weapons perfectly and whenever in trouble he either ran the ball himself or improvised brilliant plays which had never before been seen on a Canadian football gridiron. Flutie finished the game completing 22 (62.9%) of his passes for 302 yards, and carrying the ball 13 times for 98 yards. He also scored a major and was named the game's most valuable player.

Delighted with the victory, after the game Flutie said: "There's one in the critics' face. It's like, 'Shut up and let's move on'. This should dispel all the myths."

The Grey Cup games from 1989 through 1996 represented the best Canadian football had to offer. They featured great plays and showcased the talents of many of Canadian football's best players. While Doug Flutie, Henry Williams, Tom Burgess, Matt Dunigan, Damon Allen, David Sapunjis, Lui Passaglia and Dave Ridgway may never become as legendary as Ron Lancaster, Russ Jackson, Garney Henley, Jackie Parker, or Joe Krol, these players and their teammates showed that Canadian football was exciting and worth watching.

# CONCLUSION

When I began writing this book Raghib 'Rocket' Ismail was a Canadian Football League superstar, and Toronto was one of the best teams in an eight-team league. A lot has changed since then. The Rocket jumped the Argonaut ship to join the National Football League, the C.F.L. expanded and retrenched, and the Grey Cup headed south of the border. A 'new' C.F.L. was born, and then it became 'Radically Canadian'.

As the history of the Grey Cup shows, Canadian football has undergone many changes. Yet throughout those changes the game has remained exciting to watch. A rich history has been created; we should never forget it. In

Canada and the United States clash in the 1994 Cup. Here, Baltimore's Charles Anthony and B.C.'s Ray Alexander (No. 88) battle for possession. (Photo by John E. Sokolowski)

order to sustain the game we should draw a link between the past, the present and the future, and remember the exploits of Hugh Gall, Harry Batstone, Frank Leadlay, Ted Reeve, Annis Stukus, Joe Krol, Jackie Parker, Angelo Mosca, Russ Jackson, Ron Lancaster, Garney Henley, Tony Gabriel, Tom Wilkinson, Warren Moon, Brian Kelly, Doug Flutie and Lui Passaglia. These are men that we should not just remember occasionally; these are men who should be foremost in our minds when we think of great sport legends. These men should be honoured for their football exploits, and the game they have played should also be honoured.

We should remember that Canadian football is about having fun, about great plays, about great players, and about Canada. The Grey Cup is a Canadian tradition, and is the only truly Canadian professional sports championship remaining. The spirit of this great game was once again exemplified in 1996 when C.F.L. fans Mark Sproxton and Duane Melchert covered over 3,000 kilometres (1,864 miles) to attend the Grey Cup game in Hamilton. The pair started in Yellowknife, N.W.T. and travelled one-and-a-half hours to Edmonton. Then they took a four-hour flight to Toronto and hopped on public transit to take them to Hamilton.

*Heroes of the Game* has taken you on a journey through Canadian football's historic championship past. All of the Grey Cup games have been featured along with great individual performers. The games have left a rich tradition and indicate that Canadian football has a potentially bright future.

# STATISTICS

The following statistics are supplied by courtesy of the Canadian Football League, except for Participants and Coaches, Individual Statistics, and Game Statistics.

## GREY CUP RESULTS

| YEAR | DATE | SITE | SCORE | | | | ATTENDANCE |
|------|------|------|-------|---|---|---|------------|
| 1996 | Nov. 24 | Hamilton | Toronto Argonauts | 43 | Edmonton Eskimos | 37 | 38,595 |
| 1995 | Nov. 19 | Regina | Baltimore Stallions | 37 | Calgary Stampeders | 20 | 52,564 |
| 1994 | Nov. 27 | Vancouver | B.C. Lions | 26 | Baltimore Football Club | 23 | 55,097 |
| 1993 | Nov. 28 | Calgary | Edmonton Eskimos | 33 | Winnipeg Blue Bombers | 23 | 50,035 |
| 1992 | Nov. 29 | Toronto | Calgary Stampeders | 24 | Winnipeg Blue Bombers | 10 | 45,863 |
| 1991 | Nov. 24 | Winnipeg | Toronto Argonauts | 36 | Calgary Stampeders | 21 | 51,985 |
| 1990 | Nov. 25 | Vancouver | Winnipeg Blue Bombers | 50 | Edmonton Eskimos | 11 | 46,968 |
| 1989 | Nov. 26 | Toronto | Saskatchewan Roughriders | 43 | Hamilton Tiger-Cats | 40 | 54,088 |
| 1988 | Nov. 27 | Ottawa | Winnipeg Blue Bombers | 22 | B.C. Lions | 21 | 50,604 |
| 1987 | Nov. 29 | Vancouver | Edmonton Eskimos | 38 | Toronto Argonauts | 36 | 59,478 |
| 1986 | Nov. 30 | Vancouver | Hamilton Tiger-Cats | 39 | Edmonton Eskimos | 15 | 59,621 |
| 1985 | Nov. 24 | Montreal | B.C. Lions | 37 | Hamilton Tiger-Cats | 24 | 56,723 |
| 1984 | Nov. 18 | Edmonton | Winnipeg Blue Bombers | 47 | Hamilton Tiger-Cats | 17 | 60,081 |
| 1983 | Nov. 27 | Vancouver | Toronto Argonauts | 18 | B.C. Lions | 17 | 59,345 |
| 1982 | Nov. 28 | Toronto | Edmonton Eskimos | 32 | Toronto Argonauts | 16 | 54,741 |
| 1981 | Nov. 22 | Montreal | Edmonton Eskimos | 26 | Ottawa Rough Riders | 23 | 52,478 |
| 1980 | Nov. 23 | Toronto | Edmonton Eskimos | 48 | Hamilton Tiger-Cats | 10 | 54,661 |
| 1979 | Nov. 25 | Montreal | Edmonton Eskimos | 17 | Montreal Alouettes | 9 | 65,113 |
| 1978 | Nov. 26 | Toronto | Edmonton Eskimos | 20 | Montreal Alouettes | 13 | 54,695 |
| 1977 | Nov. 27 | Montreal | Montreal Alouettes | 41 | Edmonton Eskimos | 6 | 68,318 |
| 1976 | Nov. 28 | Toronto | Ottawa Rough Riders | 23 | Saskatchewan Roughriders | 20 | 53,467 |
| 1975 | Nov. 23 | Calgary | Edmonton Eskimos | 9 | Montreal Alouettes | 8 | 32,454 |
| 1974 | Nov. 24 | Vancouver | Montreal Alouettes | 20 | Edmonton Eskimos | 7 | 34,450 |
| 1973 | Nov. 25 | Toronto | Ottawa Rough Riders | 22 | Edmonton Eskimos | 18 | 36,653 |
| 1972 | Dec. 3 | Hamilton | Hamilton Tiger-Cats | 13 | Saskatchewan Roughriders | 10 | 33,993 |
| 1971 | Nov. 28 | Vancouver | Calgary Stampeders | 14 | Toronto Argonauts | 11 | 34,484 |
| 1970 | Nov. 28 | Toronto | Montreal Alouettes | 23 | Calgary Stampeders | 10 | 32,669 |
| 1969 | Nov. 30 | Montreal | Ottawa Rough Riders | 29 | Saskatchewan Roughriders | 11 | 33,172 |
| 1968 | Nov. 30 | Toronto | Ottawa Rough Riders | 24 | Calgary Stampeders | 21 | 32,655 |
| 1967 | Dec. 2 | Ottawa | Hamilton Tiger-Cats | 24 | Saskatchewan Roughriders | 1 | 31,358 |
| 1966 | Nov. 26 | Vancouver | Saskatchewan Roughriders | 29 | Ottawa Rough Riders | 14 | 36,553 |
| 1965 | Nov. 27 | Toronto | Hamilton Tiger-Cats | 22 | Winnipeg Blue Bombers | 16 | 32,655 |
| 1964 | Nov. 28 | Toronto | B.C. Lions | 34 | Hamilton Tiger-Cats | 24 | 32,655 |
| 1963 | Nov. 30 | Vancouver | Hamilton Tiger-Cats | 21 | B.C. Lions | 10 | 36,545 |
| 1962 | Dec. 1-2* | Toronto | Winnipeg Blue Bombers | 28 | Hamilton Tiger-Cats | 27 | 32,655 |
| 1961 | Dec. 2** | Toronto | Winnipeg Blue Bombers | 21 | Hamilton Tiger-Cats | 14 | 32,651 |
| 1960 | Nov. 26 | Vancouver | Ottawa Rough Riders | 16 | Edmonton Eskimos | 6 | 38,102 |
| 1959 | Nov. 28 | Toronto | Winnipeg Blue Bombers | 21 | Hamilton Tiger-Cats | 7 | 33,133 |
| 1958 | Nov. 29 | Vancouver | Winnipeg Blue Bombers | 35 | Hamilton Tiger-Cats | 28 | 36,567 |
| 1957 | Nov. 30 | Toronto | Hamilton Tiger-Cats | 32 | Winnipeg Blue Bombers | 7 | 27,051 |
| 1956 | Nov. 24 | Toronto | Edmonton Eskimos | 50 | Montreal Alouettes | 27 | 27,425 |
| 1955 | Nov. 26 | Vancouver | Edmonton Eskimos | 34 | Montreal Alouettes | 19 | 39,417 |
| 1954 | Nov. 27 | Toronto | Edmonton Eskimos | 26 | Montreal Alouettes | 25 | 27,321 |
| 1953 | Nov. 28 | Toronto | Hamilton Tiger-Cats | 12 | Winnipeg Blue Bombers | 6 | 27,313 |
| 1952 | Nov. 29 | Toronto | Toronto Argonauts | 21 | Edmonton Eskimos | 11 | 27,391 |
| 1951 | Nov. 24 | Toronto | Ottawa Rough Riders | 21 | Saskatchewan Roughriders | 14 | 27,341 |
| 1950 | Nov. 25 | Toronto | Toronto Argonauts | 13 | Winnipeg Blue Bombers | 0 | 27,101 |
| 1949 | Nov. 26 | Toronto | Montreal Alouettes | 28 | Calgary Stampeders | 15 | 20,087 |

| 1948 | Nov. 28 | Toronto | Calgary Stampeders | 12 | Ottawa Rough Riders | 7 | 20,013 |
|------|---------|---------|--------------------|----|---------------------|----|--------|
| 1947 | Nov. 29 | Toronto | Toronto Argonauts | 10 | Winnipeg Blue Bombers | 9 | 18,885 |
| 1946 | Nov. 30 | Toronto | Toronto Argonauts | 28 | Winnipeg Blue Bombers | 6 | 18,960 |
| 1945 | Dec. 1 | Toronto | Toronto Argonauts | 35 | Winnipeg Blue Bombers | 0 | 18,660 |
| 1944 | Nov. 25 | Hamilton | St. Hyacinthe-Donnacona Navy Combines | 7 | Hamilton Wildcats | 6 | 3,871 |
| 1943 | Nov. 27 | Toronto | Hamilton Flying Wildcats | 23 | Winnipeg R.C.A.F. Bombers | 14 | 16,423 |
| 1942 | Dec. 5 | Toronto | Toronto R.C.A.F. Hurricanes | 8 | Winnipeg R.C.A.F. Bombers | 5 | 12,455 |
| 1941 | Nov. 29 | Toronto | Winnipeg Blue Bombers | 18 | Ottawa Rough Riders | 16 | 19,065 |
| 1940 | Nov. 30 | Toronto | Ottawa Rough Riders | 8 | Balmy Beach | 2 | 4,998 |
|  | Dec. 7 | Ottawa | Ottawa Rough Riders | 12 | Balmy Beach | 5 | 1,700 |
| 1939 | Dec. 9 | Ottawa | Winnipeg Blue Bombers | 8 | Ottawa Rough Riders | 7 | 11,738 |
| 1938 | Dec. 10 | Toronto | Toronto Argonauts | 30 | Winnipeg Blue Bombers | 7 | 18,778 |
| 1937 | Dec. 11 | Toronto | Toronto Argonauts | 4 | Winnipeg Blue Bombers | 3 | 11,522 |
| 1936 | Dec. 5 | Toronto | Sarnia Imperials | 26 | Ottawa Rough Riders | 20 | 5,883 |
| 1935 | Dec. 7 | Hamilton | Winnipeg 'Pegs | 18 | Hamilton Tigers | 12 | 6,405 |
| 1934 | Nov. 24 | Toronto | Sarnia Imperials | 20 | Regina Roughriders | 12 | 8,900 |
| 1933 | Dec. 9 | Sarnia | Toronto Argonauts | 4 | Sarnia Imperials | 3 | 2,751 |
| 1932 | Dec. 3 | Hamilton | Hamilton Tigers | 25 | Regina Roughriders | 6 | 4,806 |
| 1931 | Dec. 5 | Montreal | Montreal Winged Wheelers | 22 | Regina Roughriders | 0 | 5,112 |
| 1930 | Dec. 6 | Toronto | Balmy Beach | 11 | Regina Roughriders | 6 | 3,914 |
| 1929 | Nov. 30 | Hamilton | Hamilton Tigers | 14 | Regina Roughriders | 3 | 1,906 |
| 1928 | Dec. 1 | Hamilton | Hamilton Tigers | 30 | Regina Roughriders | 0 | 4,767 |
| 1927 | Nov. 26 | Toronto | Balmy Beach | 9 | Hamilton Tigers | 6 | 13,676 |
| 1926 | Dec. 4 | Toronto | Ottawa Senators | 10 | University of Toronto | 7 | 8,276 |
| 1925 | Dec. 5 | Ottawa | Ottawa Senators | 24 | Winnipeg Tammany Tigers | 1 | 6,900 |
| 1924 | Nov. 29 | Toronto | Queen's University | 11 | Balmy Beach | 3 | 5,978 |
| 1923 | Dec. 1 | Toronto | Queen's University | 54 | Regina Roughriders | 0 | 8,629 |
| 1922 | Dec. 2 | Kingston | Queen's University | 13 | Edmonton Elks | 1 | 4,700 |
| 1921 | Dec. 3 | Toronto | Toronto Argonauts | 23 | Edmonton Eskimos | 0 | 9,558 |
| 1920 | Dec. 4 | Toronto | University of Toronto | 16 | Toronto Argonauts | 3 | 10,088 |
| 1916-18 No games, World War I; 1919 No Playoff Games | | | | | | | |
| 1915 | Nov. 20 | Toronto | Hamilton Tigers | 13 | Toronto Rowing & Athl. Assn. | 7 | 2,808 |
| 1914 | Dec. 5 | Toronto | Toronto Argonauts | 14 | University of Toronto | 2 | 10,500 |
| 1913 | Nov. 29 | Hamilton | Hamilton Tigers | 44 | Parkdale Canoe Club | 2 | 2,100 |
| 1912 | Nov. 30 | Hamilton | Hamilton Alerts | 11 | Toronto Argonauts | 4 | 5,337 |
| 1911 | Nov. 25 | Toronto | University of Toronto | 14 | Toronto Argonauts | 7 | 13,687 |
| 1910 | Nov. 26 | Hamilton | University of Toronto | 16 | Hamilton Tigers | 7 | 12,000 |
| 1909 | Dec. 4 | Toronto | University of Toronto | 26 | Parkdale Canoe Club | 6 | 3,807 |

* Halted by fog on Dec. 1. Final 9 minutes and 29 seconds were played on Dec. 2.  ** Overtime.

# SCORING SUMMARIES

**1996** at Ivor Wynne Stadium, Hamilton. **Toronto** (43) – TDs, Jimmy Cunningham, Robert Drummond, Doug Flutie, Adrion Smith; FGs Mike Vanderjagt (5); cons. Vanderjagt (4). **Edmonton** (37) – TDs, Eddie Brown, Jim Sandusky, Henry Williams, Eric Blount, Mark Tobert; cons. Sean Fleming (5); safety touch.

**1995** at Taylor Field, Regina. **Baltimore** (37) – TDs, Alvin Walton, Tracy Ham, Chris Wright; FGs, Carlos Huerta (5); cons., Huerta (3); single, Josh Miller. **Calgary** (20) – TDs, Doug Flutie, Marvin Pope; FGs, Mark McLoughlin (2); cons., McLoughlin (2).

**1994** at B.C. Place Stadium, Vancouver. **B.C.** (26) – TDs, Charles Gordon, Danny McManus; FGs, Lui Passaglia (4); cons. Passaglia (2). **Baltimore** (23) – TDs, Tracy Ham, Karl Anthony; FGs, Donald Igwebuike (3); cons. Igwebuike (2).

**1993** at McMahon Stadium, Calgary. **Edmonton** (33) – TDs, Lucius Floyd, Jim Sandusky; FGs, Sean Fleming (6); cons., Fleming (2); single, Fleming. **Winnipeg** (23) – TDs, Michael Richardson, Sammy Garza; FGs, Troy Westwood (3); cons., Westwood (2).

**1992** at SkyDome, Toronto. **Calgary** (24) – TDs, David Sapunjis, Allen Pitts; FGs, Mark McLoughlin (3); cons., McLoughlin (2); single, McLoughlin. **Winnipeg** (10) – TD, Gerald Alphin; FG, Troy Westwood; con., Westwood.

**1991** at Winnipeg Stadium, Winnipeg. **Toronto** (36) – TDs, Ed Berry, Darrell K. Smith, Raghib Ismail, Paul Masotti; FGs, Lance Chomyc (2); cons., Chomyc (4); singles, Chomyc (2). **Calgary** (21) – TDs, Danny Barrett, Allen Pitts; FGs, Mark McLoughlin (2); cons., McLoughlin (2); single, McLoughlin.

**1990** at B.C. Place Stadium, Vancouver. **Winnipeg** (50) – TDs, Warren Hudson (2), Lee Hull, Greg Battle, Perry Tuttle, Rick House; FGs, Trevor Kennerd (2); cons., Kennerd (6), safety touch. **Edmonton** (11) – TD, Larry Willis; FG, Ray Macoritti; con., Macoritti; single, Macoritti.

**1989** at SkyDome, Toronto. **Saskatchewan** (43) – TDs, Ray Elgaard, Jeff Fairholm, Donald Narcisse, Tim McCray; FGs, David Ridgway (4); cons., Ridgway (4); single, Terry Baker; safety touch. **Hamilton** (40) – TDs, Tony Champion (2), Derrick McAdoo (2); FGs, Paul Osbaldiston (4); cons., Osbaldiston (4).

**1988** at Landsdowne Park, Ottawa. **Winnipeg** (22) – TD, James Murphy; FGs, Trevor Kennerd (4); con., Kennerd; singles, Kennerd, Bob Cameron (2). **B.C.** (21) – TDs, Anthony Cherry, David Williams; FG, Lui Passaglia; cons., Passaglia (2); singles, Passaglia (2); safety touch.

**1987** at B.C. Place Stadium, Vancouver. **Edmonton** (38) – TDs, Henry Williams, Marco Cyncar, Brian Kelly, Damon Allen; FGs, Jerry Kauric (3); cons., Kauric (4); single, Kauric. **Toronto** (36) – TDs, Gill Fenerty (2), Doug Landry, Danny Barrett; FGs, Lance Chomyc (3); cons., Chomyc (3).

**1986** at B.C. Place Stadium, Vancouver. **Hamilton** (39) – TDs, Steve Stapler, James Rockford, Ron Ingram; FGs, Paul Osbaldiston (6); cons., Osbaldiston (3). **Edmonton** (15) – TDs, Damon Allen, Brian Kelly; 2 pt-con., Allen; con., Tom Dixon.

**1985** at Olympic Stadium, Montreal. **B.C.** (37) – TDs, Ned Armour (2), Jim Sandusky; FGs, Lui Passaglia (5); cons., Passaglia (3); single, Passaglia. **Hamilton** (24) – TDs, Ron Ingram, Johnny Shepherd, Steve Stapler; FG, Bernie Ruoff; cons., Ruoff (3).

**1984** at Commonwealth Stadium, Edmonton. **Winnipeg** (47) – TDs, Willard Reaves (2), Joe Poplawski, Stan Mikawos, Jeff Boyd; FGs, Trevor Kennerd (4), cons., Kennerd (5). **Hamilton** (17) – TDs, Dieter Brock, Rocky DiPietro; FG, Bernie Ruoff; cons., Ruoff (2).

**1983** at B.C. Place Stadium, Vancouver. **Toronto** (18) – TDs, Jan Carinci, Cedric Minter; FG, Hank Ilesic; con., Ilesic; singles, Ilesic (2). **B.C.** (17) – TDs, Mervyn Fernandez, John Henry White; FG, Lui Passaglia; cons., Passaglia (2).

**1982** at Exhibition Stadium, Toronto. **Edmonton** (32) – TDs, Brian Kelly (2), Neil Lumsden; FGs, Dave Cutler (4); cons., Cutler (2). **Toronto** (16) – TDs, Emanuel Tolbert, Terry Greer; cons., Dean Dorsey (2); safety touch.

**1981** at Olympic Stadium, Montreal. **Edmonton** (26) – TDs, Warren Moon (2), Jim Germany; FG, Dave Cutler; 2 pt-con., Marco Cyncar; cons., Cutler (2); single, Cutler. **Ottawa** (23) – TDs, Jim Reid, Sam Platt; FGs, Gerry Organ (3); cons., Organ (2).

**1980** at Exhibition Stadium, Toronto. **Edmonton** (48) – TDs, Tom Scott (3), Jim Germany (2), Brian Kelly; FGs, Dave Cutler (2); cons., Cutler (6). **Hamilton** (10) – FGs, Bernie Ruoff (3); single, Ruoff.

**1979** at Olympic Stadium, Montreal. **Edmonton** (17) – TDs, Waddell Smith, Tom Scott; FG, Dave Cutler; cons., Cutler (2). **Montreal** (9) – FGs, Don Sweet (3).

**1978** at Exhibition Stadium, Toronto. **Edmonton** (20) – TD, Jim Germany; FGs, Dave Cutler (4); con., Cutler; single, Cutler. **Montreal** (13) – TD, Joe Barnes; FGs; Don Sweet (2); con., Sweet.

**1977** at Olympic Stadium, Montreal. **Montreal** (41) – TDs, Peter Dalla Riva, John O'Leary, Bob Gaddis; FGs, Don Sweet (6); cons., Sweet (3); singles, Sweet (2). **Edmonton** (6) – FGs, Dave Cutler (2).

**1976** at Exhibition Stadium, Toronto. **Ottawa** (23) – TDs, Bill Hatanaka, Tony Gabriel; FGs, Gerry Organ (3); cons., Organ (2). **Saskatchewan** (20) – TDs, Steve Mazurak, Bob Richardson; FGs, Bob Macoritti (2); cons., Macoritti (2).

**1975** at McMahon Stadium, Calgary. **Edmonton** (9) – FGs, Dave Cutler (3). **Montreal** (8) – FGs, Don Sweet (2); singles, Sweet (2).

**1974** at Empire Stadium, Vancouver. **Montreal** (20) – TD, Larry Sherrer; FGs, Don Sweet (4); con., Sweet; single, Sweet. **Edmonton** (7) – TD, Calvin Harrell; con., Dave Cutler.

**1973** at Exhibition Stadium, Toronto. **Ottawa** (22) – TDs, Rhome Nixon, Jim Evenson; FGs, Gerry Organ (2); cons., Organ (2); safety touch. **Edmonton** (18) – TDs, Roy Bell, Garry Lefebvre; FG, Dave Cutler; cons., Cutler (2); single, Lefebvre.

**1972** at Ivor Wynne Stadium, Hamilton. **Hamilton** (13) – TD, Dave Fleming; FGs, Ian Sunter (2); con., Sunter. **Saskatchewan** (10) – TD, Tom Campana; FG, Jack Abendschan; con., Abendschan.

**1971** at Empire Stadium, Vancouver. **Calgary** (14) – TDs, Herman Harrison, Jesse Mims; cons., Larry Robinson (2). **Toronto** (11) – TD, Roger Scales; FG, Ivan MacMillan; con., MacMillan; single, MacMillan.

**1970** at Exhibition Stadium, Toronto. **Montreal** (23) – TDs, Ted Alflen, Tom Pullen, Garry Lefebvre; FG, George Springate; cons., Springate (2). **Calgary** (10) – TD, Hugh McKinnis; FG, Larry Robinson; con., Robinson.

**1969** at Autostade, Montreal. **Ottawa** (29) – TDs, Ron Stewart (2), Jim Mankins, Jay Roberts; cons., Don Sutherin (4); single, Sutherin. **Saskatchewan** (11) – TD, Alan Ford; con., Jack Abendschan; singles, Ford, Abendschan; safety touch.

**1968** at Exhibition Stadium, Toronto. **Ottawa** (24) – TDs, Russ Jackson, Vic Washington, Margene Adkins; FG, Don Sutherin; cons., Sutherin (2); single, Wayne Giardino. **Calgary** (21) – TDs, Terry Evanshen (2), Peter Liske; cons., Larry Robinson (3).

**1967** at Landsdowne Park, Ottawa. **Hamilton** (24) – TDs, Joe Zuger, Ted Watkins, Billy Ray Locklin; cons., Tommy Joe Coffey (2); singles, Zuger (3), Coffey. **Saskatchewan** (1) – Single, Alan Ford.

**1966** at Empire Stadium, Vancouver. **Saskatchewan** (29) – TDs, Jim Worden, Alan Ford, Hugh Campbell, George Reed; cons., Jack Abendschan (4); single, Ford. **Ottawa** (14) – TDs, Whit Tucker (2); con., Moe Racine; single, Bill Cline.

**1965** at Exhibition Stadium, Toronto. **Hamilton** (22) – TDs, Dick Cohee, Willie Bethea; cons., Don Sutherin (2); singles, Sutherin, Joe Zuger; safety touches (3). **Winnipeg** (16) – TDs, Art Perkins, Leo Lewis; FG, Norm Winton; con., Winton.

**1964** at Exhibition Stadium, Toronto. **B.C.** (34) – TDs, Bill Munsey (2), Jim Carphin, Bob Swift, Willie Fleming; cons., Peter Kempf (4). **Hamilton** (24) – TDs, Johnny Counts, Stan Crisson, Tommy Grant; cons., Don Sutherin (2); singles, Joe Zuger (2); safety touch.

**1963** at Exhibition Stadium, Vancouver. **Hamilton** (21) – TDs, Willie Bethea, Hal Patterson, Art Baker; cons., Don Sutherin (3). **B.C.** (10) – TD, Mack Burton; FG, Peter Kempf; con., Kempf.

**1962** at Exhibition Stadium, Toronto. **Winnipeg** (28) – TDs, Leo Lewis (2), Charlie Shepard (2); cons., Gerry James (4). **Hamilton** (27) – TDs, Garney Henley (2), Bobby Kuntz, Dave Viti; cons., Don Sutherin (2); single, Sutherin.

**1961** at Exhibition Stadium, Toronto. **Winnipeg** (21) – TDs, Gerry James, Ken Ploen (in overtime); FGs, James (2); cons., James (2); single, Jack Delveaux. **Hamilton** (14) – TDs, Paul Dekker, Ralph Goldston; cons., Don Sutherin (2).

**1960** at Empire Stadium, Vancouver. **Ottawa** (16) – TDs, Bill Sowalski, Kaye Vaughan; FG, Gary Schreider; con., Schreider. **Edmonton** (6) – TD, Jim Letcavits.

**1959** at Exhibition Stadium, Toronto. **Winnipeg** (21) – TDs, Charlie Shepard, Ernie Pitts; FG, Gerry James; cons., James (2); singles, Shepard (4). **Hamilton** (7) – FGs, Steve Oneshuk (2); single, Vince Scott.

**1958** at Empire Stadium, Vancouver. **Winnipeg** (35) – TDs, Jim Van Pelt (2), Norm Rauhaus, Charlie Shepard; FGs, Van Pelt (2); cons., Van Pelt (4); single, Shepard. **Hamilton** (28) – TDs, Ron Howell (2), Ralph Goldston, Gerry McDougall; cons., Steve Oneschuk (4).

**1957** at Varsity Stadium, Toronto. **Hamilton** (32) – TDs, Ray Bawel, Bernie Faloney, Gerry McDougall, Cookie Gilchrist (2); cons., Steve Oneschuk (2). **Winnipeg** (7) – TD, Dennis Mendyk; con., Ken Ploen.

**1956** at Varsity Stadium, Toronto. **Edmonton** (50) – TDs, Jackie Parker (3), Don Getty (2), Johnny Bright (2); FG, Joe Mobra; cons., Mobra (4); single, Parker. **Montreal** (27) – TDs, Hal Patterson (2), Sam Etcheverry, Pat Abbruzzi; cons., Bill Bewley (3).

**1955** at Empire Stadium, Vancouver. **Edmonton** (34) – TDs, Normie Kwong (2), Johnny Bright (2), Bob Heydenfeldt; FG, Bob Dean; cons., Dean (5); single, Dean. **Montreal** (19) – TDs, Hal Patterson (2) Pat Abbruzzi; cons., Bud Korchak (3); single, Korchak.

**1954** at Varsity Stadium, Toronto. **Edmonton** (26) – TDs, Earl Lindley, Bernie Faloney, Glenn Lippman, Jackie Parker; FG, Bob Dean; cons., Dean (3). **Montreal** (25) – TDs, Red O'Quinn (2), Chuck Hunsinger, Joey Pal; cons., Jim Poole (4); single, Poole.

**1953** at Varsity Stadium, Toronto. **Hamilton** (12) – TDs, Vito Ragazzo, Ed Songin; cons., Tip Logan (2). **Winnipeg** (6) – TD, Gerry James; con., Bud Korchak.

**1952** at Varsity Stadium, Toronto. **Toronto** (21) – TDs, Nobby Wirkowski, Billy Bass, Zeke O'Connor; cons., Red Ettinger (3); FG, Ettinger. **Edmonton** (11) – TDs, Normie Kwong (2); con., Wilbur Snyder.

**1951** at Varsity Stadium, Toronto. **Ottawa** (21) – TDs, Benny MacDonnel, Pete Karpuk, Alton Baldwin; cons., Bob Gain (3); singles, Bruce Cummings (2), Tom O'Malley. **Saskatchewan** (14) – TDs, Jack Nix, Sully Glasser; cons., Red Ettinger (2); singles, Glenn Dobbs (2).

**1950** at Varsity Stadium, Toronto. **Toronto** (13) – TD, Al Dekdebrun; FGs, Nick Volpe (2); singles, Joe Krol (2). **Winnipeg** (0).

**1949** at Varsity Stadium, Toronto. **Montreal** (28) – TDs, Virgil Wagner (2), Bob Cunningham, Herb Trawick; cons., Ches McCance (3); FG, McCance; singles, McCance, Fred Kijek. **Calgary** (15)- TDs, Harry Hood, Sugarfoot Anderson; cons., Vern Graham (2); single, Keith Spaith; safety touch.

**1948** at Varsity Stadium, Toronto. **Calgary** (12) – TDs, Normie Hill, Pete Thodos; cons., Fred Wilmot (2). **Ottawa** (7) – TD, Bob Paffrath; con., Eric Chipper; single, Tony Golab.

**1947** at Varsity Stadium, Toronto. **Toronto** (10) – TD, Royal Copeland; con., Joe Krol; singles, Krol (4). **Winnipeg** (9) – TDs, Bob Sandberg; con., Don Hiney; FG, Hiney.

**1946** at Varsity Stadium, Toronto. **Toronto** (28) – TDs, Royal Copeland, Joe Krol, Rod Smylie, Byron Karrys, Boris Tipoff; cons., Krol (3). **Winnipeg** (6) – TD, Wally Dobler; con., Dobler.

**1945** at Varsity Stadium, Toronto. **Toronto** (35) – TDs, Doug Smylie (2), Billy Myers (2), Royal Copeland, Joe Krol; cons. Krol (2), Smylie, Frank Hickey; single, Art Skidmore. **Winnipeg** (0).

**1944** at Civic Stadium, Hamilton. **St. Hyacinthe-Donnacona Navy** (7) – TD, Johnny Taylor; singles, Dutch Davey (2). **Hamilton Wildcats** (6) – TD, Paul Miocinovich; con., Joe Krol.

**1943** at Varsity Stadium, Toronto. **Hamilton Flying Wildcats** (23) – TDs, Doug Smith, Jimmy Fumio, Mel Lawson; cons., Joe Krol (3); FG, Krol; singles, Krol, Smith. **Winnipeg R.A.F. Bombers** (14) – TDs, Garney Smith, Dave Berry; cons., Ches McCance (2); singles, Brian Quinn (2).

**1942** at Varsity Stadium, Toronto. **Toronto R.C.A.F. Hurricanes** (8) – TD, John Poplowski; singles, Fred Kijek (2), Don Crowe (1). **Winnipeg R.C.A.F. Bombers** (5) – TD, Lloyd Boivin.

**1941** at Varsity Stadium, Toronto. **Winnipeg Blue Bombers** (18) – TDs, Mel Wilson, Bud Marquardt; cons., Ches McCance (2); FGs, McCance (2). **Ottawa** (16) – TD, Tony Golab; con., George Fraser; FGs, Fraser (3); single, Fraser.

**1940** at Varsity Stadium, Toronto. **Ottawa** (8) – TD, Dave Sprague; con., Rick Perley; singles, Sammy Sward (2). **Balmy Beach** (2) – Singles, Bobby Porter (2). At Lansdowne Park, Ottawa. **Ottawa** (12) – TD, Tommy Daley; con., Tiny Herman; singles, Sammy Sward (5), Herman. **Balmy Beach** (5) – TD, Bobby Porter.

**1939** at Lansdowne Park, Ottawa. **Winnipeg Blue Bombers** (8) – TD, Andy Bieber; singles, Greg Kabat (2), Art Stevenson. **Ottawa** (7) – TD, Andy Tommy; con., Tiny Herman; single, Herman.

**1938** at Varsity Stadium, Toronto. **Toronto** (30) – TDs, Red Storey (3), Art West, Bernie Thornton; cons., Bill Stukus (2), Annis Stukus (2); single, Annis Stukus. **Winnipeg Blue Bombers** (7) – FGs, Greg Kabat (2); single, Art Stevenson.

**1937** at Varsity Stadium, Toronto. **Toronto** (4) – FG, Earl Selkirk; single, Bob Isbister. **Winnipeg Blue Bombers** (3) – Singles, Steve Olander (2), Greg Kabat.

**1936** at Varsity Stadium, Toronto. **Sarnia** (26) – TDs, Ormond Beach (2), Mike Hedgewick (2); cons., Alex Hayes (4); singles, Bummer Stirling (2). **Ottawa** (20) – TDs, Andy Tommy, Bunny Wadsworth, Arnie Morrison; cons., Tiny Herman (2); singles, Morrison (2), Jack Leore.

**1935** at A.A.A. Grounds, Hamilton. **Winnipeg 'Pegs** (18) – TDs, Bud Marquardt, Greg Kabat, Fritz Hanson; cons., Russ Rebholz (2); single, Kabat. **Hamilton Tigers** (12) – TD, Wilf Patterson; FG, Frank Turville; singles, Turville (2); safety touch.

**1934** at Varsity Stadium, Toronto. **Sarnia** (20) – TDs, Gordon Paterson, Johnny Manore; cons., Alex Hayes (2); FG, Hayes; singles, Bummer Stirling (5). **Regina** (12) – TDs, Ted Olson, Steve Adkins; con., Paul Kirk; single, Olson.

**1933** at Davis Field, Sarnia. **Toronto** (4) – FG, Tommy Burns; single, Ab Box. **Sarnia** (3) – Singles, Bummer Stirling (3).

**1932** at A.A.A. Grounds, Hamilton. **Hamilton Tigers** (25) – TDs, Dinny Gardner, Beano Wright, Jimmy Simpson; cons., Gardner (2), Frank Turville; singles, Turville, Ray Boadway; FG, Gardner; safety touch. **Regina** (6) – TD, Austin DeFrate; con., Curt Schave.

**1931** at Molson Stadium, Montreal. **Montreal Winged Wheelers** (22) – TDs, Pete Jotkus, Kenny Grant, Wally Whitty; FG, Huck Welch; cons., Welch, Warren Stevens; singles, Welch (2). **Regina** (0).

**1930** at Varsity Stadium, Toronto. **Balmy Beach** (11) – TD, Bobby Reid; singles, Claude Harris (3), Ab Box (3). **Regina** (6) – TD, Fred Brown; single, Saul Bloomfield.

**1929** at A.A.A. Grounds, Hamilton. **Hamilton Tigers** (14) – TD, Jimmy Simpson; singles, Pep Leadlay (3), Huck Welch (6). **Regina** (3) – Singles, Saul Bloomfield (2), Jerry Erskine.

**1928** at A.A.A. Grounds, Hamilton. **Hamilton Tigers** (30) – TDs, Jimmy Simpson (2), Brian Timmis (2), Ken Walker; cons., Pep Leadlay (3); singles, Huck Welch (2). **Regina** (0).

**1927** at Varsity Stadium, Toronto. **Balmy Beach** (9) – TD, Alex Ponton Sr.; singles, Yip Foster (3), Ernie Crowhurst. **Hamilton Tigers** (6) – TD, Tebor McKelvey; single, Pep Leadlay.

**1926** at Varsity Stadium, Toronto. **Ottawa Senators** (10) – TD, Charlie Lynch; singles, Joe Miller (5). **U. of Toronto** (7) – Singles, Trimble (5), Snyder (2).

**1925** at Lansdowne Park, Ottawa. **Ottawa Senators** (24) – TDs, Charlie Connell (2), Edgar Mulroney, Don Young; singles, Charlie Lynch (4). **Winnipeg Tammany Tigers** (1) – Single, Eddie Grant.

**1924** at Varsity Stadium, Toronto. **Queen's U.** (11) – TDs, James Wright; con., Pep Leadlay; singles, Leadlay (3); safety touch. **Balmy Beach** (3) – Singles, Morris Hughes (3).

**1923** at Varsity Stadium, Toronto. **Queen's U.** (54) – TDs, Harry Batstone (2), Bill Campbell (2), Johnny Evans (2), N.L. Walker, Carl Quinn, Roy Reynolds; cons., Pep Leadlay (4), Batstone (2); singles, Leadlay (3). **Regina** (0).

**1922** at Richardson Stadium, Kingston. **Queen's U.** (13) – TDs, Charlie Mundell, Dave Harding; con., Pep Leadlay; singles, Leadlay (2). **Edmonton Elks** (1) – Single, Jack Fraser.

**1921** at Varsity Stadium, Toronto. **Toronto Argonauts** (23) – TDs, Lionel Conacher (2), Shrimp Cochrane; con., Harry Batstone; FG, Conacher; singles, Conacher (2), Glenn Sullivan (2). **Edmonton Eskimos** (0).

**1920** at Varsity Stadium, Toronto. **U. of Toronto** (16) – TDs, Warren Snyder, Jo-Jo Stirrett, Red Mackenzie; con., Mackenzie. **Toronto Argonauts** (3) – Singles, Dunc Munro (3).

**1915** at Varsity Stadium, Toronto. **Hamilton Tigers** (13) – TDs, Jack Erskine, N. Lutz; con., Sam Manson; singles, Manson (2). **Toronto Rowing** (7) – FG, George Bickle; singles, Hal DeGruchy (2), Bickle (2).

**1914** at Varsity Stadium, Toronto. **Toronto Argonauts** (14) – TDs, Glad Murphy, Freddie Mills; con., Jack O'Connor; FG, O'Connor. **U. of Toronto** (2) – Singles, J.W. MacKenzie, L. Saunders.

**1913** at Hamilton Cricket Grounds, Hamilton. **Hamilton Tigers** (44) – TDs, Art Wilson (3), Ross Craig (2), Bob Isbister Sr., Harry Glassford; cons., Manson (4); singles, Manson (4), Billy Mallett. **Toronto Parkdale** (2) – Singles, Hughie Gall (2).

**1912** at Hamilton Cricket Grounds, Hamilton. **Hamilton Alerts** (11) – TD, Ross Craig; con., Craig; singles, Tout Leckie (5). **Toronto Argonauts** (4) – Singles, Crossen Clarke (2); safety touch.

**1911** at Varsity Stadium, Toronto. **U. of Toronto** (14) – TDs, Allan Ramsay, Frank Knight; cons., Jack Maynard (2); singles, Maynard (2). **Toronto Argonauts** (7) – FG, Ross Binkley; singles, Binkley (3), Bill Mallett.

**1910** at Hamilton Cricket Grounds, Hamilton. **U. of Toronto** (16) – TDs, Red Dixon, Jack Maynard; con., Maynard; singles, Hughie Gall (2), Dixon (2), Maynard. **Hamilton Tigers** (7) – FG, Kid Smith; singles, Ben Simpson (3), Smith.

**1909** at Rosedale Field, Toronto. **U. of Toronto** (26) – TDs, Hughie Gall, Murray Thomson, Smirle Lawson; con., Bill Ritchie; singles, Gall (8), Lawson (2). **Toronto Parkdale** (6) – TD, Tom Meighan; single, Percy Killaly.

# PARTICIPANTS AND COACHES

**1909 – University of Toronto:** Dixon, Lawson, Newton, Gall, Foulds, Ritchie, Bell, Rankin, Kingston, Muir, Lajoie, Hume, Thomson, Gage, Cruickshank, Park, MacDonald, Dickson, Jones. Coach: Harry Griffith. **Parkdale Canoe Club:** Brady, Moore, Killaly, Cromar, J. Dissette, Leonard, Duncan, Addison, Ross, F. Dissette, Meaghan, Harper, Barber, Brockbank. Coach: Ed Livingstone.

**1910 – University of Toronto:** Dixon, Gage, Gall, Maynard, Foulds, Carroll, Bell, Leonard, Lajoie, Grass, Kingston, Clark, M. Thomson, Kennedy, Cory, German, Thompson, Park, Green, Gardner, Dawson. Coach: Harry Griffith. **Hamilton Tigers:** Kid Smith, Simpson, Moore, Burton, Awrey, Barron, Pfeiffer, Craig, McFarlane, Marshall, Potticary, Isbister, Glassford, Gatenby. Coach: Seppi DuMoulin.

**1911 – University of Toronto:** Taylor, Maynard, Greene, Ramsay, Campbell, Curtis, Knight, Bell, Clark, Cory, German, Grass, Sinclair, Hassard, Dales, Knox, Wood, Sifton, Thompson, Lorimer, Frith, MacDonald, Cruickshank. Coach: Dr. A.B. Wright. **Toronto Argonauts:** Smith, Lawson, Binkley, Mallett, O'Connor, Sinclair, Russell, Kent, Gale, Arnoldt, Murphy, Wigle, Moore, Murray. Coach: Billy Foulds.

**1912 – Hamilton Alerts:** Flannery, Carr, Leckie, Becker, Harper, Pfeiffer, McCarthy, J. Craig, Grey, R. Craig, Clark, Bleakley, Fisher, Smith, Fickley, Spence, Fitzgerald, McLeod, Gooddale, Fitzpatrick, Gerrard, Sheridan, Snyder. Coach: Liz Marriott. **Toronto Argonauts:** Meeghan, Lawson, Binkley, O'Connor, Dissette, Greer, Mulligan, Sinclair, Galt, Foster, Murphy, Heuther, Murray, Reaume, Clark, Patterson. Coach: Jack Newton.

**1913 – Hamilton Tigers:** Isbister, Mallett, Manson, McKelvey, Chagnon, Meyers, Young, Woodley, Craig, Wilson, Shuart, Clark, Gatenby, Glassford, Smith, Dixon, O'Heir, Myles. Coach: Liz Marriott. **Parkdale Canoe Club:** Boddy, Bickle, Gall, Zimmerman, Birnie, Dudley, Davidson, Leyfield, Potticary, Miller, Hughes, Robinson, Simpson, Gardner, Doan, Barber, McEachern. Coach: Ed Livingstone.

**1914 – Toronto Argonauts:** Murphy, Smith, O'Connor, Holmes, Mills, Patterson, Davison, Simpson, McFarlane, Foster, Motley, Burkart, Murray, Knight, Duff, Skippon, Lawson, Lobraico, Duke, McDonald, Dibble, Bickle, Murray, Alan, Lepper, Gonter. Coach: Billy Foulds. **University of Toronto:** Gage, McKenzie, Sheehy, Doyle, Saunders, Stratton, Horner, Gardiner, Nicholson, O'Reilly, McMullen, Bryon, Hughes, Cassels, Clarkson, Adelard, Sinclair. Coach: Hugh Gall.

**1915 – Hamilton Tigers:** Erskine, Manson, J. McKelvey, C. McKelvey, N. Lutz, Brydges, Glassford, Myles, Ireland, McFarlane, Vansickle, Shuart, Clark, Fisher, Clements, Meyers, Wilson. Coach: Liz Marriott. **Toronto Argonauts:** MacLaren, De Gruchy, Broderick, Bickle, Hobbs, Brown, Duncan, O'Leary, Woolnough, Crawford, Holden, Whale, Burkart, Moore. Coach: Ed Livingstone.

**1920 – University of Toronto:** Duncan, Breen, Snyder, McKenzie, Murray, N. Taylor, Douglas, Ferguson, Carew, Wesman, Wallace, G. Stirrett, Fisher, Rolph, Sullivan, J. Taylor, Allan, J. Stirrett, Earle, Carruthers, Ketchum, Hyde, Houston, Weaver, Hobbs. Coach: Laddie Cassels. **Toronto Argonauts:** Gilhooley, Batstone, O'Connor, Munro, Cochrane, Polson, Shoebottom, Sinclair, Huestis, Romeril, Sullivan, Hay, Greey, Britnell, Garrett, Pugh, Henderson, Young, Fear, Parke, Laurie, Murphy. Coach: Mike Rodden.

**1921 – Toronto Argonauts:** Stirrett, Batstone, Conacher, McCormack, Cochrane, Douglas, G. Sullivan, Hay, Romeril, Earle, Fear, Britnell, F. Sullivan, MacKenzie, Bradfield, Abbott, A. Sinclair, Heustis, Thom, Burkart, Pugh, Young, Burt, Clarke, Polson, Wallace. Coach: Sinc McEvenue. **Edmonton Eskimos:** Sheard, Dunsworth, Dorman, Fraser, Rankin, Shieman, Fowler, Stevens, Palmer, Yancey, Day, Burnett, Harrison, Emery, Moore, Creighton, Seeley, Darling, Pilgrim, Bill. Coach: Deacon White.

**1922 – Queen's University:** McLeod, Batstone, Leadlay, Harding, Evans, Lewis, Muirhead, Carson, McKelvey, Mundell, Walker, Thomas, Delahey, Dolan, Veale, Reynolds, Johnson, Nichols, Grondin, McNeil, Bond, Burns, Campbell. Coach: Billy Hughes. **Edmonton Elks:** Dorman, Fraser, Dunsworth, Creighton, Brown, Shieman, Carrigan, Duke, Palmer, Yancey, Cullinane, Burnett, Seeley, Adams, McAllister, Spence, Day, Brunson, McColl. Coach: Deacon White.

**1923 – Queen's University:** Campbell, Batstone, Leadlay, G. McKelvey, Evans, Lewis, Adams, Muirhead, R. McKelvey, Reynolds, Walker, Thomas, Quinn, McNeil, Bond, Aird, Anglin, McLeod, Grondin, Mundell, Brown, Baldwin, Delahay. Coach: Billy Hughes. **Regina Roughriders:** Milne, Arnott, McEachern, Rowand, Sandstrom, Creighton, Bates, Kerr, Rennebohm, Crapper, Leigh, Brown, Peebles, Rogers, Foster, Wood, Otton, Gilhooly, Smith. Coach: Jack Eddis.

**1924 – Queen's University:** McLeod, Leadlay, G. McKelvey, Batstone, Baldwin, Lewis, Muirhead, Brown, Reynolds, Airth, Thomas, Wright, Chantler, Hannon, Adams, Grondin, Skelton, Burley, Abernethi, J. McKelvey, McDonnell, Howard, Norrie, Voss. Coach: Billy Hughes. **Balmy Beach:** Ponton, Britton, Hughes, Cawkell, Buett, Commins, Keith, Smythe, Reeves, Bell, McLean, Stewart, Foster, Whetter, Snyder, Stronach, Polson, Ogden, Robinson, Guthrie. Coaches: M. Rodden, A. Buett.

**1925 – Ottawa Senators:** Emerson, Tubman, Mulroney, Connell, Lynch, Bruce, Wright, Humphrey, Timmis, Monahan, Starr, Young, Ault, James, Ketchum, Anderson, Buells, Herbert, Short, Curry, Chevrier, Cote, Pritchard, Miller, Grosvenor, Dunne, Kealey, Brassington, McMillan, Kirby. Coach: Dave McCann. **Winnipeg Tammany Tigers:** Buckingham, Warren, Laing, Van Vliet, Shaw, Delman, Hovey, Binney, Roth, McLeod, Redpath, Puttee, Grant, Counsell, Coultry, Milledge, McMahon, Bullock. Coach: Harold Roth.

**1926 – Ottawa Senators:** Emerson, Miller, Tubman, Connell, Lynch, Bruce, Ketchum, Humphrey, Starr, Dunne, D. Young, Brassington, McMillan, Wright, Kehoe, Herbert, Kirby, Grosvenor, Ackland, Fournier, Phillips, Dunlop, Stevenson, Mulroney, Paget, Conn, Fraser, Gilles, Cote, Kealey, Pritchard, Snelling. Coach: Dave McCann. **University of Toronto:** A. Young, Sinclair, W. Snyder, Trimble, Roos, Morgan, D. Carrick, Marritt, Stollery, Dundas, Irwin, M. Snyder, Carroll, McFayden, Hargraft, J. Carrick, Long, Wood, Daly. Coach: Ron McPherson.

**1927 – Balmy Beach:** Snyder, Moore, Foster, Smith, Ponton, Commins, Hendry, Amer, Hamlin, Crowhurst, Keith, Manzies, Hobbs, Cawkell, Dewitt, Metcalfe, Wright, McNichol, Trimble, Billings, Johnson, Newman, Robertson, Crozier, Reeve, Reid, Lewis. Coach: Dr. H. Hobbs. **Hamilton Tigers:** Small, Wright, Leadlay, Languay, McKelvey, Cox, Denman, French, Baker, Timmis, Veale, Bowman, Walker, Shuttleworth, Nolan, McRae, Gibb, Wager, Springstead, Charters, Robinson, Boden. Coach: Mike Rodden.

**1928 – Hamilton Tigers:** Small, Gibb, Welch, Boadway, Walker, Cox, Denman, Elford, Baker, Timmis, Simpson, Veale, Leadlay, Wright, Murphy, Fitzpatrick, Inksetter, Chappell, Crawford, Tope, Baker. Coach: Mike Rodden. **Regina Roughriders:** Grubb, Wilson, Erskine, Grassick, Sandstrom, Gilhooly, Pitman, Patrick, Bates, Arnott, Busch, Duff, Bloomfield, James, Doctor, Currie, Urness, Warner, McDougall, Traynor, Mitchell. Coach: Howie Milne.

**1929 – Hamilton Tigers:** Small, Welch, B. Wright, Languay, Walker, Cox, Denman, Inksetter, Timmis, Elford, Fear, Simpson, E. Wright, Gibb, Leadlay, Boadway, Chapple, Clark, J. Wright, French, Dagg, Stevens, Murphy. Coach: Mike Rodden. **Regina Roughriders:** Traynor, Bloomfield, Grubb, James, Mitchell, Campbell, Patrick, Clark, Meyers, Gilhooly, Duff, Wood, Grassick, Erskine, McDougall, Dwyer, Brown, Gerber, Barber, Goodman. Coach: Al Ritchie.

**1930 – Balmy Beach:** Harris, MacKenzie, Box, Foster, Kirkpatrick, Commins, Reid, Taylor, Hendry, Trimble, Snyder, Keith, T. Kirkland, Reeve, Jones, Knowles, Northam, Stewart, May, A. Kirkland, Botsford. Coach: Alex Ponton. **Regina Roughriders:** Grubb, Traynor, Bloomfield, Currie, Mitchell, Campbell, Thompson, Patrick, Urness, Meyer, Busch, Brown, Grassick, Garuik, Williams, Gilhooly, Jackson, Barber, Goodman. Coach: Al Ritchie.

**1931 – Montreal Winged Wheelers:** Stevens, Whitty, Perry, Welch, Haynes, Tellier, Pigeon, Adams, Burns, Hempey, Grant, Garbarino, Bennett, Sheppard, Hutton, Jotkus, McCaig, Stark, Wanless, McBrearty, Stevenson, Monty, Corsaro, Delahey, Robinson. Coach: Clary Foran. **Regina Roughriders:** Grubb, Schave, James, Goodman, Mitchell, Gilhooly, Garuik, Clark, Thompson, Urness, Busch, Warner, Traynor, Auld, Patrick, Beattie, Barber, Grassick, Campbell, Bloomfield. Coach: Al Ritchie.

**1932 – Hamilton Tigers:** Small, Turville, Gardner, Boadway, Sutton, Barker, Denman, Clarke, Timmis, Sprague, Simpson, Wilson, Walker, Wright, Reed, Friday, Tedford, Summerhayes, Patterson, Woelke, Parker, Crawford, Thornton. Coach: Billy Hughes. **Regina Roughriders:** Schave, Roseborough, Harrison, Young, De Frate, Campbell, Mjogdalen, Thompson, Garuik, Barber, Hilts, Busch, Mitchell, Jacobsen, Warner, Grassick, York, Stinson, Carswell, Gilhooly, Remick, Thompson, Traynor, Christie, Deacon, Lapoint, Lockhart. Coach: Al Ritchie.

**1933 – Toronto Argonauts:** Smith, Box, J.R. Taylor, Morris, Mullan, Wright, Palmer, McNichol, Burns, Tindall, Cutler, Moore, Munro, Upper, Stevenson, Griffiths, Wilson, Miller, Staughton, Vail, DeDiana, Valeriote, Keith, Ferris, Bell, Snyder, J.M. Taylor, Chepesuik. Coach: Lew Hayman. **Sarnia Imperials:** Harris, Brown, Stirling, Perry, Hayes, Molloy, Spears, Butler, Putman, Smith, Reeves, Manore, Patterson, Parsaca, Geary, Baker, McKay, Clark, Burr, Welch, McLean, Parsons. Coach: Pat Ouellette.

**1934 – Sarnia Imperials:** Beach, Paterson, Stirling, Perry, Hayes, Molloy, Butler, Spears, Putnam, Smith, Manore, Reeves, Parsaca, Macvicar, Vanhorne, McKay, Fraser, Baker, Parsons, Harris, McLean, Thorpe, Wickware, Chilton, Buxton, Morre, Scott, Geary. Coach: Art Massucci. **Regina Roughriders:** Achtzener, Young, Kirk, Pierce, Olson, Lydiard, Hegan, Garuik, Walker, Sprague, Adkins, Miller, Sandstrom, Renwick, Renix, Busch, Chiga, Partridge, Tomecko, Wood. Coach: Greg Grassick.

**1935 – Winnipeg 'Pegs:** Kabat, Rebholz, Hanson, James, Fritz, Adelman, Kushner, Oja, Mogul, Peschel, Marquardt, Perpich, Lane, Kobrinsky, Coulter, Harris, Ceretti, Patrick, Christie, Mobberley, Roseborough, Pagones, Harding, Nicklin, Law, Grant, Daigle. Coach: Bob Fritz. **Hamilton Tigers:** Ferraro, Welch, Smiley, Craig, Paterson, Brock, Summerhayes, Friday, Timmis, Wright, Wilson, Simpson, Turville, Reed, Gurney, Thornton, Agnew, Stull, G. Mountain, Dunn. Coach: Fred Veale.

**1936 – Sarnia Imperials:** Beach, Hedgewick, Stirling, Parsaca, Hayes, Burr, Rutter, Paterson, Clawson, Parsons, Norris, Stevenson, Van Horne, Woodcock, McLean, Harris, France. Coach: Art Massucci. **Ottawa Rough Riders:** Zelicovitz, Tommy, Roccano, Daley, Morrison, Moynahan, Herman, Fraser, Ross, Sprague, Perley, McCarthy, McCauley, Wood, Leore, Burke, Saunders, Donaldson, Casserley, Ussher, Wadsworth, Higgs. Coach: Billy Hughes.

**1937 – Toronto Argonauts:** Morris, West, Isbister, W. MacPherson, B. Stukus, Barker, Palmer, Staughton, Burt, Evans, Cutler, Bryers, Vail, Young, Ferris, Selkirk, Miller, Deadey, Storey, Zock, Mingay, Barber, Booth, Gairdner, Conquergood, Reid, Sonshine, Riddell, D. MacPherson, A. Stukus, Edwards, Lewis, Wedley. Coach: Lew Hayman. **Winnipeg Blue Bombers:** Kabat, Hanson, Olander, Stevenson, Fritz, Adelman, Mogul, Ceretti, Peschel, Oja, Marquardt, Nicklin, Roseborough, Kobrinsky, James, Harris, Mobberley, Nairn, Lucid, McCance. Coach: Bob Fritz.

**1938 – Toronto Argonauts:** Morris, West, Isbister, MacPherson, B. Stukus, Hees, Staughton, Palmer, Burt, Evans, Thornton, Cutler, Vail, Levantis, A. Stukus, Selkirk, Reid, Miller, Storey, McLean, Barber, Munro, Booth, Wedley, Ferris, Zock, Mingay, F. Stukus, Clark. Coach: Lew Hayman. **Winnipeg Blue Bombers:** Kabat, Hanson, Boivin, James, Stevenson, Wilson, Ceretti, Peschel, Gainor, Mogul, Marquardt, Roseborough, Kushner, Hatskin, Mobberley, Bieber, Nairn, Badger, McCance. Coach: Reg Threlfall.

**1939 – Winnipeg Blue Bombers:** Nicklin, Badger, Bieber, Hanson, Kabat, Wilson, Ceretti, Nairn, Gainor, Mogul, Platz, McCance, Sheley, Krisko, Boivin, Mobberley, Kushner, Peschel, Roseborough, Marquardt, Stevenson, Lear, Hatskin, Haycock, Mulvey, Iannone, Manners, Lake, Davidson. Coach: Reg Threlfall. **Ottawa Rough Riders:** Sward, Griffin, Tommy, Daley, Burke, Taylor, Herman, Fraser, G. Sprague, D. Sprague, Perley, McCarthy, Moynahan, Wadsworth, Seguin, Golab, O'Neil, McWatters, Trembley, Chipper, Ross, Edwards. Coach: Ross Trimble.

**1940 – Ottawa Rough Riders:** Sward, Griffin, Tommy, Daley, Burke, Moynahan, Fraser, Herman, Wadsworth, Seguin, McCarthy, Perley, Sprague, Sims, Taylor, Haigh, Chipper, O'Connor, Golab, O'Neil, McWatters, McGarry, Trembley, Langley, Norton, Edwards, Charbonneau, Fraser, Pilon. Coach: Ross Trimble. **Balmy Beach:** Seymour, Porter, Crowe, Drinkwater, Manson, Turner, Reid, Barron, Shields, Downard, Deadey, Salter, Foderingham, Frizelle, Morin, Marchant, Holden, Giles, Shuba, Tunnicliffe, Walker, Alexander, Brasser, Turnbull, Goodwin. Coach: Alex Ponton.

**1941 – Winnipeg Blue Bombers:** McCance, Lindsay, Hanson, Sheley, Lander, Wilson, Roseborough, Lear, Mogul, Manners, Marquardt, Thornton, Shore, Hatskin, Draper, Peschel, Kolisnyk, Boivin, McFayden, Daniels, Evenson, Ludwig, Chikowski, Preston. Coach: Reg Threlfall. **Ottawa Rough Riders:** Tommy, Daley, Golab, Griffin, Burke, Moynahan, Fraser, Seguin, McGarry, Sprague, McCarthy, O'Connor, Wadsworth, Langley, Taylor, Haigh, Klimenko, Chipper, O'Neil, McWatters, Charbonneau, Fripp, Trembley, Sims. Coach: Ross Trimble.

**1942 – Toronto R.C.A.F. Hurricanes:** Kijek, Thompson, Alexander, Parry, B. Stukus, Gaudaur, McGarry, Langley, Evans, Durno, Poscavage, Burton, Crowe, Partridge, Buckmaster, Taylor, Foderingham, Oliphant, West, Saruis, Poplowski, Prince, Reynolds, Richman, Murray, Kennedy, Ozarko, Kenricks, Carney, Richards, Jackson. Coach: Lew Hayman. **Winnipeg R.C.A.F. Bombers:** McCance, Branigan, Mathers, Lake, Sheley, Wilson, Roseborough, Lear, Ludwig, Mogul, Boivin, Moorehouse, McPhee, Johnston, Ahoff, Shore, Frobister, Lavitt, Finnson, Charlton, McFayden, Chikowski, Fritz. Coach: Reg Threlfall.

**1943 – Hamilton Flying Wildcats:** Hickey, Krol, D. Smith, Peterson, Lawson, Breza, Remigis, Gibb, Zvonkin, Bovaird, Simpson, Fumio, Stollery, Miocinovich, Crowe, Irvin, Groom, Travele, Cousins, Santucci, Brown, McDonald, Langford, Manorek, Burkhart, Capelli, J. Smith, Jones, Withers. Coach: Brian Timmis. **Winnipeg R.C.A.F. Bombers:** McCance, Smith, Capraru, Quinn, Greenberg, Shore, Shields, Lear, Ludwig, Lucid, Chikowski, Durno, Duncan, Olsen, Miller, Lavitt, Berry, Branigan, Sheldon, Ahoff, Geller, Border, McFayden, Lake. Coach: Reg Threlfall.

**1944 – St. Hyacinthe-Donnacona Navy Combines:** Barclay, Kirbyson, Davey, MacLeod, Hurley, Crncich, Bainbridge, Levantis, Santucci, Taylor, Montague, Ellis, McFall, Kotavich, Campbell, Sims, Raymon, Patch, Reid, Spicer, Baker, Chard, Abbott, Leonard, Swarbrick, Wedley, Ellis, Charron, Scully. Coach: Glen Brown. **Hamilton Wildcats:** Hickey, Krol, Manorek, Peterson, Capriotti, Breaza, Mountain, Remigis, Paul, Wheeler, G. Lawson, Fumio, Schwenger, M. Lawson, Miocinovich, Zvonkin, Simpson, Miller, Cousins, Awrey, Brown, Jones, Wright, Agnew, Dyack. Coach: Eddie McLean.

**1945 – Toronto Argonauts:** Skidmore, Smylie, Copeland, B. Karrys, Doty, Glenn, Morris, Zock, Ascott, Levantis, Cassidy, Wedley, Krol, Waldon, Bell, Richardson, Carr-Harris, Hickey, Leeming, Myers, S. Karrys, Pruski, Geyer, Curtin, Berwesser, Roe, Brown, Bainbridge, Graham, Sullivan, Foy, Reid, Materyn, Tommy, Hiltz, Courtney. Coach: Ted Morris. **Winnipeg Blue Bombers:** McCance, Johnson, Boivin, Frobister, Shore, Wilson, Iannone, Irvine, Manners, Ludwig, McFadden, Mulvey, Hobson, Pollock, Border, Draper, Daniels, Bohunicki, Geller, Hood, Lucid, Vidruk, Evanson, Ogelski, Summers. Coach: Bert Warwick.

**1946 – Toronto Argonauts:** S. Karrys, B. Karrys, Krol, Copeland, Bell, Loney, Zock, Morris, Ascott, S. Levantis, Reid, Wedley, Courtney, B. Levantis, Tipoff, Camilerri, Glenn, Deadey, P. Titanic, Robinson, Grice, Santucci, Smylie, West, Waldon, Sullivan, O'Brien, Carr-Harris, Myers, Skidmore, Booker, Pruski, McKim, Jacobs, Richardson, Cassidy, M. Titanic, Neale. Coach: Ted Morris. **Winnipeg Blue Bombers:** Smith, Hood, Ordway, Gauthier, Dobler, Wilson, Ceretti, Hammond, Manners, Gainor, Shore, Fitzgibbons, Hiney, Draper, Irving, Iannone, Geller, Macdonald, Vidruk, Ahoff, Chikowski, Frederickson, Grant, Passman. Coach: Jack West.

**1947 – Toronto Argonauts:** McKay, Copeland, Krol, Karrys, Doty, Turner, Morris, Zock, J. Levantis, Ascott, Wedley, P. Titanic, Robinson, Hazel, Pyzer, Brown, B. Stukus, Fleet, Grass, Reid, Trumbull, Meen, Cassidy, Briggs, S. Levantis, Harrison, Camilerri, Sullivan, Croyhers, Haddleton, Sakell, Bell, Courtney, Skidmore, Huntley, Pruski, McKim, Foderingham, Carr-Harris, Hickey. Coach: Ted Morris. **Winnipeg Blue Bombers:** Reagan, Don Smith, Hood, Sandberg, Hiney, Wilson, Ahoff, Iannone, Bob Smith, Passman, Gord Smith, Westrum, Perry, Ceretti, Vidruk, Irving, Lucid, Wood, Williams, Turner, Geller, Badger, Bergson, Hobson. Coach: Jack West.

**1948 – Calgary Stampeders:** Mitchener, Gyles, Hanson, Rowe, Spaith, C. Anderson, Iannone, Tomlinson, Pullar, Aguirre, Chikowski, Berry, Hood, Kwong, Hill, Thodos, Kliewer, Wilmot, Ludwig, Lear, Strode, Carter, H. Anderson, Pantages, Wusyk, Adams. Coach: Les Lear. **Ottawa Rough Riders:** Asquini, Turner, Smylie, Golab, Paffrath, Loney, Lefebvre, Steck, Canavan, Wagoner, Haigh, Anthony, Michaels, Powell, Greene, Dawson, McFaul, Chipper, Dunlap, Rogers, Karpuk, Lynch, Karrys, Tremblay. Coach: Wally Masters.

**1949 – Montreal Alouettes:** McCance, Cunningham, Festeryga, Wagner, Filchock, Keys, Quandamatteo, Hammond, Gladchuk, Trawick, Toohy, English, Vidruk, Segatore, Sheridan, Stevenson, Smith, Taylor, Douglas, Manastersky, Coulter, McParland, Harper, Kijek. Coach: Lew Hayman. **Calgary Stampeders:** Graham, Hood, Thodos, Pantages, Spaith, Wilson, Matheson, Iannone, Keir, Aguirre, Strode, E. Anderson, Kwong, Hill, Kliewer, Berry, Carter, Choukalos, Rowe, Turner, French, Hajash, Lear, H. Anderson. Coach: Les Lear.

**1950 – Toronto Argonauts:** R. Smylie, Curtis, Toogood, Bass, Dekdebrun, Hirsch, Black, McCormick, Parkin, Kerns, Scott, Whaley, Fowler, Dunlap, Bennett, Shore, McKenzie, Ascott, Wedley, Volpe, Krol, Karrys, Westlake, Stocks, P. Titanic. Coach: Frank Clair. **Winnipeg Blue Bombers:** Gibb, Casey, Ford, Stroppa, Jacobs, Brown, McPherson, Delecuw, Johnson, Tinsley, Henke, Aguirre, McPhail, Korchak, Petrow, Knowles, Vaccher, Irving, Sokol, Chambura, Wiley, Konarski, Gardiner, Norvack. Coach: Frank Larson.

**1951 – Ottawa Rough Riders:** Stanton, Turner, MacDonell, Cummings, O'Malley, Loney, Steck, Wagner, Bovey, Gain, Baldwin, Simpson, Crowe, Asquini, Anthony, Morneau, F. Dunlap, J. Dunlap, Rogers, Karpuk, Aull, Hatfield, Brennan, Carson, Hall. Coach: Clem Crowe. **Saskatchewan Roughriders:** Pelling, Glasser, Bodine, Charlton, Dobbs, Ettinger, McEwan, Iannone, Ruby, Cassidy, Wedley, Nix, Hungle, Springstein, Choukalis, Ortman, Radley, Pyne, Bell, McFaul, Wright, Wardien, Maguire, Clarke, McKim, Finlay, Yakymyk, Tremblay, Greene, Weir, Kelly, Martin, Becker, Russell, Sandberg. Coach: Harry Smith.

**1952 – Toronto Argonauts:** R. Smylie, Bass, Pyzer, Curtis, Wirkowski, Ettinger, Black, McKenzie, Carpenter, Parkin, Bruno, O'Connor, Shore, Roberts, Marshall, Ascott, Bennett, Soergel, Gray, Harpley, Scullion, Krol, D. Smylie, Karrys, Toogood, Copeland. Coach: Frank Clair. **Edmonton Eskimos:** King, Kwong, Miles, Pantages, Arnold, Keys, Quandamatteo, DeMarco, Blanchard, Snyder, Prather, Anderson, Morris, Zock, Paptroski, Bendiak, Briggs, Lord, Tully, Paffrath, Festeryga, Filchock, Mendryk, Chambers, Enright, McWhinney. Coach: Frank Filchock.

**1953 – Hamilton Tiger-Cats:** Miksza, Toohy, Custis, Dawson, Kusserow, Truant, Fraser, D. Brown, Bailey, Hapes, Songin, Gaudaur, Armstrong, Berezowski, Bevan, Darch, Scott, Wooley, B. Brown, Cross, Muzyka, Mazza, Ragazzo, Logan, Neumann, McTaggert, Garside. Coach: Carl Voyles. **Winnipeg Blue Bombers:** Korchak, Casey, James, McAlister, Kelly, Sokol, Meltzer, Skrien, Zaleski, Jacobs, Crain, Baxter, Bandiera, McPherson, Patrick, Rogers, Vidruk, Wiley, Huffman, Tinsley, Young, Armstrong, Grant, Lumsden, Hill, Pearce, Harpley. Coach: George Trafton.

**1954 – Edmonton Eskimos:** McWhinney, Parker, Miles, Kwong, Lippmann, Willsey, Mendryk, West, Kruger, Hayton, Bright, King, Faloney, Keys, Briggs, Barry, McLeod, Morris, Quandamatteo, Tully, Hodgson, Dean, Nelson, Zock, Anderson, Prather, Lindley, Bendiak. Coach: Frank Ivy. **Montreal Alouettes:** Pal, Mitchener, Moran, Webster, Adrian, Wagner, Belec, Hunsinger, Grigg, Bewley, Etcheverry, B. Coulter, Hugo, Sheridan, Blaicher, Cicia, Kovac, Trawick, Martinello, Hogan, Staton, Capozzi, T. Coulter, Elsby, Poole, Miller, O'Quinn, McNichol. Coach: Doug Walker.

**1955 – Edmonton Eskimos:** Miles, Simon, Kwong, Kruger, Willsey, Bright, Kelly, Lindley, Kimoff, Parker, Getty, Burris, Briggs, Barry, Morris, Tully, King, Hodgson, Walker, Cook, Dean, Volcan, Meinert, Stevenson, Heydenfeldt, Anderson, Mendryk, Bendiak, West, Quandamatteo. Coach: Frank Ivy. **Montreal Alouettes:** Pal, Moran, Korchak, Abbruzzi, Belec, Caroline, Darragh, Bewley, Blaicher, Williams, Klein, Etcheverry, B. Coulter, Hugo, MacLellan, Makowiecki, Trawick, Martinello, Kovac, Sheridan, T. Coulter, Staton, Elsby, Capozzi, O'Quinn, Patterson, McNichol, Miller. Coach: Doug Walker.

**1956 – Edmonton Eskimos:** McMillan, Shipka, Miles, Kwong, Bright, Kelly, Kimoff, Woyat, Kruger, Simon, Getty, Parker, Tatum, Barry, Briggs, A. Walker, Anderson, Morris, King, Kimech, Henderson, Nelson, Cook, Stevenson, Volcan, B. Walker, Mobra, Rowekamp, Bendiak, Mendryk, Tully. Coach: Frank Ivy. **Montreal Alouettes:** Abbruzzi, James, Pascal, Bewley, Pal, Blaicher, Dwyer, Karpuk, Tonegusso, Etcheverry, B. Coulter, Hugo, McLellan, Gibbons, Trawick, Kovac, Sheridan, Martinello, Baillie, Staton, T. Coulter, Shipp, Kirby, O'Quinn, Patterson, Miller, McNichol, Moran, Elsby. Coach: Doug Walker.

**1957 – Hamilton Tiger-Cats:** Howell, Grant, Fraser, Goldston, Curcillo, Macon, Graham, McDougall, Fedosoff, Gilchrist, Truant, Oneschuk, Faloney, Kelly, Miksza, Davis, DeNobile, Scott, Bevan, Suminski, Underwood, Barrow, Hughes, Dekker, Lampman, Bawel, Neumann, Toohy. Coach: Jim Trimble. **Winnipeg Blue Bombers:** Lewis, James, Rowland, Taylor, Miller, Shepard, Latourelle, Mendyk, Ploen, Roseborough, Druxman, Whitley, Bilicki, Gray, Michels, Piper, Savoie, Patrick, Tinsley, Hobart, Canakes, Rauhaus, Vincent, Gilliam, Pitts, Meadmore, Pearce, Luining. Coach: Bud Grant.

**1958 – Winnipeg Blue Bombers:** Varone, Shepard, Lewis, Ploen, Rowland, Latourelle, Kehrer, Miller, Potter, Van Pelt, Druxman, Warren, Bilicki, Burkholder, Gray, Kotowich, Piper, Savoie, Patrick, Tinsley, Hobert, Rigney, Rauhaus, Luining, Gilliam, Pitts, Meadmore, Pearce. Coach: Bud Grant. **Hamilton Tiger-Cats:** Howell, Grant, Campbell, McDougall, Fraser, Goldston, Macon, Graham, Karcz, Oneschuk, Sutherin, Hughes, Miksza, Bevan, Scott, DeNobile, Underwood, Barrow, Mosca, Suminski, Dekker, Lampman, Neumann, Toohy. Coach: Jim Trimble.

**1959 – Winnipeg Blue Bombers:** Janzen, Potter, Latourelle, Miller, Shepard, Shannon, Delveaux, Rowland, James, Lewis, Ploen, Druxman, Warren, Bilicki, Gray, Kotowich, Piper, Meadmore, Burkholder, Tinsley, Rigney, Savoie, Patrick, Pitts, Funston, Luining, Rauhaus, Ross. Coach: Bud Grant. **Hamiton Tiger-Cats:** McDougall, Wood, Howell, Grant, Oneschuk, Goldston, Macon, Chandler, Graham, Fraser, Faloney, Dawson, Miksza, Taylor, Scott, Bevan, Danjean, DeNobile, Barrow, Mosca, Suminski, Dekker, Lampman, Jones, Neumann, Paquette, Bell, Karcz. Coach: Jim Trimble.

**1960 – Ottawa Rough Riders:** Thelen, Stewart, Kelly, Brancato, Schreider, Nesbitt, Poirier, West, Daigneault, Conroy, Jackson, Lancaster, Bitkowski, Stracina, Scoccia, Bevan, Robinson, Vaughan, Koes, Mosca, Jones, Racine, Archambault, Graham, Simpson, Sowalski, Bruce, Reynolds, Bove, Collins, Selinger, Smith, Merz, Smale, Hayes, Kelly, Jelacic, Hamelin. Coach: Frank Clair. **Edmonton Eskimos:** Bright, Kwong, Shipka, Miles, J.B. Smith, Schumm, Kruger, Parker, Getty, Stephenson, Barry, Stevenson, Tully, Ecuyer, Kmech, Fracas, Gray, Volcan, Dye, Deese, Lamb, Nelson, Chapman, Coffey, B. Smith, Letcavits, Bendiak, Toon. Coach: Eagle Keys.

**1961 – Winnipeg Blue Bombers:** Potter, Delveaux, Miller, Jauch, Nagle, Rowland, James, Lewis, Latourelle, Janzen, Hagberg, Ploen, Ledyard, Druxman, Warren, Gray, Humeniuk, Kotowich, Meadmore, Hamelin, Savoie, Patrick, Piper, Rigney, Wright, Funston, Rauhaus, Pitts, Luining, Burkholder, Shepard, Fraser. Coach: Bud Grant. **Hamilton Tiger-Cats:** Rogers, Karcz, Klien, McKee, Grant, Shannon, Goldston, Sutherin, Palmer, McDougall, Henley, Howell, Hickman, Faloney, Cosentino, Miksza, Cureton, Scott, Caraway, Kelly, Barrow, DeNobile, Minihane, Ray, Moran, Fraser, Neumann, Dekker, Patterson. Coach: Jim Trimble.

**1962 – Winnipeg Blue Bombers:** Latourelle, Lewis, Shepard, Delveaux, Miller, Janzen, James, Rauhaus, Potter, William, Ploen, Ledyard, Thornton, Bruzell, Druxman, Warren, Thorson, Humeniuk, Gray, Burkholder, Ash, Rigney, Piper, Hamelin, Thomas, Patrick, Savoie, Pitts, Luining, Funston, Whisler, Rowland, Hagberg. Coach: Bud Grant. **Hamilton Tiger-Cats:** Kuntz, Henley, Reid, Patterson, Easterly, Caleb, Karcz, Sutherin, Grant, Goldston, Fernandez, McKee, Schreider, Zuger, Cosentino, Walton, Miksza, Cureton, Kelly, Barrow, Scott, Nagurski, DeNobile, Mosca, Minihane, Ray, Dekker, Viti, Neumann, Kilrea. Coach: Jim Trimble.

**1963 – Hamilton Tiger-Cats:** Krouse, Hmiel, Bethea, Grant, Cannavino, Sutherin, Goldston, Kuntz, Baker, Henley, Pace, Faloney, Cosentino, Zuger, Ceppetelli, Miksza, Cureton, Kilrea, Kelly, Gossage, Nagurski, Barrow, DeNobile, Pikula, Mosca, Viti, McKee, Karcz, Neumann, Patterson, Page. Coach: Ralph Sazio. **British Columbia Lions:** Morris, Fleming, Munsey, Homer, Shafer, Beaumont, Kempf, Lasseter, Beamer, Vicic, Bailey, Kapp, Ohler, Hagemoen, Bilicki, Therrien, Hinton, Cotter, Brown, Dennis, Martin, Cacic, Frank, Fouts, Seale, Fieldgate, Burton, Janes, Claridge, Findlay. Coach: Dave Skrien.

**1964 – British Columbia Lions:** Fleming, Morris, Munsey, Homer, Shafer, Beaumont, Kempf, Lasseter, Swift, Bailey, Kapp, Ohler, Schwertfeger, Findlay, Bilicki, Williams, Hinton, Cotter, Brown, Kasapis, Dennis, Cacic, Sugarman, Martin, Fouts, Seale, Carphin, Fieldgate, Burton, Claridge. Coach: Dave Skrien. **Hamilton Tiger-Cats:** Baker, Counts, Grant, Bethea, Kuntz, Zuger, Sutherin, Henley, Krouse, Cimba, Cohee, Faloney, Cosentino, Miksza, Kelly, Gossage, Metras, Ceppetelli, Barrow, DeNobile, Mosca, Nagurski, Pikula, Hoerster, Patterson, Crisson, Viti, Karcz, Neumann, Goldston. Coach: Ralph Sazio.

**1965 – Hamilton Tiger-Cats:** Zuger, Cosentino, Bethea, Anthony, Cohee, Henley, Krouse, Page, Grant, Cimba, McDougall, Sutherin, Kuntz, Wayte, Ceppetelli, Metras, Walton, Barrow, Danychuk, Paterra, Reynolds, Karcz, Kelly, Nagurski, Mosca, Martinello, Patterson, Viti, Crisson, Locklin. Coach: Ralph Sazio. **Winnipeg Blue Bombers:** Ploen, Perkins, Lewis, Raimey, Ulmer, Wozney, Hanson, Thornton, Janzen, Palmer, Cooper, Rauhaus, Pitts, Desjardins, Robson, Minnick, Rothiser, Gray, Thorson, Miller, Piper, Rigney, Dennis, Hamelin, Kiffen, Winton, Funston, Nielsen, Taylor, Mariani. Coach: Bud Grant.

**1966 – Saskatchewan Roughriders:** West, Dorsch, Buchanan, Wlasiuk, Ford, Kosid, Dumelie, Petmanis, Dushinski, Campbell, G. Reed, Lancaster, Bennett, Urness, Levesque, Abendschan, Dempsey, W. Shaw, C. Shaw, K. Reed, Atchison, McQuarters, Whitehouse, Beynon, Benecick, Brock, Barwell, Worden, Ekstran, Gerhardt, Wahlmeier, Ringer, Dudley. Coach: Eagle Keys. **Ottawa Rough Riders:** Stewart, Tucker, Dillard, Scott, Poirier, Gaines, Gilbert, O'Billovich, Conroy, Blum, DeGraw, McCarthy, Jackson, Cline, Specht, Lehmann, Selinger, Perdrix, Walderzak, Cain, Racine, Harrison, Shirk, Shaw, Collins, Brown, Booth, Watkins, Roberts, Thompson. Coach: Frank Clair.

**1967 – Hamilton Tiger-Cats:** Redell, Krouse, Bethea, Page, Grant, Cimba, Storey, Fleming, Richardson, Henley, Hansen, Turek, Smith, Brewer, Zuger, Ceppetelli, Michaluk, Danychuk, Hohman, Stover, Kelly, Barrow, Steiner, Turner, Mosca, Locklin, Viti, Coffey, Watkins, Christian, Patterson, Mitchell, Cohee, Gibbs. Coach: Ralph Sazio. **Saskatchewan Roughriders:** Buchanan, G. Reed, Ford, Campbell, Dumelie, W. Shaw, Duschinski, West, Bennett, Kosid, Wlasiuk, Dorsch, Brandt, Dempsey, Lancaster, Urness, Wahlmeier, Abendschan, Atamian, Atchison, Bahnuik, Beynon, Brock, K. Reed, McQuarters, Barwell, Worden, Carphin, Ekstran, Gerhardt, Kaye, C. Shaw, Benecick. Coach: Eagle Keys.

**1968 – Ottawa Rough Riders:** Cooper, Tucker, Pullen, Adkins, Roberts, Beynon, Racine, Schuette, Specht, Braggins, Selinger, Scott, Coleman, Stewart, Jackson, Van Burkleo, Booth, Shirk, Cain, Collins, Perdrix, Lehmann, Campbell, K. Shaw, Giardino, Joyner, Sutherin, Washington, Poirier, Gaines, Ardern, Dever. Coach: Frank Clair. **Calgary Stampeders:** Evanshen, Harrison, G. Shaw, Zickefoose, James, Roy, Spitzer, Lueck, Boleski, Schumm, Kramer, Liske, Vander Kelen, Cranmer, Linterman, McCarthy, Froese, Watson, Woods, Luzzi, Liggins, Suderman, Payne, Forzani, Furlong, Stewart, Harris, Keeling, Wilson, Andruski, R. Shaw. Coach: Jerry Williams.

**1969 – Ottawa Rough Riders:** Thomas, Stewart, Sutherin, Van Burkleo, Mankins, Poirier, Ardern, Giardino, Gaines, Cooper, Thompson, Black, Dever, Jackson, Selinger, Specht, Perdrix, Cain, Campbell, Braggins, Schuette, Joyner, Shirk, Smith, Beynon, Booth, Collins, Lehmann, Tucker, Pullen, Adkins, Roberts, Washington, Racine. Coach: Frank Clair. **Saskatchewan Roughriders:** DeGraw, Dorsch, Molnar, Ford, Kosid, Thompson, Duschinski, Bennett, G. Reed, Lancaster, Wyche, Urness, Brandt, Aldag, Abendschan, Bahnuik, McQuarters, Baker, Galloway, Brock, W. Shaw, C. Shaw, Dempsey, Seaman, Kyle, Campbell, K. Reed, Frith, Rankin, Barwell, Worden, Fletcher, McKinnie, Gainer. Coach: Eagle Keys.

**1970 – Montreal Alouettes:** Storey, Denson, Van Ness, Wade, Passander, Lefebvre, Evanshen, Alflen, Dalla Riva, Pullen, Ceppetelli, Randall, Raffin, George, Canale, Desjardins, Phaneuf, Code, Fairholm, Thompson, Gaines, Couture, Highsmith, Smear, Judges, C. Collins, Webster, Widger, T. Collins, Kuisma, Kosmos, Springate, Booras, Wormith, Cook, Davis. Coach: Sam Etcheverry. **Calgary Stampeders:** Linterman, McKinnis, Cranmer, Keeling, Lawrence, Holm, Crabbe, Johnson, Silye, Marcil, Shaw, Harrison, Bark, Boleski, Kramer, Roy, Schumm, Atamian, Starks, Stewart, Robinson, Wilson, Andruski, Perez, Koinzan, Suderman, James, Liggins, Helton, Harris, Furlong, Forzani. Coach: Jim Duncan.

**1971 – Calgary Stampeders:** Linterman, Mims, Crabbe, Holmes, Silye, McKinnis, Rankin, Keeling, Lindsey, Marcil, Shaw, Senst, Harrison, Bark, Liggins, Schumm, Joe Forzani, Atamian, Bond, Boleski, Starks, Robinson, Henderson, Wilson, Andruski, James, Helton, Koinzan, Suderman, Harris, Furlong, John Forzani, Van Burkleo, Taylor. Coach: Jim Duncan. **Toronto Argonauts:** Raimey, Abofs, Cranmer, McQuay, Symons, Theismann, Barton, Eben, Moro, Henderson, Profit, Desjardins, Scales, Wells, Bray, Nykoluk, Kelly, Paquette, Thornton, Anderson, Luster, Barrett, Stillwagon, Knechtel, Brame, Vijuk, Corrigall, Mack, Martin, MacMillan, Andrusyshyn, Aldridge. Coach: Leo Cahill.

**1972 – Hamilton Tiger-Cats:** Fleming, Buchanan, Richardson, Wesolowski, Ealey, Van Burkleo, Henley, Gabriel, Coffey, Christian, Mitchell, Chalupka, Hohman, Papai, Danychuck, Gantt, Williams, Shaw, Brenner, Sternberg, Clarke, Porter, Mosca, Smith, Kudryk, Inskeep, Wells, Blum, Kosmos, Krouse, Ferguson, Sunter. Coach: Jerry Williams. **Saskatchewan Roughriders:** Reed, Thompson, Campana, Molnar, Lancaster, Wyche, Pearce, Ford, Barwell, Manchuk, Bailey, Bird, Reid, Brandt, Abendschan, Brock, Galloway, Cook, Kosid, Bennett, Robinson, Duchinski, Steele, Walter, Bahnuik, McCord, Perdone, Roth, Baker, Shaw, Svitak, Collins, Dempsey, Pyne, Seaman, McQuarters. Coach: Dave Skrien.

**1973 – Ottawa Rough Riders:** Green, Evenson, Wellesley, Keeling, Cassata, Foley, Nixon, Oldham, Schultz, Pullen, McKeown, Perdrix, Schuette, Reid, Brandon, Racine, Smith, Sims, Collins, Piaskoski, Krupe, Law, Tosh, Giardino, Woodward, Marcelin, Adams, Laputka, Smith, Dever, Kosmos, Campbell, Organ. Coach: Jack Gotta. **Edmonton Eskimos:** Bell, Harrell, Warrington, McGregor, Lemmerman, Wilkinson, Lefebvre, Cooper, Walls, McGowan, Travis, Howes, Martin, Scales, Watkins, Turner, Adam, Lagrone, Molstad, Highbaugh, Dupuis, Farlinger, Henshall, Huff, Beaton, Estay, Forwick, Knechtel, Clarke, Belser, Britts, Cutler. Coach: Ray Jauch.

**1974 – Montreal Alouettes:** Florio, Sherrer, Ferrughelli, L. Smith, Jones, Wade, Mofford, Eaman, Rodgers, Dalla Riva, Mitchell, Conrad, Bonnett, Braggins, Watrin, Randall, Weir, George, Critchlow, Price, Harris, Gaines, Proudfoot, Luster, W. Smith, Judges, Ah You, Widger, Buono, Crennel, Zapiec, Sweet, Edgson, Yochum, Chown, Gantt, Zumbach, D. Smith. Coach: Marv Levy. **Edmonton Eskimos:** Bell, Harrell, Warrington, Campbell, Markle, Lemmerman, Wilkinson, Lefebvre, Lang, Walls, McGowan, Howes, Martin, Scales, Worobec, Turner, Smith, Fennell, LaGrone, Watkins, Highbaugh, Dupuis, Noble, Beaton, Farlinger, Estay, Forwick, Jones, Potter, Lambros, McDonough, McLaren, Cutler. Coach: Ray Jauch.

**1975 – Edmonton Eskimos:** Bell, Harrell, Konihowski, Lemmerman, Wilkinson, Lefebvre, Lang, Walls, McGowan, Howes, Turner, Martin, Scales, Worobec, Watkins, Lavorato, Matherne, Highbaugh, Dupuis, Farlinger, Fink, Norrie, Estay, Stevenson, Laputka, Fennell, James, Towns, Potter, Kepley, McLaren, Cutler, Britts, Beaton, Warrington. Coach: Ray Jauch. **Montreal Alouettes:** Florio, Rodgers, Ferrughelli, L. Smith, Jones, Wade, Mofford, Eaman, Petty, Crennel, Conrad, Evans, Watrin, Chown, Ah You, Randall, Weir, Price, Harris, Gaines, Cook, Rhino, Yochum, Bonnett, Judges, Pomarico, Proudfoot, Dalla Riva, Widger, Buono, Fanucci, Sweet. Coach: Marv Levy.

**1976 – Ottawa Rough Riders:** Foley, Green, Palazeti, Clements, Robinson, Holloway, Hatanaka, Avery, Stenerson, Kuzyk, Gabriel, Schuette, Brandon, Smith, Turcotte, Coode, Raines, Crepin, Brenner, Tosh, Woodward, Myrick, Monds, Allemang, Fanucci, Piaskoski, Hedges, Sims, Kosmos, Cameron, Moore, Organ, Falconer, Code, Jackson. Coach: George Brancato. **Saskatchewan Roughriders:** O'Hara, Molnar, Campana, Holmes, McGee, Pettersen, Syme, Lancaster, Dawson, Mazurak, B. Richardson, Brandt, Galloway, Dirks, Hopson, Holden, Miller, Provost, Odums, Graham, L. Richardson, McEachern, Marshall, Williams, O'Neal, Wells, Cherkas, Landy, Roth, Clare, Goree, Vann, Manchuk, Macoritti, Holden. Coach: John Payne.

**1977 – Montreal Alouettes:** Dattilio, Mofford, O'Leary, McMann, L. Smith, Barnes, Wade, Gaddis, Dalla Riva, Conrad, D. Smith, Bonnett, Watrin, Randall, Huber, Yochum, Ardern, Harris, Rhino, Proudfoot, Crump, Perry, Gregoire, Ah You, Weir, Davis, Judges, Buono, Crennel, Zapiec, Sweet, Belton, Strayhorn, Alapa, Aynsley, Chown, Burrow, Beaton, Hopkins. Coach: Marv Levy. **Edmonton Eskimos:** Lang, Santucci, Germany, Strickland, Lemmerman, Wilkinson, Warrington, W. Smith, Konihowski, McGowan, Ribbins, Howes, Martin, Scales, Upton, Dobbins, Turner, Lavorato, Highbaugh, Montagano, Farlinger, Jones, Butler, Hollimon, Estay, Boone, Stevenson, Fennell, Hentschel, Potter, Bryans, Kepley, Ilesic, Cutler, Towns. Coach: Hugh Campbell.

**1978 – Edmonton Eskimos:** Warrington, Santucci, Germany, McNeil, Washington, Moon, Lemmerman, Wilkinson, Lang, Scott, Smith, Konihowski, McGowan, Fryer, Howes, Milian, Upton, Stevenson, Pothier, Martin, Turner, Lavorato, Butler, Highbaugh, Holliman, Estay, Boone, Jackson, Fennell, Hentschel, Towns, Bryans, Kepley, Farlinger, Ilesic, Cutler, Jones, Potter. Coach: Hugh Campbell. **Montreal Alouettes:** Mofford, Green, O'Leary, Barnes, Wade, Dattilio, Gaddis, Anonsen, McMann, L. Smith, Dalla Riva, Labbett, Bonnett, D. Smith, Watrin, Halsall, Payton, Yochum, Kahl-Winter, Uteck, Burrow, Harris, Morris, Proudfoot, Taylor, Perry, Luke, Gregoire, Cowlings, Ah You, Weir, Judges, Buono, Olenchalk, Friesen, Crennel, Zapiec, Rhino, Sweet. Coach: Joe Scannella.

**1979 – Edmonton Eskimos:** Lang, Warrington, Scott, Santucci, Germany, Moon, Wilkinson, Lemmerman, Kelly, Smith, Konihowski, Cyncar, Fryer, Howes, Milian, Upton, Stevenson, Pothier, Blanchard, Wilson, Lavorato, Jones, Butler, Fraietta, Highbaugh, Holliman, Estay, Boone, Walker, Hentschel, Towns, Potter, Kepley, Zacharko, Crennel, Bryans, Ilesic, Cutler, Fennell. Coach: Hugh Campbell. **Montreal Alouettes:** Green, O'Leary, Barnes, Calgagni, Dattilio, Baker, Gaddis, McMann, L. Smith, Dalla Riva, Arakgi, Hameluck, D. Smith, Watrin, Mangold, Payton, Yochum, Pfohl, Uteck, Marshall, Burrow, Harris, Proudfoot, Gelley, Petruccio, Gregoire, Ah You, Judges, Weir, Buono, Cousineau, Friesen, Hampton, Sweet. Coach: Joe Scannella.

**1980 – Edmonton Eskimos:** Lang, Warrington, Scott, Santucci, Germany, Lumsden, Moon, Wilkinson, Kelly, Smith, Konihowski, Pough, Buggs, Fryer, Howes, Milian, Upton, Pothier, Yochum, Stevenson, Highbaugh, McLeod, Jones, Butler, Hollimon, Fraietta, Estay, Boone, Parker, Kearns, Fennell, Hentschel, Towns, Potter, Kepley, Ilesic, Cutler, Broomell, Wilson, Lavorato, Blanchard, Barber, Wald. Coach: Hugh Campbell. **Hamilton Tiger-Cats:** Graves, McCorquindale, Crawford, Colwell, Marler, Rozantz, DiPietro, Cyncar, Paterson, Pettersen, Holland, Labbett, Waszczuk, Redl, Moffat, Fulton, George, Martin, Woods, Graham, Anderson, Paul, Nielsen, Shaw, Heighton, Taylor, Woznesensky, Smith, Ramey, Muller, Ward, Zambiasi, Priestner, Clare, Blair, Crennel, Ruoff, Robinson. Coach: John Payne.

**1981 – Edmonton Eskimos:** Lang, Scott, Santucci, Germany, Lumsden, Moon, Wilkinson, Cyncar, Kelly, Smith, Howes, Milian, Upton, Blanchard, Pothier, Stevenson, Lavorato, Highbaugh, McLeod, Jones, Hayes, Hollimon, Fraietta, Boone, Estay, Kearns, Fennell, Towns, Potter, Parker, Kepley, Ilesic, Cutler, Manchuk, Pointer, Fryer, Walter, Broomell. Coach: Hugh Campbell. **Ottawa Rough Riders:** Stoqua, Park, Platt, Reid, Starkey, Watts, Kirk, Avery, Gary Cook, Taylor, Beckstead, Gabriel, Tittley, Phillips, Belcher, Staub, Inglis, Powell, Brazley, Hardee, Glenn Cook, Sutton, Brune, Marshall, Piaskowski, Raines, Seymour, Ward, Mitchell, Sowieta, Glassford, Organ. Coach: George Brancato.

**1982 – Edmonton Eskimos:** Scott, Germany, Cyncar, Kehoe, Lumsden, Fryer, DeBrueys, Moon, Olander, Kelly, Smith, Milian, Upton, Blanchard, Stevenson, Pothier, Connop, Highbaugh, Jones, Hayes, Hollimon, Fraietta, Kearns, Boone, Tuinei, Fennell, Towns, Potter, Parker, Kepley, Manchuk, Ilesic, Cutler, McLeod, Butcher, Marshall, Dixon, Bolzon, W. Williams, Santucci, Estay, M. Williams, Walter, Levenseller. Coach: Hugh Campbell. **Toronto Argonauts:** Minter, Pearson, Carinci, Townsend, Newman, Bronk, Holloway, Barnes, Greer, McGhee, Holmes, Mangold, Ferrone, Malinosky, Trifaux, Woods, D. Wilson, Heath, Ackroyd, Gray, Walker, Henderson, Del Col, Mohr, Olsen, Lyskiewicz, E. Wilson, Elser, Moen, Pointer, Berryman, Jackson, Dorsey, Hameluck, Smith. Coach: Bob O'Billovich.

**1983 – Toronto Argonauts:** Tolbert, Minter, Pearson, Carinci, Palazeti, Holloway, Barnes, Greer, Townsend, Holmes, Hameluck, Antunovic, Norton, Ferrone, Trifaux, Malinosky, Pruenster, Brazley, D. Wilson, McEachern, Ackroyd, Del Col, Mohr, E. Wilson, King, Curry, Elser, Moen, Mitchell, Lawson, Nicholson, Ilesic, Paul, Greene, Teague, Forbes, Bronk, Adams, Meacham, Smith. Coach: Bob O'Billovich. **British Columbia Lions:** DeBrueys, Taylor, White, Pankratz, Potter, Strong, Chapdelaine, Dewalt, Paopao, Armour, Fernandez, Wilson, Miles, Leonhard, Roper, Swafford, Guevin, Blain, Martin, Glier, Byrd, Parker, Heath, Crawford, Jones, Klassen, Cherkas, Racette, Moore, Vaughan, Konar, Jackson, McNeel, Passaglia. Coach: Don Matthews.

**1984 – Winnipeg Blue Bombers:** Reaves, Cantner, Kehoe, Clements, Hufnagel, Neiles, Murphy, Erdman, House, Boyd, Poplawski, Bonk, Moors, Bauer, Nemeth, Walby, Bastaja, Flagel, Rose, Hailey, Turner, Ploughman, Shaw, Norman, Sturdivant, MacIver, Racette, Mikawos, Jones, Robinson, Brown, Pahl, Fowler, Kennerd, Cameron, Hons, Patterson, Palma, Gibbs, Pitts, Huclack. Coach: Cal Murphy. **Hamilton Tiger-Cats:** Shepherd, Bragagnolo, Graffi, Brock, Tedford, Johnson, Jett, Lee, Crawford, DiPietro, Kearns, Waszczuk, Brady, Francis, Riley, Allemang, Scholz, Best, Fields, Streeter, Bennett, McIntyre, Wright, Skillman, Walker, Lyszkiewicz, Price, Covington, Sauve, Zambiasi, Priestner, Gataveckas, Ezerins, Ruoff. Coach: Al Bruno.

**1985 – British Columbia Lions:** Sims, Robinson, White, Pankratz, Potter, Watson, Dewalt, Cowan, Sandusky, Armour, Fernandez, DeBrueys, Wilson, Leonhard, Sinclair, Roper, Blain, Buis, Illerbrun, Clash, Martin, Blier, Byrd, Barnett, K. Parker, Gooch, Crawford, A. Jones, J. Parker, Hebeler, B. Jones, Gray, Klassen, Konar, Jackson, Ulmer, Crews, Passaglia, Guevin, Jenkins, Emery, Glier. Coach:

Don Matthews. **Hamilton Tiger-Cats:** Lee, Shepherd, Crawford, DiPietro, Rybansky, Jackson, Hobart, Porras, Champion, Stapler, Collie, Ingram, Brady, Allemang, Arp, Sanderson, Riley, Scholz, Derks, Bess, Browne, Fields, Streeter, Rose, Bennett, Lehne, Skillman, Covington, Fournier, Lyszkiewicz, Price, Zambiasi, Priestner, Gataveckas, Cary, Mathis, Ezerins, Ruoff. Coach: Al Bruno.

**1986 – Hamilton Tiger-Cats:** Champion, Lee, Shepherd, Zachary, DiPietro, Bender, Tommy, Kerrigan, Hobart, Porras, Ingram, Stapler, Brady, Allemang, Sanderson, Riley, Scholz, Malinosky, Gorrell, Derks, Browne, Fields, Streeter, Rockford, Bennett, Shields, Lehne, Skillman, Covington, Napiorkowski, Sauve, Walker, Lyszkiewicz, Price, Gataveckas, F. Robinson, Ezerins, M. Robinson, Zambiasi, Osbaldiston, Ruoff, Jackson, Andrews, Huclack, Riley. Coach: Al Bruno. **Edmonton Eskimos:** Richards, Cyncar, House, M. Jones, Skinner, Sedun, Johnstone, Da. Allen, Taylor, Dunigan, Williams, Do. Allen, Wilkerson, S. Jones, Dermott, Chapman, Blanchard, Sparenberg, Stevenson, Connop, Phillips, Harding, Jackson, Toney, Bell, Howard, George, Volpe, P. Jones, DesLauriers, Hill, Tuinei, Mandarich, Zachery, Kearns, Bass, Green, Shaffer, McLean, Wruck, Balkovec, Dixon, Kelly, Howlett. Coach: Jackie Parker.

**1987 – Edmonton Eskimos:** Cyncar, M. Jones, Skinner, House, Marshall, Richards, Johnstone, Dunigan, Da. Allen, Ham, S. Jones, Kelly, Williams, Connop, Dermott, Stevenson, Blanchard, Phillips, Pothier, Bowles, Benjamin, Howard, Robinson, Wilson, Blair, Toney, Norman, Kearns, Hill, Tuinei, McCormack, Palumbis, Mandarich, Zachery, Wruck, Bass, Shaffer, Balkovec, Warren, DesLauriers, Kauric. Coach: Joe Faragalli. **Toronto Argonauts:** D. Smith, Fenerty, Johns, Pearson, Edwards, Hudson, Renfroe, Congemi, Thomas, J. Smith, Beckstead, Ambrosie, Ferrone, Kardash, Skemp, Pruenster, Schultz, Pleasant, Clash, Daniels, Vaughan, Drain, Ryan, Kulka, Sellers, Baylis, Schmidt, Harding, Pless, Elliott, Moen, Landry, Chomyc, Ilesic. Coach: Bob O'Billovich.

**1988 – Winnipeg Blue Bombers:** Fabi, Johns, Pahl, Jessie, Cochrane, Rhymes, Salisbury, Saltz, Winey, Shorten, Murphy, Bauer, Molle, Tierney, Bastaja, Black, Rodehutskors, Hill, Hailey, Sampson, Pettway, Jefferson III, Thompson, Allen, Andrews, Clatney, Fears, Gray, Mikawos, Hatziioannou, Brown, West, Fowler, Kennerd, Cameron, Wicklum. Coach: Mike Riley. **British Columbia Lions:** Carinci, Taras, A. Parker, Cooper, Cherry, Taylor, Lecky, Murray, Dunigan, Foggie, Streater, Williams, Sinclair, Vanden Bos, Buis, Coflin, Roper, Clarkson, Smith, Francis, Thomas, Drawhorn, Gooch, Ryan, Wiseman, Ballard, Derban, J. Parker, Belway, Moore, Konar, Glier, Braswell, Ulmer, Stumon, Passaglia. Coach: Larry Donovan.

**1989 – Saskatchewan Roughriders:** Fairholm, Elgaard, M. Jones, McCray, Austin, Burgess, Narcisse, Guy, Anderson, Poley, Aldag, Moore, Stevenson, Skipper, Hall, Hogue, Wiggins, Jurasin, Goldsmith, Lewis, Klingbeil, Rashovich, Albright, Lowe, Suitor, Ridgway, Baker, Bentrim, Hoffman, Daniels, Walling, Crane, Urness, Payne, Drinkwalter, Ellingson, Alipate, Brown, McCormack, Wright. Coach: John Gregory. **Hamilton Tiger-Cats:** Estell, DiPietro, McAdoo, Tommy, Kerrigan, Dillon, Champion, Zatylny, Sanderson, Harle, Riley, Gorrell, Derks, Shields, Gordon, Jordan, Lewis, Covington, Lorenz, Glanton, Walker, Robinson, Corbin, Giftopoulos, Rockford, Osbaldiston, Winfield, Grant, Knight, Castello, Loucks, Gataveckas, Robirtis, Henry, Jackson, Napiorkowski. Coach: Al Bruno.

**1990 – Winnipeg Blue Bombers:** Mimbs, Pearce, Hudson, McManus, Garza, Burgess, Tuttle, Winey, House, Hull, Crifo, Streater, Bauer, Benjamin, Molle, Black, Redl, Walby, Rodehutskors, Hill, Browne, Hailey, Bovell, Sampson, Allen, Q. Williams, Croonen, Hatziioannou, Gray, Mikawos, Battle, Jones, Randolph, West, A. Williams, Kennerd, Cameron. Coach: Mike Riley. **Edmonton Eskimos:** Marshall, Cyncar, Gaertner, Soles, Ellis, Walling, Smith, Johnstone, Jones, Ham, Taylor, H. Williams, Wright, Willis, Connop, Vercheval, McConnell, Dermott, Storme, Bowles, Mathis, Francis, Gooch, Shelton, Jackson, DuMaresq, Walker, B. Williams, Bourgeau, Davidson, Bass, Braswell, McLean, Wruck, Blugh, Norman, Macoritti. Coach: Joe Faragalli.

**1991 – Toronto Argonauts:** Clack, Clemons, Izquierdo, Masotti, Murray, Nastasiuk, Smellie, Smith, Dunigan, Foggie, Gillus, Ismail, Williams, Schmidt, Beckstead, Ferrone, Kardash, Coflin, Pruenster, Schultz, Berry, Bovell, Brazley, Pleasant, Rockford, Van Belleghem, Wilson, Campbell, Hallman, Warren, Johnson, Braswell, Castello, Elliott, Ford, Gaines, Moen, Chomyc, Ilesic, Skemp, Thomas, Harding. Coach: Adam Rita. **Calgary Stampeders:** Pitts, Jenkins, Sapunjis, Spoletini, Toner, Beals, Barrett, Taylor, Renfroe, Hopkins, Simien, Crawford, Bland, Smith, Davies, Hinds, Cafazzo, Blanchard, Henry, Moore, Fairbanks, Hall, Thurman, Tucker, Anthony, Leonard, Watson, W. Johnson, Cofield, Zizakovic, Hasselbach, Warnock, Laird, C. Johnson, A. Johnson, Barandon, Kopp, Peterson, McLoughlin, Kauric, Clatney, McVey, Wicklum, Finlay. Coach: Wally Buono.

**1992 – Calgary Stampeders:** Anthony, Bland, Brewster, Cafazzo, Clatney, Cofield, Covernton, Crawford, Davies, Finlay, Flutie, Forde, Hall, Hasselbach, Jenkins, A. Johnson, W. Johnson, Knox, Laird, Leonard, MacDonald, Marof, Martino, McLoughlin, McVey, Mitchel, Moore, Peterson, Pitts, Pope, Romano, Sapunjis, Singer, Smith, Taylor, Thurman, Torrance, Tucker, Warnock, Watson, Zerr, Zizakovic. Coach: Wally Buono. **Winnipeg Blue Bombers:** Crifo, Thompson, Martin, Pillow, Alphin, Richardson, Pearce, Hudson, Garza, McManus, Dunigan, Cameron, Westwood, Black, MacNeil, Vankoughnett, Walby, Molle, Gorrell, Benjamin, Gray, Grant, Mikawos, Booker, Baker, Battle, Rogers, Randolph, Tsangaris, West, Thomas, Hill, Evans, Plummer, Smith, Dzikowicz, Sampson. Coach: Urban Bowman.

**1993 – Edmonton Eskimos:** Allen, Ambrosie, Berry, Blugh, Bourgeau, E. Brown, T. Brown, Christensen, Connop, Dermott, Dickson, Dumaresq, Fleming, Floyd, Foggie, Goods, Harper, Holland, Hunter, Izquierdo, Johnson, Krupey, Lolar, Lyons, Marshall, Martin, Mitchel, C. Morris, G. Morris, Muecke, Murphy, Parrish, Pless, Roberts, Rogers, Sandusky, Shelton, Soles, Walling, Williams, Wilson, Woods, Wruck. Coach: Ron Lancaster. **Winnipeg Blue Bombers:** Williams, Jackson, Bryant, Alphin, Wilcox, Richardson, Johnstone, Forde, Pearce, Garza, Porras, McCant, Westwood, Cameron, Gorrell, MacNeil, Vankoughnett, Black, Walby, Benjamin, Lewis, Mikawos, Booker, Hatziioannou, Payton, Clark, Battle, Randolph, Tsangaris, Rogers, Smith, Evans, Dzikowicz, Sampson, Phillips, Brown, Boyko. Coach: Cal Murphy.

**1994 – British Columbia Lions:** Alexander, Austin, Browne, Caravatta, Chatman, Chaytors, Chronopoulos, Clark, Clarke, Collier, Europe, Flutie, Forde, Foudy, Furdyk, Gordon, Hanson, Jackson, Jefferson, Mantyka, McLennan, McManus, Millington, Newby, Passaglia, Petersen, Philpot, Robertson, Scrivener, Sinclair, Smith, Snipes, Stevenson, Stewart, Taras, Trevathan, Wilburn, Wright. Coach: Dave Ritchie. **Baltimore Football Club:** Alexander, C. Anthony, K. Anthony, Armstrong, Ballard, Baylis, Beals, Benson, Bornelli, Brigance, Brooks, Canley, B. Clark, R. Clark, Congemi, Drummond, G. Earle, J. Earle, Fort, Malcolm Goodwin, Matt Goodwin, Gravely, Ham, Igwebuike, Jones, J. Miller, S. Miller, Payton, Petry, Pourdanesh, Presbury, Pringle, I. Smith, L. Smith, Subis, Tuipulotu, Walton, Washington, Watson, Wilson. Coach: Don Matthews.

**1995 – Baltimore Stallions:** Culver, Alphin, Armstrong, Cook, Clark, Drummond, Pringle, Wright, Tuipulotu, Ham, Jones, Crowley, Huerta, Miller, Subis, Earle, Dixon, Withycombe, Fort, Pourdanesh, Carter, Payton, Davis, Baylis, Maxie, Walton, Gravely, Bryant, Benson, Goodwin, Brigance, Johnson, Anthony, Craft, Smith, Watson, Griffin. Coach: Don Matthews. **Calgary Stampeders:** Vaughan, Pitts, Sapunjis, Williams, Reid, Danielson, Stewart, Edwards, Daniels, Brenner, Garcia, Moore, Flutie, Martino, McLoughlin, McNeil, Chronopoulos, Romano, Beaton, Crysdale, Pandelidis, Laird, W. Johnson, Floyd, Pope, Zizakovic, Finlay, McClanahan, Biggs, A. Johnson, Kellogg, Frers, Knox, Coleman, Jordan, Leonard, Vaughn. Coach: Wally Buono.

**1996 – Toronto Argonauts:** Flutie, Berry, Harris, Simmons, Vanderjagt, A. Smith, Fleetwood, Izquierdo, D. Smith, Wilson, Nimako, Dmytryshyn, Drummond, Clemons, L. Smith, Benson, Givens, C. Harris, O'Shea, Canter, Payne, Gioskos, Vercheval, Raposo, Perez, Kiselak, Stevenson, Stewart, Morreale, Casola, Williams, Cunningham, Masotti, Maxie, Waldrop, Giles. Coach: Don Matthews. **Edmonton Eskimos:** Williams, Hagan, Brown, Pleasant, Sandusky, Ledbetter, Frank, Fleming, McManus, Harper, Blair, Reed, Rogers, Mobley, T. Brown, Hamilton, Tobert, Burse, Blount, Dickson, Martin, Pless, Goods, Roberts, Miller, Hunter, Dermott, Green, Rayam, Groenewegen, Morris, Connop, MacCready, Mazzoli, Flutie, Blugh. Coach: Ron Lancaster.

# INDIVIDUAL STATISTICS

(Not available for every game)

**1947 – Rushing: Argonauts** — B. Karrys 12-65, Copeland 6-35, Doty 5-30, Krol 5-18, B. Stukus 6-15, Brown 5-15; **Blue Bombers** — Sandberg 22-95, Don Smith 12-52, Hiney 4-22, Hood 9-28, Reagan 1-2.

**1948 – Rushing: Stampeders** — Thodos 7-53, Gyles 7-35, Hood 5-24, Rowe 5-24, Pantages 4-18; **Rough Riders** — Turner 11-130, Golab 23-107.

**1949 – Rushing: Alouettes** — Cunningham 15-90, Wagner 17-60, Festeryga 9-25, Manastersky 1-1; **Stampeders** — Rowe 9-51, Hood 12-50, Thodos 5-30, Kwong 4-20, Pantages 4-10.

**1953 – Rushing: Tiger-Cats** — Brown 2-4, Songin 3-minus 17, Hapes 12-53, Custis 7-50, Kusserow 2-13, Bailey 5-31; **Blue Bombers** — James 12-49, Meltzer 2-14, Casey 4-29, Jacobs 2-minus 26, Sokol 2-7. **Receiving: Tiger-Cats** — Custis 2-26, Logan 2-27, Kusserow 2-19, Ragazzo 3-84, Toohy 1-20, Hapes 1-7; **Blue Bombers** — Armstrong 10-140, Meltzer 3-37, Grant 2-14, Korchak 1-14, Sokol 4-41, James 2-15, Pearce 2-45, Casey 5-39, McAllister 1-1, Huffman 1-11. **Passing: Tiger-Cats** — Songin 10-22-1-163, Kusserow 1-1-0-20; **Blue Bombers** — Jacobs 31-48-2-357. **Punt Returns: Tiger-Cats** — Custis 3-21, Brown 5-32, Bailey 1-7; **Blue Bombers** — James 6-41, Meltzer 1-4, Casey 3-38. **Kick-off Returns: Tiger-Cats** — Custis 1-30, Brown 1-9; **Blue Bombers** — James 2-56, Skrien 1-8. **Field Goals: Tiger-Cats** — Hapes 0-1; **Blue Bombers** — Korchak 0-1.

**1954 – Rushing: Eskimos** — Faloney 7-30, Parker 8-60, Kwong 16-85, Miles 5-26, Lippman 7-54, Kruger 3-18; **Alouettes** — Webster 18-113, Hunsinger 12-71, Etcheverry 8-20, Wagner 2-11, Bewley 2-33, Belec 1-1. **Receiving: Eskimos** — Parker 3-58, Lindley 2-11, Bendiak 4-77, McWhinney 1-15; **Alouettes** — O'Quinn 13-316, Poole 3-31, Pal 3-71, Webster 2-31, Hunsinger 1-4, Wagner 1-minus 1. **Passing: Eskimos** — Faloney 7-17-2-114, Miles 3-3-0-47, Parker 0-3-0-0; **Alouettes** — Etcheverry 22-31-2-407. **Punt Returns: Eskimos** — West 2-14, Willsey 1-8, Kruger 1-10; **Alouettes** — Griggs 1-4, Bewley 5-35, Hunsinger 1-5, Pal 2-9, Etcheverry 1-12. **Kick-off Returns: Eskimos** — West 1-13, Miles 1-29, Kwong 1-7, Bendiak 1-5, Lippman 1-23; **Alouettes** — Webster 3-86, Griggs 1-0. **Field Goals: Eskimos** — Deans 0-1.

**1955 – Rushing: Eskimos** — Kwong 30-145, Parker 8-75, Bright 7-77, Miles 7-71, Lindley 6-50, Getty 2-6, Kimoff 1-7, Kelly 1-7; **Alouettes** — Etcheverry 8-12, Abbruzzi 7-17, Caroline 5-18, Belec 4-22. **Receiving: Eskimos** — Kwong 3-20, Bright 1-23, Miles 1-30, Bendiak 1-15, Lindley 1-25, Heydenfeldt 1-15; **Alouettes** — O'Quinn 8-134, Patterson 5-99, Pal 4-62, Belec 3-29, Bewley 3-38, Moran 3-37, Abbruzzi 2-55, Caroline 1-42, Miller 1-12. **Passing: Eskimos** — Parker 8-16-1-128; **Alouettes** — Etcheverry 30-41-2-508. **Punt Returns: Eskimos** — Kruger 3-26, Miles 2-0, Simon 1-4, Kelly 1-4; **Alouettes** — Pal 3-7, Bewley 2-4, Williams 1-17, Coulter 1-0. **Kick-off Returns: Eskimos** — Miles 2-59, Kruger 1-14, Bright 1-13; **Alouettes** — Patterson 1-25, Caroline 1-16, Bewley 1-7, Hugo 1-7, Sheridan 1-3. **Field Goals: Eskimos** — Dean 1-2; **Alouettes** — Korchak 0-1.

**1956 – Rushing: Eskimos** — Bright 28-171, Parker 19-120, Kwong 19-80, Miles 11-66, Kruger 2-9, Getty 4-9; **Alouettes** — Abbruzzi 14-77, James 7-46, Patterson 1-9, Pascal 9-40, Etcheverry 10-minus 32. **Receiving: Eskimos** — Miles 1-19, Walker 1-17, Parker 2-25, Bright 3-40; **Alouettes** — Pascal 2-21, O'Quinn 3-36, Patterson 6-139, Pal 1-20, James 3-89, Abbruzzi 1-24. **Passing: Eskimos** — Getty 7-15-1-101; **Alouettes** — Etcheverry 16-38-4-329. **Punt Returns: Eskimos** — Mendryk 5-44, Miles 3-16, Kruger 1-6; **Alouettes** — Karpuk 5-9, Pal 5-16, Patterson 1-14. **Kick-off Returns: Eskimos** — Kwong 1-4, Parker 1-25, Miles 1-4, Mobra 1-9, Kruger 1-8; **Alouettes** — Pal 2-34, James 1-12, Patterson 2-59, Hugo 1-9. **Field Goals: Eskimos** — Mobra 1-1, Parker 0-1.

**1957 – Rushing: Tiger-Cats** — McDougall 10-86, Gilchrist 18-48, Faloney 2-13, Grant 1-10, Graham 1-3; **Blue Bombers** — Ploen 9-54, Miller 5-19, Lewis 11-38, James 16-62, Mendyk 5-19, Roseborough 1-0. **Receiving: Tiger-Cats** — Gilchrist 2-30, Dekker 1-19, Grant 1-13, McDougall 1-5; **Blue Bombers** — Pitts 8-93, Gilliam 3-33, James 0-8, Mendyk 4-42, Canakes 0-1. **Passing: Tiger-Cats** — Faloney 5-15-0-67; **Blue Bombers** — Ploen 11-20-2-97, Mendyk 0-2-0-0, Roseborough 4-6-0-80. **Punt Returns: Tiger-Cats** — Howell 4-26, Fedosoff 5-15; **Blue Bombers** — Latourelle 10-37, Rowland 4-26, Pearce 1-1. **Kick-off Returns: Tiger-Cats** — Bawel 1-26, Lampman 1-0; **Blue Bombers** — Lewis 2-93, Michels 1-8, Pearce 2-0, Canakes 1-0. **Field Goals: Tiger-Cats** — Oneschuk 0-1.

**1958 – Rushing: Blue Bombers** — Shepard 14-120, Ploen 1-1, Lewis 13-69, Van Pelt 6-26, Varone 8-33; **Tiger-Cats** — McDougall 11-57, Faloney 12-24, Sutherin 3-19, Campbell 7-43. **Receiving: Blue Bombers** — Gilliam 2-26, Pitts 2-36, Lewis 2-24, Ploen 2-54, Shepard 2-35, Van Pelt 1-20; **Tiger-Cats** — Dekker 5-75, McDougall 5-53, Howell 4-76, Macon 1-22, Lampman 1-7. **Passing: Blue Bombers** — Van Pelt 8-15-0-140, Ploen 2-2-0-35, Lewis 1-2-0-20; **Tiger-Cats** — Faloney 16-25-2-233. **Punt Returns: Blue Bombers** — Latourelle 5-32, Rowland 2-26, Rauhaus 1-22; **Tiger-Cats** — Macon 4-7, Howell 1-5. **Kick-off Returns: Blue Bombers** — Varone 1-0, Lewis 1-14, Ploen 2-35; **Tiger-Cats** — Howell 2-29, Grant 2-19, Macon 1-18. **Field Goals: Blue Bombers** — Van Pelt 2-2; **Tiger-Cats** — Sutherin 0-1.

**1959 – Rushing: Blue Bombers** — Shepard 17-57, Ploen 8-minus 8, James 9-31, Lewis 9-30, Shannon 5-29; **Tiger-Cats** — McDougall 21-62, Goldston 9-38, Faloney 3-minus 30, Wood 4-4. **Receiving: Blue Bombers** — Pitts 2-57, Funston 1-41, James 1-9, Shannon 1-18; **Tiger-Cats** — Howell 3-36, McDougall 4-34, Chandler 1-8, Goldston 1-8, Lampman 1-11. **Passing: Blue Bombers** — Ploen 4-11-0-116, Lewis 1-1-0-9; **Tiger-Cats** — Faloney 9-21-0-89, Fraser 1-1-0-8. **Punt Returns: Blue Bombers** — Latourelle 8-60, Janzen 7-30; **Tiger-Cats** — Howell 5-37, Macon 1-5, Wood 4-22, Goldston 2-2. **Kick-off Returns: Blue Bombers** — James 1-8; **Tiger-Cats** — McDougall 1-11, Wood 2-23. **Field Goals: Blue Bombers** — James 1-1; **Tiger-Cats** — Oneschuk 2-2.

**1960 – Rushing: Rough Riders** — Stewart 18-99, Thelen 21-118, Jackson 5-35, Lancaster 2-minus 12, Kelly 4-14; **Eskimos** — Bright 5-15, Kwong 7-7, Shipka 5-22, Parker 9-0. **Receiving: Rough Riders** — Sowalski 2-56, Simpson 1-17, Graham 1-16, Thelen 1-11, Kelly 1-2; **Eskimos** — Smith 3-35, Letcavits 6-132, Parker 1-11, Schumm 1-12, Coffey 1-7. **Passing: Rough Riders** — Jackson 5-11-1-100, Lancaster 1-4-0-2; **Eskimos** — Parker 10-22-1-179, Getty 2-2-1-18. **Punt Returns: Rough Riders** — Daigneault 1-6, West 3-22, Stewart 9-38; **Eskimos** — Miles 8-32, Smith 3-31. **Kick-off Returns: Rough Riders** — Daigneault 1-27, Sowalski 1-11; **Eskimos** — Parker 1-74, Miles 1-22, Smith 1-29. **Field Goals: Rough Riders** — Schreider 1-1.

**1961 – Rushing: Blue Bombers** — Ploen 9-71, Lewis 16-96, Hagberg 18-81, James 13-47; **Tiger-Cats** — Faloney 8-19, McDougall 7-11, Shannon 5-13, Cosentino 1-minus 3, Hickman 3-20, Goldston 1-minus 4. **Receiving: Blue Bombers** — Pitts 4-83, Funston 2-59, James 3-22, Latourelle 3-56; **Tiger-Cats** — Patterson 7-105, Dekker 3-115, McDougall 4-38, Grant 3-26, Goldston 4-55, Henley 2-11. **Passing: Blue Bombers** — Ploen 8-17-0-140, Ledyard 4-6-1-80; **Tiger-Cats** — Faloney 23-37-0-350. **Punt Returns: Blue Bombers** — Latourelle 13-90, Janzen 4-8; **Tiger-Cats** — Henley 4-17, Sutherin 2-15, Howell 4-37. **Kick-off Returns: Blue Bombers** — Lewis 1-29, Janzen 2-44, Jauch 1-17; **Tiger-Cats** — McDougall 3-49, Shannon 1-22. **Field Goals: Blue Bombers** — James 2-2.

**1962 – Rushing: Blue Bombers** — Lewis 10-41, Ploen 3-41, James 3-15, Latourelle 2-1, Shepard 1-4; **Tiger-Cats** — Kuntz 16-49, Zuger 6-49, Henley 4-99, Cosentino 2-33, Caleb 2-8. **Receiving: Blue Bombers** — Lewis 7-77, Funston 6-65, Pitts 4-51, Shepard 2-24, Latourelle 1-7; **Tiger-Cats** — Henley 5-118, Patterson 3-62, Viti 1-36, Dekker 1-10, Easterly 1-17, Caleb 1-8. **Passing: Blue Bombers** — Ledyard 14-19-1-175, Ploen 5-11-0-34, Lewis 1-1-0-15; **Tiger-Cats** — Zuger 12-30-0-190, Cosentino 4-7-0-61. **Punt Returns: Blue Bombers** — Janzen 6-25, Latourelle 2-13; **Tiger-Cats** — Grant 5-42, Henley 2-9, Sutherin 4-22. **Kick-off Returns: Blue Bombers** — Lewis 3-116, Janzen 1-10; **Tiger-Cats** — Caleb 4-66, Goldston 1-16. **Field Goals: Tiger-Cats** — Sutherin 0-2.

**1963 – Rushing: Tiger-Cats** — Bethea 4-41, Pace 11-32, Baker 10-50, Faloney 9-54; **Lions** — Beamer 11-56, Fleming 5-12, Morris 1-4, Kapp 8-19, Lasseter 3-15. **Receiving: Tiger-Cats** — Grant 6-100, Patterson 3-95, Bethea 2-14, Henley 1-40, Viti 1-12; **Lions** — Morris 2-14, Lasseter 1-4, Burton 4-40, Homer 1-8, Janes 3-72, Beamer 1-7, Findlay 2-45, Claridge 3-44. **Passing: Tiger-Cats** — Faloney 13-20-1-261; **Lions** — Kapp 17-33-1-234. **Punt Returns: Tiger-Cats** — Grant 3-14, Sutherin 6-25; **Lions** — Beaumont 4-10, Shaffer 5-12. **Kick-off Returns: Tiger-Cats** — Bethea 1-34, Barrow 1-19; **Lions** — Morris 3-52, Lasseter 1-33. **Field Goals: Tiger-Cats** — Sutherin 0-1; **Lions** — Kempf 1-1.

**1964 – Rushing: Lions** — Fleming 6-67, Munsey 8-57, Kapp 3-17, Swift 7-17, Morris 1-3; **Tiger-Cats** — Baker 7-41, Bethea 8-33, Kuntz 4-10, Faloney 12-55, Counts 5-59. **Receiving: Lions** — Morris 4-64, Homer 3-46, Fleming 2-35, Carphin 1-8; **Tiger-Cats** — Grant 7-102, Patterson 5-91, Crisson 3-29, Counts 3-14. **Passing: Lions** — Kapp 9-21-1-145, Ohler 1-1-0-8; **Tiger-Cats** — Faloney 18-33-0-236, Sutherin 0-1-1-0. **Field Goals: Lions** — Kempf 0-1.

**1965 – Rushing: Tiger-Cats** — Cohee 4-44, Bethea 12-68, Kuntz 3-6, Anthony 1-3, McDougall 2-3, Cosentino 4-minus 9, Zuger 6-27; **Blue Bombers** — Lewis 13-84, Perkins 14-28, Raimey 9-37, Thornton 2-5, Cooper 1-minus 13, Ploen 11-33. **Receiving: Tiger-Cats** — Bethea 2-71; **Blue Bombers** — Perkins 3-11, Raimey 2-40, Nielson 1-8, Funston 1-9. **Passing: Tiger-Cats** — Zuger 2-4-0-71, Cosentino 0-1-0-0; **Blue Bombers** — Ploen 6-12-1-54, Lewis 1-1-0-14. **Punt Returns: Tiger-Cats** — Henley 2-15, Sutherin 1-3, Grant 3-3, Karcz 1-0; **Blue Bombers** — Ulmer 1-12, Wozney 4-10. **Kick-off Returns: Tiger-Cats** — Bethea 1-3, McDougall 1-25; **Blue Bombers** — Raimey 2-28, Lewis 2-59. **Field Goals: Blue Bombers** — Winton 1-2.

**1966 – Rushing: Roughriders** — Reed 23-133, Buchanan 10-54, Ford 2-5, Lancaster 1-4; **Rough Riders** — Scott 8-15, Dillard 9-29, Stewart 8-23, Jackson 4-25. **Receiving: Roughriders** — Campbell 3-28, Barwell 1-46, Worden 3-48, Buchanan 2-19, Ford 1-19; **Rough Riders** — Roberts 2-21, Tucker 4-174. **Passing: Roughriders** — Lancaster 10-20-0-160; **Rough Riders** — Jackson 6-15-1-195, Stewart 0-1-1-0. **Punt Returns: Roughriders** — Kosid 1-3, Wlasiuk 8-34; **Rough Riders** — Cline 4-4, Gilbert 4-15. **Kick-off Returns: Roughriders** — Buchanan 3-78; **Rough Riders** — Scott 2-53, Gaines 3-77, Thompson 1-0. **Field Goals: Roughriders** — Abendschan 0-3.

**1967 – Rushing: Tiger-Cats** — Bethea 7-30, Fleming 2-8, Smith 10-22, Turek 1-minus 1, Zuger 6-11; **Roughriders** — G. Reed 21-92, Buchanan 6-13, Ford 2-3, Dorsch 2-10, Lancaster 1-2. **Receiving: Tiger-Cats** — Coffey 1-13, Watkins 2-86, Bethea 5-65; **Roughriders** — Campbell 1-7, Buchanan 4-99, Ford 1-0, Reed 1-9, Worden 1-4. **Passing: Tiger-Cats** — Zuger 8-20-1-164, Turek 0-1-0-0; **Roughriders** — Lancaster 8-20-3-119. **Punt Returns: Tiger-Cats** — Grant 5-18, Page 2-4, Henley 6-48; **Roughriders** — Wlasiuk 10-17, Kosid 4-32, K. Reed 1-1. **Kick-off Returns: Tiger-Cats** — Bethea 1-17, Smith 1-23; **Roughriders** — Ford 1-19, Buchanan 2-30. **Field Goals: Tiger-Cats** — Coffey 0-1; **Roughriders** — Abendschan 0-1.

**1968 – Rushing: Rough Riders** — Washington 13-138, Scott 15-38, Jackson 4-43, Stewart 1-3; **Stampeders** — Woods 9-17, Linterman 4-16, Watson 5-13, Liske 5-31, Stewart 1-minus 6, Evanshen 1-3. **Receiving: Rough Riders** — Adkins 2-93, Washington 3-25, Roberts 2-43, Stewart 1-24; **Stampeders** — Shaw 7-75, McCarthy 6-86, Evanshen 5-68, Harrison 2-16, Watson 2-13. **Passing: Rough Riders** — Jackson 8-17-0-185; **Stampeders** — Liske 21-36-1-258. **Punt Returns: Rough Riders** — Cooper 4-10, Ardern 4-9, Sutherin 1-14; **Stampeders** — Robinson 7-17, McCarthy 2-7, Linterman 1-9, Robinson 2-39. **Kick-off Returns: Rough Riders** — Cooper 2-26, Washington 1-22, Schuette 1-0; **Stampeders** — Woods 3-73, Robinson 1-34. **Field Goals: Rough Riders** — Sutherin 1-4; **Stampeders** — Robinson 0-1.

**1969 – Rushing: Rough Riders** — Giardino 11-27, Mankins 10-72, Stewart 5-41, Jackson 5-31; **Roughriders** — Reed 11-28, Thompson 5-19, Molnar 2-21, Lancaster 1-minus 5. **Receiving: Rough Riders** — Mankins 5-56, Roberts 3-36, Stewart 2-112, Tucker 1-34, Giardino 1-11, Cooper 1-5; **Roughriders** — Campbell 4-57, Molnar 4-43, Thompson 2-22, Ford 2-44, Fletcher 2-18, Reed 1-55. **Passing: Rough Riders** — Jackson 13-22-0-254; **Roughriders** — Lancaster 15-30-1-239. **Punt Returns: Rough Riders** — Ardern 4-22, Cooper 4-6; **Roughriders** — DeGraw 5-36, Kosid 6-11. **Kick-off Returns: Rough Riders** — Cooper 2-50, Ardern 1-15; **Roughriders** — Ford 2-101, Thompson 1-19, Reed 1-19. **Field Goals: Rough Riders** — Sutherin 0-1; **Roughriders** — Abendschan 0-1.

**1970 – Rushing: Alouettes** — Denson 16-66, Van Ness 8-30, Pullen 1-7; **Stampeders** — McKinnis 12-48, Cranmer 4-16, Linterman 5-5, Holm 1-minus 3. **Receiving: Alouettes** — Lefebvre 2-20, Denson 1-4, Van Ness 3-25, Evanshen 6-95, Dalla Riva 2-23, Pullen 4-38, Alflen 1-10; **Stampeders** — Linterman 3-23, Shaw 3-28, Harrison 3-22, Cranmer 2-14, Johnson 2-11, McKinnis 3-15, Sillye 1-6. **Passing: Alouettes** — Wade 16-34-3-159, Van Ness 2-2-0-46, Denson 1-1-0-10; **Stampeders** — Keeling 16-37-2-119, Laurence 0-2-0-0. **Punt Returns: Alouettes** — Couture 8-57, Fairholm 5-20, Storey 2-4; **Stampeders** — Sillye 8-48, Perez 3-13, Starks 1-10. **Kick-off Returns: Alouettes** — Thompson 1-25; **Stampeders** — Starks 2-43, McKinnis 1-18, Crabbe 1-7. **Field Goals: Alouettes** — Springate 1-1, Canale 0-1; **Stampeders** — Robinson 1-1.

**1971 – Rushing: Stampeders** — Mims 11-37, McKinnis 12-52, Linterman 5-5, Henderson 1-0, Keeling 4-9; **Argonauts** — Theismann 6-26, McQuay 12-39, Symons 11-33. **Receiving: Stampeders** — Linterman 2-68, Harrison 1-14, McKinnis 1-8, Shaw 1-15, Henderson 1-6; **Argonauts** — McQuay 2-24, Profit 2-67, Thornton 1-14, Henderson 1-43, Symons 1-0, Eben 3-44. **Passing: Stampeders** — Keeling 6-16-3-111; **Argonauts** — Theismann 8-14-0-189, Barton 2-5-0-3, Symons 0-1-0-0. **Punt Returns: Stampeders** — Silye 7-19, Rankin 4-18, Starks 2-5; **Argonauts** — Paquette 5-9, Abofs 6-16, Symons 1-5. **Kick-off Returns: Stampeders** — Rankin 1-11, Crabbe 1-19; **Argonauts** — Raimey 2-19, McQuay 0-35, Moro 1-0. **Field Goals: Argonauts** — MacMillan 1-3.

**1972 – Rushing: Tiger-Cats** — Buchanan 16-22, Ealey 9-63, Fleming 5-16; **Roughriders** — Reed 22-93, Thompson 6-14, Molnar 1-4, Campana 1-0. **Receiving: Tiger-Cats** — Henley 7-98, Coffey 3-61, Gabriel 3-54, Fleming 2-28, Porter 1-23, Richardson 1-12, Buchanan 1-15; **Roughriders** — Campana 9-83, Barwell 5-43, Ford 3-41, Pearce 2-66, Reed 1-6. **Passing: Tiger-Cats** — Ealey 18-29-2-291; **Roughriders** — Lancaster 20-29-2-239. **Punt Returns: Tiger-Cats** — Clarke 6-24, Sternbert 1-0, Krouse 1-0; **Roughriders** — Molnar 5-5, Walter 1-8, Kosid 3-8. **Kick-off Returns: Tiger-Cats** — Porter 1-14, Clarke 1-16; **Roughriders** — Thompson 1-26, Molnar 1-8. **Field Goals: Tiger-Cats** — Sunter 2-2; **Roughriders** — Abendschan 1-2.

**1973 – Rushing: Rough Riders** — Evenson 11-53, Green 6-25, Foley 2-7, Cassata 5-29, Adams 1-5; **Eskimos** — Bell 12-46, Harrell 7-43, Wilkinson 3-3. **Receiving: Rough Riders** — Pullen 3-26, Nixon 4-72, Wellesley 0-7, Green 4-56; **Eskimos** — McGowan 5-58, Harrell 4-51, Highbaugh 1-8, Wells 7-61, Lefebvre 2-16, Bell 1-14. **Passing: Rough Riders** — Cassata 11-23-2-161; **Eskimos** — Wilkinson 10-20-0-107, Lemmerman 10-22-0-101. **Punt Returns: Rough Riders** — Foley 3-15, Adams 3-11, Woodward 3-9, Marcelin 1-0; **Eskimos** — Dupuis 3-8, Cooper 3-8, Farlinger 1-1, Highbaugh 2-2. **Kick-off Returns: Rough Riders** — Marcelin 2-49, Organ 1-0; **Eskimos** — Butts 1-7, Highbaugh 2-36. **Field Goals: Rough Riders** — Organ 2-3; **Eskimos** — Cutler 1-1.

**1974 – Rushing: Alouettes** — Ferrughelli 13-59, Sherrer 11-50, Rodgers 2-minus 3, L. Smith 2-6, Wade 3-minus 3; **Eskimos** — Bell 13-22, Harrell 4-10, Wilkinson 2-2, Warrington 1-15. **Receiving: Alouettes** — Rodgers 4-67, Sherrer 3-41, L. Smith 1-14, Dalla Riva 1-14, Eamon 1-10, Ferrughelli 2-5; **Eskimos** — McGowan 1-85, Harrell 4-22, Warrington 1-13, Lefebvre 1-6. **Passing: Alouettes** — Wade 10-25-0-139, Jones 2-4-0-12; **Eskimos** — Wilkinson 7-16-1-64, Lemmerman 4-8-1-62, Lefebvre 0-1-0-0. **Punt Returns: Alouettes** — Florio 6-19, Eamon 4-36; **Eskimos** — Highbaugh 1-35, Lang 1-5, Campbell 5-21, Dupuis 1-3, Beaton 1-2. **Kick-off Returns: Alouettes** — Florio 1-21, Sherrer 1-15, Harris 1-20; **Eskimos** — Lambros 1-0, Bell 0-10. **Field Goals: Alouettes** — Sweet 4-6.

**1975 – Rushing: Eskimos** — Bell 11-46, Harrell 6-17, Wilkinson 4-10, Lemmerman 1-minus 3; **Alouettes** — Ferrughelli 14-85, Rodgers 9-34, Smith 3-4, Jones 2-15. **Receiving: Eskimos** — McGowan 9-98, Konihowski 3-26, Lang 2-27, Wells 1-14; **Alouettes** — Smith 8-55, Ferrughelli 2-20, Petty 3-88, Dalla Riva 1-14, Eamon 1-6. **Passing: Eskimos** — Wilkinson 10-16-105, Lemmerman

5-11-1-60; **Alouettes** — Jones 12-18-1-115, Wade 3-3-0-68. **Punt Returns: Eskimos** — Highbaugh 5-39, Fink 2-4; **Alouettes** — Rodgers 7-72, Harris 2-7. **Kick-off Returns: Eskimos** — Fink 1-11, Bell 1-9; **Alouettes** — Buono 1-0. **Field Goals: Eskimos** — Cutler 3-4; **Alouettes** — Sweet 2-4.

**1976 – Rushing: Rough Riders** — Green 19-75, Organ 1-52, Clements 5-37, Palazeti 3-7, Foley 1-2; **Roughriders** — Molnar 13-46, McGee 3-11, Campana 4-4. **Receiving: Rough Riders** — Gabriel 7-124, Green 1-15, Avery 1-14, Foley 1-14, Kuzyk 1-7; **Roughriders** — Pettersen 7-80, Richardson 5-78, McGee 5-48, Mazurak 2-31, Dawson 2-25, Campana 1-1. **Passing: Rough Riders** — Clements 11-25-3-174; **Roughriders** — Lancaster 22-36-0-263. **Punt Returns: Rough Riders** — Hatanaka 2-86, Green 5-41, Myrick 2-20; **Roughriders** — Marshall 1-3, Campana 1-3, Pettersen 2-7, Mazurak 2-20. **Kick-off Returns: Rough Riders** — Organ 3-166; **Roughriders** — Macoritti 3-137. **Field Goals: Rough Riders** — Organ 3-4; Roughriders — Macoritti 2-3.

**1977 – Rushing: Alouettes** — O'Leary 9-40, Wade 5-1, Belton 12-36, Smith 1-3, Mofford 1-4; **Eskimos** — Lemmerman 2-minus 2, German 3-6, Strickland 8-39, Santucci 6-23, Wilkinson 4-minus 10. **Receiving: Alouettes** — O'Leary 6-90, Gaddis 4-108, Belton 4-30, Smith 1-12, Dattilio 2-39, Dalla Riva 3-42, Mofford 2-19; **Eskimos** — Lang 4-65, McGowan 1-9, Germany 1-0, Konihowski 1-11, Strickland 1-4. **Passing: Alouettes** — Wade 22-40-1-340, Smith 1-0-0-0; **Eskimos** — Lemmerman 5-22-4-74, Wilkinson 3-7-0-15. **Punt Returns: Alouettes** — Rhino 4-88, Harris 4-29; **Eskimos** — Butler 5-22, Highbaugh 1-minus 1. **Kick-off Returns: Alouettes** — Rhino 2-46; **Eskimos** — Santucci 4-109, Hollimon 3-44, Highbaugh 0-25. **Field Goals: Alouettes** — Sweet 6-7; **Eskimos** — Cutler 2-2.

**1978 – Rushing: Eskimos** — Germany 19-49, Santucci 6-29, Wilkinson 3-9, Moon 1-3, Warrington 2-3; **Alouettes** — O'Leary 7-31, Barnes 5-29, Green 12-22, Wade 2-minus 6. **Receiving: Eskimos** — Scott 6-53, Germany 3-26, Santucci 5-25, Smith 1-11, McGowan 1-4; **Alouettes** — Gaddis 4-78, O'Leary 5-37, Green 2-6, Dalla Riva 1-17, Smith 1-9. **Passing: Eskimos** — Wilkinson 16-26-1-119; **Alouettes** — Barnes 6-9-0-73, Wade 7-17-0-74. **Punt Returns: Eskimos** — Butler 7-53, Scott 1-12, Highbaugh 1-5, Lavorato 1-0, Hollimon 1-0; **Alouettes** — Rhino 7-82, Mofford 2-0. **Kick-off Returns: Eskimos** — Butler 2-39, Hollimon 1-29, Bryans 1-9; **Alouettes** — Green 2-35. **Field Goals: Eskimos** — Cutler 4-5; **Alouettes** — Sweet 2-2.

**1979 – Rushing: Eskimos** — Germany 15-70, Santucci 2-6, Moon 5-18; **Alouettes** — Green 21-142, O'Leary 3-11, Pfohl 1-5, Barnes 8-46. **Receiving: Eskimos** — Lang 1-9, W. Smith 4-90, Santucci 1-7, Scott 3-70, Kelly 2-27; **Alouettes** — Baker 2-14, Gaddis 3-53, O'Leary 3-44, Green 4-30, L.Smith 1-10. **Passing: Eskimos** — Wilkinson 6-10-1-107, Moon 5-11-0-96; **Alouettes** — Barnes 13-23-1-151, Baker 0-1-0-0. **Punt Returns: Eskimos** — Butler 4-29, Fraietta 3-14, Crennel 1-8; **Alouettes** — Baker 2-13, Harris 4-29. **Kick-off Returns: Eskimos** — Fraietta 1-16; **Alouettes** — Baker 3-60. **Field Goals: Eskimos** — Cutler 1-1; **Alouettes** — Sweet 3-3.

**1980 – Rushing: Eskimos** — Lumsden 8-85, Moon 7-71, Wilkinson 2-27, Germany 7-15, Santucci 3-7; **Tiger-Cats** — Graves 12-67, Marler 4-45. **Receiving: Eskimos** — Scott 12-174, Kelly 4-104, Fryer 4-77, Buggs 3-73; **Tiger-Cats** — Pettersen 3-47, Holland 2-43, Cyncar 2-37, Paterson 2-24. **Passing: Eskimos** — Moon 21-33-1-398, Wilkinson 2-6-0-30; **Tiger-Cats** — Marler 9-22-3-151, Rozantz 0-5-1-0. **Punt Returns: Eskimos** — Butler 6-31, Fraietta 1-3; **Tiger-Cats** — Graves 1-8. **Kick-off Returns: Eskimos** — Holliman 1-23; **Tiger-Cats** — Graves 7-132. **Field Goals: Eskimos** — Cutler 2-2; **Tiger-Cats** — Ruoff 3-4.

**1981 – Rushing: Eskimos** — Germany 13-56, Moon 12-23, Lumsden 1-2; **Rough Riders** — Platt 12-48, Watts 5-29, Stoqua 0-5, Reid 1-1. **Receiving: Eskimos** — Lumsden 8-91, Cyncar 7-61, Kelly 4-46, Scott 2-44, Germany 1-14, Smith 1-5; **Rough Riders** — Gabriel 6-76, Platt 4-29, Kirk 2-32, Reid 2-29, Stoqua 1-34, Avery 1-4. **Passing: Eskimos** — Moon 13-27-3-181, Wilkinson 10-13-0-80; **Rough Riders** — Watts 16-29-3-204. **Punt Returns: Eskimos** — Fraietta 5-28, Cyncar 3-15, Hayes 1-6; **Rough Riders** — Brazley 5-47, Kirk 4-33. **Kick-off Returns: Eskimos** — Hayes 2-46, Fraietta 1-13; **Rough Riders** — Brazley 4-96. **Field Goals: Eskimos** — Cutler 1-2; **Rough Riders** — Organ 3-3.

**1982 – Rushing: Eskimos** — Germany 12-70, Moon 9-91, Lumsden 7-39; **Argonauts** — Minter 1-minus 1, Holloway 7-54. **Receiving: Eskimos** — Scott 3-59, Fryer 4-55, Kelly 6-111, Lumsden 2-29, Smith 4-47, Germany 1-18; **Argonauts** — Greer 7-105, Minter 7-105, Tolbert 1-84, Bronk 1-13, Pearson 1-12. **Passing: Eskimos** — Moon 21-33-1-319; **Argonauts** — Holloway 17-35-1-319, Greer 0-2-0-0. **Punt Returns: Eskimos** — Hayes 6-27, Fraietta 1-7; **Argonauts** — Carinci 2-23, Newman 1-1. **Kick-off Returns: Eskimos** — Holliman 2-30; **Argonauts** — Heath 4-67, Greer 1-19. **Field Goals: Eskimos** — Cutler 4-4.

**1983 – Rushing: Argonauts** — Minter 8-36, Barnes 3-36, Holloway 2-24; **Lions** — Strong 6-35, White 3-10, Dewalt 1-1. **Receiving: Argonauts** — Minter 6-68, Greer 4-73, Tolbert 3-45, Pearson 2-34, Townsend 2-20, Carinci 2-16, Palazeti 2-14; **Lions** — White 8-92, Fernandez 7-130, Strong 6-33, Armour 4-42, Pankratz 1-12, Chapdelaine 1-8, DeBrueys 1-8. **Passing: Argonauts** — Barnes 14-24-0-175, Holloway 7-15-1-95; **Lions** — Dewalt 28-47-1-325. **Punt Returns: Argonauts** — Brazley 9-58, Minter 1-10; **Lions** — Crawford 9-37, Heath 1-4. **Kick-off Returns: Argonauts** — Brazley 3-82; **Lions** — Crawford 1-22, Strong 1-19. **Field Goals: Argonauts** — Ilesic 1-4; **Lions** — Passaglia 1-1.

**1984 – Rushing: Blue Bombers** — Kehoe 12-89, Reaves 15-64, Cantner 1-16, Clements 4-8; **Tiger-Cats** — Brock 2-17, Bragagnolo 3-5, Shepherd 2-4, Ledford 1-1, Crawford 1-minus 3, Graffi 1-1. **Receiving: Blue Bombers** — Poplawski 5-101, Murphy 3-53, Kehoe 5-47, Cantner 2-35, Boyd 3-28, House 2-26, Reaves 3-21; **Tiger-Cats** — Bragagnolo 7-48, Jett 6-45, DiPietro 4-64, Shepherd 3-27, Johnson 2-23, Francis 1-0. **Passing: Blue Bombers** — Clements 20-29-2-281, Hufnagel 3-3-0-30; **Tiger-Cats** — Brock 22-42-1-198, Tedford 1-1-0-9. **Punt Returns: Blue Bombers** — Neiles 8-43, Kehoe 2-31, Shaw 1-10, Hailey 1-8; **Tiger-Cats** — Crawford 4-41. **Kick-off Returns: Blue Bombers** — Cantner 1-18, Brown 1-11, Flagel 1-7; **Tiger-Cats** — Crawford 7-98, Shepherd 2-25, Graffi 1-18. **Field Goals: Blue Bombers** — Kennerd 4-4; **Tiger-Cats** — Ruoff 1-1.

**1985 – Rushing: Lions** — Sims 19-98, Passaglia 1-13, Dewalt 4-5, White 4-5; **Tiger-Cats** — Hobart 14-110, Shepherd 14-88. **Receiving: Lions** — Armour 3-151, Sandusky 6-135, Pankratz 3-79, White 2-29; **Tiger-Cats** — Ingram 3-107, Stapler 5-55, Crawford 2-12, DiPietro 1-10. **Passing: Lions** — Dewalt 14-28-0-394; **Tiger-Cats** — Hobart 10-32-1-174, Porras 1-3-1-10. **Punt Returns: Lions** — Clash 12-105; **Tiger-Cats** — Crawford 8-37, Bennett 2-8. **Kick-off Returns: Lions** — Byrd 1-29, Leonhard 1-16, Sims 1-21; **Tiger-Cats** — Crawford 4-83, Shepherd 1-18. **Field Goals: Lions** — Passaglia 5-6; **Tiger-Cats** — Ruoff 1-1.

**1986 – Rushing: Tiger-Cats** — Huclack 10-48, Bender 4-9, Hobart 3-9, Tommy 4-7, Kerrigan 2-7; **Eskimos** — Dunigan 7-22, Da. Allen 4-20, Johnstone 3-14, Skinner 2-2, M. Jones 3-13. **Receiving: Tiger-Cats** — Stapler 4-130, Ingram 4-100, Champion 3-49, DiPietro 3-14, Huclack 2-16; **Eskimos** — M. Jones 5-84, House 2-51, Do. Allen 3-48, Johnston 1-20, Skinner 2-31, Richards 1-9, Cyncar 1-6, Kelly 3-37. **Passing: Tiger-Cats** — Kerrigan 15-32-2-304, Hobart 1-3-1-5; **Eskimos** — Dunigan 11-26-1-158, Da. Allen 7-12-1-128. **Punt Returns: Tiger-Cats** — Bennett 5-37, Lee 2-11; **Eskimos** — Richard 3-28, Howlett 3-3. **Kick-off Returns: Tiger-Cats** — Bender 1-15, Fields 1-24, DiPietro 1-0; **Eskimos** — Richards 5-119, Jackson 1-16. **Field Goals: Tiger-Cats** — Osbaldiston 6-6.

**1987 – Rushing: Eskimos** — Dunigan 3-18, M. Jones 9-76, Allen 6-46, Johnstone 1-minus 3; **Argonauts** — Renfroe 2-15, Fenerty 17-106, Barrett 1-25, Hudson 5-25. **Receiving: Eskimos** — Kelly 3-59, S. Jones 3-41, House 7-134, Cyncar 1-6, M. Jones 4-52, Skinner 3-28, Johnstone 2-39; **Argonauts** — Thomas 2-29, J. Smith 2-33, D. Smith 3-51, Pearson 4-38, Fenerty 1-1, Jones 1-1. **Passing: Eskimos** — Dunigan 8-12-1-104, Allen 15-20-0-255; **Argonauts** — Renfroe 9-19-0-153, Barrett 4-12-0-60. **Punt Returns: Eskimos** — Williams 5-157, Robinson 1-4; **Argonauts** — Clash 4-18, J. Smith 1-6. **Kick-off Returns: Eskimos** — S. Jones 2-32, Richards 4-68, Williams 1-23; **Argonauts** — D. Smith 8-132, Edwards 0-8. **Field Goals: Eskimos** — Kauric 3-4; **Argonauts** — Chomyc 3-5.

**1988 – Rushing: Blue Bombers** — Jessie 8-35, Johns 9-23; **Lions** — Cherry 23-133, Dunigan 7-49, A. Parker 7-36. **Receiving: Blue Bombers** — Murphy 5-165, Johns 3-38, Winey 1-16, Rhymes 1-9, Fabi 1-12, Jessie 1-6; **Lions** — Williams 3-78, Carinci 4-59, Lecky

3-34, Parker 1-1, Cherry 3-24. **Passing: Blue Bombers** — Salisbury 12-32-0-246; **Lions** — Dunigan 14-32-2-196. **Punt Returns: Blue Bombers** — Pettway 3-16, Cochrane 1-7, Shorten 3-21; **Lions** — Drawhorn 8-21, Carinci 2-6, Wiseman 2-1. **Kick-off Returns: Blue Bombers** — Jefferson 1-33, Rhymes 1-21, Cochrane 1-0; **Lions** — Cherry 1-29, Drawhorn 5-134. **Field Goals: Blue Bombers** — Kennerd 4-5; **Lions** — Passaglia 1-3.

**1989 – Rushing: Roughriders** — McCray 8-22, Jones 4-11, Austin 2-8; **Tiger-Cats** — McAdoo 21-83, Tommy 2-6. **Receiving: Roughriders** — Guy 4-100, Narcisse 5-98, Fairholm 2-97, Elgaard 6-73, McCray 4-42, Ellingson 5-64; **Tiger-Cats** — Champion 8-106, DiPietro 5-54, Estell 3-33, Zatylny 1-13, McAdoo 2-29, Winfield 2-34, Knight 2-34. **Passing: Roughriders** — Austin 26-41-1-474; **Tiger-Cats** — Kerrigan 22-35-1-303. **Punt Returns: Roughriders** — Hall 4-34, Guy 1-6, Suitor 1-2; **Tiger-Cats** — Winfield 2-25, Gordon 0-32, Zatylny 2-24. **Kick-off Returns: Roughriders** — Guy 4-127, McCray 6-169; **Tiger-Cats** — McAdoo 3-75, Zatylny 3-53, Gataveckas 1-15, Jackson 1-0. **Field Goals: Roughriders** — Ridgway 4-5; **Tiger-Cats** — Osbaldiston 4-4.

**1990 – Rushing: Blue Bombers** — Mimbs 11-55, Burgess 7-26, Hudson 4-7; **Eskimos** — Ham 11-84, Marshall 13-54, Johnstone 1-11, Soles 1-8, Walling 1-minus 1. **Receiving: Blue Bombers** — House 6-107, Tuttle 3-70, Winey 3-67, Hudson 4-66, Hull 2-26, Streater 2-17, Mimbs 1-14; **Eskimos** — Ellis 8-131, Willis 4-46, Cyncar 2-24, Soles 2-17, Wright 1-11, Walling 1-10, Smith 1-8, Marshall 1-6. **Passing: Blue Bombers** — Burgess 18-31-0-286, McManus 2-2-0-66, Garza 1-4-1-15; **Eskimos** — Ham 20-37-3-253. **Punt Returns: Blue Bombers** — Winey 4-83, Streater 2-17; **Eskimos** — H. Williams 6-24, Shelton 1-2. **Kick-off Returns: Blue Bombers** — Halley 2-55, Winey 1-10; **Eskimos** — Smith 3-33, H. Williams 3-78, Walling 1-6. **Field Goals: Blue Bombers** — Kennerd 2-2; **Eskimos** — Macoritti 1-1.

**1991 – Rushing: Argonauts** — Dunigan 7-44, Smellie 5-11, Clemons 3-minus 2; **Stampeders** — Jenkins 7-28, Sapunjis 2-27, P. Smith 1-16, Barrett 9-14. **Receiving: Argonauts** — D.K. Smith 3-62, Masotti 2-45, Williams 3-14, Ismail 2-7, Clemons 1-7, Smellie 1-7; **Stampeders** — Bland 11-136, Beals 7-67, Pitts 4-66, Sapunjis 4-45, P. Smith 4-39, Simien 2-13, Jenkins 2-11. **Passing: Argonauts** — Dunigan 12-29-0-142; **Stampeders** — Barrett 34-56-3-377. **Punt Returns: Argonauts** — Ismail 5-70, Clemons 2-12, Brazley 1-1; **Stampeders** — Smith 6-46, Tucker 4-2. **Kick-off Returns: Argonauts** — Ismail 4-183, Clemons 1-43, Smith 1-18; **Stampeders** — P. Smith 3-36, Jenkins 2-29. **Field Goals: Argonauts** — Chomyc 2-4; **Stampeders** — McLoughlin 2-2.

**1992 – Rushing: Stampeders** — Jenkins 9-25, Flutie 4-20, McVey 2-3; **Blue Bombers** — Richardson 8-27, Dunigan 2-9. **Receiving: Stampeders** — Crawford 6-162, Bland 8-116, Sapunjis 7-85, Pitts 7-75, Smith 3-33, Jenkins 2-9; **Blue Bombers** — Alphin 5-103, Pillow 1-42, Richardson 3-18, Thompson 1-15, Crifo 2-14, Hudson 1-10. **Passing: Stampeders** — Flutie 33-49-0-480; **Blue Bombers** — Dunigan 6-19-0-47, McManus 7-18-1-155. **Punt Returns: Stampeders** — Crawford 7-70, Smith 3-2; **Blue Bombers** — Plummer 4-28, Smith 1-0. **Kick-off Returns: Stampeders** — Crawford 1-1, Smith 1-18; **Blue Bombers** — Plummer 3-49. **Field Goals: Stampeders** — McLoughlin 3-4; **Blue Bombers** — Westwood 1-1.

**1993 – Rushing: Eskimos** — Allen 14-90, Floyd 14-53, Soles 5-4; **Blue Bombers** — Richardson 10-26, Garza 5-10, Johnstone 1-6. **Receiving: Eskimos** — E. Brown 4-114, Soles 4-46, Sandusky 3-36, Christensen 2-25, Floyd 4-5; **Blue Bombers** — Williams 7-118, Jackson 4-57, Alphin 3-55, Richardson 4-44, Wilcox 4-30, Johnstone 1-9. **Passing: Eskimos** — Allen 17-29-1-226; **Blue Bombers** — Garza 20-43-2-322. **Punt Returns: Eskimos** — Williams 5-4; **Blue Bombers** — Boyko 5-16. **Kick-off Returns: Eskimos** — Floyd 4-94; **Blue Bombers** — Bryant 2-22, Boyko 1-9. **Field Goals: Eskimos** — Fleming 6-7; **Blue Bombers** — Westwood 3-3.

**1994 – Rushing: Lions** — Philpott 17-109, Millington 13-85, Flutie 2-18, McManus 1-1; **Baltimore** — Pringle 18-71, Ham 9-88, Drummond 1-12. **Receiving: Lions** — Alexander 5-119, Flutie 2-25, Murphy 1-9, Clark 1-9; **Baltimore** — Washington 2-72, Wilson 2-52, Drummond 2-38, Pringle 2-18, Armstrong 1-13. **Passing: Lions** — Austin 6-16-3-69, McManus 3-7-0-93; **Baltimore** — Ham 9-24-2-193, Congemi 0-0-0-0. **Punt Returns: Lions** — Flutie 7-30, McLennan 1-6; **Baltimore** — L. Smith 4-39, K. Anthony 1-0. **Kick-off Returns: Lions** — McLennan 3-54; **Baltimore** — Smith 3-58, Pringle 2-37. **Field Goals: Lions** — Passaglia 4-6; **Baltimore** — Igwebuike 3-5.

**1995 – Rushing: Baltimore** — Pringle 21-137, Ham 7-24, Alphin 1-minus 11; **Calgary** — Flutie 10-45, Stewart 10-33. **Receiving: Baltimore** — Drummond 3-47, Clark 3-44, Armstrong 3-27, Alphin 2-40, Tuipulotu 2-21, Culver 2-18, Pringle 2-16; **Calgary** — Sapunjis 8-113, Stewart 7-58, Pitts 3-54, T. Vaughn 3-46, Williams 1-13, Pope 1-3. **Passing: Baltimore** — Ham 17-29-213-0-0; **Calgary** — Flutie 23-49-287-1-1. **Punt Returns: Baltimore** — Wright 4-93; **Calgary** — T. Vaughn 1-6, Stewart 1-0, G. Vaughn; 1-0. **Kick-off Returns: Baltimore** — Wright 3-37; **Calgary** — Stewart 2-32, T. Vaughn 1-31, Coleman 1-16. **Field Goals: Baltimore** — Huerta 5-6; **Calgary** — McLoughlin 2-3.

**1996 – Rushing: Toronto** — Flutie 13-98, Drummond 12-50; **Edmonton** — Blount 8-29, Burse 4-14, Tobert 1-5. **Receiving: Toronto** — Masotti 6-100, Drummond 6-77, Cunningham 4-58, Clemons 3-29, Williams 1-20, Izquierdo 3-18; **Edmonton** — E. Brown 5-125, Sandusky 3-120, Da. Flutie 7-84, Tobert 4-59, Burse 2-11, Mazzoli 1-8, Blount 3-7. **Passing: Toronto** — Flutie 22-35-302-0-0; **Edmonton** — McManus 25-38-414-1-3. **Field Goals: Toronto** — Vanderjagt 5-5; **Edmonton** — Fleming 0-3. **Punt Returns: Toronto** — Cunningham 2-81; **Edmonton** — Williams 3-38. **Kick-off Returns: Toronto** — Clemons 5-96, O'Shea 1-15, Drummond 1-0; **Edmonton** — Williams 3-117, Goods 1-11, Blount 1-9, Martin 1-0.

# GAME STATISTICS

(Statistics are not available for every Grey Cup game)

| 1921 | Argonauts | Eskimos |
|---|---|---|
| First Downs | 20 | 17 |
| Kicks | 23 | 18 |
| Punts Kicked Back | 5 | 0 |
| Drop-kicks Attempted | 4 | 2 |
| Drop-kicks Made | 1 | 0 |
| Penalty, Yards | 90 | 40 |
| Ball Lost on Downs | 1 | 4 |
| Ball Lost on Fumble | 0 | 4 |
| Ball Lost on Penalty | 1 | 2 |

| 1924 | Queen's | Balmy Beach |
|---|---|---|
| First Downs | 11 | 4 |
| Kicks | 30 | 29 |
| Punts Kicked Back | 1 | 1 |
| Drop-kicks Attempted | 2 | 0 |
| Drop-kicks Made | 0 | 0 |
| Penalty, Yards | 55 | 20 |
| Ball Lost on Downs | 1 | 2 |
| Ball Lost on Fumble | 1 | 1 |
| Ball Lost on Penalty | 2 | 1 |

| 1930 | Balmy Beach | Roughriders |
|---|---|---|
| First Downs | 6 | 6 |
| Yds from Scrimmage | 263 | 201 |
| Average Yds per Kick | 31 | 27 |
| Fumbles lost | 2 | 3 |
| Yds Returns | 78 | 39 |

| 1931 | Winged Wheelers | Roughriders |
|---|---|---|
| First Downs | 14 | 10 |
| Yds from Scrimmage | 336 | 170 |
| Average Yds per Kick | 43.8 | 37.5 |
| Yds Returns | 232 | 68 |
| Intercepts By | 2 | 1 |
| Fumbles lost | 4 | 2 |

| 1932 | Tigers | Roughriders |
|---|---|---|
| First Downs | 13 | 11 |
| Yds Rushing | 328 | 181 |
| Yds Passing | 48 | 97 |
| Intercepts By | 6 | 0 |
| Average Punt | 41 | 38 |
| Fumbles lost | 7 | 6 |

| 1933 | Argonauts | Imperials |
|---|---|---|
| First Downs | 7 | 9 |
| Yds Rushing | 86 | 91 |
| Yds Passing | 39 | 80 |
| Intercepts By | 1 | 1 |
| Average Punt | 40 | 39 |
| Runbacks | 144 | 181 |
| Fumbles lost | 0 | 1 |

| 1934 | Imperials | Roughriders |
|---|---|---|
| First Downs | 8 | 4 |
| Yds Rushing | 173 | 60 |
| Yds Passing | 93 | 106 |
| Intercepts By | 4 | 0 |
| Average Punt | 46 | 42 |
| Runbacks | 49 | 135 |
| Fumbles lost | 1 | 3 |

| 1935 | 'Pegs | Tigers |
|---|---|---|
| First Downs | 9 | 3 |
| Yds Rushing | 125 | 48 |
| Yds Passing | 87 | 38 |
| Intercepts By | 2 | 1 |
| Average Punt | 38 | 45 |
| Runbacks | 367 | 95 |
| Fumbles lost | 1 | 0 |

| 1936 | Imperials | Rough Riders |
|---|---|---|
| First Downs | 9 | 15 |
| Yds Rushing | 223 | 291 |
| Yds Passing | 42 | 51 |
| Intercepts By | 3 | 2 |
| Average Punt | 49 | 40 |
| Runbacks | 128 | 161 |
| Fumbles lost | 3 | 3 |

| 1937 | Argonauts | Blue Bombers |
|---|---|---|
| First Downs | 9 | 5 |
| Yds Rushing | 159 | 125 |
| Yds Passing | 0 | 65 |
| Intercepts By | 4 | 2 |
| Average Punt | 54.6 | 46.4 |
| Runbacks | 150 | 71 |
| Fumbles lost | 5 | 1 |

| 1938 | Argonauts | Blue Bombers |
|---|---|---|
| First Downs | 16 | 7 |
| Yds Rushing | 148 | 88 |
| Yds Passing | 149 | 146 |
| Intercepts By | 4 | 3 |
| Average Punt | 46.1 | 43.0 |
| Runbacks | 93 | 27 |
| Fumbles lost | 3 | 2 |

| 1939 | Blue Bombers | Rough Riders |
|---|---|---|
| First Downs | 8 | 3 |
| Yds Rushing | 126 | 116 |
| Yds Passing | 23 | 99 |
| Intercepts By | 0 | 3 |
| Average Punt | 35 | 39 |
| Runbacks | 46 | 14 |
| Fumbles lost | 0 | 3 |

| 1940 (Game 1) | Rough Riders | Balmy Beach |
|---|---|---|
| First Downs | 12 | 5 |
| Yds Rushing | 200 | 97 |
| Yds Passing | 14 | 22 |
| Intercepts By | 0 | 0 |
| Average Punt | 37.3 | 34.6 |
| Runbacks | 174 | 77 |
| Fumbles lost | 2 | 2 |

| 1940 (Game 2) | Rough Riders | Balmy Beach |
|---|---|---|
| First Downs | 5 | 10 |
| Yds Rushing | 114 | 146 |
| Yds Passing | 43 | 70 |
| Intercepts By | 4 | 1 |
| Average Punt | 38.8 | 34.1 |
| Runbacks | 98 | 61 |
| Fumbles lost | 1 | 2 |

| 1941 | Blue Bombers | Rough Riders |
|---|---|---|
| First Downs | 7 | 11 |
| Yds Rushing | 130 | 192 |
| Yds Passing | 108 | 23 |
| Intercepts By | 2 | 3 |
| Average Punt | 37 | 38 |
| Runbacks | 46 | 67 |
| Fumbles lost | 1 | 4 |

| 1942 | Hurricanes | R.C.A.F. Bombers |
|---|---|---|
| First Downs | 10 | 10 |
| Yds Rushing | 217 | 65 |
| Yds Passing | 24 | 121 |
| Intercepts By | 4 | 0 |
| Average Punt | 41.2 | 39.8 |
| Runbacks | 111 | 73 |
| Fumbles lost | 2 | 0 |

| 1943 | Wildcats | R.C.A.F. Bombers |
|---|---|---|
| First Downs | 5 | 11 |
| Yds Rushing | 126 | 199 |
| Yds Passing | 39 | 51 |
| Intercepts By | 3 | 3 |
| Average Punt | 45.6 | 36.3 |
| Runbacks | 100 | 57 |
| Fumbles lost | 2 | 2 |

| 1945 | Argonauts | Blue Bombers |
|---|---|---|
| First Downs | 19 | 9 |
| Yds Rushing | 360 | 132 |
| Yds Passing | 77 | 13 |
| Intercepts By | 1 | 1 |
| Average Punt | 37 | 32 |
| Runbacks | 110 | 11 |
| Fumbles lost | 2 | 4 |

| 1946 | Argonauts | Blue Bombers |
|---|---|---|
| First Downs | 6 | 11 |
| Yds Rushing | 82 | 146 |
| Yds Passing | 214 | 133 |
| Intercepts By | 2 | 2 |
| Average Punt | 37.4 | 41.7 |
| Runbacks | 63 | 52 |
| Fumbles lost | 1 | 0 |

| 1947 | Argonauts | Blue Bombers |
|---|---|---|
| First Downs | 15 | 15 |
| Yds Rushing | 172 | 210 |
| Yds Passing | 91 | 39 |
| Intercepts By | 1 | 1 |
| Average Punt | 38 | 38 |
| Runbacks | 137 | 43 |
| Fumbles lost | 4 | 2 |

| 1948 | Stampeders | Rough Riders |
|---|---|---|
| First Downs | 16 | 18 |
| Yds Rushing | 177 | 311 |
| Yds Passing | 132 | 55 |
| Intercepts By | 2 | 0 |
| Average Punt | 39 | 41 |
| Runbacks | 28 | 121 |
| Fumbles lost | 0 | 5 |

| 1949 | Alouettes | Stampeders |
|---|---|---|
| First Downs | 23 | 17 |
| Yds Rushing | 193 | 165 |
| Yds Passing | 210 | 178 |
| Intercepts By | 4 | 1 |
| Average Punt | 38.9 | 41.6 |
| Runbacks | 85 | 58 |
| Fumbles lost | 4 | 1 |

| 1950 | Argonauts | Blue Bombers |
|---|---|---|
| First Downs | 11 | 3 |
| Yds Rushing | 229 | 111 |
| Yds Passing | 7 | 48 |
| Intercepts By | 2 | 0 |
| Average Punt | 36.6 | 36.8 |
| Runbacks | 70 | 125 |
| Fumbles lost | 1 | 2 |

| 1951 | Rough Riders | Roughriders |
|---|---|---|
| First Downs | 14 | 18 |
| Yds Rushing | 187 | 194 |
| Yds Passing | 127 | 141 |
| Intercepts By | 1 | 2 |
| Average Punt | 45 | 46 |
| Runbacks | 149 | 126 |
| Fumbles lost | 3 | 3 |

| 1952 | Argonauts | Eskimos |
|---|---|---|
| First Downs | 15 | 18 |
| Yds Rushing | 149 | 139 |
| Yds Passing | 235 | 261 |
| Intercepts By | 2 | 0 |
| Average Punt | 39 | 42 |
| Fumbles lost | 1 | 2 |

| 1953 | Tiger-Cats | Blue Bombers |
|---|---|---|
| First Downs | 17 | 21 |
| Yds Rushing | 134 | 73 |
| Yds Passing | 183 | 357 |
| Intercepts By | 1 | 1 |
| Average Punt | 40 | 35 |
| Fumbles lost | 1 | 1 |

| 1954 | Eskimos | Alouettes |
|---|---|---|
| First Downs | 25 | 34 |
| Yds Rushing | 273 | 249 |
| Yds Passing | 161 | 407 |
| Intercepts By | 2 | 2 |
| Average Punt | 36.8 | 37.2 |
| Fumbles lost | 3 | 6 |

| 1955 | Alouettes | Eskimos |
|---|---|---|
| First Downs | 30 | 34 |
| Yds Rushing | 69 | 438 |
| Yds Passing | 508 | 128 |
| Intercepts By | 1 | 2 |
| Average Punt | 38 | 40 |
| Fumbles lost | 3 | 2 |

| 1956 | Alouettes | Eskimos |
|---|---|---|
| First Downs | 25 | 36 |
| Yds Rushing | 140 | 455 |
| Yds Passing | 329 | 101 |
| Intercepts By | 4 | 2 |
| Average Punt | 37 | 33 |
| Fumbles lost | 3 | 1 |

| 1957 | Tiger-Cats | Blue Bombers |
|---|---|---|
| First Downs | 10 | 21 |
| Yds Rushing | 160 | 192 |
| Yds Passing | 67 | 177 |
| Intercepts By | 2 | 0 |
| Average Punt | 43.1 | 37.9 |
| Fumbles lost | 2 | 6 |

| 1958 | Blue Bombers | Tiger-Cats |
|---|---|---|
| First Downs | 26 | 22 |
| Yds Rushing | 249 | 143 |
| Yds Passing | 195 | 233 |
| Intercepts By | 2 | 0 |
| Average Punt | 43 | 38 |
| Fumbles lost | 3 | 1 |

| 1959 | Blue Bombers | Tiger-Cats |
|---|---|---|
| First Downs | 11 | 10 |
| Yds Rushing | 139 | 74 |
| Yds Passing | 125 | 97 |
| Intercepts By | 0 | 0 |
| Average Punt | 45 | 40 |
| Fumbles lost | 2 | 2 |

| 1960 | Rough Riders | Eskimos |
|---|---|---|
| First Downs | 17 | 14 |
| Yds Rushing | 254 | 44 |
| Yds Passing | 102 | 197 |
| Intercepts By | 2 | 1 |
| Average Punt | 41 | 43 |
| Fumbles lost | 2 | 3 |

| 1961 | Blue Bombers | Tiger-Cats |
|---|---|---|
| First Downs | 20 | 18 |
| Yds Rushing | 295 | 56 |
| Yds Passing | 220 | 350 |
| Intercepts By | 0 | 1 |
| Average Punt | 44 | 39 |
| Fumbles lost | 2 | 0 |

| 1962 | Blue Bombers | Tiger-Cats |
|---|---|---|
| First Downs | 21 | 21 |
| Yds Rushing | 102 | 238 |
| Yds Passing | 224 | 251 |
| Intercepts By | 0 | 1 |
| Average Punt | 41.1 | 43.6 |
| Fumbles lost | 1 | 1 |

| 1963 | Tiger-Cats | Lions |
|---|---|---|
| First Downs | 19 | 22 |
| Yds Rushing | 177 | 106 |
| Yds Passing | 261 | 234 |
| Intercepts By | 1 | 1 |
| Average Punt | 36.6 | 37.9 |
| Fumbles lost | 0 | 0 |

| 1964 | Lions | Tiger-Cats |
|---|---|---|
| First Downs | 15 | 24 |
| Yds Rushing | 161 | 198 |
| Yds Passing | 153 | 236 |
| Intercepts By | 1 | 1 |
| Average Punt | 34.1 | 41.8 |
| Fumbles lost | 1 | 2 |

| 1965 | Tiger-Cats | Blue Bombers |
|---|---|---|
| First Downs | 7 | 18 |
| Yds Rushing | 142 | 174 |
| Yds Passing | 71 | 68 |
| Intercepts By | 1 | 0 |
| Average Punt | 32 | 24 |
| Fumbles lost | 5 | 1 |

| 1966 | Roughriders | Rough Riders |
|---|---|---|
| First Downs | 18 | 12 |
| Yds Rushing | 196 | 92 |
| Yds Passing | 160 | 195 |
| Intercepts By | 2 | 0 |
| Average Punt | 36.4 | 37.1 |
| Fumbles lost | 0 | 1 |

| 1967 | Tiger-Cats | Roughriders |
|---|---|---|
| First Downs | 9 | 11 |
| Yds Rushing | 70 | 120 |
| Yds Passing | 164 | 119 |
| Intercepts By | 3 | 1 |
| Average Punt | 45.4 | 38.2 |
| Fumbles lost | 0 | 2 |

| 1968 | Rough Riders | Stampeders |
|---|---|---|
| First Downs | 13 | 24 |
| Yds Rushing | 222 | 74 |
| Yds Passing | 185 | 258 |
| Intercepts By | 1 | 0 |
| Average Punt | 42.5 | 38 |
| Fumbles lost | 2 | 2 |

| 1969 | Rough Riders | Roughriders |
|---|---|---|
| First Downs | 17 | 13 |
| Yds Rushing | 171 | 63 |
| Yds Passing | 254 | 239 |
| Intercepts By | 1 | 0 |
| Average Punt | 41.5 | 39.5 |
| Fumbles lost | 2 | 3 |

| 1970 | Alouettes | Stampeders | | 1971 | Stampeders | Argonauts |
|---|---|---|---|---|---|---|
| First Downs | 18 | 9 | | First Downs | 8 | 13 |
| Yds Rushing | 103 | 66 | | Yds Rushing | 103 | 98 |
| Yds Passing | 215 | 119 | | Yds Passing | 111 | 192 |
| Intercepts By | 2 | 3 | | Intercepts By | 0 | 3 |
| Average Punt | 36.7 | 37.6 | | Average Punt | 38 | 40.2 |
| Fumbles lost | 2 | 2 | | Fumbles lost | 1 | 3 |

| 1972 | Tiger-Cats | Roughriders | | 1973 | Rough Riders | Eskimos |
|---|---|---|---|---|---|---|
| First Downs | 23 | 24 | | First Downs | 12 | 19 |
| Yds Rushing | 101 | 111 | | Yds Rushing | 119 | 92 |
| Yds Passing | 291 | 239 | | Yds Passing | 161 | 208 |
| Intercepts By | 2 | 2 | | Intercepts By | 0 | 2 |
| Average Punt | 39 | 37 | | Average Punt | 42 | 36 |
| Fumbles lost | 0 | 1 | | Fumbles lost | 1 | 2 |

| 1974 | Alouettes | Eskimos | | 1975 | Eskimos | Alouettes |
|---|---|---|---|---|---|---|
| First Downs | 16 | 8 | | First Downs | 13 | 14 |
| Yds Rushing | 109 | 49 | | Yds Rushing | 70 | 138 |
| Yds Passing | 151 | 126 | | Yds Passing | 165 | 183 |
| Intercepts By | 2 | 0 | | Intercepts By | 1 | 1 |
| Average Punt | 43.6 | 38.6 | | Average Punt | 34 | 39 |
| Fumbles lost | 1 | 2 | | Fumbles lost | 1 | 1 |

| 1978 | Eskimos | Alouettes | | 1979 | Eskimos | Alouettes |
|---|---|---|---|---|---|---|
| First Downs | 15 | 10 | | First Downs | 16 | 21 |
| Yds Rushing | 93 | 76 | | Yds Rushing | 94 | 204 |
| Yds Passing | 119 | 147 | | Yds Passing | 203 | 151 |
| Intercepts By | 0 | 1 | | Intercepts By | 1 | 1 |
| Average Punt | 41 | 30 | | Average Punt | 40.4 | 45.5 |
| Fumbles lost | 2 | 2 | | Fumbles lost | 0 | 0 |

| 1980 | Eskimos | Tiger-Cats | | 1981 | Eskimos | Rough Riders |
|---|---|---|---|---|---|---|
| First Downs | 31 | 12 | | First Downs | 21 | 14 |
| Yds Rushing | 205 | 112 | | Yds Rushing | 81 | 83 |
| Yds Passing | 428 | 151 | | Yds Passing | 261 | 204 |
| Intercepts By | 4 | 1 | | Intercepts By | 3 | 3 |
| Average Punt | 42 | 46 | | Average Punt | 48 | 43 |
| Fumbles lost | 3 | 1 | | Fumbles lost | 1 | 1 |

| 1982 | Eskimos | Argonauts | | 1983 | Argonauts | Lions |
|---|---|---|---|---|---|---|
| First Downs | 31 | 17 | | First Downs | 21 | 19 |
| Yds Rushing | 200 | 53 | | Yds Rushing | 96 | 46 |
| Yds Passing | 319 | 319 | | Yds Passing | 270 | 325 |
| Intercepts By | 1 | 1 | | Intercepts By | 1 | 1 |
| Average Punt | 43.0 | 37.8 | | Average Punt | 46 | 42 |
| Fumbles lost | 1 | 1 | | Fumbles lost | 1 | 1 |

| 1984 | Blue Bombers | Tiger-Cats | | 1985 | Lions | Tiger-Cats |
|---|---|---|---|---|---|---|
| First Downs | 27 | 14 | | First Downs | 16 | 17 |
| Yds Rushing | 177 | 25 | | Yds Rushing | 121 | 198 |
| Yds Passing | 311 | 207 | | Yds Passing | 394 | 184 |
| Intercepts By | 1 | 2 | | Intercepts By | 2 | 0 |
| Average Punt | 43.0 | 39.9 | | Average Punt | 41 | 46 |
| Fumbles lost | 1 | 1 | | Fumbles lost | 1 | 1 |

| 1986 | Tiger-Cats | Eskimos | | 1987 | Eskimos | Argonauts |
|---|---|---|---|---|---|---|
| First Downs | 16 | 19 | | First Downs | 25 | 20 |
| Yds Rushing | 80 | 71 | | Yds Rushing | 137 | 171 |
| Yds Passing | 309 | 286 | | Yds Passing | 359 | 213 |
| Intercepts By | 2 | 3 | | Intercepts By | 0 | 1 |
| Average Punt | 35.8 | 43.7 | | Average Punt | 44.7 | 44 |
| Fumbles lost | 1 | 6 | | Fumbles lost | 2 | 0 |

| 1988 | Blue Bombers | Lions | | 1989 | Roughriders | Tiger-Cats |
|---|---|---|---|---|---|---|
| First Downs | 12 | 24 | | First Downs | 28 | 23 |
| Yds Rushing | 58 | 218 | | Yds Rushing | 41 | 89 |
| Yds Passing | 246 | 196 | | Yds Passing | 474 | 303 |
| Intercepts By | 2 | 0 | | Intercepts By | 1 | 2 |
| Average Punt | 47.3 | 45.7 | | Average Punt | 46 | 47 |
| Fumbles lost | 0 | 1 | | Fumbles lost | 0 | 0 |

| 1990 | Blue Bombers | Eskimos | | 1991 | Argonauts | Stampeders |
|---|---|---|---|---|---|---|
| First Downs | 23 | 23 | | First Downs | 7 | 28 |
| Yds Rushing | 88 | 156 | | Yds Rushing | 53 | 85 |
| Yds Passing | 367 | 253 | | Yds Passing | 142 | 377 |
| Intercepts By | 3 | 1 | | Intercepts By | 3 | 0 |
| Average Punt | 37 | 45 | | Average Punt | 36 | 28 |
| Fumbles lost | 1 | 4 | | Fumbles lost | 3 | 2 |

| 1992 | Stampeders | Blue Bombers |
|---|---|---|
| First Downs | 25 | 12 |
| Yds Rushing | 48 | 36 |
| Yds Passing | 480 | 202 |
| Intercepts By | 1 | 0 |
| Average Punt | 34 | 44 |
| Fumbles lost | 1 | 1 |

| 1993 | Eskimos | Blue Bombers |
|---|---|---|
| First Downs | 19 | 23 |
| Yds Rushing | 147 | 42 |
| Yds Passing | 226 | 322 |
| Intercepts By | 2 | 1 |
| Average Punt | 49 | 45 |
| Fumbles lost | 2 | 5 |

| 1994 | Lions | Baltimore |
|---|---|---|
| First Downs | 16 | 15 |
| Yds Rushing | 213 | 171 |
| Yds Passing | 162 | 193 |
| Intercepts By | 2 | 3 |
| Average Punt | 38 | 39 |
| Fumbles lost | 0 | 1 |

| 1995 | Baltimore | Calgary |
|---|---|---|
| First Downs | 18 | 21 |
| Yds Rushing | 150 | 78 |
| Yds Passing | 213 | 287 |
| Intercepts By | 1 | 0 |
| Average Punt | 49.5 | 34 |
| Fumbles lost | 1 | 2 |

| 1996 | Toronto | Edmonton |
|---|---|---|
| First Downs | 30 | 21 |
| Yds Rushing | 148 | 48 |
| Yds Passing | 302 | 414 |
| Intercepts By | 1 | 0 |
| Average Punt | 41 | 33 |
| Fumbles lost | 0 | 0 |

# TEAM RECORDS

(Scoring and appearances records date from 1909; all other records date from 1953)

**Highest attendance**
68,318 – Montreal 41 Edmonton 6, Montreal, Nov. 27, 1977
65,113 – Edmonton 17 Montreal 9, Montreal, Nov. 25, 1979
60,081 – Winnipeg 47 Hamilton 17, Edmonton, Nov. 18, 1984

**All-time most points against**
497 – Edmonton
465 – Hamilton
458 – Winnipeg
419 – Toronto
340 – Saskatchewan

**Most points both teams one game**
83 – Saskatchewan vs Hamilton, Nov. 26, 1989
80 – Toronto vs Edmonton, Nov. 24, 1996
77 – Edmonton vs Montreal, Nov. 24, 1956

**Most points one team first quarter**
18 – Hamilton vs Winnipeg, Nov. 27, 1943
17 – Hamilton vs Edmonton, Nov. 30, 1986
   – Edmonton vs Winnipeg, Nov. 28, 1993

**Most points one team third quarter**
28 – Winnipeg vs Edmonton, Nov. 25, 1990
20 – Montreal vs Edmonton, Nov. 27, 1977
18 – Edmonton vs Montreal, Nov. 24, 1956

**Fewest points winning team**
4 – Toronto vs Sarnia, Dec. 9, 1933
   – Toronto vs Winnipeg, Dec. 11, 1937
7 – St. Hyacinthe vs Hamilton, Nov. 25, 1944

**Highest shutout**
54-0 – Queen's vs Regina, Dec. 1, 1923
35-0 – Toronto vs Winnipeg, Dec. 1, 1945
30-0 – Hamilton vs Regina, Dec. 1, 1928

**Most touchdowns one team one game**
9 – Queen's vs Regina, Dec. 1, 1923
7 – Hamilton vs Toronto, Nov. 29, 1913
   – Edmonton vs Montreal, Nov. 24, 1956

**All-time most converts**
50 – Hamilton
44 – Edmonton
39 – Toronto
37 – Winnipeg

**Most converts both teams one game**
9 – Toronto vs Edmonton, Nov. 24, 1996
8 – Edmonton vs Montreal, Nov. 26, 1955
   – Winnipeg vs Hamilton, Nov. 29, 1958
   – Saskatchewan vs Hamilton, Nov. 26, 1989

**All-time most points scored**
545 – Hamilton
490 – Toronto
445 – Edmonton
375 – Winnipeg
276 – Ottawa

**Most points one team one game**
54 – Queen's vs Regina, Dec. 1, 1923
50 – Edmonton vs Montreal, Nov. 24, 1956
   – Winnipeg vs Edmonton, Nov. 25, 1990
48 – Edmonton vs Hamilton, Nov. 23, 1980

**Most points one team one quarter**
28 – Winnipeg vs Edmonton (3rd), Nov. 25, 1990
27 – Winnipeg vs Hamilton (2nd), Nov. 18, 1984
   – Toronto vs Edmonton (2nd), Nov. 24, 1996

**Most points one team second quarter**
27 – Winnipeg vs Hamilton, Nov. 18, 1984
   – Toronto vs Edmonton, Nov. 24, 1996
21 – Winnipeg vs Hamilton, Dec. 1, 1962
   – Toronto vs Edmonton, Nov. 29, 1987
   – Saskatchewan vs Hamilton, Nov. 26, 1989

**Most points one team fourth quarter**
24 – Toronto vs Winnipeg, Dec. 10, 1938
19 – Hamilton vs Winnipeg, Nov. 30, 1957
18 – Winnipeg vs Hamilton, Nov. 28, 1959

**Fewest points both teams one game**
7 – Toronto vs Sarnia, Dec. 9, 1933
   – Toronto vs Winnipeg, Dec. 11, 1937
10 – Ottawa vs Balmy Beach, Nov. 30, 1940

**All-time most touchdowns**
66 – Hamilton
58 – Toronto
51 – Edmonton
42 – Winnipeg
33 – Ottawa
26 – Montreal

**Most touchdowns both teams one game**
11 – Edmonton vs Montreal, Nov. 24, 1956
9 – Queen's vs Regina, Dec. 1, 1923
   – Toronto vs Edmonton, Nov. 24, 1996

**Most converts one team one game**
6 – Queen's vs Regina, Dec. 1, 1923
   – Edmonton vs Hamilton, Nov. 23, 1980
   – Winnipeg vs Edmonton, Nov. 25, 1990

**All time most field goals**
31 – Edmonton
23 – Winnipeg
22 – Hamilton
19 – Montreal

**Most field goals one team one game**
6 – Montreal vs Edmonton, Nov. 27, 1977
– Hamilton vs Edmonton, Nov. 30, 1986
– Edmonton vs Winnipeg, Nov. 28, 1993

**All time most singles**
79 – Toronto                29 – Ottawa
46 – Hamilton

**Most singles both teams one game**
12 – Ottawa vs U. Toronto, Dec. 4, 1926
– Hamilton vs Regina, Nov. 30, 1929
11 – U. Toronto vs Toronto Parkdale, Dec. 4, 1909

**Most safety touches one team one game**
3 – Hamilton vs Winnipeg, Nov. 27, 1965

**Fewest first downs one team one game**
7 – Hamilton vs Winnipeg, Nov. 27, 1965
– Toronto vs Calgary, Nov. 24, 1991
8 – Calgary vs Toronto, Nov. 28, 1971
– Edmonton vs Montreal, Nov. 24, 1974

**Most total yards both teams one game**
1,115 – Edmonton vs Montreal, Nov. 26, 1955
1,090 – Edmonton vs Montreal, Nov. 27, 1954
1,018 – Edmonton vs Montreal, Nov. 24, 1956

**Fewest total yards both teams one game**
376 – Winnipeg vs Hamilton, Nov. 18, 1984
389 – Edmonton vs Montreal, Nov. 24, 1974
391 – Winnipeg vs Hamilton, Nov. 27, 1965
– Edmonton vs Montreal, Nov. 26, 1978

**Fewest yards rushing one team one game**
24 – Hamilton vs Winnipeg, Nov. 18, 1984
36 – Winnipeg vs Calgary, Nov. 29, 1992
41 – Montreal vs Edmonton, Nov. 26, 1955
– Saskatchewan vs Hamilton, Nov. 26, 1989

**Most passes attempted one team one game**
56 – Calgary vs Toronto, Nov. 24, 1991
49 – Calgary vs Winnipeg, Nov. 29, 1992
– Calgary vs Baltimore, Nov. 19, 1995

**Most passes completed one team one game**
34 – Calgary vs Toronto, Nov. 24, 1991
33 – Calgary vs Winnipeg, Nov. 29, 1992
31 – Winnipeg vs Hamilton, Nov. 28, 1953

**Most yards passing one team one game**
508 – Montreal vs Edmonton, Nov. 26, 1955
480 – Calgary vs Winnipeg, Nov. 29, 1992
474 – Saskatchewan vs Hamilton, Nov. 26, 1989

**Most touchdowns passing one team one game**
4 – Ottawa vs Saskatchewan, Nov. 30, 1969
– Edmonton vs Hamilton, Nov. 23, 1980
– Winnipeg vs Edmonton, Nov. 25, 1990

**Most fumbles one team one game**
7 – Edmonton vs Hamilton, Nov. 30, 1986
6 – Montreal vs Edmonton, Nov. 27, 1954
– Winnipeg vs Hamilton, Nov. 30, 1957
– Edmonton vs Winnipeg, Nov. 25, 1990

**Most interception returns one team one game**
4 – Edmonton vs Montreal, Nov. 24, 1956
– Montreal vs Edmonton, Nov. 27, 1977
– Edmonton vs Hamilton, Nov. 23, 1980

**Most field goals both teams one game**
9 – Edmonton vs Winnipeg, Nov. 28, 1993
8 – Montreal vs Edmonton, Nov. 27, 1977
– Saskatchewan vs Hamilton, Nov. 26, 1989

**Most singles one team one game**
10 – U. Toronto vs Toronto Parkdale, Dec. 4, 1909
9 – Hamilton vs Regina, Nov. 30, 1929
7 – U. Toronto vs Ottawa, Dec. 4, 1926

**All-time most safety touches**
6 – Hamilton

**Most first downs one team one game**
36 – Edmonton vs Montreal, Nov. 24, 1956
34 – Montreal vs Edmonton, Nov. 27, 1954
– Edmonton vs Montreal, Nov. 26, 1955

**Most total yards one team one game**
656 – Montreal vs Edmonton, Nov. 27, 1954
606 – Edmonton vs Hamilton, Nov. 23, 1980
566 – Edmonton vs Montreal, Nov. 26, 1955

**Fewest total yards one team one game**
102 – Edmonton vs Montreal, Nov. 27, 1977
155 – Edmonton vs Montreal, Nov. 24, 1974
171 – Hamilton vs Winnipeg, Nov. 28, 1959

**Most yards rushing one team one game**
456 – Edmonton vs Montreal, Nov. 24, 1956
438 – Edmonton vs Montreal, Nov. 26, 1955
295 – Winnipeg vs Hamilton, Dec. 2, 1961

**Most touchdowns rushing one team one game**
4 – Edmonton vs Montreal, Nov. 26, 1955
– Edmonton vs Montreal, Nov. 24, 1956
– Hamilton vs Winnipeg, Nov. 30, 1957

**Fewest passes attempted one team one game**
5 – Hamilton vs Winnipeg, Nov. 27, 1965
12 – Winnipeg vs Hamilton, Nov. 28, 1959
13 – Winnipeg vs Hamilton, Nov. 27, 1965

**Fewest passes completed one team one game**
2 – Hamilton vs Winnipeg, Nov. 27, 1965
5 – Winnipeg vs Hamilton, Nov. 28, 1959
6 – Hamilton vs Winnipeg, Nov. 30, 1957
– Ottawa vs Edmonton, Nov. 26, 1960
– Ottawa vs Saskatchewan, Nov. 26, 1966

**Fewest yards passing one team one game**
68 – Winnipeg vs Hamilton, Nov. 27, 1965
71 – Hamilton vs Winnipeg, Nov. 27, 1965
83 – Hamilton vs Winnipeg, Nov. 30, 1957

**Most turnovers one team one game**
10 – Winnipeg vs Hamilton, Nov. 30, 1957
(6 fumb., 2 int., 2 lost poss.)
– Edmonton vs Montreal, Nov. 27, 1977
(4 fumb., 4 int., 2 lost poss.)
– Edmonton vs Hamilton, Nov. 30, 1986
(6 fumb., 2 int., 2 lost poss.)

**Most fumbles lost one team one game**
6 – Montreal vs Edmonton, Nov. 27, 1954
– Winnipeg vs Hamilton, Nov. 30, 1957
– Edmonton vs Hamilton, Nov. 30, 1986

**Most interception returns both teams one game**
6 – Edmonton vs Montreal, Nov. 24, 1956
– Ottawa vs Edmonton, Nov. 22, 1981
5 – Calgary vs Montreal, Nov. 28, 1970
– Montreal vs Edmonton, Nov. 27, 1977
– Edmonton vs Hamilton, Nov. 23, 1980
– Edmonton vs. Hamilton, Nov. 30, 1986
– Baltimore vs B.C., Nov. 27, 1994

## Most punts one team one game
18 – Hamilton vs Winnipeg, Nov. 28, 1959
 – Hamilton vs Saskatchewan, Dec. 2, 1967
17 – Winnipeg vs Hamilton, Nov. 28, 1959
 – Hamilton vs Winnipeg, Dec. 2, 1961

## Most yards punted one team one game
818 – Hamilton vs Saskatchewan, Dec. 2, 1967
782 – Winnipeg vs Hamilton, Nov. 28, 1959
703 – Hamilton vs Winnipeg, Dec. 2, 1963

## Most punt returns one team one game
17 – Winnipeg vs Hamilton, Dec. 2, 1961
15 – Winnipeg vs Hamilton, Nov. 28, 1959
 – Saskatchewan vs Hamilton, Dec. 2, 1967
 – Montreal vs Calgary, Nov. 28, 1970

## Most yards punt returns one team one game
128 – Ottawa vs Saskatchewan, Nov. 28, 1976
117 – Montreal vs Edmonton, Nov. 27, 1977
105 – B.C. vs Hamilton, Nov. 24, 1985

## Most kick-off returns one team one game
10 – Hamilton vs B.C., Nov. 28, 1964
 – Hamilton vs Winnipeg, Nov. 18, 1984
 – Saskatchewan vs Hamilton, Nov. 26, 1989

## Most yards kick-off returns one team one game
296 – Saskatchewan vs Hamilton, Nov. 26, 1989
244 – Toronto vs Calgary, Nov. 24, 1991
178 – Edmonton vs Montreal, Nov. 27, 1977

## Most punts both teams one game
33 – Hamilton vs Winnipeg, Nov. 28, 1959
32 – Hamilton vs Saskatchewan, Dec. 2, 1967
31 – Winnipeg vs Hamilton, Dec. 2, 1961

## Most yards punted both teams one game
1,417 – Hamilton vs Winnipeg, Nov. 28, 1959
1,353 – Hamilton vs Saskatchewan, Dec. 2, 1967
1,316 – Winnipeg vs Hamilton, Dec. 2, 1961

## Most punt returns both teams one game
28 – Saskatchewan vs Hamilton, Dec. 2, 1967
27 – Winnipeg vs Hamilton, Nov. 28, 1959
 – Winnipeg vs Hamilton, Dec. 2, 1961
 – Montreal vs Calgary, Nov. 28, 1970

## Most yards punt returns both teams one game
167 – Winnipeg vs Hamilton, Dec. 2, 1961
161 – Ottawa vs Saskatchewan, Nov. 28, 1976
156 – Winnipeg vs Hamilton, Nov. 28, 1959

## Most kick-off returns both teams one game
18 – Saskatchewan vs Hamilton, Nov. 26, 1989
15 – Edmonton vs Toronto, Nov. 29, 1987
13 – Winnipeg vs Hamilton, Nov. 18, 1984
 – Edmonton vs Toronto, Nov. 24, 1996

## Most yards kick-off returns both teams one game
439 – Saskatchewan vs Hamilton, Nov. 26, 1989
309 – Toronto vs Calgary, Nov. 24, 1991
263 – Edmonton vs Toronto, Nov. 29, 1987

# INDIVIDUAL RECORDS

**All-time most games played**
9 – Tommy Grant, Ham.; John Barrow, Ham.; Angelo Mosca, Ott.-Ham.; Dave Cutler, Edm.; Larry Highbaugh, Edm.; Hank Ilesic, Edm.-Tor.

**All-time most points**
72 – Dave Cutler, Edm. 1969-84
61 – Don Sweet, Mtl.-Ham 1972-85
45 – Lui Passaglia, B.C. 1976-96

**All-time most touchdowns**
5 – Hal Patterson, Mtl.-Ham. 1954-67
 – Brian Kelly, Edm. 1979-87

**All-time most converts**
17 – Don Sutherin, Ham.-Ott.-Tor. 1958-70
16 – Dave Cutler, Edm. 1969-84
12 – Pep Leadlay, Queen's-Ham. Tigers 1925-29
 – Trevor Kennerd, Wpg. 1980-91

**All-time most field goals**
18 – Dave Cutler, Edm. 1969-84
17 – Don Sweet, Mtl.-Ham. 1972-85
11 – Lui Passaglia, B.C. 1976-94

**Longest field goals**
53 – Carlos Huerta, Balt. vs. Cal. Nov. 19, 1995
52 – Dave Cutler, Edm. vs Mtl. Nov. 23, 1975
51 – Bob Macoritti, Sask. vs Ott. Nov. 28, 1976

**Most singles one game**
8 – Hugh Gall, U. Toronto vs Tor. Parkdale Dec. 4, 1909
6 – Huck Welch, Ham. Tigers vs Regina Nov. 30, 1929
5 – Tout Leckie, Ham. Alerts vs Tor. Argos Nov. 30, 1912
 – Joe Miller, Ott. Sen. vs U. Toronto Dec. 4, 1926
 – Charles Trimble, U. Toronto vs Ott. Sen. Dec. 4, 1926
 – Bummer Stirling, Sarnia vs Regina Nov. 24, 1934
 – Sammy Sward, Ott. vs Balmy Beach Dec. 7, 1940

**Most times rushed one game**
30 – Normie Kwong, Edm. vs Mtl. Nov. 26, 1955
28 – Johnny Bright, Edm. vs Mtl. Nov. 24, 1956
23 – George Reed, Sask. vs Ott. Nov. 26, 1966
 – Tony Cherry, B.C. vs Wpg. Nov. 27, 1988

**All-time most games won**
7 – Jack Wedley, Tor.-St. Hyacinthe-Donnacona Combines; Bill Stevenson, Edm.; Hank Ilesic, Edm.-Tor.

**Most points one game**
23 – Don Sweet, Mtl. vs Edm. Nov. 27, 1977
22 – Jim Van Pelt, Wpg. vs Ham. Nov. 29, 1958
21 – Paul Osbaldiston, Ham. vs Edm. Nov. 30, 1986
 – Sean Fleming, Edm. vs Wpg. Nov. 28, 1993

**Most touchdowns one game**
3 – Art Wilson, Ham. vs Tor. Parkdale Nov. 29, 1913
 – Red Storey, Tor. vs Wpg. Dec. 10, 1938
 – Jackie Parker, Edm. vs Mtl. Nov. 24, 1956
 – Tommy Scott, Edm. vs. Ham. Nov. 23, 1980

**Most converts one game**
6 – Dave Cutler, Edm. vs Ham. Nov. 23, 1980
 – Trevor Kennerd, Wpg. vs Edm. Nov. 25, 1990
5 – Bob Dean, Edm. vs Mtl. Nov. 26, 1955
 – Trevor Kennerd, Wpg. vs Ham. Nov. 18, 1984
 – Sean Fleming, Edm. vs Toronto, Nov. 24, 1996

**Most field goals one game**
6 – Don Sweet, Mtl. vs Edm. Nov. 27, 1977
 – Paul Osbaldiston, Ham. vs. Edm. Nov. 30, 1986
 – Sean Fleming, Edm. vs Wpg. Nov. 28, 1993

**All-time most singles**
12 – Hugh Gall, U. Toronto vs Tor. Parkdale 1909-12
 – Pep Leadlay, Queen's vs Ham. Tigers 1922-29
10 – Huck Welch, Ham. Tigers vs Mtl. W.W. 1928-37
 – Bummer Stirling, Sarnia 1931-37

**All-time most times rushed**
77 – George Reed, Sask. 1963-75
72 – Normie Kwong, Edm. 1951-60
 – Leo Lewis, Wpg. 1955-66

**All-time most yards rushed**
359 – Leo Lewis, Wpg. 1955-66
346 – George Reed, Sask. 1963-75
318 – Normie Kwong, Edm. 1951-60

**Most yards rushed one game**
171 – Johnny Bright, Edm. vs Mtl. Nov. 24, 1956
145 – Normie Kwong, Edm. vs Mtl. Nov. 26, 1955
142 – David Green, Mtl. vs Edm. Nov. 25, 1979

**All-time most touchdowns rushing**
4 – Johnny Bright, Edm. 1954-64
  – Normie Kwong, Edm. 1951-60
  – Jim Germany, Edm. 1977-83

**All-time most pass receptions**
29 – Hal Patterson, Mtl. vs Ham. 1954-67
26 – Tommy Scott, Edm. 1978-83
22 – Red O'Quinn, Mtl. 1952-59
  – Brian Kelly, Edm. 1979-87

**All-time most yards on pass receptions**
580 – Hal Patterson, Mtl.-Ham. 1954-67
441 – Red O'Quinn, Mtl. 1952-59
400 – Tommy Scott, Edm. 1978-83

**Longest completed pass**
90 – Red O'Quinn, from Etcheverry, Mtl. vs Edm. Nov. 27, 1954
  – Paul Dekker, from Faloney, Ham. vs Wpg. Dec. 2, 1961
85 – Whit Tucker, from Jackson, Ott. vs Sask. Nov. 26, 1966

**Most TDs on pass receptions one game**
3 – Tommy Scott, Edm. vs Ham. Nov. 23, 1980

**Most passes one game**
56 – Danny Barrett, Cal. vs Tor. Nov. 24, 1991
49 – Doug Flutie, Cal. vs Wpg. Nov. 29, 1992
  – Doug Flutie, Cal. vs Balt. Nov. 19, 1995

**Most passes completed one game**
34 – Danny Barrett, Cal. vs Tor. Nov. 24, 1991
33 – Doug Flutie, Cal. vs Wpg. Nov. 29, 1992
31 – Jack Jacobs, Wpg. vs Ham. Nov. 28, 1953

**Most yards passing one game**
508 – Sam Etcheverry, Mtl. vs Edm. Nov. 26, 1955
480 – Doug Flutie, Cal. vs Wpg. Nov. 29, 1992
474 – Kent Austin, Sask. vs Ham. Nov. 26, 1989

**Most touchdown passes one game**
4 – Russ Jackson, Ott. vs Sask. Nov. 30, 1969

**Most interceptions one game thrown**
4 – Sam Etcheverry, Mtl. vs Edm. Nov. 24, 1956
  – Bruce Lemmerman, Edm. vs Mtl. Nov. 27, 1977

**Most fumbles one game**
4 – Gerry James, Wpg. vs Ham. Nov. 30, 1957
3 – Johnny Bright, Edm. vs Mtl. Nov. 24, 1956
  – Matt Dunigan, Edm. vs Ham. Nov. 30, 1986
  – Matt Dunigan, Tor. vs Cal. Nov. 24, 1991

**Most punts one game**
17 – Charlie Shepard, Wpg. vs Ham. Nov. 28, 1959
  – Joe Zuger, Ham. vs Sask. Dec. 2, 1967
15 – Cam Fraser, Ham. vs Wpg. Nov. 28, 1959
  – Cam Fraser, Ham. vs Wpg. Dec. 2, 1961
  – Ron Stewart, Cal. vs Mtl. Nov. 28, 1970

**Most yards punting one game**
782 – Charlie Shepard, Wpg. vs Ham. Nov. 28, 1959
760 – Joe Zuger, Ham. vs Sask. Dec. 2, 1967
621 – Cam Fraser, Ham. vs Wpg. Dec. 2, 1961

**All-time most punt returns**
37 – Ron Latourelle, Wpg. 1955-64
22 – Greg Butler, Edm. 1977-80
20 – Garney Henley, Ham. 1960-75

**Longest run**
80 – Vic Washington, Ott. vs Cal. Nov. 30, 1968
74 – Garney Henley, Ham. vs Wpg. Dec. 1-2, 1962
58 – Bernie Faloney (1), Johnny Counts (57), Ham. vs. B.C. Nov. 28, 1964

**Most touchdowns rushing one game**
3 – Art Wilson, Ham. Tigers vs Tor. Parkdale Nov. 29, 1913
  – Red Storey, Tor. vs Wpg. Dec. 10, 1938

**Most pass receptions one game**
13 – Red O'Quinn, Mtl. vs Edm. Nov. 27, 1954
12 – Tommy Scott, Edm. vs Ham. Nov. 23, 1980
11 – Carl Bland, Cal. vs Tor. Nov. 24, 1991

**Most yards on pass receptions one game**
316 – Red O'Quinn, Mtl. vs Edm. Nov. 27, 1954
174 – Whit Tucker, Ott. vs Sask. Nov. 26, 1966
  – Tommy Scott, Edm. vs Ham. Nov. 23, 1980

**All-time most TDs on pass receptions**
5 – Brian Kelly, Edm. 1979-87
4 – Hal Patterson, Mtl.-Ham. 1954-67
  – Tommy Scott, Edm. 1978-83

**All-time most passes thrown**
169 – Bernie Faloney, Edm.-Ham.-Mtl.-B.C. 1954-67
139 – Ron Lancaster, Ott.-Sask. 1960-78
133 – Doug Flutie, B.C.-Cal.-Tor 1990-96

**All-time most passes completed**
92 – Bernie Faloney, Edm.-Ham.-Mtl.-B.C. 1954-67
78 – Doug Flutie, B.C.-Cal.-Tor. 1990-96
76 – Ron Lancaster, Ott.-Sask. 1960-78

**All-time most yards passing**
1,369 – Bernie Faloney, Edm.-Ham.-Mtl.-B.C. 1954-67
1,244 – Sam Etcheverry, Mtl. 1952-60
1,069 – Doug Flutie, B.C.-Cal.-Tor. 1990-96

**All-time most touchdown passes**
8 – Bernie Faloney, Edm.-Ham.-Mtl.-B.C. 1954-67
  – Russ Jackson, Ott. 1958-69
7 – Ron Lancaster, Ott.-Sask. 1960-78
  – Joe Krol, Ham.-Tor. 1945-55

**All-time most interceptions thrown**
8 – Sam Etcheverry, Mtl. 1952-60
6 – Ron Lancaster, Ott.-Sask. 1960-78
  – Bernie Faloney, Edm.-Ham.-Mtl.-B.C. 1954-67

**Longest interception return**
74 – Vern Perry, Mtl. vs Edm. Nov. 27, 1977
56 – Greg Battle, Wpg. vs Edm. Nov. 25, 1990
54 – Dick Thornton, Tor. vs Cal. Nov. 30, 1971

**Most fumble returns one game**
3 – Phil Minnick, Wpg. vs Ham. Nov. 27, 1965
2 – Ray Bawel, Ham. vs Wpg. Nov. 30, 1957
  – Ben Zambiasi, Ham. vs Edm. Nov. 30, 1986
  – David Bovell, Wpg. vs Edm. Nov. 25, 1990
  – Keith Castello, Tor. vs Cal. Nov. 24, 1991

**All-time most yards punting**
2,735 – Hank Ilesic, Edm.-Tor. 1977-93
2,166 – Joe Zuger, Ham. 1962-71
2,092 – Cam Fraser, Ham.-Mtl. 1951-69

**Longest punts**
87 – Alan Ford, Sask. vs Ham. Dec. 2, 1967
85 – Garry Lefebvre, Edm. vs Ott. Nov. 25, 1973
84 – Lui Passaglia, B.C. vs Wpg. Nov. 27, 1988

**Most punt returns one game**
13 – Ron Latourelle, Wpg. vs Ham. Dec. 2, 1961
12 – Darnell Clash, B.C. vs Ham. Nov. 24, 1985
10 – Gene Wlasiuk, Sask. vs Ham. Dec. 2, 1967

**All-time most yards on punt returns**
250 – Ron Latourelle, Wpg. 1955-64
170 – Randy Rhino, Mtl. 1976-80
137 – Garney Henley, Ham. 1960-75

**Longest punt return**
82 – Chris Wright, Balt. vs Cal. (TD) Nov. 19, 1995
80 – Jimmy Cunningham, Tor. vs Edm. (TD) Nov. 24, 1996
79 – Bill Hatanaka, Ott. vs Sask. (TD) Nov. 28, 1976

**Most kick-offs one game**
10 – Trevor Kennerd, Wpg. vs Ham. Nov. 18, 1984
   – Paul Osbaldiston, Ham. vs Sask. Nov. 26, 1989

**Most yards on kick-offs one game**
622 – Paul Osbaldiston, Ham. vs Sask. Nov. 26, 1989
551 – Trevor Kennerd, Wpg. vs Ham. Nov. 18, 1984
440 – Dave Ridgway, Sask. vs Ham. Nov. 26, 1989

**All-time most kick-off returns**
11 – Rufus Crawford, Ham. 1979-85
10 – Leo Lewis, Wpg. 1955-66
 9 – Tom Richards, Edm. 1986-90

**All-time most yards on kick-off returns**
306 – Leo Lewis, Wpg. 1955-66
218 – Henry Williams, Edm. 1986-96
187 – Tom Richards, Edm. 1986-90

**Longest kick-off return**
91 – Henry Williams, Edm. vs. Tor. (TD) Nov. 24, 1996
87 – Raghib Ismail, Tor. vs Cal. (TD) Nov. 24, 1991
78 – Alan Ford, Sask. vs Ott. Nov. 30, 1969

**Most yards on punt returns one game**
105 – Darnell Clash, B.C. vs Ham. Nov. 24, 1985
 93 – Chris Wright, Balt. vs Cal. Nov. 19, 1995
 90 – Ron Latourelle, Wpg. vs Ham. Dec. 2, 1961

**All-time most kick-offs**
31 – Dave Cutler, Edm. 1969-84
29 – Don Sutherin, Ham.-Ott.-Tor. 1958-70
23 – Trevor Kennerd, Wpg. 1980-91

**Yards on kick-offs**
1,623 – Don Sutherin, Ham.-Ott.-Tor. 1958-70
1,412 – Dave Cutler, Edm. 1969-84
1,305 – Trevor Kennerd, Wpg. 1980-91

**Longest kick-off**
100 – Dave Cutler, Edm. vs Tor. Nov. 28, 1982
 77 – Peter Kempf, B.C. vs Ham. Nov. 30, 1963
    – Don Sutherin, Ham. vs Wpg. Nov. 27, 1965
    – Bernie Ruoff, B.C. vs Ham. Nov. 24, 1985

**Most kick-off returns one game**
8 – Dwight Edwards, Tor. vs Edm. Nov. 29, 1987
7 – Obie Graves, Ham. vs Edm. Nov. 23, 1980
  – Rufus Crawford, Ham. vs Wpg. Nov. 18, 1984

**Most yards on kick-off returns one game**
183 – Raghib Ismail, Tor. vs Cal. Nov. 24, 1991
169 – Tim McCray, Sask. vs Ham. Nov. 26, 1989
134 – Anthony Drawhorn, B.C. vs Wpg. Nov. 27, 1988

**Longest unsuccessful field goal return**
115 – Henry Williams, Edm. vs Tor. (TD) Nov. 29, 1987

# M.V.P.S

1996 – Most Valuable Player, Doug Flutie, QB, Toronto; Most Valuable Canadian, Mike Vanderjagt, K, Toronto
1995 – Most Valuable Player, Tracy Ham, QB, Baltimore; Most Valuable Canadian, David Sapunjis, SB, Calgary
1994 – Most Valuable Player, Karl Anthony, DB, Baltimore; Most Valuable Canadian, Lui Passaglia, K, B.C.
1993 – Most Valuable Player, Damon Allen, QB, Edmonton; Most Valuable Canadian, Sean Fleming, K, Edmonton
1992 – Most Valuable Player, Doug Flutie, QB, Calgary; Most Valuable Canadian, David Sapunjis, SB, Calgary
1991 – Most Valuable Player, Raghib Ismail, WR, Toronto; Most Valuable Canadian, David Sapunjis, SB, Calgary
1990 – Offence, Tom Burgess, QB, Winnipeg; Defence, Greg Battle, LB, Winnipeg; Canadian, Warren Hudson, FB, Winnipeg
1989 – Offence, Kent Austin, QB, Saskatchewan; Defence, Chuck Klingbeil, DT, Saskatchewan; Canadian, Dave Ridgway, K, Saskatchewan
1988 – Offence, James Murphy, WR, Winnipeg; Defence, Michael Gray, DT, Winnipeg; Canadian, Bob Cameron, P. Winnipeg
1987 – Offence, Damon Allen, QB, Edmonton; Defence, Stewart Hill, DE, Edmonton; Canadian, Milson Jones, RB, Edmonton
1986 – Offence, Mike Kerrigan, QB, Hamilton; Defence, Grover Covington, DE, Hamilton; Canadian, Paul Osbaldiston, K/P, Hamilton
1985 – Offence, Roy Dewalt, QB, B. C. ; Defence, James Parker, DE, B.C.; Canadian, Lui Passaglia, P/K, B.C.
1984 – Offence, Tom Clements, QB, Winnipeg; Defence, Tyrone Jones, LB, Winnipeg; Canadian, Sean Kehoe, RB, Winnipeg
1983 – Offence, Joe Barnes, QB, Toronto; Defence, Carl Brazley, DB, Toronto; Canadian Rick Klassen, DT, B.C.
1982 – Offence, Warren Moon, QB, Edmonton; Defence, Dave Fennell, DT, Edmonton; Canadian, Dave Fennell, DT, Edmonton
1981 – Offence, J.C. Watts, QB, Ottawa; Defence, John Glassford, LB, Ottawa; Canadian, Neil Lumsden, RB, Edmonton
1980 – Offence, Warren Moon, QB, Edmonton; Defence, Dale Potter, LB, Edmonton; Canadian, Dale Potter, LB, Edmonton
1979 – Offence, David Green, RB, Montreal; Defence, Tom Cousineau, LB, Montreal; Canadian, Don Sweet, K, Montreal
1978 – Offence, Tom Wilkinson, QB, Edmonton; Defence, Dave Fennell, DT, Edmonton; Canadian, Angelo Santucci, RB, Edmonton
1977 – Offence, Sonny Wade, QB, Montreal; Defence, Glen Weir, DT, Montreal; Canadian, Don Sweet, K, Montreal
1976 – Offence, Tom Clements, QB, Ottawa; Defence, Cleveland Vann, LB, Saskatchewan; Canadian, Tony Gabriel, TE, Ottawa
1975 – Offence, Steve Ferrughelli, RB, Montreal; Defence, Lewis Cook, DB, Montreal; Canadian, Dave Cutler, K, Edmonton
1974 – Offence, Sonny Wade, QB, Montreal; Defence, Junior Ah You, DE, Montreal; Canadian, Don Sweet, K, Montreal
1973 – Most Valuable Charlie Brandon, DE, Ottawa; Canadian, Garry Lefebvre, DB, Edmonton
1972 – Most Valuable Chuck Ealey, QB, Hamilton; Canadian, Ian Sunter, K, Hamilton
1971 – Most Valuable Player, Wayne Harris, LB, Calgary; Canadian, Dick Suderman, DE, Calgary
1970 – Most Valuable Player, Sonny Wade, QB, Montreal
1969 – Most Valuable Player, Russ Jackson, QB, Ottawa
1968 – Most Valuable Player, Vic Washington, RB, Ottawa
1967 – Most Valuable Player, Joe Zuger, QB, Hamilton
1962 – Most Valuable Player, Leo Lewis, RB, Winnipeg
1961 – Most Valuable Player, Ken Ploen, QB, Winnipeg
1960 – Most Valuable Player, Ron Stewart, RB, Ottawa
1959 – Most Valuable Player, Charlie Shepard, RB, Winnipeg

# WINNERS BY CITY AND TEAM

**20 – Toronto**
Argonauts (13) – 1914, 1921, 1933, 1937, 1938, 1945, 1946, 1947, 1950, 1952, 1983, 1991, 1996
Balmy Beach (2) – 1927, 1930
University of Toronto (4) – 1909, 1910, 1911, 1920
R.C.A.F. Hurricanes (1) – 1942

**14 – Hamilton**
Alerts (1) – 1912
Tigers (5) – 1913, 1915, 1928, 1929, 1932
Flying Wildcats (1) – 1943
Tiger-Cats (7) – 1953, 1957, 1963, 1965, 1967, 1972, 1986

**11 – Edmonton**
Eskimos - 1954, 1955, 1956, 1975, 1978, 1979, 1980, 1981, 1982, 1987, 1993

**10 – Winnipeg**
'Pegs (1) – 1935
Blue Bombers (9) – 1939, 1941, 1958, 1959, 1961, 1962, 1984, 1988, 1990

**9 – Ottawa**
Senators (2) – 1925, 1926
Rough Riders (7) – 1940, 1951, 1960, 1968, 1969, 1973, 1976

**6 – Montreal**
Winged Wheelers (1) – 1931
St. Hyacinthe-Donnacona Navy Combines (1) – 1944
Alouettes (4) – 1949, 1970, 1974, 1977

**3 – Vancouver**
British Columbia Lions – 1964, 1985, 1994

**3 – Calgary**
Stampeders – 1948, 1971, 1992

**3 – Kingston**
Queen's University – 1922, 1923, 1924

**2 – Sarnia**
Imperials – 1934, 1936

**2 – Regina**
Saskatchewan Roughriders – 1966, 1989

**1 – Baltimore**
Stallions – 1995

# YEAR-BY-YEAR PLAYOFF SCORES

**1996**
West Semi-Final – Edmonton Eskimos 68, Winnipeg Blue Bombers 7
East Semi-Final – Montreal Alouettes 22, Hamilton Tiger-Cats 11
West Final – Edmonton Eskimos 15, Calgary Stampeders 12
East Final – Toronto Argonauts 43, Montreal Alouettes 7
Grey Cup – Toronto Argonauts 43, Edmonton Eskimos 37

**1994**
West Semi-Finals – B.C. Lions 24, Edmonton Eskimos 23
West Semi-Finals – Calgary Stampeders 36, Saskatchewan Roughriders 3
East Semi-Finals – Toronto Argonauts 15, Baltimore Football Club 34
East Semi-Finals – Winnipeg Blue Bombers 26, Ottawa Rough Riders 16
West Final – B.C. Lions 37, Calgary Stampeders 36
East Final – Baltimore Football Club 14, Winnipeg Blue Bombers 12
Grey Cup – B.C. Lions 26, Baltimore Football Club 23

**1992**
West Semi-Final – Saskatchewan Roughriders 20, Edmonton Eskimos 22
East Semi-Final – Ottawa Rough Riders 28, Hamilton Tiger-Cats 29
West Final – Edmonton Eskimos 22, Calgary Stampeders 23
East Final – Hamilton Tiger-Cats 11, Winnipeg Blue Bombers 59
Grey Cup – Calgary Stampeders 24, Winnipeg Blue Bombers 10

**1990**
West Semi-Final – Saskatchewan Roughriders 27, Edmonton Eskimos 43
East Semi-Final – Ottawa Rough Riders 25, Toronto Argonauts 34
West Final – Edmonton Eskimos 43, Calgary Stampeders 23
East Final – Toronto Argonauts 17, Winnipeg Blue Bombers 20
Grey Cup – Winnipeg Blue Bombers 50, Edmonton Eskimos 11

**1988**
West Semi-Final – B.C. Lions 42, Saskatchewan Roughriders 18
East Semi-Final – Winnipeg Blue Bombers 35, Hamilton Tiger-Cats 28
West Final – B.C. Lions 37, Edmonton Eskimos 19
East Final – Winnipeg Blue Bombers 27, Toronto Argonauts 11
Grey Cup – Winnipeg Blue Bombers 22, B.C. Lions 21

**1986**
West Semi-Final – B.C. Lions 21, Winnipeg Blue Bombers 14
West Semi-Final – Edmonton Eskimos 27, Calgary Stampeders 18
West Final – Edmonton Eskimos 41, B.C. Lions 5
East Finals – Game 1 – Toronto Argonauts 31, Hamilton Tiger-Cats 17
East Finals – Game 2 – Hamilton Tiger-Cats 42, Toronto Argonauts 25
(Hamilton won 2 game total-points series 59-56)
Grey Cup – Hamilton Tiger-Cats 39, Edmonton Eskimos 15

**1995**
North Semi-Finals – Hamilton Tiger-Cats 13, Calgary Stampeders 31
North Semi-Finals – B.C. Lions 15, Edmonton Eskimos 26
South Semi-Finals – Winnipeg Blue Bombers 21, Baltimore Stallions 36
South Semi-Finals – Birmingham Barracudas 9, San Antonio Texans 52
North Final – Edmonton Eskimos 4, Calgary Stampeders 37
South Final – San Antonio Texans 11, Baltimore Stallions 21
Grey Cup – Baltimore Stallions 37, Calgary Stampeders 20

**1993**
West Semi-Finals – Saskatchewan Roughriders 13, Edmonton Eskimos 51
West Semi-Finals – B.C. Lions 9, Calgary Stampeders 17,
East Semi-Final – Ottawa Rough Riders 10, Hamilton Tiger-Cats 21
West Final – Edmonton Eskimos 29, Calgary Stampeders 15
East Final – Hamilton Tiger-Cats 19, Winnipeg Blue Bombers 20
Grey Cup – Edmonton Eskimos 33, Winnipeg Blue Bombers 23

**1991**
West Semi-Final – B.C. Lions 41, Calgary Stampeders 43
East Semi-Final – Ottawa Rough Riders 8, Winnipeg Blue Bombers 26
West Final – Calgary Stampeders 38, Edmonton Eskimos 36
East Final – Winnipeg Blue Bombers 3, Toronto Argonauts 42
Grey Cup – Toronto Argonauts 36, Calgary Stampeders 21

**1989**
West Semi-Final – Saskatchewan Roughriders 33, Calgary Stampeders 26
East Semi-Final – Winnipeg Blue Bombers 30, Toronto Argonauts 7
West Final – Saskatchewan Roughriders 32, Edmonton Eskimos 21
East Final – Winnipeg Blue Bombers 10, Hamilton Tiger-Cats 14
Grey Cup – Saskatchewan Roughriders 43, Hamilton Tiger-Cats 40

**1987**
West Semi-Final – Edmonton Eskimos 30, Calgary Stampeders 16
East Semi-Final – Toronto Argonauts 29, Hamilton Tiger-Cats 13
West Final – Edmonton Eskimos 31, B.C. Lions 7
East Final – Toronto Argonauts 19, Winnipeg Blue Bombers 3
Grey Cup – Edmonton Eskimos 38, Toronto Argonauts 36

**1985**
West Semi-Final – Winnipeg Blue Bombers 22, Edmonton Eskimos 15
East Semi- Final – Montreal Alouettes 30, Ottawa Rough Riders 20
West Final – B.C. Lions 42, Winnipeg Blue Bombers 22
East Final – Hamilton Tiger-Cats 50, Montreal Alouettes 26
Grey Cup – B.C. Lions 37, Hamilton Tiger-Cats 24

**1984**
West Semi-Final – Winnipeg Blue Bombers 55, Edmonton Eskimos 20
East Semi-Final – Hamilton Tiger-Cats 17, Montreal Alouettes 11
West Final – Winnipeg Blue Bombers 31, B.C. Lions 14
East Final – Hamilton Tiger-Cats 14, Toronto Argonauts 13 (overtime)
Grey Cup – Winnipeg Blue Bombers 47, Hamilton Tiger-Cats 17

**1982**
West Semi-Final – Winnipeg Blue Bombers 24, Calgary Stampeders 3
East Semi-Final – Ottawa Rough Riders 30, Hamilton Tiger-Cats 20
West Final – Edmonton Eskimos 24, Winnipeg Blue Bombers 21
East Final – Toronto Argonauts 44, Ottawa Rough Riders 7
Grey Cup – Edmonton Eskimos 32, Toronto Argonauts 16

**1980**
West Semi-Final – Calgary Stampeders 14, Winnipeg Blue Bombers 32
East Semi-Final – Ottawa Rough Riders 21, Montreal Alouettes 25
West Final – Winnipeg Blue Bombers 24, Edmonton Eskimos 34
East Final – Montreal Alouettes 13, Hamilton Tiger-Cats 24
Grey Cup – Edmonton Eskimos 48, Hamilton Tiger-Cats 10

**1978**
West Semi-Final – Winnipeg Blue Bombers 4, Calgary Stampeders 38
East Semi-Final – Hamilton Tiger-Cats 20, Montreal Alouettes 35
West Final – Calgary Stampeders 13, Edmonton Eskimos 26
East Final – Montreal Alouettes 21, Ottawa Rough Riders 16
Grey Cup – Edmonton Eskimos 20, Montreal Alouettes 13

**1976**
West Semi-Final – Edmonton Eskimos 14, Winnipeg Blue Bombers 12
East Semi-Final – Hamilton Tiger-Cats 23, Montreal Alouettes 0
West Final – Saskatchewan Roughriders 23, Edmonton Eskimos 13
East Final – Ottawa Rough Riders 17, Hamilton Tiger-Cats 15
Grey Cup – Ottawa Rough Riders 23, Saskatchewan Roughriders 20

**1974**
West Semi-Final – Saskatchewan Roughriders 24, B.C. Lions 14
East Semi-Final – Ottawa Rough Riders 21, Hamilton Tiger-Cats 19
West Final – Edmonton Eskimos 31, Saskatchewan Roughriders 27
East Final – Montreal Alouettes 14, Ottawa Rough Riders 4
Grey Cup – Montreal Alouettes 20, Edmonton Eskimos 7

**1972**
West Semi-Final – Saskatchewan Roughriders 8, Edmonton Eskimos 6
East Semi-Final – Montreal Alouettes 11, Ottawa Rough Riders 14
West Final – Saskatchewan Roughriders 27, Winnipeg Blue Bombers 24
East Final – Hamilton Tiger-Cats 7, Ottawa Rough Riders 19
East Final – Ottawa Rough Riders 8, Hamilton Tiger-Cats 23
Grey Cup – Hamilton Tiger-Cats 13, Saskatchewan Roughriders 10

**1970**
West Semi-Final – Calgary Stampeders 16, Edmonton Eskimos 9
East Semi-Final – Montreal Alouettes 16, Toronto Argonauts 7
West Finals – Calgary Stampeders 28, Saskatchewan Roughriders 11
West Finals – Saskatchewan Roughriders 11, Calgary Stampeders 3
West Finals – Calgary Stampeders 15, Saskatchewan Roughriders 14
East Finals – Hamilton Tiger-Cats 22, Montreal Alouettes 32
East Finals – Montreal Alouettes 11, Hamilton Tiger-Cats 4
Grey Cup – Calgary Stampeders 10, Montreal Alouettes 23

**1968**
West Semi-Final – Edmonton Eskimos 13, Calgary Stampeders 29
East Semi-Final – Hamilton Tiger-Cats 21, Toronto Argonauts 33
West Finals – Calgary Stampeders 32, Sasktchewan Roughriders 0
West Finals – Saskatchewan Roughriders 12, Calgary Stampeders 25
    (overtime)
East Finals – Ottawa Rough Riders 11, Toronto Argonauts 13
East Finals – Toronto Argonauts 14, Ottawa Rough Riders 36
Grey Cup – Calgary Stampeders 21, Ottawa Rough Riders 24

**1966**
West Semi-Final – Edmonton Eskimos 8, Winnipeg Blue Bombers 16
East Semi-Final – Montreal Alouettes 14, Hamilton Tiger-Cats 24
West Finals – Winnipeg Blue Bombers 7, Saskatchewan Roughriders 14
West Finals – Saskatchewan Roughriders 21, Winnipeg Blue Bombers 19
East Finals – Ottawa Rough Riders 30, Hamilton Tiger-Cats 1
East Finals – Hamilton Tiger-Cats 16, Ottawa Rough Riders 42
Grey Cup – Saskatchewan Roughriders 29, Ottawa Rough Riders 14

**1983**
West Semi-Final – Winnipeg Blue Bombers 49, Edmonton Eskimos 22
East Semi-Final – Hamilton Tiger-Cats 33, Ottawa Rough Riders 31
West Final – B.C. Lions 39, Winnipeg Blue Bombers 21
East Final – Toronto Argonauts 41, Hamilton Tiger-Cats 36
Grey Cup – Toronto Argonauts 18, B.C. Lions 17

**1981**
West Semi-Final – B.C. Lions 15, Winnipeg Blue Bombers 11
East Semi-Final – Montreal Alouettes 16, Ottawa Rough Riders 20
West Final – Edmonton Eskimos 22, B.C. Lions 16
East Final – Ottawa Rough Riders 17, Hamilton Tiger-Cats 13
Grey Cup – Edmonton Eskimos 26, Ottawa Rough Riders 23

**1979**
West Semi-Final – B.C. Lions 2, Calgary Stampeders 37
East Semi-Final – Hamilton Tiger-Cats 26, Ottawa Rough Riders 29
West Final – Calgary Stampeders 7, Edmonton Eskimos 19
East Final – Ottawa Rough Riders 6, Montreal Alouettes 17
Grey Cup – Edmonton Eskimos 17, Montreal Alouettes 9

**1977**
West Semi-Final – B.C. Lions 33, Winnipeg Blue Bombers 32
East Semi-Final – Ottawa Rough Riders 21, Toronto Argonauts 16
West Final – Edmonton Eskimos 38, B.C. Lions 1
East Final – Montreal Alouettes 21, Ottawa Rough Riders 18
Grey Cup – Montreal Alouettes 41, Edmonton Eskimos 6

**1975**
West Semi-Final – Saskatchewan Roughriders 42, Winnipeg Blue
Bombers 24
East Semi-Final – Montreal Alouettes 35, Hamilton Tiger-Cats 12
West Final – Edmonton Eskimos 30, Saskatchewan Roughriders 18
East Final – Montreal Alouettes 20, Ottawa Rough Riders 10
Grey Cup – Edmonton Eskimos 9, Montreal Alouettes 8

**1973**
West Semi-Final – Saskatchewan Roughriders 33, B.C. Lions 13
East Semi-Final – Montreal Alouettes 32, Toronto Argonauts 10 (overtime)
West Final – Edmonton Eskimos 25, Saskatchewan Roughriders 23
East Final – Ottawa Rough Riders 23, Montreal Alouettes 14
Grey Cup – Ottawa Rough Riders 22, Edmonton Eskimos 18

**1971**
West Semi-Final – Winnipeg Blue Bombers 23, Saskatchewan
Roughriders 34
East Semi-Final – Ottawa Rough Riders 4, Hamilton Tiger-Cats 23
West Finals – Saskatchewan Roughriders 21, Calgary Stampeders 30
West Finals – Calgary Stampeders 23, Saskatchewan Roughriders 21
East Finals – Toronto Argonauts 23, Hamilton Tiger-Cats 8
East Finals – Hamilton Tiger-Cats 17, Toronto Argonauts 11
Grey Cup – Calgary Stampeders 14, Toronto Argonauts 11

**1969**
West Semi-Final – B.C. Lions 21, Calgary Stampeders 35
East Semi-Final – Hamilton Tiger-Cats 9, Toronto Argonauts 15
West Finals – Calgary Stampeders 11, Saskatchewan Roughriders 17
West Finals – Saskatchewan Roughriders 36, Calgary Stampeders 13
East Finals – Ottawa Rough Riders 14, Toronto Argonauts 22
East Finals – Toronto Argonauts 3, Ottawa Rough Riders 32
Grey Cup – Saskatchewan Roughriders 11, Ottawa Rough Riders 29

**1967**
West Semi-Final – Edmonton Eskimos 5, Saskatchewan Roughriders 21
East Semi-Final – Toronto Argonauts 22, Ottawa Rough Riders 38
West Finals – Saskatchwan Roughriders 11, Calgary Stampeders 15
West Finals – Calgary Stampeders 9, Saskatchewan Roughriders 11
West Finals – Saskatchewan Roughriders 17, Calgary Stampeders 13
East Finals – Hamilton Tiger-Cats 11, Ottawa Rough Riders 3
East Finals – Ottawa Rough Riders 0, Hamilton Tiger-Cats 26
Grey Cup – Saskatchewan Roughriders 1, Hamilton Tiger-Cats 24

**1965**
West Semi-Final – Saskatchewan Roughriders 9, Winnipeg Blue
Bombers 15
East Semi-Final – Montreal Alouettes 7, Ottawa Rough Riders 36
West Finals – Winnipeg Blue Bombers 9, Calgary Stampeders 27
West Finals– Calgary Stampeders 11, Winnipeg Blue Bombers 15
West Finals – Winnipeg Blue Bombers 19, Calgary Stampeders 12
East Finals – Hamilton Tiger-Cats 18, Ottawa Rough Riders 13
East Finals – Ottawa Rough Riders 7, Hamilton Tiger-Cats 7
Grey Cup – Winnipeg Blue Bombers 16, Hamilton Tiger-Cats 22

**1964**
West Semi-Finals – Calgary Stampeders 25, Saskatchewan Roughriders 34
West Semi-Finals – Saskatchewan Roughriders 6, Calgary Stampeders 51
East Semi-Final – Montreal Alouettes 0, Ottawa Rough Riders 27
West Finals – B.C. Lions 24, Calgary Stampeders 10
West Finals – Calgary Stampeders 14, B.C. Lions 10
West Finals – Calgary Stampeders 14, B.C. Lions 33
East Finals – Hamilton Tiger-Cats 13, Ottawa Rough Riders 30
East Finals – Ottawa Rough Riders 8, Hamilton Tiger-Cats 26
Grey Cup – B.C. Lions 34, Hamilton Tiger-Cats 24

**1962**
West Semi-Finals – Saskatchewan Roughriders 0, Calgary Stampeders 25
West Semi-Finals – Calgary Stampeders 18, Saskatchewan Roughriders 7
East Semi-Final – Montreal Alouettes 18, Ottawa Rough Riders 17
West Finals -Winnipeg Blue Bombers 14, Calgary Stampeders 20
West Finals – Calgary Stampeders 11, Winnipeg Blue Bombers 19
West Finals – Calgary Stampeders 7, Winnipeg Blue Bombers 12
East Finals – Hamilton Tiger-Cats 28, Montreal Alouettes 17
East Finals – Montreal Alouettes 21, Hamilton Tiger-Cats 30
Grey Cup – Winnipeg Blue Bombers 28, Hamilton Tiger-Cats 27

**1960**
West Semi-Finals – Calgary Stampeders 7, Edmonton Eskimos 30
West Semi-Finals – Edmonton Eskimos 40, Calgary Stampeders 21
East Semi-Final – Montreal Alouettes 14, Ottawa Rough Riders 30
West Finals- Winnipeg Blue Bombers 22, Edmonton Eskimos 16
West Finals – Edmonton Eskimos 10, Winnipeg Blue Bombers 5
West Finals – Edmonton Eskimos 4, Winnipeg Blue Bombers 2
East Finals – Toronto Argonauts 21, Ottawa Rough Riders 33
East Finals – Ottawa Rough Riders 21, Toronto Argonauts 20
Grey Cup – Edmonton Eskimos 6, Ottawa Rough Riders 16

**1958**
West Semi-Finals – Edmonton Eskimos 27, Saskatchewan Roughriders 11
West Semi-Finals – Saskatchewan Roughriders 1, Edmonton Eskimos 31
East Semi-Final – Ottawa Rough Riders 26, Montreal Alouettes 12
West Finals – Winnipeg Blue Bombers 30, Edmonton Eskimos 7
West Finals – Edmonton Eskimos 30, Winnipeg Blue Bombers 7
West Finals – Edmonton Eskimos 7, Winnipeg Blue Bombers 23
East Finals – Hamilton Tiger-Cats 35, Ottawa Rough Riders 7
East Finals – Ottawa Rough Riders 7, Hamilton Tiger-Cats 19
Grey Cup – Winnipeg Blue Bombers 35, Hamilton Tiger-Cats 28

**1956**
West Semi-Finals – Winnipeg Blue Bombers 7, Saskatchewan
　　　　　　　　　Roughriders 42
West Semi-Finals – Saskatchewan Roughriders 8, Winnipeg Blue
　　　　　　　　　Bombers 19
East Semi-Final – Ottawa Rough Riders 21, Hamilton Tiger-Cats 46
West Finals – Edmonton Eskimos 22, Saskatchewan Roughriders 23
West Finals – Saskatchewan Roughriders 12, Edmonton Eskimos 20
West Finals – Saskatchewan Roughriders 7, Edmonton Eskimos 51
East Finals – Montreal Alouettes 30, Hamilton Tiger-Cats 21
East Finals – Hamilton Tiger-Cats 41, Montreal Alouettes 48
Grey Cup – Edmonton Eskimos 50, Montreal Alouettes 27

**1954**
West Semi-Finals – Winnipeg Blue Bombers 14, Saskatchewan
　　　　　　　　　Roughriders 14
West Semi-Finals – Winnipeg Blue Bombers 13, Saskatchewan
　　　　　　　　　Roughriders 11
West Finals – Winnipeg Blue Bombers 3, Edmonton Eskimos 9
West Finals – Edmonton Eskimos 6, Winnipeg Blue Bombers 12
West Finals – Winnipeg Blue Bombers 5, Edmonton Eskimos 10
East Finals – Montreal Alouettes 14, Hamilton Tiger-Cats 9
East Finals – Montreal Alouettes 24, Hamilton Tiger-Cats 19
Grey Cup Semi-Final – Edmonton Eskimos 28, Kitchener-Waterloo
　　　　　　　　　Dutchmen 6
Grey Cup – Edmonton Eskimos 26, Montreal Alouettes 25

**1952**
West Semi-Finals – Edmonton Eskimos 12, Calgary Stampeders 31
West Semi-Finals – Calgary Stampeders 7, Edmonton Eskimos 30
East Semi-Finals – Toronto Argonauts 22, Hamilton Tiger-Cats 6
East Semi-Finals – Hamilton Tiger-Cats 27, Toronto Argonauts 11
East Semi-Finals – Toronto Argonauts 12, Hamilton Tiger-Cats 7
West Finals – Winnipeg Blue Bombers 28, Edmonton Eskimos 12
West Finals – Edmonton Eskimos 18, Winnipeg Blue Bombers 12
West Finals – Edmonton Eskimos 22, Winnipeg Blue Bombers 11
East Final – Toronto Argonauts 34, Sarnia Imperials 15
Grey Cup – Toronto Argonauts 21, Edmonton Eskimos 11

**1963**
West Semi-Finals – Saskatchewan Roughriders 9, Calgary Stampeders 35
West Semi-Finals – Calgary Stampeders 12, Saskatchewan Roughriders 39
East Semi-Final – Montreal Alouettes 5, Ottawa Rough Riders 17
West Finals – B.C. Lions 19, Saskatchewan Roughriders 7
West Finals – Saskatchewan Roughriders 13, B.C. Lions 8
West Finals – Saskatchewan Roughriders 1, B.C. Lions 36
East Finals – Hamilton Tiger-Cats 45, Ottawa Rough Riders 0
East Finals – Ottawa Rough Riders 35, Hamilton Tiger-Cats 18
Grey Cup – B.C. Lions 10, Hamilton Tiger-Cats 21

**1961**
West Semi-Finals – Edmonton Eskimos 8, Calgary Stampeders 10
West Semi-Finals – Calgary Stampeders 17, Edmonton Eskimos 18
East Semi-Final – Toronto Argonauts 43, Ottawa Rough Riders 19
West Finals – Winnipeg Blue Bombers 14, Calgary Stampeders 1
West Finals – Calgary Stampeders 14, Winnipeg Blue Bombers 43
East Finals – Hamilton Tiger-Cats 7, Toronto Argonauts 25
East Finals – Toronto Argonauts 2, Hamilton Tiger-Cats 48 (overtime)
Grey Cup – Winnipeg Blue Bombers 21, Hamilton Tiger-Cats 14 (overtime)

**1959**
West Semi-Finals – Edmonton Eskimos 20, B.C. Lions 8
West Semi-Finals – B.C. Lions 7, Edmonton Eskimos 41
East Semi-Final – Montreal Alouettes 0, Ottawa Rough Riders 43
West Finals – Winnipeg Blue Bombers 19, Edmonton Eskimos 11
West Finals – Edmonton Eskimos 8, Winnipeg Blue Bombers 16
East Finals – Hamilton Tiger-Cats 5, Ottawa Rough Riders 17
East Finals – Ottawa Rough Riders 7, Hamilton Tiger-Cats 21
Grey Cup – Winnipeg Blue Bombers 21, Hamilton Tiger-Cats 7

**1957**
West Semi-Finals – Calgary Stampeders 13, Winnipeg Blue Bombers 13
West Semi-Finals – Winnipeg Blue Bombers 15, Calgary Stampeders 3
East Semi-Finals – Montreal Alouettes 24, Ottawa Rough Riders 15
West Finals – Edmonton Eskimos 7, Winnipeg Blue Bombers 19
West Finals – Winnipeg Blue Bombers 4, Edmonton Eskimos 5
West Finals – Winnipeg Blue Bombers 17, Edmonton Eskimos 2 (overtime)
East Finals – Hamilton Tiger-Cats 17, Montreal Alouettes 10
East Finals – Montreal Alouettes 1, Hamilton Tiger-Cats 39
Grey Cup – Winnipeg Blue Bombers 7, Hamilton Tiger-Cats 32

**1955**
West Semi-Finals – Winnipeg Blue Bombers 16, Saskatchewan
　　　　　　　　　Roughriders 7
West Semi-Finals – Saskatchewan Roughriders 9, Winnipeg Blue
　　　　　　　　　Bombers 8
East Semi-Final – Toronto Argonauts 32, Hamilton Tiger-Cats 28
West Finals – Edmonton Eskimos 29, Winnipeg Blue Bombers 6
West Finals – Winnipeg Blue Bombers 6, Edmonton Eskimos 26
East Final – Toronto Argonauts 36, Montreal Alouettes 38
Grey Cup – Edmonton Eskimos 34, Montreal Alouettes 19

**1953**
West Semi-Finals – Saskatchewan Roughriders 5, Winnipeg
　　　　　　　　　Blue Bombers 43
West Semi-Finals – Winnipeg Blue Bombers 17, Saskatchewan
　　　　　　　　　Roughriders 18
West Finals – Winnipeg Blue Bombers 7, Edmonton Eskimos 25
West Finals – Edmonton Eskimos 17, Winnipeg Blue Bombers 21
West Finals – Winnipeg Blue Bombers 30, Edmonton Eskimos 24
East Finals – Hamilton Tiger-Cats 37, Montreal Alouettes 12
East Finals – Hamilton Tiger-Cats 22, Montreal Alouettes 11
Grey Cup Semi-Final – Winnipeg Blue Bombers 24, Balmy Beach 4
Grey Cup – Hamilton Tiger-Cats 12, Winnipeg Blue Bombers 6

**1951**
West Semi-Final – Winnipeg Blue Bombers 1, Edmonton Eskimos 4
East Semi-Finals – Ottawa Rough Riders 17, Hamilton Tiger-Cats 7
East Semi-Finals – Ottawa Rough Riders 11, Hamilton Tiger-Cats 9
West Finals – Saskatchewan Roughriders 11, Edmonton Eskimos 15
West Finals – Edmonton Eskimos 5, Saskatchewan Roughriders 12
West Finals – Edmonton Eskimos 18, Saskatchewan Roughriders 19
East Final – Ottawa Rough Riders 43, Sarnia Imperials 17
Grey Cup – Ottawa Rough Riders 21, Saskatchewan Roughriders 14

**1950**
West Semi-Final – Edmonton Eskimos 24, Saskatchewan Roughriders 1
East Semi-Finals – Hamilton Tiger-Cats 13, Toronto Argonauts 11
East Semi-Finals – Toronto Argonauts 24, Hamilton Tiger-Cats 6
West Finals – Winnipeg Blue Bombers 16, Edmonton Eskimos 17
West Finals – Edmonton Eskimos 12, Winnipeg Blue Bombers 22
West Finals – Edmonton Eskimos 6, Winnipeg Blue Bombers 29
East Final – Toronto Argonauts 43, Balmy Beach 13
Grey Cup – Toronto Argonauts 13, Winnipeg Blue Bombers 0

**1948**
East Semi-Finals – Montreal Alouettes 21, Ottawa Rough Riders 19
East Semi-Finals – Ottawa Rough Riders 15, Montreal Alouettes 7
West Finals – Calgary Stampeders 4, Saskatchewan Roughriders 4
West Finals – Saskatchewan Roughriders 6, Calgary Stampeders 17
East Final – Ottawa Rough Riders 19, Hamilton Tigers 0
Grey Cup – Calgary Stampeders 12, Ottawa Rough Riders 7

**1946**
East Semi-Final – Toronto Argonauts 12, Montreal Alouettes 6
West Finals – Winnipeg Blue Bombers 18, Calgary Stampeders 21
West Finals – Calgary Stampeders 0, Winnipeg Blue Bombers 12
East Final – Toronto Argonauts 20, Balmy Beach 12
Grey Cup – Toronto Argonauts 28, Winnipeg Blue Bombers 6

**1944**
Grey Cup – St. Hyacinthe-Donnacona Navy 7, Hamilton Wildcats 6

**1942**
East Final – Toronto R.C.A.F. Hurricanes 18, Ottawa R.C.A.F. Uplands 13
West Final – Winnipeg R.C.A.F. Bombers 13, Regina Navy 6
Grey Cup – Toronto R.C.A.F. 8 Hurricanes, Winnipeg R.C.A.F. Bombers 5

**1940**
West Finals – Winnipeg Blue Bombers 7, Calgary Bronks 0
West Finals – Calgary Bronks 2, Winnipeg Blue Bombers 23
(West did not compete in Grey Cup)
Grey Cup Semi-Finals – Ottawa Rough Riders 12, Toronto Argonauts 1
Grey Cup Semi-Finals – Ottawa Rough Riders 8, Toronto Argonauts 1
Grey Cup – (Game 1) Ottawa Rough Riders 8, Balmy Beach 2
　　　　　　 (Game 2) Ottawa Rough Riders 12, Balmy Beach 5
　　　　　　 Ottawa won round 20-7

**1938**
West Semi-Final – Regina Roughriders 0, Winnipeg Blue Bombers 13
East Semi-Finals – Toronto Argonauts 9, Ottawa Rough Riders 1
East Semi-Finals – Toronto Argonauts 5, Ottawa Rough Riders 3
West Finals – Winnipeg Blue Bombers 12, Calgary Bronks 7
West Finals – Calgary Bronks 2, Winnipeg Blue Bombers 13
East Final – Toronto Argonauts 25, Sarnia Imperials 8
Grey Cup – Toronto Argonauts 30, Winnipeg Blue Bombers 7

**1936**
West Semi-Finals – Winnipeg Blue Bombers 7, Regina Roughriders 4
West Semi-Finals – Regina Roughriders 20, Winnipeg Blue Bombers 5
West Final – Regina Roughriders 3, Calgary Bronks 1
(West did not compete in Grey Cup)
Grey Cup Semi-Finals – Ottawa Rough Riders 5, Toronto Argonauts 1
Grey Cup Semi-Finals – Ottawa Rough Riders 17, Toronto Argonauts 5
Grey Cup – Sarnia Imperials 26, Ottawa Rough Riders 20

**1934**
West Semi-Finals – Vancouver Meralomas 5, University of Alberta 0
West Semi-Finals – Vancouver Meralomas 8, University of Alberta 6
West Semi-Finals – Regina Roughriders 8, Winnipeg Rugby Club 0
West Finals – Regina Roughriders 22, Vancouver Meralomas 2
West Finals – Regina Roughriders 7, Vancouver Meralomas 2
East Final – Sarnia Imperials 11, Hamilton Tigers 4
Grey Cup – Sarnia Imperials 20, Regina Roughriders 12

**1949**
East Semi-Finals – Montreal Alouettes 22, Ottawa Rough Riders 7
East Semi-Finals – Montreal Alouettes 14, Ottawa Rough Riders 13
West Finals – Calgary Stampeders 18, Saskatchewan Roughriders 12
West Finals – Saskatchewan Roughriders 9, Calgary Stampeders 4
East Final – Montreal Alouettes 40, Hamilton Tigers 0
Grey Cup – Montreal Alouettes 28, Calgary Stampeders 15

**1947**
East Semi-Finals – Toronto Argonauts 3, Ottawa Rough Riders 0
East Semi-Finals – Toronto Argonauts 21, Ottawa Rough Riders 0
West Finals – Calgary Stampeders 4, Winnipeg Blue Bombers 16
West Finals – Winnipeg Blue Bombers 3, Calgary Stampeders 15
West Finals – Calgary Stampeders 3, Winnipeg Blue Bombers 10
East Final – Toronto Argonauts 22, Ottawa Trojans 1
Grey Cup – Toronto Argonauts 10, Winnipeg Blue Bombers 9

**1945**
West Semi-Finals – Calgary Stampeders 3, Regina Roughriders 1
West Semi-Finals – Regina Roughriders 0, Calgary Stampeders 12
East Semi-Finals – Toronto Argonauts 27, Ottawa Rough Riders 8
East Semi-Finals – Toronto Argonauts 6, Ottawa Rough Riders 10
West Final – Calgary Stampeders 6, Winnipeg Blue Bombers 9
East Final – Toronto Argonauts 14, Balmy Beach 2
Grey Cup – Toronto Argonauts 35, Winnipeg Blue Bombers 0

**1943**
East Final – Hamilton Flying Wildcats 7, Lachine R.C.A.F. 6
West Finals – Winnipeg R.C.A.F. Bombers 1, Regina All-Services 0
West Finals – Winnipeg R.C.A.F. Bombers 11, Regina All-Services 0
Grey Cup – Hamilton Flying Wildcats 23, Winnipeg R.C.A.F. 14

**1941**
East Semi-Finals – Toronto Argonauts 16, Ottawa Rough Riders 8
East Semi-Finals – Ottawa Rough Riders 10, Toronto Argonauts 1
West Finals – Winnipeg Blue Bombers 6, Regina Roughriders 8
West Finals – Regina Roughriders 12, Winnipeg Blue Bombers 18
West Finals – Regina Roughriders 2, Winnipeg Blue Bombers 8
East Final – Ottawa Rough Riders 7, Hamilton Wildcats 2
Grey Cup – Winnipeg Blue Bombers 18, Ottawa Rough Riders 16

**1939**
West Semi-Final – Calgary Bronks 24, Regina Roughriders 17
East Semi-Finals – Ottawa Rough Riders 11, Toronto Argonauts 0
East Semi-Finals – Ottawa Rough Riders 28, Toronto Argonauts 6
West Finals – Calgary Bronks 13, Winnipeg Blue Bombers 7
West Finals – Winnipeg Blue Bombers 28, Calgary Bronks 7
East Final – Ottawa Rough Riders 23, Sarnia Imperials 1
Grey Cup – Winnipeg Blue Bombers 8, Ottawa Rough Riders 7

**1937**
East Semi-Finals – Ottawa Rough Riders 15, Toronto Argonauts 11
East Semi-Finals – Toronto Argonauts 10, Ottawa Rough Riders 1
West Finals – Calgary Bronks 13, Winnipeg Blue Bombers 10
West Finals – Winnipeg Blue Bombers 9, Calgary Bronks 1
East Final – Toronto Argonauts 10, Sarnia Imperials 6
Grey Cup – Toronto Argonauts 4, Winnipeg Blue Bombers 3

**1935**
West Semi-Finals – Calgary Bronks 14, Vancouver Meralomas 0
West Semi-Finals – Winnipeg 'Pegs 13, Regina Roughriders 6
West Final – Winnipeg 'Pegs 7, Calgary Bronks 0
East Semi-Final – Hamilton Tigers 44, Queen's University 4
East Final – Hamilton Tigers 22, Sarnia Imperials 3
Grey Cup – Winnipeg 'Pegs 18, Hamilton Tigers 12

**1933**
West Semi-Finals – Winnipeg Rugby Club 11, Regina Roughriders 1
West Semi-Finals – Calgary Altomahs 13, Vancouver Meralomas 11
West Final – Winnipeg Rugby Club 15, Calgary Altomahs 1
East Semi-Final – University of Toronto refuses to compete
Grey Cup Semi-Final – Toronto Argonauts 13, Winnipeg Rugby Club 0
Grey Cup – Toronto Argonauts 4, Sarnia Imperials 3

**1932**
West Semi-Finals – Regina Roughriders 9, Winnipeg St. John's 1
West Semi-Finals – Calgary Altomahs 6, Vancouver Meralomas 4
West Semi-Finals – Vancouver Meralomas 6, Calgary Altomahs 5
West Final – Regina Roughriders 30, Calgary Altomahs 2
East Semi-Final – Hamilton Tigers 15, Sarnia Imperials 11
East Final – Hamilton Tigers 9, University of Toronto 3
Grey Cup – Hamilton Tigers 25, Regina Roughriders 6

**1930**
West Quarter-Final – Regina Roughriders 23, Winnipeg St. John's 0
West Semi-Final – Regina Roughriders 9, Calgary Tigers 6
West Finals – Regina Roughriders 17, Vancouver Meralomas 0
West Finals – Regina Roughriders 4, Vancouver Meralomas 0
East Semi-Final – Hamilton Tigers 8, Queen's University 3
East Final – Balmy Beach 8, Hamilton Tigers 5
Grey Cup – Balmy Beach 11, Regina Roughriders 6

**1928**
West Final – Regina Roughriders 12, Winnipeg St. John's 1
East Semi-Final – McGill University refuses to compete
East Final – Hamilton Tigers 28, University of Toronto Seconds 5
Grey Cup – Hamilton Tigers 30, Regina Roughriders 0

**1926**
West Semi-Finals – Regina Roughriders 13, Winnipeg St. John's 5
    (Overtime)
West Semi-Finals – University of Alberta 21, Victoria, B.C. 2
West Final – Regina Roughriders 13, University of Alberta 5
(West did not compete in Grey Cup)
East Semi-Final – Ottawa Senators 7, Balmy Beach 6
Grey Cup – Ottawa Senators 10, University of Toronto 7

**1924**
West Semi-Final – Winnipeg Victorias 22, Regina Roughriders 5
West Final – Winnipeg Victorias 11, Calgary 50th Battalion 9
West did not compete in Grey Cup
East Semi-Final – Queen's University 11, Hamilton Tigers 1
Grey Cup – Queen's University 11, Balmy Beach 3

**1922**
West Semi-Final – Edmonton Elks 13, Regina Rugby Club 8
West Final – Edmonton Elks 19, Winnipeg Victorias 6
East Semi-Final – Toronto Argonauts 20, Parkdale Canoe Club 1
East Final – Queen's University 12, Toronto Argonauts 11
Grey Cup – Queen's University 13, Edmonton Elks 1

**1920**
Grey Cup Semi-Final – Toronto Argonauts 5, Toronto Rugby Club 2
Grey Cup – University of Toronto 16, Toronto Argonauts 3

**1915**
Grey Cup Semi-Final – No game. Intercollegiate competition suspended
Grey Cup – Hamilton Tigers 13, Toronto Rowing and Athletic Association 7

**1913**
Grey Cup Semi-Final – McGill University refused to compete
Grey Cup – Hamilton Tigers 44, Parkdale Canoe Club 2

**1911**
Grey Cup Semi-Final – Toronto Argonauts 9, Hamilton Alerts 2
Grey Cup – University of Toronto 14, Toronto Argonauts 7

**1909**
Grey Cup Semi-Final – University of Toronto 31, Ottawa Rough Riders 7
Grey Cup – University of Toronto 26, Parkdale Canoe Club 6

**1931**
West Semi-Finals – Regina Roughriders 47, Winnipeg St. John's 5
West Semi-Finals – Calgary Altomahs 6, Vancouver Athletic Club 4
West Semi-Finals – Calgary Altomahs 14, Vancouver Athletic Club 1
East Semi-Final – University of Western Ontario 7, Sarnia Imperials 1
East Final – Montreal Winged Wheelers 22, University of Western
    Ontario 0
Grey Cup – Montreal Winged Wheelers 22, Regina Roughriders 0

**1929**
West Semi-Final – Regina Roughriders 19, Winnipeg St. John's 3
West Final – Regina Roughriders 15, Calgary Tigers 8
East Semi-Final – Hamilton Tigers 14, Sarnia Imperials 2
East Final – Hamilton Tigers 14, Queen's University 3
Grey Cup – Hamilton Tigers 14, Regina Roughriders 3

**1927**
West Semi-Final – Regina Roughriders 17, Winnipeg Tammany Tigers 2
West Finals – Regina Roughriders 13, University of B.C. 1
West Finals – Regina Roughriders 19, University of B.C. 0
(West did not compete in the Grey Cup)
East Semi-Final – Hamilton Tigers 21, Queen's University 6
Grey Cup – Balmy Beach 9, Hamilton Tigers 6

**1925**
West Semi-Final – University of Alberta did not compete
West Final – Winnipeg Tammany Tigers 11, Regina Roughriders 1
East Semi-Final – Queen's University 21, Balmy Beach 9
East Final – Ottawa Senators 11, Queen's University 2
Grey Cup – Ottawa Senators 24, Winnipeg Tammany Tigers 1

**1923**
West Semi-Final – Regina Roughriders 9, Edmonton Eskimos 6
West Final – Regina Roughriders 11, Winnipeg Victorias 1
East Semi-Final – Hamilton Tigers 24, Hamilton Rowing Club 1
East Final – Queen's University 13, Hamilton Tigers 5
Grey Cup – Queen's University 54, Regina Roughriders 0

**1921**
West Quarter-Final – Winnipeg Victorias 16, Saskatoon Quakers 1
West Semi-Final – Edmonton Eskimos 16, Winnipeg Victorias 6
East Semi-Final – Toronto Argonauts 20, University of Toronto 12
East Final – Toronto Argonauts 16, Parkdale Canoe Club 8
Grey Cup – Toronto Argonauts 23, Edmonton Eskimos 0

**1916-1919**
No Grey Cup competition

**1914**
Grey Cup Semi-Final – Toronto Argonauts 16, Hamilton Rowing Club 14
Grey Cup – Toronto Argonauts 14, University of Toronto 2

**1912**
Grey Cup Semi-Final – McGill University refused to compete
Grey Cup – Hamilton Alerts 11, Toronto Argonauts 4

**1910**
Grey Cup Semi-Final – University of Toronto 22, Toronto A.A.C. 3
Grey Cup – University of Toronto 16, Hamilton Tigers 7

# ACKNOWLEDGMENTS

*Heroes of the Game* is a dream come true. While watching a C.F.L. match and wondering if the game would survive into the 21st century, I found myself envisioning writing a book immortalizing Canadian football. The end product was clear, but the process was cloudy. The endeavour was large and would never have been completed without the assistance of many dedicated individuals.

I am especially grateful to Louise Froggett of the Canadian Football Hall of Fame & Museum, Hamilton. Louise was instrumental throughout the research of this book. As a passionate football fan, she realized the importance of seeing that it was published.

I am also grateful to Leif Pettersen. I never had the opportunity to play professional football and thus I was unsure if *Heroes of the Game* captured from a player's perspective the tradition of the Grey Cup. After Leif reviewed the book and enthusiastically supported it my spirits were lifted.

The C.F.L. has also been of great assistance. At various stages it helped to move the book forward by permitting access to statistical information and to photographs.

Many others have been involved in this dream. I am thankful for the efforts of Neil Henderson, Jim Nagata, Ian Hutchison, Dan Ferrone, Chris Markwell, Roger Yachetti, Bob Nicholson, Mike Cosentino, Dave Watkins, Professor Bob Calder, Rob Sanders, Judge Hugh Locke, Judge David Humphrey, Jake Gaudaur, Jack Gordon, Damon Allen, Garney Henley, David Sapunjis, Mike Clemons, Russ Jackson, Tony Gabriel, Cam Fraser, Joe Krol, Bill Stukus, Wayne Shaw, Ted Urness, Joe Heit, Tina Powell, Professor Reginald Bibby, Janice Smith, Sandra Campbell-Fraser, Elizabeth Dagg and Gregory B. Fulton. At one stage or another each of these people contributed to the making of *Heroes of the Game*.

I am of course extremely grateful to the team at Moulin Publishing. Without Ed Boyce, Chris Boyce, Norman Holt, Heidy Lawrance and Maya Mavjee the memories of Canadian football would have remained buried.

I am most grateful to my wife, Prema. Her encouragement was without equal. Notwithstanding the frustrations experienced in trying to achieve my dream, Prema continued to keep it focused. She is as much a hero of the game as any player who ever participated in a Grey Cup championship.

# SOURCES

The most important resources used in the compilation of *Heroes of the Game* were newspaper articles from 1909 through 1996. The author has relied upon the accounts of the Grey Cup games as provided in *The Varsity, The Toronto Daily News, The Toronto Telegram, The Toronto (Daily) Star, The Globe and Mail, The Toronto Sun, The Ottawa Citizen, The Montreal Gazette, The Hamilton Spectator, The Kingston Whig Standard, The Winnipeg Free Press, The Calgary Herald, The Regina Leader Post, The Vancouver Province,* and *The Vancouver Sun* as available on microfilm at York University, The University of Toronto and the Metro Toronto Reference Library.

With the assistance of the Canadian Football Hall of Fame & Museum, Hamilton, the author also relied upon game programmes and film footage. Radio coverage housed at the CBC Archives in Toronto was researched as well.

Photographs have been obtained from the University of Toronto Archives, The City of Toronto Archives, The Hamilton Public Library, The Canadian Football Hall of Fame & Museum, The Canadian Football League, Imperial Oil Limited, Art Martin and John Sokolowski.

Quotations from *Rider Pride* are reprinted by courteous permission of the authors, Bob Calder and Garry Andrews.

Allan, Tony. *Football Today and Yesterday.* Winnipeg: Harlequin, 1961.

Calder, Bob and Andrews, Garry. *Rider Pride.* Saskatoon: Western Producer Prairie Books, 1984.

Cosentino, Frank. *Canadian Football – The Grey Cup Years.* Toronto: Musson Books, 1969.

Currie, Gordon. *100 Years of Canadian Football.* Toronto: Pagurian Press, 1968.

Gabriel, Tony and Fillmore, Stanley. *Double Trouble.* Toronto: Gage, 1978.

Sullivan, Jack. *The Grey Cup Story.* Don Mills: Greywood Publishing, 1971.

Teitel, Jay. *The Argo Bounce.* Toronto: Lester & Orpen Dennys Ltd., 1982.

Walker, Gordon. *Grey Cup Tradition.* Edmonton: E.S.P. Marketing & Communications Ltd., 1987.

*1996 Facts, Figures and Records.* Toronto: C.F.L., 1996.

# INDEX

(David Brown Photography, Saskatoon)

Stephen Thiele graduated from Osgoode Hall and
is a research lawyer and legal editor for Butterworths
Canada Limited. He has spent five years researching
and writing *Heroes of the Game*. The book is an
expression of the passion Stephen possesses for the
sport and the history of Canadian football.
He lives in Toronto with his wife, Prema.